HUMAN ECOLOGY

A THEORY OF COMMUNITY STRUCTURE

By

AMOS H. HAWLEY

ASSOCIATE PROFESSOR OF SOCIOLOGY
UNIVERSITY OF MICHIGAN

THE RONALD PRESS COMPANY · NEW YORK

Copyright, 1950, by

THE RONALD PRESS COMPANY

———

All Rights Reserved

To

RODERICK D. MCKENZIE

PREFACE

This volume attempts to develop a full and coherent theory of human ecology. Working from the assumption that there is continuity in the life patterns of all organic forms, the argument begins with the contributions of plant and animal ecologists and seeks to elaborate the logical implications of general ecological theory. This leads to the investigation of a fundamental yet long neglected sociological problem, namely, the nature and development of community structure. Such an interpretation of ecology represents a deliberate limitation of the subject. Too often ecology is viewed as an all-inclusive point of view—a study of all of life in relation to all of environment. That, in effect, is an invitation to the student to spend himself in the mere extension of his reach. If it is to have substance, ecology must have bounds. This is no less true of its application to human social phenomena than of its use in the study of similar matters involving other forms of life.

Perhaps it is unnecessary to state that the final answer to the ecological problem is not achieved here. Although it has accomplished much in the three decades since its inception, human ecology is still a fledgling discipline, if indeed it may be called a discipline. Thus the reader will do well to regard this as a book of hypotheses, as a point of departure for research and subsequent theoretical development.

The publication of this volume marks the completion of a work begun a number of years ago by the late Professor R. D. McKenzie. At his death, in 1940, I assumed responsibility for accomplishing the task. At the outset it was intended that the finished work would be published under the joint authorship of Professor McKenzie and myself. Circumstances over which I have had no control, however, altered that arrangement. But the change in the original plan in no way minimizes my great indebtedness to Professor McKenzie. If those who knew him well read the book carefully, they will detect his influence, not to mention his ideas, in many of the passages. At this late date it can only be hoped that this heritage has been justly treated. For that I willingly accept responsibility.

Many others have played an important part in the fulfillment of this work. Mrs. R. D. McKenzie's constant encouragement and penetrating criticism have been of inestimable assistance. The manuscript was read wholly or in part by many friends and colleagues, including Doctors R. C. Angell, Rupert Vance, Jessie Steiner, Don J. Bogue, Ronald Freedman, Werner Landecker, Peter Ostafin and Edward Swanson. From all these I have drawn many valuable suggestions and criticisms. My colleagues in the Metropolitan Community Seminar, especially Dr. E. M. Hoover, have served unwittingly as a rich source of ideas and stimulation. I am also greatly indebted to Marion Dunlap Rickel, Arthur Hinman, Jack Kantner, Samuel Pratt, and all the other graduate students who possessed the fortitude to sit through my seminar on human ecology. Needless to say, none of these persons is culpable for the book's deficiencies.

AMOS H. HAWLEY

Ann Arbor, Michigan
   March 15, 1950

CONTENTS

PART I

Ecology and Human Ecology

PART II

The Human Aggregate

PART IV

Change and Development

ILLUSTRATIONS

TABLES

PART I

ECOLOGY AND HUMAN ECOLOGY

Chapter 1

INTRODUCTION

The word ecology is derived from the Greek *oikos*—a house or place to live in; also from this root come the more familiar terms *economy* and *economics*. Ernst Haeckel, the German biologist, is credited with being the first to use the term *ecology,* employing it in his study of plants in 1868.[1] But the science of ecology did not get under way until the turn of the twentieth century, when textbooks began to appear such as those of Eugenus Warming, *Oecology of Plants,* 1909; F. E. Clements, *Research Methods in Ecology,* 1905, and *Plant Physiology and Ecology,* 1907. Since then a vast literature has accumulated and the subject has become generally recognized as an important branch of the biological sciences.

Ecology is commonly defined as the study of "the relation of organisms or groups of organisms to their environment."[2] It is based upon the perception of the world of life as a system of dynamic interdependences. Every organism, plant and animal—including man—is in constant process of adjustment to an environment external to itself. The life of an organism, in other words, is inescapably bound up with the conditions of the environment, which comprise not only topography, climate, drainage, etc., but other organisms and their activities as well. The universal life triad, declares Bews, is "environment—function—organism."[3] All organisms are engaged in activities which have as their logical conclusion adjustment to environment.

It is often said that ecology is but a new name for an old subject, and in many respects this is true. Ever since man was able to record his observations there is evidence that he was aware of the relation of life to environment. Geography—the so-called mother of sciences—from earliest antiquity has been concerned, among other things, with the study of the relation of life to variations in the physical environment. And for many centuries students of natural history have been observing and recording the varieties of life and the intri-

---

[1] *History of Creation* (1868).
[2] *Encyclopaedia Britannica* (14th ed.), X, 152.
[3] *Human Ecology* (Oxford, 1937), 18.

cate connections among the different life forms. Yet ecology is distinctly a new product, an outgrowth of modern science.

Science develops by the mechanisms of observation and conceptualization.

Our coordinated knowledge, which in the general sense of the term is science, is formed by the meeting of two orders of experience. One order is constituted by the direct, immediate discriminations of particular observations. The other order is constituted by our general way of conceiving the Universe. They will be called, the Observational Order, and the Conceptual Order. The first point to remember is that the observational order is invariably interpreted in terms of the concepts supplied by the conceptual order. . . . We inherit an observational order, namely types of things which we do in fact discriminate; and we inherit a conceptual order, namely a rough system of ideas in terms of which we do in fact interpret.[4]

We observe and we invent concepts to describe and classify our observations. Science progresses in this twofold manner. What distinguishes ecology as a new science from the older natural history or biogeography is not so much the focus of attention as the method of approach. The emergence of concepts, which facilitated both observation and the integration of data observed as well as the development of more efficient methods of investigation, brought the subject matter of natural history under the purview of a new set of procedures and problems. Instead of viewing the adaptations of organisms to environment from the standpoint of their anecdotal value or with a view to proving the theory of natural selection, ecology concerns itself with the detailed analysis of the processes by which adaptations are reached and maintained.

It is important to recognize that ecology developed as a biological rather than as a geographical or social science in spite of the fact that the relation of organisms to environment has pronounced geographic and social aspects. This is the more remarkable in view of the dependence of the founders of modern ecology upon social science and related disciplines for many of their descriptive concepts.[5] These

---

[4] Alfred N. Whitehead, *Adventures of Ideas*, 198. Copyright 1933 by The Macmillan Company and used with their permission.

[5] An example of this interchange of concepts between disciplines is reported by Charles Darwin: "In October, 1838, that is fifteen months after I had begun my systematic enquiry, I happened to read for amusement 'Malthus on Population,' and being well prepared to appreciate the struggle for existence which everywhere goes on from long-continued observation of the habits of animals and plants, it at once struck me that under these circumstances, favourable variations would tend to be preserved, and unfavourable ones to be destroyed. The result of this would be the formation of new species. Here then I had at last got a theory by which to work; but I was so anxious to avoid prejudice, that I determined not for some time to write even the briefest sketch of it." Francis Darwin (ed.), *The Life and Letters of Charles Robert Darwin* (New York: Appleton-Century-Crofts, Inc., 1919), 68.

borrowed concepts were refined and given specific biological content and, along with many concepts indigenous to biology, have acquired general usage in all phases of ecology, including human ecology.

The basis of modern ecology, as of all other branches of the biological sciences and to a large extent of the social sciences as well, lies in the work by the great biologists, Darwin and Wallace. In particular, Darwin's *Origin of Species,* published in 1859, and his *Descent of Man,* 1871, set the stage for a new era in biological research. Attention shifted from a preoccupation with cosmological problems, such as the ultimate meaning of each form of life for every other which followed from the assumption of immutability of species, to a search for specific causes responsible for the existence of species, based upon accumulated evidence of change in the organic world. Final causes were forsaken in favor of necessary and sufficient causes. In the ferment of biological empiricism of the nineteenth century a scientific natural history began to take form.

In his works Darwin formulated the basic ideas which were later brought together to constitute the theoretical understructure, the frame of reference, of modern ecology. All life was his province and he perceived it as a moving system of vital relationships in which were implicated every organism and species of life. This general conception, which he described metaphorically as the "web of life," has been elaborated by succeeding students and has become the key idea in ecological research. Organisms are related to one another in the web, Darwin pointed out, on the basis of a struggle for existence. Struggle for existence is a broad and general term, referring to the organism's relationships with both the inorganic and the organic elements of the environment. It includes in its meaning the competition among forms of life and also the cooperation and mutual aid that develop among organisms, which was emphasized later by Kropotkin and other Neo-Darwinists. Through struggle for existence order develops and the web of life unfolds as organisms become adjusted to one another and to the physical environment. Finally, Darwin demonstrated the limiting and constraining effects of environment upon forms of life. Of considerable importance in this connection is his extension of the term *environment* to include all factors external to the organism and exerting an influence on its behavior. Thus there is an organic as well as an inorganic environment, and the organism's place in one is affected by and in turn affects its place in the other.

Scientific ecology, then, is indebted to Darwin for the main outlines of its theory, the essential conceptions being: (1) the web of life in which organisms are adjusted or are seeking adjustment to one another, (2) the adjustment process as a struggle for existence, and (3) the environment comprising a highly complex set of conditions of adjustment. But Darwin's contribution to ecology went beyond the development of a point of view. He provided numerous exemplary models of research in his studies of the geographical distribution of species and also in his studies of habitual or instinctive behavior. Nevertheless, the immediate effect of Darwin's work on natural science was to send botanists and zoologists back into their laboratories to study the morphology and physiology of specimens and to work on problems of description and classification.[6] This work was a necessary preliminary to scientific field study because species and varieties had to be identified accurately before they could be studied effectively in the field. The classifications of earlier naturalists, particularly that of Linnaeus, were valuable but lacked the refinement and completeness necessary for work in scientific ecology.

Botanists quickly accomplished the major part of their taxonomic work and thus were first to begin research in the field of scientific ecology. Zoologists were later in concluding their identification and classification of species, because, as Elton explains, there are more species of animals than of plants, and plants do not rush away when an attempt is made to collect them.[7] In consequence, plant ecology has reached a high degree of development while animal ecology, though its progress has been rapid in recent years, is still an immature body of theory and method. Students of human life have plunged into ecological research with their taxonomic task only partially completed. In fact, even today the determination and classification of data are not generally recognized as of primary importance for the advancement of social science. Human ecologists, therefore, like their colleagues in other branches of social science, are hampered by persistent disagreements concerning the nature of their data and the techniques of study that are amenable to them. As no workable theoretical system can be built upon anything other than a coherent and inclusive classification of data, the progress of human ecology promises to be slow until this task is done.

The three phases of scientific ecology—plant, animal, and human—have developed and remain as more or less distinct branches of the discipline. This has been due, in part, to the long established diversity of interest among students of life, which has carried over into ecology from the parent disciplines. Also, the temporal order in which the ecological viewpoint entered into established fields of inquiry is prob-

---

[6] Charles Elton, *Animal Ecology* (New York, 1927), 3.
[7] *Ibid.*

ably an important factor in effecting a diversification of the field. Botanists, zoologists, and finally sociologists were successively attracted by the merits of the ecological approach for their separate fields of interest and the resulting differentiation in extent of progress seems to lend support to the initial subdivision of ecology. But the explanation cannot be entirely a historical one; certain differences in subject matter and in the applicability of research technique provide a legitimate basis for the threefold subdivision. For example, the basic difference in food habits between plants and animals and the consequent differences in the modes of interrelationship set the vegetable and the animal kingdoms apart for ecologists as well as for biologists generally. Furthermore, there are important differences in locomotive powers and in the variability and adaptability of behavior, not only between plants and animals but within the animal kingdom itself. Such differences give rise to special problems which make for a division of labor within a scientific discipline.

The subdivision of ecology into smaller units of study is not in itself a matter for consternation. While science is committed to the formulation of fruitful generalizations, it must at the same time be sensitive to differences among the units of observation. The delimitation of areas of similarity and margins of difference in the field of observation is a necessary function of science. New disciplines arise when it becomes evident that certain units of observation are so different from others that existing assumptions and generalizations cannot without the loss of precision be extended to describe them. Ecologists recognize striking similarities among all forms of life but they also observe highly important differences which require detailed examination. The subdivision of the general field reflects the normal progress of scientific analysis. It is necessary however to guard against any compartmentalization of research activity that threatens to impede communication among workers in the three divisions.

Plant ecology got its start in the latter part of the nineteenth century with the works of Haeckel and Warming. In subsequent years its growth was rapid, both with respect to the development and refinement of research tools and the accumulation of literature. At present plant ecology occupies a recognized position in textbooks on general botany and in college curricula. By virtue of its strategic priority plant ecology furnished animal and human ecologists with many of their initial concepts [8] and set the pattern for much of their research work. But, as might be expected, the development of these

---

[8] For evidence of this see J. Richard Carpenter, *An Ecological Glossary* (Norman, Oklahoma, 1938).

more recent fields has progressively dissociated them from the authority of plant ecology and is establishing them on a more or less independent footing.

Animal ecology is a product of the twentieth century. While its roots reach far back into the old natural history investigations, all the literature employing the term *animal ecology* has appeared since the beginning of the twentieth century and largely in the last three decades. C. C. Adams' *Guide to the Study of Animal Ecology,* 1913, and V. E. Shelford's *Animal Communities in Temperate America,* 1913, were among the first contributions in this field. Animal ecologists developed their field in close relation to plant ecology. They have the same general conception of the nature of their task and employ much the same terminology. But, owing to its relative youth and perhaps also to the greater complexity of its subject matter, animal ecology has not yet become so well systematized as plant ecology.

The term *human ecology* made its appearance in 1921 in the volume, *An Introduction to the Science of Sociology* by R. E. Park and E. W. Burgess.[9] Its meaning has not always been clear, however, despite the fact that sociologists and, to a lesser extent, anthropologists have given the term widespread currency in numerous special studies and textbooks. Although sociologists assumed responsibility for defining and delimiting the field of human ecology, they have neglected this in their concern with special and often minute problems of ecological research. Analysis, in other words, has seldom been followed by synthesis and as a result analysis has frequently been misguided so far as the progress of ecology is concerned. Nevertheless, human ecology has shown remarkable vitality and gives evidence of having achieved a permanent ranking among the social sciences. A clarification of its definition is the more imperative, therefore, if it is to hold and develop its present position.

The distinctions between the three branches of ecology, however, are sometimes ignored and their commonalities emphasized in what is known as general or bio-ecology. The term is usually construed to mean the study of relations among all life forms. Since all forms of life are biological organisms having similar elemental requirements and hence displaying comparable habits of behavior, the study of all life may be embraced within a single conceptual scheme. To illustrate, C. C. Adams, speaking of the relation of general ecology to human ecology, says that "emphasis is placed upon the continuity of the processes and sequences of change which are revealed in the sub-

---

9 (Chicago, 1921), 161-216.

human biological world, rather than to emphasize their distinctness from the conditions found in the human communities." [10] But general ecology is not to be confused with an uncritical analogical reasoning from plant to animal to human behavior. Such an oversimplification belies the observable facts and, as Thomson and Geddes declare, "is a 'biologism,' just as it is a materialism to insist that life is adequately describable in chemico-physical terms." [11]

The conception of a general ecology carries another implication. Ecology, on occasion, is regarded in its fullest possible extension as an exhaustive inquiry into the vast and intricate pattern that is nature, the study of the relation of each thing to everything else. This is known as the holistic point of view popularized by General Smuts, the distinguished South African philosopher and statesman.[12] Holism views life in all its manifestations as a single system in process of interaction with the inorganic environment. Life is held to be a self-building and self-replenishing whole, rotating in time, beginning with inorganic matter and returning thereto, yet expanding and spreading against the opposing forces of the environment, diversifying and adapting to fill every niche and crevice. All nature, in effect, is merged in an ever-renewing chemical synthesis.[13] The organism, in this view, is an abstraction and is not to be understood apart from the context in its entirety. W. P. Taylor and J. W. Bews are representatives of the holistic outlook. Ecology, Taylor declares, must be defined as the study of "*all* relations of *all* organisms to *all* their environment." [14] He states further: "Ecology is not confined to animals, neither is it limited to plants. Indeed ecology is not a restricted subject. In its very essence it is comprehensive. Its stimulating key words are integration, *Einheit,* correlation, coordination, synthesis." [15] Bews concurs, stating that: "Environment, function, and organism constitute together what has been called the fundamental biological triad. The triad must be studied as one complete whole, and this study is essentially what we mean by ecology." [16]

The holistic viewpoint, as a philosophy of science, is both a confession of faith and a goal to be pursued; and as such it has great significance. In describing nature as one integrated system it reveals

---

[10] "The Relation of General Ecology to Human Ecology." *Ecology,* XVI: 3 (July, 1935), 328.
[11] *Life: Outlines of General Biology* (London, 1931), Vol. I, 129.
[12] *Evolution and Holism* (London, 1926).
[13] Cf. H. G. Wells, J. S. Huxley, and G. P. Wells, *The Science of Life,* Vol. III, 926-67.
[14] "What is Ecology and What Good is It?" *Ecology,* XVII (July, 1936), 335.
[15] *Ibid.,* 335.
[16] *Op. cit.,* 1-2.

the scientist's faith in a universe of cause and effect relationships, the whole of which is capable of being made intelligible to the normal mind. At the same time it points to the essential unity of science with respect to its problems and its ultimate goal. However, the holistic viewpoint harbors certain dangers for the scientist. If the magnitude of the picture it presents does not stagnate activity, it is apt to encourage hasty generalization and immature synthesis. The scientist is a finite creature and in order to work effectively within his limited capacities he must devote his attention to the study of an infinitesimal part of the whole. Ecologists are no exception in this respect. Like their colleagues in other branches of scientific endeavor, they must occupy themselves with details in order to shed any light on the problems of life in general. Certainly it is beyond the capacity of any one individual to explore the entire field.

In point of fact, a science is delimited by what it does rather than by any a priori definition of its field. General ecology and also the holistic characterization of ecology are of the nature of generic terms. They describe in broad outline the point of view of ecology, but they fail to provide any identifying clues by which the ecologist at work can be recognized apart from the workers in other fields such as parasitology, entomology, geography, economics, psychology, etc. In order to be more than a point of view ecology must have a domain wherein it is autonomous. This is not to say that it must have a subject matter uniquely its own, but it must bring into focus a set of problems not included within the scope of other disciplines to which scientific techniques can be, and in fact are being, applied.

The following chapters in this introductory section develop the point of view and hence the definition of ecology in much greater detail. In Chapters 2 and 3 the essential assumptions and the hypothesis of ecology are set forth. Chapter 4 attempts to formulate a working definition of human ecology and to show its relation to the various social sciences.

SUPPLEMENTARY REFERENCES

ADAMS, C. C. "The Relation of Human Ecology to General Ecology," *Ecology*, XVI (July, 1935), 316-35.
PARK, R. E., and Burgess, E. W. *An Introduction to the Science of Sociology.* Chicago: The University of Chicago Press, 1921. Chaps. iii and viii.
TAYLOR, W. P. What is Ecology and What Good Is it?" *Ecology*, XVII (July, 1936), 333-46.
WARMING, E. *Oecology of Plants: An Introduction to the Study of Plant Communities.* Oxford: Clarendon Press, 1909.

Chapter 2

ORGANISM AND ENVIRONMENT

The definition of ecology as the study of the relation of organisms to environment may be adequate for general purposes but it lacks the precision requisite to the delimitation of a field of scientific inquiry. Since all the life sciences—biological and social—deal with the relationship between organisms and environment we need to make clear what aspect of this problem is the peculiar concern of ecology. Let us begin with the elements of the problem.

Living and Nonliving Matter.—We are all familiar with life. It is everywhere about us. In fact, so well acquainted are we with life that the task of distinguishing between living and nonliving things would seem to present no great difficulty. Yet when we attempt to describe the essential differentiating quality between these two types of matter most of us find ourselves confronted with a perplexing problem. The more sophisticated may take comfort in the knowledge that not even the biologists have satisfied themselves on this point. Biological knowledge is far from complete and the question of the nature of life is still a challenging issue. After reviewing various definitions of life, A. J. Lotka wrote: "Little harm, and perhaps much gain, can come from a frank avowal that we are unable to state clearly the difference between living and nonliving matter. This does not in any way commit us to the view that no such difference exists." [1] We shall then venture a resolution of this difficulty which, though lacking in exactness, may serve our immediate purpose.

Briefly, the distinctive feature of living matter is its peculiar dynamic quality. There is activity in all things, but only living things are capable of the type of activity represented in growth and reproduction. Nonliving objects are at best mere reservoirs of energy and temporary ones at that: they cannot retain energy without loss. Living matter, on the other hand, possesses the power of absorbing energy continuously and cumulatively. Any particular manifestation of life, it is true, is of limited duration—it has its day and ceases to be. But the organism is reincarnated in manifold progeny and the cumulative

---

[1] *Elements of Physical Biology* (Baltimore, 1925), 19.

process tends to be accelerated at each renewal of the life cycle. This difference between the two kinds of matter appears to run deeper than many of us realize. Indeed, the physical universe appears gradually to be disintegrating, for inorganic matter passes steadily into energy which is progressively dissipated.[2] Animate nature, on the other hand, seems to be following a countertrend: it is a "building-up" in which life is swelling to ever larger dimensions. The one kind of matter, then, can do no more than persist; the other grows, enlarges, multiplies.

This dynamic quality of life shows itself in another and equally important manner—in its capacity for unlimited variation. Living matter is irritable, responsive to external circumstances; hence it is always seeking to embody itself in some organic form appropriate to its surroundings. Thus, while all life is essentially the same in chemical composition and process, the forms in which life actually expresses itself vary greatly in size and shape. At opposite extremes stand the microscopic bacterium and the giant tree; the tiny amoeba and the massive whale; the stationary plant and the mobile animal. Between these remote extremes are more or less continuous gradations of life forms. Moreover, the types of life in existence at any one time are not permanently fixed; not only are they highly varied, they are constantly varying. As the record of paleontology reveals, forms of life have been regularly eliminated and replaced by new and different forms. Numerous evidences indicate that what occurred in the past is occurring in the present. The spectacle of life is in truth one of seething restlessness and endless change.

It is already apparent that life cannot be considered alone and *in vacuo*. There are forces other than those developed within the organism that operate to bring about the effects which greet the eye of the observer. Living things require space in which to carry on necessary activities, and food with which to maintain vital processes. These elemental requirements cause life to be irrevocably implicated in the external physical world. Life is a synthesis of organism and environment; the two form a partnership so intimate that it can be resolved only in theory.

Environment is a generic concept under which are subsumed all external forces and factors to which an organism or aggregate of organisms is actually or potentially responsive. The very breadth of the concept restricts its use for purposes of precise description. In general, however, environment refers to the medium in which an or-

---

2 Sir James Jeans, *The Mysterious Universe* (New York, 1937), 13-15.

ganism exists. Environment comprises the raw materials of life and the conditions, both favorable and unfavorable, that affect the use of those materials. The supply of necessary materials and the circumstances which attend their use are such as to constitute an ever-present problem for living creatures.

In the first place, the total amount of space available to living forms, in which may be found the essential ingredients of life, is quite small. If measured on the grand scale of the universe, it is infinitesimal. The surface of the earth does not exceed two hundred million square miles—fifty-five million square miles of land and one hundred forty-five million square miles of water. Furthermore, the biosphere, as the vertical life space is called, is a thin zone, extending but a few miles in either direction from the earth's surface. It is only within this brief vertical span that temperatures are neither too hot nor too cold for life-giving chemical processes; and air pressure is neither too great nor too small for the frail structures in which life manifests itself. Living forms, therefore, are held close to the surface of the earth. Ever since life first appeared, hundreds of millions of years ago, it has been steadily enlarging its range both vertically and horizontally and there is no reason to think that this process will not continue. But, since the bounds of the biosphere are pressed back at a rate that is measured on a geological time-scale, the world at any given time is fixed and unchangeable in the amount of life it can support.

Despite the meager dimensions of the available life space, it provides an almost limitless variety of places that may be occupied by living creatures. "There are first the differences in medium—earth, air, water; differences in salinity from almost pure water to the Dead Sea's more than 20 per cent of salts; differences in temperature from hot springs that are nearly boiling down to many degrees below freezing; differences in pressure from well below half an atmosphere on high mountains to several hundred atmospheres in the deep sea; differences in light from the intense tropical sun to the utter darkness of caves, of the oceanic abyss or of an animal's gut."[3] These variations combine in numerous ways to form a great number of more or less distinct life zones. Beginning with the abyssal depths of the sea there is a vertical layering of life zones extending up to the highest mountain peak. At the earth's surface there is a horizontal zonation from the equator to the poles—tropical, subtropical, temperate, subarctic, and arctic. In addition, there are many interstitial and marginal zones,

[3] H. G. Wells, J. S. Huxley, and G. P. Wells, *The Science of Life,* Vol. III, 829. By permission of Mrs. Marjorie Wells.

such as littoral, subterranean, atmospheric, and organic. With greater attention to detail the number and variety of habitats that might be listed would fill a thick volume.

Moreover, the physical world is itself subject to change under the stresses and strains developed within the earth's crust, with the erosive movements of wind and water and with the exploitation by plants and animals in pursuit of their sustenance needs. Apart from these major changes, which are always in process, there are numerous minor fluctuations from season to season, from day to day, and from one hour to the next. Temperature, precipitation, light, air pressure, etc., oscillate everywhere between more or less wide extremes, the range of variation being least in tropical latitudes and greatest in the so-called temperate zones. Restlessness characterizes the inorganic as well as the organic world. But while the dynamics of life is expressed in growth and reproduction, that in the physical world reveals itself as recurrence and a ceaseless redistribution of materials. The two kinds of change, in other words, are entirely different.

Organism and environment are therefore two indefinitely variable factors. Living matter is a highly dynamic substance which possesses both a capacity for indeterminate expansion and a tendency to express itself in specific plant and animal forms. Environment provides countless combinations of conditions which, although constantly subject to change, are always limited in the opportunities they afford living things.[4] The relation between the two is a fundamental dependence of one on the other, of organism on environment. It is this relationship which constitutes our primary concern.

The Struggle for Existence.—The relation of organisms to the external world is usually characterized in its generality as a struggle for existence. This phrase has very broad implications. Darwin used it in a "large and metaphorical sense" to include every effort exerted by organisms, singly or in combination, to extend individual existence to the limits imposed by physiology and yet be successful in leaving progeny. "Struggle for existence" should no more create an image of nature "red of tooth and claw" than of nature as a Utopia of altruistic beings. In simple terms, it means that life is earnest and that it is so because of the difficulties with which it is beset.

Fundamentally, the struggle for existence in nature arises from the different modes of change in organic and inorganic matter. Organic life is recalcitrant and insurgent, seeking always to expand beyond its

---

[4] R. H. Whitbeck and O. J. Thomas, *The Geographic Factor* (New York, 1932), 21.

local environs.   Environment is a passive but rigorous censor, imposing restrictions on living forms and tending to shape them to its pattern.   This may be simply illustrated.

The power of reproduction is so great in every kind of life that,
lacking any interference, one species could literally fill the earth with
its offspring in a relatively short time.   A single microbe, for instance,
is capable of multiplying its number to a thirty-digit figure in one
day.[5] Linnaeus estimated than an annual plant with only two seeds
could be represented by over a million descendants in twenty-one
years.   Even the slow-breeding elephant, according to Darwin's figures, could cover all the land space of the earth with the progeny of
one pair in less than 750 years.[6] It is unnecessary that we restrict
ourselves to such inferences.   The tremendous fecundity of life is evident on every hand.   A codfish is said to produce two million eggs,
a conger eel ten million and an oyster twenty million.   The prickly
pear, when introduced into Australia, covered thousands of square
miles of land in a few years, and at the height of its spread was invading a new acre every minute of the day.[7] In certain parts of the world
today mankind is reproducing at a rate that may more than double
the population in less than a generation.   We must also take account
of the fact that celibacy in nature is an exception rather than a common occurrence.   Virtually every adult individual, plant or animal,
attempts to participate in populating the earth.   Thus, as Malthus said
of man, the tendency to increase in a geometric ratio is inherent in all
life.   There is no theoretical limit to the geometric progression.

Actually, however, living forms seldom if ever realize their maximum reproductive capacity.   The flora and fauna of any area do not
seem to increase significantly over a period of years.   There are, to be
sure, fluctuations in the numbers of organisms.   One year there may
be a superabundance of rabbits; the next year the field mice may be
swarming over the fields; and in still another season a species of insect
may appear in unusually large numbers.   Sometimes increases of this
sort reach catastrophic proportions, as in the plagues of insects and
rodents that periodically occur in different parts of the world.   But
such outbursts are temporary, for in every case the *status quo* tends
to be restored, usually by a sudden destruction of the offending species.
On the whole, the population of living things in an area appears to remain fairly stable.

---

[5] J. A. Thomson and P. Geddes, *Life: Outlines of General Biology* (London,
1931), 22.
[6] Charles Darwin, *Origin of Species* (New York, 1925), 6th ed., 80.
[7] Wells, Huxley, and Wells, *op. cit.*, 997.

Such stability, though more apparent than real, is subtle evidence of the struggle of organisms with environment. It represents at least a partial resolution of the opposition between contending forces. He who looks beneath the surface, however, will note many signs of a continuing struggle. Great numbers of dead organisms indicate a tremendous mortality rate, especially among the young of species.[8] Even more obvious and important is the manifold and incessant activity of living organisms. Individuals are constantly on the move, searching for food and other necessities, seeking to attain more advantageous positions, trying and erring, and otherwise striving not only to live but to live better and more abundantly. The struggle for existence is inexorable and inescapable; wherever there is life there is resistance to life. For this reason the struggle for existence is one of the great creative principles in organic nature. Adaptation is a term used to refer to the struggle for existence in its specific, creative aspect.

Adaptation.—The central problem of life is adaptation to those external conditions which provide the materials for existence but which also impede and limit expansion. For every form of life there is an irreducible minimum of materials and conditions without which growth and reproduction are impossible. Light, temperature, humidity, food elements, etc., in varying degrees and combinations, are essential to all species. Variations in these qualities of the environment, together with the presence of competitors and predators, impose restrictions on the number of beings that may occupy an area. It is thus imperative that the organism gain control, through one device or another, over the factors that constitute its environment. Adaptation is the securing and conserving of control over the environment.

Thus the organism is responsive to those environing conditions that are relevant to its needs. It cannot exist without them or without taking them into account. But the converse of this is not true. The elements of the environment, with certain exceptions, exist independently of any particular individual or species. Although the conditions that compose the environment are ever in process of change, they possess no inclination to accommodate themselves to the needs of the organism. The sun, for example, does not vary its intensity to suit the requirements of individual plants. Moreover the sun is but one among a complex of factors each having its own principle of variation. So far as the organism is concerned, therefore, the occurrence of environmental factors in a combination congenial to its survival is, to a large extent, fortuitous. This is less true, of course, as the organism

---

8 Darwin, *op. cit.*, 55-57.

gains control over its own behavior and thereby acquires the ability to manipulate factors in the external world to fit its needs. Nevertheless, the organism is at all times the active and responsible agent. The dependence of organism on the physical environment is a one-way relationship. Environmental change, moreover, proceeds without regard for the welfare of organisms or of species of organisms. Consequently the equipment of the organism which fits it for a given habitat tends always to become outmoded. Adaptation is therefore a continuous process to which there appears to be no ultimate termination.

The problem of survival, then, rests with the organism, not with the environment. As Darwin pointed out, it is in response to the varied sustaining qualities of environment that life becomes differentiated and distributed over the earth. Each form of life represents at least a temporary adaptation to local conditions and its activities reveal the tendency to achieve an even more satisfactory state of adjustment. The relation of organism to environment, referred to earlier as an elemental dependence, may be more aptly described as adaptation, the most generalized form of which is the struggle for existence.

The environment of any life form is a set of manifold external circumstances which influence, positively or negatively, the activities of the organism. Any attempt to enumerate the components of environment involves one in an endless task; for each species and type of life responds to a variety of stimuli in a way more or less peculiar to itself. It is possible for general purposes, however, to avoid the extreme multiplicity of factors included in the meaning of environment by reverting to the simple classification we have been using, namely: (1) inorganic; and (2) organic. In the former are included all the mechanical and nonliving conditions that surround the organism, such as light, air pressure, humidity, temperature, minerals, topography, etc. The latter, the organic environment, comprises all manifestations of life whose activities impinge upon the individual or group of individuals. This includes other members of the same species as well as representatives of different species present in the area. Thus man's organic environment is composed of the vegetation which impedes his movements, animals which prey upon him and upon which he preys, domesticated plants and animals, and, what is often most important, his fellowmen. The adaptive efforts of the individual organism, then, are directed toward both inorganic and organic phases of the environment.

We wish to make it clear that our use of the term adaptation does not imply perfection in the relationship between organism and environment. This might be possible were it not for the fact that both terms in the relationship are not only dynamic but differ in character and rate of change. It is obvious, however, that the organism must achieve some degree of harmony between its needs and the opportunities for their satisfaction, otherwise life would be impossible. Whether the harmony attained is ideal or perfect is a question for others to decide: we are interested in the extent to which it makes survival possible. As a process, adaptation means nothing more than a striving to establish a working relationship; as a state of being, adaptation is simply that which exists at the moment.

Furthermore, it is necessary to guard against the misconception of adaptation known as environmentalism.[9] The tendency to view environment, and especially the concrete, tangible environment, as the sole cause of behavior and even of life itself has a long history which is amply described elsewhere.[10] The defects of such a monistic view have been repeatedly shown, and most students today are well aware of them. All events are effects of multiple causation. Speaking very generally, there are always at least two causes operating where life is concerned—organic and inorganic, or organism and environment. Behavior is a product of the interaction of the two; the organism is not the only cause of its activity, nor is environment the only source of stimulation. Unfortunately, however, critics of environmental determinism have often been inclined to omit completely the environmental factor, which simply results in the substitution of a different form of determinism. Certainly the plant's form, its mode of growth, etc., are not caused entirely by the circumstances that surround it. But it is equally true that these attributes are not caused entirely by the individual plant's having been produced by progenitors with comparable traits. The specific plant is the result of organism interacting with environment. Adaptation is a way of conceiving this relationship and as such involves no judgment as to which factor is the more important.

Types of Adaptation.—The almost infinite variety of ways in which organisms meet life problems may be classified in any manner appropriate to the problem at hand. For present purposes the distinction between individual and communal adaptations will serve. Since the individual organism is the common denominator of life and the manifest source of organic energy, adaptations are always observable in the actions of individuals. It is also true, however, that individuals

---

[9] See, for example, Ruth Bunzel, "The Economic Organization of Primitive Peoples," in *General Anthropology,* ed. Franz Boas (New York, 1938), 331.

[10] Wilson D. Wallis, "Environmentalism," *Encyclopedia of the Social Sciences,* V, 561-66.

are independent in but few respects; they inevitably live together and
collaborate with their fellows in overcoming the resistances to life. To
a large extent these two aspects of adaptation represent merely a difference in perspective. Individuals are simply abstractions of the totality of life; and the totality is merely an intellectual synthesis of
individual units. We have no intention of trying to resolve this theoretical problem, except arbitrarily for the moment. It is convenient to
proceed to an understanding of adaptation with the conception of individual and collective forms. The relationship of one type of adaptation to the other should become clear in the course of the following
discussion.

Individual adaptations as they relate to these phases of the environment may be further subdivided into genetic and somatic types. That
is to say, the responses of living forms to inorganic and organic factors
may consist of either genetic or somatic changes. Genetic adaptations,
although manifested by individuals, pertain to the morphology of the
species; whereas somatic adaptations are characteristics peculiar to
the individual. A brief survey of how these adaptations are exhibited
by different organisms will enable us to grasp more fully the meaning
of adaptation and at the same time will reveal certain marked similarities in all forms of life.

Genetic and Somatic Adaptation.—The first and most elementary
problem confronting the organism is that of acquiring a physiological
equipment appropriate to its survival in a given environment. "The
necessity for definite adaptations acts upon the (flora and) fauna like
a sieve of definite mesh, allowing only more or less similar forms to
pass." [11] That is to say, each habitat imposes basic requirements upon
its occupants which must be fulfilled in the structures of the organisms.
These we term genetic adaptations. Darwin emphasized this mode of
adjustment in his explanation of the origin of species. Adaptations
of the structural order are genetically produced; they result from hereditary variation and environmental selection. Every organism is
unique to some degree in its genetic qualities. Those individuals
whose genetic qualities enable them to live in a specific environment
may establish themselves there; the rest perish or move to an environment in which they can survive.

Thus there tends to be "a definite correlation between the peculiarities of inhabitants and those of habitats." [12] Some plants live in water

---

[11] R. Hesse, W. C. Allee, and K. P. Schmidt, *Ecological Animal Geography* (New
York, 1937), 29. Parentheses are ours.
[12] Wells, Huxley, and Wells, *op. cit.*, 835.

and have practically no roots, but, in general, plants are equipped with roots with which they secure water and food materials from the soil and anchor themselves to the habitat. Plants require leaves for the evaporation of water and the absorption of light and carbon dioxide. However, species may be distinguished by the kind of leaves they possess. In tropical areas where moisture is abundant, plants have large-pored leaves; in arid regions where water must be conserved such leaves would be destructive and, consequently, small-pored leaves predominate. Some desert plants, such as cacti, possess large storage space for water. Animals in arctic and desert areas are notable for their protective colorations which seem to identify them with their environment. Marine animals are provided with locomotor and respiratory organs quite different from those of animals occupying terrestrial and aerial habitats. For both plants and animals food is a requirement of first importance, hence their principal specialized adaptations of structure are in each case related to the food factor. Since plants make their own foods, their structures are specially adapted to the mechanical and chemical phase of the environment. Animals, on the other hand, depend for their food on other living forms and their specialized adaptations, for the most part, are concerned with the organic phase of the environment. The teeth and talons of the tiger, the tube-like tongue of the ant-eater, and the glands of the spider, employed in the construction of its web, are obvious examples. "Snipe and woodcock have beaks converted into sensitive and flexible worm detectors and pincers; those of herons are converted into fish-spears, of hawks and owls into flesh-tearers." [13]

In man are found genetic adaptations of no less consequence for survival than those of lower animals and plants. A significant difference appears, however, in the matter of specialization of structure; man possesses the most highly generalized organic structure that has yet appeared in animate nature. His erect bipedal position leaves the forearms free for manipulatory activities. The opposable thumb on his hand makes possible an unparalleled dexterity in the construction and use of tools. A highly developed larynx permits the use of complex vocal symbolizations and, therefore, makes possible an extraordinarily nice adjustment of behavior in cooperative enterprises. Man is also equipped with a highly centralized and closely coordinated nervous system which affords him a high degree of sensitivity and control over his own behavior. These, in brief, constitute the essential genetic adaptation of man; and they give him an environmental

---

[13] *Ibid.*, 835.

tolerance greater than that of any other organism. There are, to be sure, other adaptations which further contribute to man's range of selectivity of environment, and in each case the lack of specialization is marked. For example, most forms of life are structurally limited in the variety of foods they may use, but man appears to be omnivorous in the fullest sense of the word. According to one writer: "He has the incisors of a rodent, the molars of a plant-eater, and the canines of a carnivore. . . . He has an added length of gut for the digestion of green foods, gastric juices for the conversion of starch to sugar, pepsin for the metabolism of proteins, and pancreatic fluid for the emulsification of fats. No animal has such a power of adapting itself to different environmental conditions, nor such a bewildering number of appetites or tastes." [14]

Long-time changes in the environment are met by genetic adaptations such as we have been describing. But at any given time for any given individual it is not sufficient that organic structure be fitted only to a particular set of external conditions. The organism must have within its structure a degree of plasticity which will enable it to accommodate itself to the cyclical variations as well as to other special conditions in the habitat. Somatic adaptation, observable in the bodily changes and forms of behavior that develop in the course of the individual's life cycle, is therefore of fundamental importance to the survival of the individual and indirectly of the species. The capacity for somatic adaptation is also genetically conditioned and may almost be considered a structural element. Plasticity is a general characteristic of all living forms, but is present in varying degrees in different species and in different individuals within a species. The somatic adaptations made by an organism reveal the inherent versatility of the organic structure in meeting local variations in the environment. Unlike genetic adaptations, however, adaptations of the somatic order are temporary; they exist in the life of an individual but are not passed on to succeeding generations.

A few illustrations will clarify what is meant by somatic adaptation. Members of the same species of plant manifest in different environments considerable variation in bodily form. Dandelions growing in short grass on a lawn hug the ground, and the blossom has a very short stem. But in deep grass a long stem raises the blossom to a position where sunlight may be had. Root systems too vary with conditions. If ground water is plentiful, root systems spread out broadly; but if surface water is scarce roots grow downward in search

[14] Audrey Richards, *Hunger and Work in a Savage Tribe* (London and Chicago: The Free Press, 1932), 7-8.

of underground moisture. Certain plants are capable of developing adventitious roots when added support for the stalk becomes necessary. Modifications are also common among animals. Biologists tell us that shellfish will produce much thicker shells when removed from warm to cold water. The same change occurs in mollusks in response to wave action. Likewise fur-bearing animals grow heavy coats of fur and then shed them for lighter ones, alternating with the seasons. A striking instance of somatic adaptation occurs in individuals of a species of Mexican salamander which, in the presence of certain environmental conditions that stimulate abnormal thyroid activity, change from marine to land habitants, undergoing a rather complete metamorphosis.[15]

The human organism is also capable of a considerable degree of somatic adaptation to food, climate, and other aspects of the environment. The digestive system though it suffers a disturbance upon a change of diet will generally become readjusted in a short time. Likewise when the body is exposed to the hot rays of the sun it will develop a protective shield, commonly referred to as skin tanning. Man's heart and lungs vary in size with the altitude at which he customarily lives, that is, with the atmospheric pressure and the proportion of oxygen in the air.[16] Somatic adaptations are also made to many of the diseases that plague mankind. It is well known in medical science that persons who have been exposed for a long time to certain diseases develop a considerable degree of immunity. The practice of vaccination rests upon this principle. The extreme severity of measles, mumps, whooping cough, and chicken-pox among savage peoples has frequently been contrasted with the relative mildness of these diseases among civilized peoples. On the other hand, tropical peoples develop an effective immunity to malaria and often carry the germ for years without showing any marked evidence of debilitation.[17]

There is a tendency to think of adaptation as confined to matters of form or structure. "Birds," says Ritter, "are more apt to be spoken of as adapted for flight than as adapted in flight."[18] Behavior, when it is not ignored in considerations of adaptation, is often regarded as a structural phase of the organism. The view of behavior as determined by certain inherent constants which predispose the organism to act in specific ways is widely held, particularly as regards lower life

---

15 H. S. Jennings, *The Biological Basis of Human Nature* (New York, 1930), 124-25.
16 Whitbeck and Thomas, *op. cit.*, 48-49.
17 G. H. L. Pitt-Rivers, *The Clash of Culture and the Contact of Races* (London, 1927), 75.
18 *The Natural History of Our Conduct* (New York, 1927), 14.

forms. These presumably fixed and unlearned ways of acting are known in their simplest forms as tropisms and in their more complex manifestations as instincts. The action of the plant in following with its leaves and blossom the changing source of light is an instance of photo-tropism. The nest-building activity of a species of spider which involves fashioning a symmetrical excavation neatly fitted with a hinged and bevel-edged trap door, all this performed without contact with any of its fellows, represents instinct. But that the fixity of behavior is ever complete is seriously to be doubted. The utility of the instinct hypothesis, in fact, has been so severely and competently criticized in recent years that it has fallen into almost complete disuse.[19]

"As a matter of actual observation," Ritter declares, "organic activity is far and away more adaptive than is organic structure." [20] Every form of life must act selectively with reference to environment; it is constantly making distinctions, seizing upon that which is appropriate to its needs and rejecting or avoiding that which is not. Each generation of organisms encounters an environment that has been modified by the activities of the parent generation and by numerous other causes of change. Furthermore, each individual is capable of putting itself into a wide variety of relations with the elements of the environment, often quite different from those experienced by the parent. Especially in the case of animals, the power of free locomotion opens up a large range of variation in experience. Adaptations of behavior constitute, therefore, the most conspicuous and important forms of somatic adaptation. The tropisms of plants are variously expressed depending on light conditions, the location of water supply, and other circumstances. Darwin, though reluctant to admit any large degree of variability in animal behavior, conceded ". . . that the mental qualities of animals of the same kind . . . vary much," and that this "could be shown by many facts." [21] During the course of his observations of the mud-dauber wasp, William McDougall punched holes in the partly completed nest while the wasp was off in search of more materials. On its return, the wasp inspected the structure and repaired the damage before continuing with the major part of the task.[22] More familiar to most of us is the process of eliminating fear in animals, known as taming. But some animals, particularly game animals, have been observed to grow more fearful of man as the result of accumulated experience with him. A very common demonstration

[19] See L. L. Bernard, *Instinct, A Study in Social Psychology* (New York, 1924).
[20] *Op. cit.,* 14.
[21] *Op. cit.,* 187.
[22] *The Energies of Men* (New York, 1933), 36-39.

of flexibility in animal behavior occurs in the frequent changes in food habits resulting from fluctuations in the supply of customary food objects.[23] Such changes have their repercussions in other phases of the animal's behavior, especially in hunting habits. Wolves, lions, and other carnivores adapt their hunting techniques to the kind and amount of food objects available. In this connection, an interesting, though perhaps inconclusive, experiment performed with cats and rats is suggestive. One group of kittens was raised with mothers who killed rats in their presence, another group was permitted no contact with rats until they were some months old, and a third group was raised with rats as companions. In the first group 85 per cent killed rats before they were four months old. Of the second group 45 per cent became rat-killers. But no cat in the third group killed any of its companion rats or any strange rats of the same species, although 16 per cent killed rats of other species.[24]

Man, as we have pointed out, is a relatively unspecialized animal. In the naked state his climatic tolerance is more restricted than that of many other animals, yet his physiological structure is so nonspecific as to allow him a far greater range of adaptability than that enjoyed by any other species of life. This is evident in the extent of man's spread over the earth which exceeds that of any other organism of comparable size; human occupancy reaches from the tropics to arctic areas and is found in all latitudes between these climatic extremes. Man's adaptability is further evident in the almost unlimited number of ways in which different peoples accomplish essentially the same end. For example, in regard to food, it is doubtful if there is any sizable nonpoisonous organism which is not a customary food object for some group of men. Again, an apparently limitless variety of techniques have been developed for the provision of shelter, for protection from enemies, for the ordering of human relationships, etc.

The primary cause of man's extraordinary adaptability is his superior mental capacity. Other features of his unspecialized physiology, such as his erect bipedal posture, his opposable thumb, and his laryngeal apparatus, contribute to the relatively unrestricted functioning of this capacity. Whereas other animals depend largely on genetic changes for adaptation to environment, man's chief form of adjustment has been through agencies external to himself but largely of his own fashioning. Instead of developing claws, wings, hard shell cov-

---

[23] Cf. P. L. Errington, "Food Habits of Iowa Red Fox During a Drought Summer," *Ecology*, XVIII (January, 1937), 53-61.

[24] Z. Y. Kuo, "Genesis of Cat's Responses to Rats," *Journal of Comparative Psychology*, XI (October, 1930), 1-35.

erings, horns, etc., man has constructed tools, clothing, weapons, and various other devices from the materials of his environment. More than any other organism he has relied upon the retention of past experience and constructive imagination to guide his adaptive efforts. This is not to say, however, as is sometimes implied, that there is a sharp demarcation between man and other animals in regard to the possession and exercise of mental capacity. Many other animals in adjusting to environment make use of agencies external to themselves. Monkeys use sticks to knock coconuts from trees, birds and insects construct nests, and beavers fell trees and build dams to refashion their natural habitats. The difference between man and other forms of life is a matter of degree rather than of kind, so far as present evidence permits generalization.

But man is not uniformly free throughout his life-cycle to realize the full potentiality of his adaptive capacity. Adaptability, it appears, is greatest at birth and declines slowly but steadily as the individual advances through his life span.[25] Each repetition of a response, each step toward the acquisition of patterned ways of acting further constricts the original flexibility of behavior, producing in the individual "an unconscious fixation of habits or learned stereotyped reactions of a relatively irreversible character."[26] The young generation readily assimilates the innovations of its time but the parents find it difficult to do so. New industries are manned predominantly by the younger generation while old industries retain large quotas of elders. Long established practice begets a cultural complacency and resistance to innovation in a population. Numerous inventions have either been delayed or prevented entirely from coming into use at least in part by this factor. In the eighteenth century the iron plow was rejected because it was thought the iron would poison the soil. Similarly the six-shooter was at first declared by the United States Army to be of little military value, though later became a most important factor in crushing Indian resistance.

An inventory of the peoples of the world would reveal a variety of modes of life much greater than the number of physically distinguishable groups and also would show each group living in terms of but a small part of the range of varied responses of which the human organism is capable. In every instance there is to be found some degree of specialization, more or less immutable. Although the evidence

---

[25] W. R. Miles, "Age and Human Ability," *Psychological Review*, XL (1933), 99-123; and "Age in Human Society," *A Handbook of Social Psychology*, ed. Carl Murchison (Worcester, Mass., 1935), 619 ff.

[26] W. I. Thomas, *Primitive Behavior* (New York, 1937), 26.

from physiology and ethnology indicates that man has a maximum food tolerance, in actual fact specific individuals and groups are usually restricted in their food habits.[27] The Hindu domesticates cattle yet he is repelled by the thought of eating beef or any other kind of meat; the Orthodox Jew refuses to eat pork; while the Westerner and the gentile consume both beef and pork with pleasure. "Moreover savage tribes, including cannibals, have a horror of eggs as food," and "tribes which eat putrid flesh and raw entrails of animals are revolted by some of our delicacies." [28] A similar bias in favor of the familiar or the customary is manifested in other forms of behavior. Preliterate as well as Oriental peoples have been observed to respond with amusement and disgust to our mode of courtship as portrayed in Hollywood motion picture productions. Responses to odors, colors, tones, materials, and other objects of experience differ greatly among peoples habituated to different stimuli. It is obvious that the persistence of customary patterns of behavior in a given group may not be explained solely on the basis of loss of plasticity through the crystallization of habits. But this nevertheless functions as a highly important factor in the limited abilities of individuals to adopt or even to appreciate the behavior of alien peoples. Habit, as James has said, is indeed the "great flywheel of society," keeping each in his place and conserving the gains that have been made.[29]

The plasticity of an organism, particularly in its behavior reactions to environmental stimuli, may be observed from a different point of view. It is easy to overemphasize the apparent perfection of adaptation, whether genetic or somatic. We are always more impressed by the successes achieved by organisms than by their failures. The latter are not so evident to the casual observer, but require the patient and practiced eye of the field worker. Early biologists were intrigued by the appropriateness of the traits of an organism, but contemporary students stress the relative frequency of maladaptation. Ritter, for example, observes in animal behavior a tendency both to excessiveness and to misdirection of effort. "The woodpecker, equipped to store nuts in holes which he has pecked in trees, pecks far more holes than he ever fills, and fills far more holes than he or his fellows ever empty." [30] Instead of storing acorns, the woodpecker frequently stores pebbles and other objects that are of no use to him. Beavers

27 See C. W. Townsend, "Food Prejudices," *Scientific Monthly,* XXVI (1928), 65-68.
28 Thomas, *op. cit.,* 28.
29 Wm. James, *Selected Papers on Philosophy,* Everyman's Library (New York, 1918), 58-66.
30 *Op. cit.,* 75-76.

often fell trees which they fail to use either in building houses or dams, or for food. Trees sometimes are cut which, because of their location or their species, are of no particular value to the beaver.[31]   In other words, a given activity does not always benefit the organism.   To a certain extent maladaptation is due to overspecialization in organic structure and habit systems which inhibit a ready adjustment to changed external conditions.   But it is probable that a very large part of maladjusted behavior is a consequence of the opportunity for error which is an inevitable accompaniment of great variability.

One particular form of somatic or functional adaptation now being studied by biologists, which often has the character of maladaptation, is the tendency for animals to live in restricted territories even though they may be structurally adapted to much wider habitats.   Birds, deer, squirrels, mice and even insects tend to delimit their habitats geographically and to protect such territory against invasion by other members of their own species.   The usual practice is for each family, or mated pair with their offspring, to establish possession over a given unit of territory.   Sometimes, as in the case of squirrels, the various family domains are separated by neutral territories over which all families may search for food unmolested.[32]   One explanation given for this phenomenon is that intimate knowledge of the habitat has survival value.   Within the limited area individuals move about and become thoroughly acquainted with all environmental conditions including food objects, their locations, and behavior characteristics.   On occasion, however, this domestic tendency takes on the aspect of maladaptation.   In some cases food shortage fails to dislodge the occupants from their domain although adjacent areas contain larger supplies of appropriate food items.   "Of the larger wild game about the Painted Woods (North Dakota) and vicinity, after the buffalo and bear, the elk were the next to disappear, which owing to a kind of domestication or attachment to the points where they were born and raised, they usually remained in the one neighborhood until exterminated by the great influx of hunters that came in with or followed the building of the Northern Pacific Railroad." [33]

Maladaptation is also common among human beings.   For the most part it results from change in environment along with the persistence of habitual ways of acting.   Thus, as we noted earlier, to the extent

---

[31] *Ibid.,* 150 f.

[32] Walter Heape, *Emigration, Migration, and Nomadism* (Cambridge, 1931), Chap. ii.

[33] J. W. Taylor, *Beavers and Their Ways,* p. 135. Quoted by W. E. Ritter, *op. cit.,* 218.

that individuals become cemented in a "cake of custom" they lose their ability to adapt to new conditions. This is one reason why many tribal peoples, such as the Tasmanians, become extinct when their territories are invaded by peoples with more efficient technologies. The specific maladaptations that appear in periods of transition are much the same whether the individuals are preliterate or civilized. The Chukchee, for example, who turned from sedentary coast-dwellers to pastoral nomads, carry with them heavy complicated shelters resembling their former permanent dwellings, instead of developing a simpler and more easily transportable type.[34] Likewise, people from northwestern Europe, notably Britain, who have sought to colonize the tropics have insisted on retaining food habits, manners of dress, and other inappropriate customs acquired in the mother country.[35] In every group may be found superstitions and customs that are no longer relevant to the conditions of life but which nevertheless are allowed to continue, creating confusion and interfering with efficient functioning.

We may suppose, however, that most of these maladaptations are temporary and will in time be corrected. Professor Ogburn has referred to the effect of unequal rates of change in human behavior as "cultural lag." [36] For example, before the Comanche separated from the Plateau tribe to become a distinct group, it was the practice upon a man's death to destroy all his possessions. Since the individual's belongings included little more than his clothing and weapons, the loss to the group was small. Later the Comanche acquired the horse, so essential to existence on the plains, and individuals often amassed great wealth, their herds of horses sometimes numbering 2,000 head. Nevertheless the old practice appears to have been continued until some time prior to 1870. By this date the custom had been revised, involving the symbolic killing of only the favorite horse of the deceased, the remainder being distributed among the relatives. The transition was not entirely complete for no definite set of rules regulating property inheritance had been devised.[37] Similar instances of lag in readjustment are numerous in the history of civilized society. The confinement of women to domestic activities continued long after the majority of these functions were transferred to industry. Many years were required for Western peoples to learn to live in great cities, and there is reason to believe the adaptation is still not complete.

---

[34] Franz Boas, *The Mind of Primitive Man* (New York, 1913), 162.
[35] A. Grenfell Price, *White Settlers in the Tropics* (New York, 1939), 217-27.
[36] *Social Change* (New York, 1922), 200 ff.
[37] Ralph Linton, *The Study of Man* (New York, 1936), 297-98.

Some cases of maladaptation appear not to have resulted from cultural lag, though the explanation of these is more or less obscure. The Japanese despite their large population restrict their agriculture to the lowlands and do not use the mountain slopes even for grazing, though the highlands comprise roughly 80 per cent of Japan's total land area. A short distance away in the Philippines, where similar topographic conditions prevail but with a much lower population density, the mountain sides are assiduously terraced and cultivated. Again, the Tasmanians inhabited an area rich in natural resources, but failed to advance their technology beyond a crude level. Yet the Eskimo, occupying one of the world's least favorable habitats, have developed a remarkably ingenious technology. Answers to these enigmas would require an extensive study of the growth and change of culture, which we are not prepared to undertake at present.

There is little agreement among scholars on standards by which a custom or set of customs may be classified as maladaptation. Such a classification is largely an ethical matter and standards vary with the observer and with the situation under observation. Who is able to assert authoritatively that maladaptation is revealed in the prevalence of exceptionally high frequencies of infanticide among certain primitive peoples, or in the destructive potlatch of the Kwakiutl Indians? How shall we regard the Hindu veneration of the cow which results in the keeping of millions of cattle at a cost of several times in excess of the total land revenue of India?[38] It might be argued that any practice which interferes with survival is maladaptation. This position has much to recommend it; but survival may take any of a number of different forms. Survival, in other words, is relative to the circumstances in which the organism lives. For this reason we have been content to define adaptation as the establishment of a working arrangement, the achievement of at least a partial equilibrium between contending forces.

Communal Adaptation.—The discussion to this point has been centered principally upon the individual as the representative of a species. But one of the first lessons learned by the conscientious observer of life is that organisms do not live as discrete units, except, possibly, for brief periods of time. They do not, in other words, achieve their adaptation to environment alone and unaided. Nothing could be more erroneous than a conception of the organic world merely as a distribution of self-sufficient and disparate units of life. Living organisms

---

[38] G. Findlay Shirras, "Indian Agriculture and Indian Peasants," *Indian Journal of Economics,* IX (October, 1928), 120.

are inevitably dependent upon their fellows in one way or another; and the organic world, viewed in its generality, is a multitude of partnerships and corporations that overlie and interpenetrate one another, thus constituting an intricate network of vital relationships.

It has been pointed out that adaptations to both inorganic and organic phases of the environment are required of all life forms. These, as we have shown, are effected through genetic and somatic means. Of particular importance, though sometimes overlooked, is the fact that adaptation to one environmental phase is impossible without adaptation to the other. The complex character of the adaptation process derives in part from the inherent physical and mental limitations of the organism, but probably to a much greater extent from the rapid reproduction rate of which living creatures are capable with the resultant tendency to overcrowding the available life space. W. G. Sumner provides us with an apt, though somewhat oversimplified, explanation of the way in which organic and inorganic environments become interrelated. When an individual, he observes, is attempting to accomplish something in an area, the fact that other individuals are trying to do the same thing in the same area is for him a highly important condition. The individual organism may ignore the others and thus, by exposing itself to the risk of unnecessary interference and conflict, increase its chances of failure in the enterprise. Or it may adjust its activities to those of its co-inhabitants and thereby enhance the probability of success.[39] In other words, through cooperation energy is conserved and the effects of chance occurrences that threaten the life of the organism are minimized. Adaptation to the physical and mechanical conditions of the environment is facilitated, in fact is secured, through the mutual adaptation of organisms.

Students of life are in general agreement that the universal tendency is for organisms to confront the environment not as individuals but as units in a cooperative effort at adaptation. For example, plants, the most independent of living forms, "do not ordinarily live alone like hermits but are found growing along with other plants in communities that usually consist of many individuals."[40] Concerning animals, Darwin wrote: "Although there is no evidence that any animal performs an action for the exclusive good of another species, yet each tries to take advantage of the instincts of the other, as each takes advantage of the weaker bodily structure of the other species."[41] Man is no exception to the general rule. Men everywhere live in associa-

---

[39] *Folkways* (New York, 1906), 16.
[40] W. B. McDougall, *Plant Ecology* (Philadelphia, 1931), 214.
[41] *Op. cit.*, 186.

tion with other forms of life as well as with their fellowmen. Few instances of solitary human beings have come to light and, while information concerning these feral creatures is far from satisfactory, it appears that survival in every case was contingent upon the individual's adapting his activities to those of other species.[42]

Thus, it is evident that adaptation is a collective phenomenon, involving all the organisms occupying a given area. The exposition of this hypothesis is the subject of the following chapter, but it may be pointed out here that the adaptive efforts of individuals culminate in a community of interorganic relationships by means of which each organism maintains itself in the habitat. To this "higher physiology of organisms" we apply the term *communal adaptation* in order to convey the idea that adaptation to environment is a population rather than an individual problem.

Communal adaptation constitutes the distinctive subject matter of ecology which is a study not of individuals but of populations of living things. Individuals and their adaptations are of importance to the ecologist only in that they serve as convenient units in the analysis of a community. Ecology concerns itself not with mere aggregations of individuals but with their organization and integration in a community. That the community is the essential adaptive mechanism may be taken as the distinctive hypothesis of ecology.

Summary.—Although ecology is concerned with a special aspect of the relation of organism to environment, an analysis of that relationship in its generality will assist in the clarification of the ecological problem. Living matter is dynamic, self-reproductive, and expansible. It is constantly seeking to embody itself in organic forms appropriate to the context of conditions in the external world. Nonliving matter, though changeable, is neither self-reproductive nor cumulative. It constitutes the substance and the elemental conditions from which life draws its sustenance. From the difference in the modes of change of living and nonliving matter arises the central problem of life, the problem, that is, of maintaining growing, multiplying life forms in a restricted but ever changing environment. The problem is one of adaptation and has been characterized as a struggle for existence. Struggle is interpreted to mean the exertion of effort whether in conflict or cooperation to maintain and expand life.

Considered in its specific manifestations rather than as a process adaptation assumes many forms. Adaptations may be classified as

---

[42] Cf. R. E. Park and E. W. Burgess, *An Introduction to the Science of Sociology* (Chicago, 1921), 239-43.

individual and communal, and the former may be subdivided into
genetic and somatic adaptations. Genetic adaptations are species
characteristics that result from hereditary variation and natural selection. They are present in all forms of life, but range from highly
specialized features that limit the organism to a very specific habitat
and type of life to generalized structural characteristics that, as in the
human species, permit the organism to occupy a great diversity of
habitats and to develop any of an almost unlimited variety of life
patterns. Somatic adaptations pertain to variations of form and of
activity that occur in the life of the individual and within the limits of
tolerance of his genetic structure. Again man exhibits the extreme
of variability in this respect particularly in regard to behavior, as is
indicated by the tremendous diversity of human culture. The differences between men and other organisms in adaptive capacity, though
great, seems to be a matter of degree rather than of kind.

Organisms live not as discrete units, but collectively in organized
unions of one kind or another. Adaptation is achieved indirectly and
with the aid of the organism's fellows: adaptation to the inorganic
phase of the environment presupposes adaptation to the organic phase.
The cooperative or organized population that emerges from the adaptive efforts of organisms is the chief, in fact the basic, means of adaptation to the inorganic environment. This is what is meant by
communal adaptation and it is this that constitutes the special subject
matter of ecology.

SUPPLEMENTARY REFERENCES

OSBORNE, HENRY FAIRFIELD. *The Origin and Evolution of Life: On the Theory of
    Action, Reaction and Interaction of Energy.* New York: Chas. Scribner's Sons,
    New York, 1918.
SEARS, PAUL B. *Life and Environment: The Interrelation of Living Things.* New
    York: Columbia University Press, 1939.
WOODWORTH, R. S. "Individual and Group Behavior," *American Journal of So-
    ciology,* XLIV (May, 1939), 823-29.

Chapter 3

INTERRELATEDNESS OF LIFE

The Web of Life.—Everybody knows in a general way that different forms of life are interrelated. The facts are so obvious that we take them for granted as we do the weather, the stars, and the landscape. Cattle and horses graze together in the meadows and seek shelter on a hot day under the shade of the trees. Robins and other birds search for worms and seeds in the lawn or in the fields. The cat steals up silently in the grass or underbrush to seize the unsuspecting bird or mouse. Squirrels rummage for nuts and escape the dogs by scurrying up trees. Bees and hummingbirds flit from flower to flower gathering nectar; while mosquitoes and other insects become so bold that we fit our houses with screens to keep them out. Dandelions and other "weeds" invade our lawns and choke out the grass—and so we might continue indefinitely.

Relationships among living creatures, however, are infinitely more complex than they appear on the surface. The oft repeated phrase "all flesh is grass and all fish is diatom" is more than a mere epigram; it is an accurate, if cryptic, expression of the subtle and highly ramified interconnectedness of life. Darwin was among the first to appreciate fully nature's intricate pattern which he described in the metaphor "web of life." This vivid concept has since become the point of departure for ecological study; it constitutes the frame of reference for an ecological, as against a physiological or psychological, analysis of life. We must, therefore, examine in some detail the meaning of this idea.

Darwin, in his description of the nexus between cats and next year's clover crop,[1] provided the now classic illustration of the network of vital linkages which bind different organisms together. Humble-bees alone, his observations disclosed, visit the red clover; other bees and insects cannot reach the nectar. But the number of humble-bees in an area depends in a great measure on the number of field-mice, since these latter invade the nests of humble-bees and rob them of their food stores. Cats, in turn, are the natural enemies of mice and hence con-

---

[1] *Origin of Species,* 59. According to J. Arthur Thomson, "... red clover imported to New Zealand did not bear fertile seeds until humble-bees were also imported." *Darwinism and Human Life* (New York, 1919), 53.

33

trol their numbers.   In areas adjacent to villages the nests of humble-bees were found to be more numerous than elsewhere, owing no doubt to the larger number of cats there.   An increase in the cat population, it may be inferred, is followed by a decrease in the number of mice, thus permitting an increase of humble-bees and, consequently, a more widespread fertilization of red clover.   Creatures that, to all outward appearances, are ". . . remote in the scale of nature . . ." are found to be linked together in a chain of relations.   Much has been accomplished since Darwin stirred the intellectual world by the publication of his observations and theories and much new light has been shed on the correlations of organisms and their collective adjustment to the varying physical environment.   Darwin and his colleagues sketched the principal outlines in nature's pattern and subsequent students have been rapidly filling in the details of the pattern with many valuable discoveries.   The deeper the analysis of the "web of life" is pushed the more meaningless becomes such a word as "independent."

In the performance of the most elementary physiological functions the two great units of the organic world, the plant and the animal kingdom, are involved in a give and take, a rudimentary division of labor.   Plants, needing carbon in the manufacture of their own food, draw carbon dioxide from the atmosphere, and give off oxygen. Conversely, animals to maintain life must have oxygen in large quantities and, in exchange, they return carbon dioxide to the atmosphere. There are, to be sure, other sources of carbon, such as volcanic action, the combustion of organic materials, and the activities of certain microbes in breaking down carbohydrates; but the largest part is released in the exhalations of animal organisms.   On the other hand, vegetable organisms are constantly replenishing the supply of oxygen available for animal use.   Priestly discovered this principle in the eighteenth century when he found that air "spoilt" by mice could once more be made capable of supporting animal life, if green plants were left in it for a period.[2]

Interdependence as seen in the circulation of matter is much more ramified than this simple exchange.   Each organism is a combination of chemicals generally essential to life—carbon, oxygen, nitrogen, hydrogen, phosphorus, calcium, iron, sulphur, and others—of which it is but a temporary custodian.   Sooner or later it must yield up the elements composing it for a renewal of the life process.   Every species is food for another species and in this way vital ingredients are transmitted from body to body.

---

[2] Sir Wm. Dampier, *A History of Science* (New York, 1932), 285.

Consider, for example, the muscles of a man. Their material may be used up—burnt or worn away—during his life, in which case it will be excreted in his breath or in his urine. Or it may be present at his death, in which case it will be fallen upon by bacteria and demolished, and the chemical bricks of which it is built make their way as before either into the air or into the soil in the form of comparatively simple molecules. In either case, sooner or later, it will be built again into a living thing. . . . Life is a continual commerce. There is a rhythm, a cycle, from inorganic substance in the air and soil to plant tissue, thence to animal, from either of these last two stages via excretion or death and decay back to the air and soil.[3]

Green plants play a fundamental role in animate nature. They are the primary manufacturies of the foods which nourish the entire animal kingdom. Through their photosynthetic activities they draw together the various inorganic materials and transform them into the compounds that animals require. In this they have the assistance of numerous species of microscopic vegetable organisms, known as bacteria, whose function it is to liberate the chemicals that become deposited in various forms for use by green plants. Myriads of these little catalysts labor at breaking down the corpses of organisms, fixating nitrogen in compounds with other elements, oxidizing ferrous metals, attacking solid accumulations of calcium, phosphorus, and other materials. Green plants could not live, much less perform their function in the organic world, without the help of micro-organisms. It is doubtful too that green plants could long survive in the absence of the animals that feed upon them, since animals are an important source of many essential compounds such as carbon dioxide, nitrates, and phosphates. Nevertheless, it does not distort the facts to regard green plants as the foundation upon which is reared the structure of the animal kingdom.

Plant materials enter the animal kingdom as the food of its vegetarian members. Herbivora convert plant into animal matter and thus act as intermediaries between the major part of the animal world and its ultimate food supply; they function as secondary manufacturies. In turn, herbivora are eaten by carnivora which themselves are food objects for larger carnivora and these again may be preyed upon by still other carnivorous feeders. Darwin's instance of the cats and the clover described just such a chain of food relationships at each link of which materials are assembled and processed for use by a succeeding link. Herbivora are but plants once removed while carnivora are plants two or more times removed.

[3] H. G. Wells, J. S. Huxley, and G. P. Wells, *The Science of Life,* Vol. III, 305-306. By permission of Mrs. Marjorie Wells.

Food chains are innumerable in nature. They are interlaced in a variety of ways through the more or less omnivorous habits of many creatures, the multifaceted lives of parasites, and the indiscriminate searchings of scavengers. In a North American forest, for example, the oak, maple, elm, and other deciduous trees support a number of interlocking food chains, as shown in Figure 1. Mice and squirrels feed on the fruit and leaves of trees. Mice are eaten by skunks which in turn serve as food for the red fox, while squirrels are food for the grey fox. Another line starts from the bark of the same tree; the bark is consumed by insects, the insects by birds and mice, and birds and mice by raccoon and fox. Insects also contribute to the support

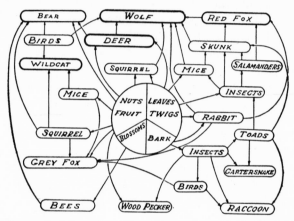

Fig. 1.—A fragment of the web of life. (From Victor E. Shelford, "The Physical Environment," in *A Handbook of Social Psychology,* ed. C. Murchison [Worcester, Mass.: Clark University Press, 1935], 568. Used by permission.)

of the raccoon by way of the garter snake and the toad. A third line may originate from the blossoms of the tree from which the bees get honey. Bees are eaten by various birds and these in turn are eaten by wildcat, bear, and wolf. Wolves also feed on red fox, skunk, mice, squirrels, and deer; the food of bears is even more diversified. Other chains might be traced from the wood-boring insects that infest the limbs and trunks of trees, the earthworms that feed upon the fallen leaves, and the parasites that live both in and on the organisms supplied indirectly by the tree.

Symbiosis.—Upon analysis of the web of life, we find that one of its most conspicuous and important components is the symbiotic relationship. The term *symbiosis* denotes a mutual dependence between unlike organisms. Because they make dissimilar demands on the environment members of different species may supplement the efforts of one another. The food-enemy relationship is of this order. The eater and the eaten are engaged in a vital cooperation, each contributing to and facilitating the circulation of life-giving matter. But their mutual assistance is also more direct. The food species produces a surplus population for the maintenance of a predator species. The latter, by its predation, exercises a control on the size of the food species population which, if it grew too large, would be exposed to extinction by contagion or by the exhaustion of its own food supply. "It is easy to see that what may be a one-sided harmful relation between individuals may be a tolerable or even beneficial relation between populations." [4] There are, however, many less sanguinary expressions of symbiosis.

Nature is replete with instances of direct mutual helpfulness between unlike organisms. Much of the complexity of the web of life is due to the prevalence of this phenomenon. The association of leguminous plants and certain nitrogen-fixating bacteria is a typical example of symbiosis. Bacteria, existing in nodules on the roots of legumes, capture nitrogen from the air and transform it into substances that these plants can absorb; the plants in turn contribute materially to the sustenance of the bacteria. For this reason, legumes such as alfalfa and clover restore the fertility of soil in which they grow and are, therefore, of great importance to man in his agriculture. Another instance of symbiosis, which strikingly reveals the intimacy of the relationship, is represented in the heather of Britain.

It grows exuberantly on mountain and moorland where few other flowering plants can make a living. There is soil, but it is unready; there is water, but it is apt to be physiologically unavailable. How does the heather flourish so well? The answer is that it has entered into a very intimate partnership with a fungus, which penetrates through and through the heather, from root to stem, into every leaf, even into the flower and its seed. What an individual could not do, a firm achieves. The heather is a dual organism; it is like a flowering lichen! If it stood alone it would be a remarkable curiosity, but it is only an instance of a kind of partnership that is now known to be common, between the highest plants and the lowest.[5]

The dependence of herbivora upon bacteria to assist in breaking down the cells of plants taken into the stomach as food; the cooperation between certain plants and animals by which the animals are provided with fruit and the plants have their seeds scattered widely

---

[4] A. E. Emerson, "The Biological Basis of Social Cooperation," *Illinois Academy of Science Transactions,* XXXIX (1946), 13.

[5] J. Arthur Thomson, *Concerning Evolution* (New Haven: Yale University Press, 1925), 104-105.

over the environment; the entrance of the little plover into the mouth of the crocodile to pick the blood-sucking leeches from the gums of that huge amphibian; the exchange of hospitality by the ant for the milk of the aphid; the partnership between man and favored plants and animals—man providing an ideal habitat devoid of natural enemies and in return having his food supplied; these and numerous other occasions of symbiosis draw the threads of interrelationship in the living world into a tight and complex fabric.

Parasitism is sometimes distinguished as a unique relationship. Unlike the symbiont, one hears it said, the parasite does not pay its way; it draws its sustenance from another plant or animal without actually, or immediately, destroying the life of its host. But a note of caution must be introduced into this way of regarding organisms classed as parasites. The characterization appears to be valid only from the point of view of the individual host, not from that of the species. According to Elton, "the difference between the methods of a carnivore and a parasite is simply the difference between living upon capital and upon income . . ." [6] and this distinction involves an evaluation often difficult to make.[7] Realistically, the parasite is but a miniature herbivore or carnivore whose small size represents a structural adaptation that permits a most intensive utilization of environment. Parasitism is thus merely a special form of symbiosis.

Still other forms of interspecific relationship may be mentioned, such as helotism—or the enslavement of one species by another as practiced by termites; and predatism—another name for the food-enemy relationship but connoting the element of wanton destruction. Yet these, like parasitism, are merely special forms of symbiosis; their use as denotative terms depends largely upon the values carried in the mind of the observer. The one incontrovertible fact, to which all such terms point, is the mutualism of life. Diverse species associating together draw heavily or lightly on the special abilities of one another and the benefits returning to each may be immediate or delayed, direct or indirect; nevertheless each plays a necessary part in the ongoing drama of life. Symbiosis, then, appropriately describes all forms of

---

[6] Charles Elton, *Animal Ecology* (New York, 1927), 72.

[7] "It is common to find parasites referred to as if they were in some way more morally oblique in their habits than other animals, as if they were taking some unfair and mean advantage of their hosts. If we once start working out such 'responsibilities' we find that the whole animal kingdom lives on the spare energy of other species or upon plants, while the latter depend upon the radiant energy of the sun. If parasites are to occupy a special place in this scheme we must, to be consistent, accuse cows of petty larceny against grass, and cactuses of cruelty to the sun." Charles Elton, *Animal Ecology*, p. 75. Published by The Macmillan Company and used with their permission.

living together of unlike organisms.[8] But symbiosis is not the only cohesive factor in the web of life.

Commensalism.—Organisms relate themselves to one another on the basis of their likenesses as well as their differences. Hence a second and equally important relation in the web of life is that which arises between similar creatures—members of a given species or rather individuals that make similar demands on the environment. This is the relation of *commensalism* which, literally interpreted, means eating from the same table.[9]

The most elementary and yet salient expression of commensalism in nature is competition, the name given to the kind of interaction in which each individual affects the behavior of every other by its effect upon the common supply of sustenance materials. Wherever individuals with like demands crowd in upon limited resources there is competition. Competition is almost as general as are the phenomena of reproduction and aggregation. These processes, in fact, are the mainsprings of competition; they tend to bring about a situation in which the assembled organisms make demands for food and living space in excess of the available supply. The ensuing interaction may be exceedingly subtle, as in the competition of plants for light and nutrients, or frankly overt, as in the rivalry among chickens for food thrown into their pen. It may be indirect and unconscious, as the grazing of cattle in a fenced pastureland, or direct and conscious, as between business men seeking to outdo one another with their advertising.

Competition varies directly, as we have suggested, with the organism-resource ratio. The intensity of the relationship, however, depends not only upon the number of individuals in an area but also upon the degree of similarity existing among them. Thus, while competition is common between members of the same species, many

---

[8] A narrower meaning is sometimes given to the term symbiosis in special studies where it is necessary to draw the distinction more finely. To Thomson and Geddes: "It means a mutually beneficial internal partnership between two organisms of different kinds." (J. A. Thomson and P. Geddes, *Life: Outlines of General Biology* (London, 1931), 133.) This definition may be taken as representative of the more precise usage of the term and is illustrated in the relationship of the heather and the fungus. F. E. Clements declares: "The term symbiosis has sometimes been rendered meaningless or at least superfluous by being extended to include practically all the phenomena of association, but is here employed in its proper sense of a specialized coaction, involving some degree of mutuality." However, he continues: "This latter may fluctuate greatly from type to type, and in our present knowledge no hard and fast limits can be set." ("Social Origins and Processes Among Plants," *Handbook of Social Psychology*, ed. C. Murchison (Worcester, Mass., 1935), 31.) See also J. R. Carpenter, *An Ecological Glossary* (Norman, Okla., 1938), 268.

[9] "Le commensal est simplement un compagnon de table." (J. Braun-Blanquet, *Plant Sociology*, trans. George D. Fuller and Henry S. Conrad (New York, 1932), 9.)

different species possess requirements sufficiently alike to make them competitors. For example, seedlings of one species of tree compete with each other for space, water, light, and nutrients, as well as with seedlings of other species and also with the parent trees.[10] Animal competition pertains primarily to food and secondarily to space in which to breed and find shelter. To the extent that different species have different food habits competition is confined to each species. But there are numerous instances of interspecies competition: deer, rabbits, and mice compete for certain kinds of grass; and toads, garter snakes, salamanders, raccoons, birds and other carnivora compete for various forms of insect life.

The significance of competition is often emphasized to the exclusion of the mutual support like organisms render one another. Organisms with similar requirements frequently combine their efforts to maintain favorable life conditions; an aggregate acting in concert can accomplish what a lone individual cannot. The number of individuals of a species banded together in an area, for instance, seems to be a factor of consequence for their survival. A large group of animals is more immune from attack by enemies than are individuals or small groups of twos and threes. This may partly account for the more pronounced herding tendency of herbivora than is exhibited by carnivora. Darling reports that "snow is less of a danger to a large mass of deer than it is to small groups. . . ." [11] Allee showed experimentally that goldfish in large numbers are better able to overcome poisons in their habitat than when they encounter such conditions individually.[12] Illustrations of this very simple form of cooperation could be recited indefinitely, for it is a very commonplace phenomenon.[13]

Thus animate nature may be likened to a fabric ever in process of being woven upon the looms of the physical environment; the warp formed of symbiotic and the woof of commensalistic relations. There is no question as to which is the more important; both warp and woof are essential to the weaving.

Plant and animal ecologists are disposed to regard symbiosis as an interspecies relationship and commensalism as an intraspecies re-

---

[10] "Morosow counted on one hectare 1,048,660 ten-year old beeches. In a fifty-year old pure stand of the same area there were 4,460; in a stand one hundred and twenty years old only 509. The completely closed growth permitted, therefore, only 1 out of about 2,000 young beeches to come to maturity." (Braun-Blanquet, *op. cit.*, 11-12.)

[11] *A Herd of Red Deer* (London, 1937), 97.

[12] *The Social Life of Animals* (New York, 1938), 53-57.

[13] P. Kropotkin, *Mutual Aid*; W. C. Allee, *Animal Aggregations* (Chicago, 1931); F. Alverdes, "The Behavior of Mammalian Herds and Packs," in *A Handbook of Social Psychology,* ed. C. Murchison, 194 ff.

lationship. This may be true by and large, especially among lower forms of life; yet the species concept is somewhat too rigid for ecological purposes.[14] Symbiosis may occur within a species and, as we have seen, commensalism often reaches across two or more species. In point of fact, taxonomic characteristics have ecological relevance only so far as they serve as indexes of behavior traits. "When an ecologist says 'there goes a badger,'" Elton declares, "he should include in his thoughts some definite idea of the animal's place in the community to which it belongs, just as if he had said 'there goes the vicar.'"[15] This is to say that the speciation of importance in ecological study is occupational rather than morphological.

The Biotic Community.—Animate nature appears at first glance as a bewildering melange of vital linkages. The web of life, however, is not a random or haphazard occurrence. Despite the many important differences in life, place, and time, the urge to live and the struggle it invokes culminate in a pattern of relationships which has its counterparts throughout the biosphere. The web of life contains numerous distinguishable configurations of relationships all of which are more or less alike in the essentials of organization.

Subdivisions of the web of life become evident when organisms are observed in the context of the physical environment. It hardly needs to be pointed out that interrelations develop in specific places, at specific times, and under particular conditions of the environment. Life, in short, is a space-time phenomenon; just as there is differentiation to constitute units of the physical environment, there is also differentiation to constitute units of associated life. These units are described as communities.

The biotic community [16] is composed of the plant-animal formation that obtains in a given area or habitat. Its unit parts are species so closely interrelated that they constitute a clearly discernible unit.

---

14 Cf. W. H. Thorpe, "Ecology and the Future of Systematics," in *The New Systematics,* ed. Julian Huxley (Oxford, 1940), 341-64; and H. C. Cowles, "An Ecological Aspect of the Conception of Species," *The American Naturalist,* XLII (1908), 265-71.

15 *Op. cit.,* 64.

16 The term *community* has been used loosely by ecologists to refer to a wide variety of associational phenomena. This is evidenced by the citations in *An Ecological Glossary* (64). The rich potential meaning of the word, probably derived from its long-standing currency in the vernacular, makes it unsuitable for technical purposes unless it be redefined along narrower lines. However, opposition to the varied usage of the concept community should be based not on lexicographical grounds but on what is regarded as an appropriate unit of observation in ecological research. Specialization of interest in ecology has given rise to the concepts "plant community," "animal community," and "human community." These have been treated as separate units although it is generally conceded that close and vital interactions and interdependences exist between them. The abstraction represented in

The community conception arises from the consideration of the species formation as a collective response to the life conditions offered by a given habitat. The formation constitutes a community in that it possesses a common habitat and serves a common end, namely, adaptation to the habitat.

Ecological interest in the biotic community is twofold in character, being concerned with (1) the form of community organization and (2) the mode of community development. We shall deal briefly with both of these phases. It should be stated, however, that the lack of detailed studies of the biotic community in its entirety makes it impossible to do more than indicate some of the principal organizational characteristics. Accordingly, the discussion of community organization will be concerned with habitat, niches, food-chains, dominance, the pyramid of numbers, and equilibrium. While it may be true that these elements of structure have not been described in all cases with the precision that is to be desired, they have been observed so repeatedly by students in the field that they have come to be regarded as universals of associated life.

Organization of the Biotic Community.—In view of the hypothesis implicit in ecological studies that the community is the agency through which an aggregate of organisms adapts itself to a common habitat, it is well to consider the nature of the habitat factor. The unit of space inhabited by a population is ordinarily described as environment. In this discussion environment is used to refer to all the externally emanating influences that impinge upon an individual or an aggregate of individuals, whichever happens to be the unit of observation. Habitat carries a narrower meaning. It embraces only the physical and chemical conditions that distinguish one unit of occupied space from another; in other words, *habitat* involves a description of the place of abode of the organism, species, or association of species, solely in terms of the inorganic features present.[17] The merit of this definition of habitat is that it draws a sharp distinction between the biotic community and the dwelling place, between the adapting organisms and that to which they must all adapt. Some definitions

each of these concepts may have value for limited purposes but it frequently does violence to an accurate description of associated life. Hence, "biotic community" is here used to avoid over-abstraction by including in the concept all that is germane to the description of the adaptation of life to a given habitat. For purposes of this study, "biotic community" may be regarded as synonymous with "biome," employed by Clements and Shelford in *Bio-Ecology* (New York, 1939), 20 ff.

[17] Clements and Shelford, *op. cit.,* 26-27. W. C. Allee states: "... the habitat includes all the environmental factors which center about the dwelling place except the competition between the animals themselves." (*Animal Life and Social Growth* (Baltimore, 1932), 16.)

of habitat confuse these two factors. Thus while the various occupants of an area may correctly be considered as environmental to one another they are not in the strict sense of the term elements of the habitat; they are elements of the community.

The habitat, as thus defined, enters into ecological thought, not as a first *cause,* but as a prior *cause* of major importance.[18] But this should not be interpreted as attributing efficient and determining power to the habitat. Rather the habitat is a cause in that it constitutes a set of stimuli to which organisms necessarily respond. The causal sequence may be formulated thus: The reactions of dynamic organisms to the habitat and the consequent interaction among themselves, which in turn produce new reactions on the habitat and again new interactions, and so on, gives rise to a biotic community having a coherent organization and pattern of growth.

The basis of the community is constituted by the vegetation of the habitat. This follows directly from the fact that the sessile and sedentary mode of life of plants gives to the association of organisms a more or less distinctive and stable unit character. The vegetation, as Phillips says, gives physiognomy to the biotic community.[19] Every association of plants includes species of varying height of stem and depth of root. The typical deciduous forest, for instance, has as its most prominent members the oak, hickory, maple, or other tall trees whose foliage forms the forest roof. Beneath the roof there is usually a second layer composed of the foliage of shrubs of medium height. A third stratum is made up of shorter-stemmed plants, such as flowers, ferns, and grasses. Finally, there is a ground covering of mosses, lichens, and other low-growing vegetation. The number of such layers seldom exceeds three or four in the deciduous forest. In a cornfield the layers may be only two in number. But in a tropical rainforest the space from roof to floor may comprise a dozen or more strata of plant life.

There is, moreover, a numerical gradation in the forest from top to bottom. The large plants have large requirements for light, water, nutrients, etc., whereas the smaller plants have, in keeping with their size, more modest requirements. Hence, there is room in a given area for more shrubs than trees, for more grasses and flowering plants than shrubs, and for more mosses than grasses and flowers. The plant

---

18 ". . . the essence of ecology lies in its giving the fullest possible value to the habitat as cause and the community as effect, the two constituting the basic phases of a unit process." (Clements and Shelford, *op. cit.,* 30.)

19 John Phillips, "The Biotic Community," *The Journal of Ecology,* XIX (February, 1931), 1-24.

association, therefore, assumes a hierarchical form, each stratum of which is symbiotically related to every other.

Vegetation lends form to the community in another respect. By virtue of its intimate connection with the physical and chemical conditions, and its reaction on these conditions, plant life functions as the intermediary between the habitat and animal life. Plants modify and translate the habitat, making it suitable or unsuitable to different animal species, and thereby exercise a selective influence upon animals. From the standpoint of herbivorous animals the plant association is a complex of food objects and as such it attracts herbivora in accordance with their food habits, and these in turn serve as a food base for various types of carnivora. In addition, the plant association exerts an important determining influence through its reaction on temperatures, humidity, and other elements of local climate, and through its provision of shelter and breeding sites. Thus the animal species composition of the community is fundamentally dependent on the plant matrix.

In consequence, different types of plant associations support different kinds of animal populations. To return to the example of the deciduous forest, it is found to possess a characteristic set of animals including a host of arboreal insects—plant lice, wood worms and wood ticks, and various chains of carnivorous birds as tits, warblers, crows, and owls. There are also certain rodents such as rabbits, squirrels, and mice, together with the carnivora that live on these creatures such as skunks, lynx, and certain species of fox. Deer, elk, bear, and other large herbivora which depend largely on shrubs and trees for food and shelter are also to be found in the community. A prairie grassland, on the other hand, has a different composition of animal life, one that is more or less peculiar to itself. It has a distinctive set of insects; of burrowing animals such as the gopher, badger, and prairie dog; of grazing herbivora represented by buffalo and pronghorn antelope; of burrowing carnivora such as wolves, foxes, and coyotes; of birds that nest on the ground, prairie chickens and meadow larks, as well as certain species of burrowing hawks and owls.

A very useful conception in the study of communities is that of the "niche" or functional role.[20] This concept focuses attention upon what organisms do in the habitat rather than upon their morphological characteristics. A community may be viewed as an organization of niches, since the activities of each class of organism influence the activities of every other class in the association.

---

[20] See Elton, *op. cit.,* 63-68; and Wells, Huxley, and Wells, *op. cit.,* 971-72.

The organism which occupies the niche of key importance in the community is called the dominant. As defined by Clements and Shelford, "A dominant is an organism with such definite relations to climate and such significant reactions upon the habitat . . . as to control the community and assign to other species subordinate positions of varying rank." [21] The tallest plants usually perform this function, for they regulate the light conditions in the habitat and thereby determine directly what other species of plants may occupy the area and indirectly, through the vegetation matrix, the animal species-composition of the community. The dominants may be "oaks in an oakwood, the grass in a field, the heather on a moor, the great trees in a tropical forest, the bulrushes in a swamp." [22] In each instance the organism best adapted to the habitat controls the composition and hence the functioning of the community.

Dominance, however, is a quality which attaches in some degree to all niches in the community. Each species exerts some control, directly or indirectly, over the activities of other species. The carnivore at the end of the food-chain, with the plant matrix, shares in the control of the animal organisms in the more basic niches of the community. But these lesser organisms, through their habits of movement and reproduction, also influence the activities of the "subdominant" carnivora. Similarly the activities of herbivorous animals not only modify but also are modified by the number and distribution of plants. Even though influence over others is exercised by every species in the biotic community such influence is very unevenly distributed. For this reason, organisms exercising lesser dominance are commonly known as *influents,* while the term *dominant* is reserved for those organisms that exercise the maximum degree of control.

Every biotic community contains, in addition to the niche of the dominant, certain broadly defined niches such as those of the microbe, the green plant, the herbivore, the carnivore, the scavenger, etc. As is the case with dominants the other roles are occupied by quite unlike organisms in different areas of the world. The green plant niche may be filled by grasses on the prairies, by shrubs and trees in the forest, or by marine plankton in the sea. The herbivore niche embraces many species of animal life ranging from the tiny sap-sucker in some habitats to the gigantic elephant in others. The principal scavenger in polar regions is the arctic fox, while in tropical areas it is the hyena. The well-known role of the earthworm in temperate areas is performed on coral reefs by land-crabs and in subarctic areas by small insects

---

[21] *Op. cit.,* 238-39.
[22] Wells, Huxley, and Wells, *op. cit.,* 968.

called spring-tails. It is apparent, as Elton points out, that there is a pronounced tendency for different organisms in widely separated places "to drift into similar occupations. . . ." [23]

Niches, the unit parts of the community, are linked together in what were earlier called food-chains, each link serving as food for the succeeding link. Each plant species may support one or more such chains, some of which comprise only two links while others may have four or five. Beginning thus with green plants and running through herbivora and several stages of carnivora, food-chains arise from a multitude of points in the plant matrix and converge ultimately in one or a very few species of carnivorous feeders. There is, in other words, a numerical grading of niches in the community based on the food habits of organisms. Numerous kinds of plant materials support an almost equally large number of herbivorous species; the carnivora that prey directly on herbivora constitute a smaller variety of life forms; and finally food-chains end with species represented by relatively few individuals.

There is also a grading of niches with respect to the number and size of organisms comprising them. The community, in other words, may be viewed as a pyramid of numbers.[24] In the niches at the base of a food-chain the organisms are comparatively numerous but small in size while in each successive link numbers decrease and size increases. The situation in the community as a whole is analogous to that which obtains in the plant matrix; more small than large organisms can occupy a given area. The grading of numbers, however, is not simply a matter of spatial mechanics; of much greater importance in the pyramiding of numbers are the interdependences of various-sized organisms. Small organisms reproduce at a faster rate than do larger creatures and are therefore able to produce a number in excess of that needed to maintain the species. This margin of excess supports a number of larger organisms. These, in turn, because of their relatively slower rates of reproduction, provide a somewhat smaller excess for the support of still larger though fewer organisms. A stage is finally reached in which the number is so small and the breeding habits such that the surplus is not sufficient to maintain a further niche in the chain of food relationships.

This inverse relation between number and size of associated organisms is further explained by another important factor limiting the food habits of animals, namely, time. Most animals are physically unable to cope with animals larger than themselves, although termites,

[23] *Op. cit.,* 65.
[24] Cf. *Ibid.,* 68-70.

wolves, and other animals band together to bring down large game. But, in general, animals are restricted to food objects that are smaller than they are, to organisms they can readily overcome with the equipment they individually possess. It is impractical, however, for an animal to attempt to feed indiscriminately on smaller organisms, for it is imperative that it satisfy its need within a given interval of time. Otherwise the cumulative deficiency would weaken the animal to a point at which it would be unable to withstand disease and the attacks of enemies. Thus time enters to fix a lower limit to the size of objects that an animal may habitually eat. A small carnivore, such as a garter snake, may feed upon insects, but for a fox, insects are too small and too widely spaced. The fox may find satisfaction from mice, rabbits, and birds, whereas the lion can do with nothing less than sheep, deer, or zebras. The lack of a suitably sized food object is sometimes compensated by large numbers. The whalebone whale is able to subsist on tiny crustacea largely because these occur in huge swarms. Similarly, large herbivora may confine their eating to blades of grass, but only where grass grows in profusion. An interesting instance in this connection is cited by Elton of the hapless sheep of Tibet which, because of the sparsity of grass, must eat on the run.[25] An organism, depending on its size, requires a minimum amount of food in its habitat, which may be expressed either in the size or the number of its food objects. The pyramid of numbers represents an adaptation of life to the time factor as manifested in the physiological rhythms of various species.[26]

Although a knowledge of the number relations between different organisms is of fundamental importance to an understanding of their collective life, a full quantitative description of a biotic community has yet to be offered. A few partial estimates have been prepared. Thomson and Geddes declare that ". . . a pound of cod's flesh requires for its making ten pounds of large whelk or 'buckie' each pound of which corresponds to ten pounds of sea worms, each pound of which corresponds to ten pounds of animalculae and organic particles. So that a pound of cod's steak represents a thousand pounds of sea-dust." [27] It has also been estimated that plankton rotifers and crustacea in Lake Mendota, Wisconsin, require food materials twelve to fifteen times their own weight.[28] A lion in Africa is said to kill approximately fifty zebras per year. Wells, Huxley, and Wells suggest that this implies

[25] *Ibid.,* 143.
[26] See Chapter 14.
[27] J. A. Thomson and P. Geddes, *Life: Outlines of General Biology,* p. 107. (London: Williams and Norgate Ltd., 1931.)
[28] Elton, *op. cit.,* 70.

a ratio of several hundred zebras to one lion, since the number of zebras eaten by lions represents only a small part of the surplus required of the species.[29]

The Regulation of Numbers.—A very important question pertaining to the organization of the community concerns the ways in which numbers in the several species are regulated so as to insure the survival of each species and the maintenance of the larger unit. Too small a number of individuals leaves a species unable to compensate through reproduction for the devastation wrought by enemies and the rigors of storm, drought, prolonged winter, etc. For example, at the turn of the century excessive killing by hunters had so reduced the number of heath hen in Massachusetts that the species was unable to survive the inclemencies of the environment and became extinct despite twenty-five years of active protection by state and private agencies.[30] Too large a population is equally detrimental since it causes a sudden depletion of the food supply and thus exposes the whole species to starvation. Overcrowding is also favorable to epidemic diseases which often, as in the case of malaria, cannot thrive when the host population is too small. There is thus for each species and mode of life an optimum number above or below which the chances for survival are considerably lessened. Such a number is most appropriate for the stability of the community.

The old conception of the organization of life as a "balance of nature" implying a highly stable system of relationships has been modified as a result of empirical investigation, especially in the field of animal life. Elton presents a great deal of evidence to support his contention that unbalance in nature is frequently more apparent than balance. His investigations reveal that the number of animals of a given species fluctuates enormously.[31] Marked variations have been observed in the number of rabbits, lynx, martens, deer and many other mammalian species; also in the number of locusts, chinch bugs, army worms, moths, and numerous other forms of insect life; as well as in rodent and bird populations. For some species there appears to be a clearly defined cycle in these variations. Lemmings, British mice,[32] and the arctic fox oscillate on a three- to four-year frequency, while larger species such as Canadian lynx, snow-shoe rabbit, and red fox

---

[29] *Op. cit.*, 992.
[30] W. C. Allee, *The Social Life of Animals*, 113-15.
[31] See Wm. E. Ritter, *The Natural History of Our Conduct;* also Clements and Shelford, *op. cit.*, 172-99.
[32] French mice experience sharp increases and decreases in number, but the variations appear to be irregular. (See Elton, *op. cit.*, 137.)

have a somewhat longer cycle, reaching a peak number every ten to twelve years.[33] At present the data on animal fluctuations are too deficient to be conclusive, nevertheless they clearly indicate that animate nature is ever in a state of flux.

Although the community is clearly not the neatly balanced arrangement it was once thought to be, it is nevertheless a well-established fact that any appreciable variation in the number of individuals in one species is followed by corresponding variations in the species associated with it. The initiating factor may be variation in climate or in other aspects of the physical environment, epidemic diseases, the migratory tendencies of different species, anything, in fact, that changes the food-enemy ratio at some point in the community.[34] Elton provides us with an interesting description of this phenomenon as it was observed in Labrador.

In a year of mouse abundance, many animals change their feeding habits to feast royally on mice. Bears and wolverines do this. In 1905 Cabot says that the grazing was so much spoilt by the mice that the caribou left this part of Labrador in a body to seek food elsewhere. In consequence of the absence of caribou, the Indians in the interior were compelled to subsist mainly upon fish, being also greatly handicapped for lack of deer skins from which to manufacture their clothes. In one area the annual crop of crowberries failed in some places, owing to the young shoots having been devoured by mice. According to Hutton, the shortage of *Empetrum* fruit, the usual and almost the only berry food of the Eskimos, gave rise to a pandemic of a puscular skin disease, due apparently to the deficiency of some food factor contained in the crowberries.[35]

Man is often unwittingly an agent in disturbing the number relations among organisms. By destroying one kind of life he eliminates an enemy of some species, a food supply of others; or by introducing a new form of life into an area he increases the enemies or the food of different species and thus upsets whatever balance may have been attained. A good illustration is the introduction of the mongoose into Jamaica. The planters, wishing to check the scourge of the Oriental rat in the Jamaica cane fields, imported the carnivorous mongoose which was well known for its ability to destroy rodents. The Oriental

---

[33] Clements and Shelford, *op. cit.*, 188-99; and Wells, Huxley, and Wells, *op. cit.*, 1002.

[34] See Elton, *op. cit.*, 141. Clements and Shelford state the causal factor differently as failure of the adults to leave the usual number of progeny resulting from a reduction in the number of breeders caused by food shortage and adverse physical conditions, disturbances in the normal functioning of the reproducing habits, or to destruction of the young by adults. (*Op. cit.*, 180.)

[35] C. E. Elton, *Animal Ecology and Evolution* (London: The Clarendon Press, 1930), 20-21.

rat was soon eliminated, and the mongoose began to feed upon the native cane-rats. Soon the cane-rat population was much reduced and the mongoose, which had increased considerably in numbers, turned its attention to poultry, and to the ground-nesting birds, lizards, and snakes which had served effectively in preventing the multiplication of various insects injurious to the cane crop. Thus the mongoose became a pest and measures had to be taken to reduce its numbers. The introduction of the English starling into New England was followed by the spread of the blackberry; and the transportation of the rabbit to Australia and New Zealand caused the starvation of thousands of sheep when the rapidly multiplying rabbit stripped the grazing land of its grass. Similar sequences have been noted on numerous other occasions when man has interfered in natural life communities. Enough has been said to indicate the nature of the number relations in a community. The prevailing tendency is for the number in each species to become adjusted to the demands of its enemies, on the one hand, and to the requirements for survival, on the other hand. Even though violent fluctuations of numbers occur, sometimes in regular and sometimes in irregular fashion, relatively few species become extinct and, as Elton says, "the species composition of most communities remains very much the same over long periods." [36] The community, in other words, approximates an equilibrium albeit a moving equilibrium, in which the numbers in each species are balanced against the needs of other species.

The Community as an Organism.—The community has often been likened to an individual organism. So intimate and so necessary are the interrelations of its parts, it has been pointed out, that any influence felt at one point is almost immediately transmitted throughout. Further, not only is the community a more or less self-sufficient entity, having inherent in it the principle of its own life process; it has also a growth or natural history with well-defined stages of youth, maturity, and senescence. [37] It is therefore a whole which is something different from the sum of its parts, possessing powers and potentialities not present in any of its components. [38] If not an organism, it is at least a super-organism.

A full review of the history of the organic conception of the community is unnecessary here. Other authors have adequately per-

---

[36] *Ibid.,* 25.
[37] Cf. F. E. Clements, *Plant Succession: An Analysis of the Development of Vegetation* (Washington, D. C., 1916), 124-25; and W. B. McDougall, *Plant Ecology* (Philadelphia, 1931), 214-16.
[38] Clements and Shelford, *op. cit.,* 20.

formed this task.[39] However, it may be pointed out in passing that the idea was first exploited by social scientists. Although Herbert Spencer was not the originator of the theory, his cogent application of it in his systematic description of human society was primarily responsible for its gaining wide currency in the latter part of the nineteenth century.[40] Later the idea fell into disrepute as the result of abuse at the hands of writers such as Lilienfeld and Novicow, together with a general reaction against the close dependence of social upon biological science. The ensuing criticism was vigorous and often unwise; it accomplished little more than a repudiation of the terminology that had accumulated in the exposition of the thought. The idea itself persisted and gathered force. At a somewhat later time students of plant and animal life took up the organic conception of collective life and found in it a fruitful generalizing tool.

The criticism leveled against the organic conception has, for the most part, consisted in the charge that it constitutes an indiscriminate use of analogy, a mere "biologism," as it were. Perhaps it will not be amiss to consider briefly the response that is made to this allegation. In general, ecologists recognize certain limitations of the analogy they draw in employing the organic conception. However, some, such as Wheeler,[41] insist that it involves not simply an analogy but a real identity. Child, too, contends that the difference between an individual organism and an organization of organisms is one of degree rather than of kind.[42] Wheeler concurs in this statement:

The distinction emphasized by Fouillee and Ferriere, that the individuals in animal and human society retain their mobility and are spatially isolated, whereas the histological elements of the organism are fixed and contiguous, is perhaps not as significant as they imagine. The blood cells are also a part of the organism and the distances separating the tissue elements are relative. Even the cells, serum, lymph, etc., are masses of electrons separated by distances so enormous that if the human body could be compressed till all its electrons were in contact with one another, it would have a total bulk of only a few cubic millimeters.[43]

[39] *Ibid.*, 21-24. See also P. A. Sorokin, *Contemporary Sociological Theories* (New York, 1928), 195-97.
[40] *Principles of Sociology* (New York, 1904), Vol. I, 449-62.
[41] "The Ant Colony as an Organism," *Journal of Morphology*, XXII (1911), 307-25. See also W. E. Ritter and E. W. Bailey, "The Organismal Conception: Its Place in Science and Its Bearing on Philosophy," *University of California Publication in Zoology*, XXXI (1938), 307-58.
[42] C. M. Child, *Physiological Foundations of Behavior* (New York, 1924), 270. "The shading of meaning which distinguishes organization from organism is in the direction of relative looseness of relation as between the parts and the whole, and relative lack of independence of conditions external to the system." (*Baldwin's Dictionary of Psychology and Philosophy*, Vol. II, 219.)
[43] W. M. Wheeler, *The Social Insects* (New York: Harcourt, Brace & Co., 1928), 305.

Allee has pointed out that failure to see the essential similarity between an individual and organization of individuals arises from inappropriate comparison. The resemblance between a loosely knit animal association and a closely integrated organism—such as a dog or a man—may not be immediately apparent, but it does not follow that the issue is therefore closed. Not all animals are so well organized as these higher types. In some species, such as sponges, it is almost impossible to determine what part of the living tissue belongs to one individual and what part to another. Again, certain animals, the starfish and the sea-anemone for example, are so poorly coordinated as to have comparatively little control over their members. With such organisms the community compares very favorably; in fact, in many instances the community has more definite organic attributes than do certain of these lower forms of life.[44]

As with many analogies, this one is an approximation to the truth. It at least calls attention to many properties of the organized aggregate that might otherwise escape notice. It also suggests problems for investigation. But it is not necessary, indeed it would not be wise, to impute an identity of community with organism.

Development of the Biotic Community.—It is important to recognize that the biotic community is by no means a static and indestructible arrangement of organisms. The species composition and the habits of life embraced in the community vary from season to season and from year to year, as indicated in our discussion of the fluctuation of numbers. Moreover, if the variations in numbers are closely observed over a period of years, they may be seen to accompany fundamental changes in the organization of the community. There is, in other words, a second kind of dynamics to be observed in the study of communities of which population cycles are often an index. We refer here to the process of community development or succession.

The community, like the individual organism, is something that grows. It proceeds from small beginnings, passes through a series of developmental stages, and eventually attains a mature state. The process may be very gradual, occupying a century or more, or it may occur as a much more rapid series of changes, requiring but a few years. In either case the developmental sequence is essentially the same, though, of course, the process seldom recurs without some variation. It involves a series of population changes, one set of species replacing another, until finally a complement of species appears which is so well adapted to the habitat as to be able to resist further invasion.

---

[44] *Animal Life and Social Growth,* 2-3.

If a boiled hay infusion were prepared and exposed to the air for several weeks, one would be able to observe under the microscope the successional development of a miniature community. Bacteria are the first living things to arrive and they quickly become abundant as they feed upon the decaying vegetable matter. When the transformation of organic matter into food suitable for animals is well advanced, tiny ciliate protozoa which subsist upon bacteria make their appearance in the liquid. These are followed by predaceous protozoa which eat the smaller vegetarian type. Other animal organisms may also make their appearance. But the entire community will soon disintegrate owing to the exhaustion of the food base. It is possible, however, that the liquid will be colonized by green plants such as algae, in which case the whole community will be reorganized on the new food base. Colonization by algae can happen, of course, only after certain organic materials have been deposited in the habitat by the animal inhabitants. With the establishment of algae a new cycle is introduced, for the little green plant brings in its wake a new set of occupants.

The initiating factor in succession outside the laboratory may be either a physical or a biological disturbance in the habitat. Any event, in fact, which destroys the relative equilibrium of a community or creates an untenanted area may mark the beginning of a succession of changes leading to a reorganization of the community. Functional disturbances undoubtedly constitute the most important category of causal factors. Organisms are constantly doing things to their habitats which render them no longer hospitable to the occupants. Plants, for instance, through the deposition of humus and the consequent change in soil composition, drive themselves out of their dwelling places. Animals likewise contribute to their own forced withdrawal through their reactions on the habitat. Each species prepares the area for its successor. It seems to be an ecological principle that any attribute of an organism which facilitates its establishment in a habitat is at the same time a passive factor in its survival there.

The developmental process has been conceived as a series of cycles leading from one stage to the next, the unit parts of each cycle being invasion, competition, and establishment or ecesis.[45] The initial alteration of conditions opens the habitat to invasion by one or more of the many alien species that are usually seeking opportunity to colonize the area. In the ensuing competition it develops that one species is better adapted than the others to the area in question. This species, therefore, wins in the struggle and succeeds in establishing

---

[45] Clements, *op. cit.*, 75.

itself in the habitat, that is, it multiplies rapidly and takes possession of the entire area. The cycle is repeated again when the habitant species modifies the habitat beyond the limits of appropriateness for its needs. This, to be sure, is an oversimplified statement of the process of community development. Nevertheless, if the process is studied with particular emphasis upon dominant species, as is often done, the invasion-competition-establishment cycle serves as a relatively accurate picture of what occurs in each stage. Actually, however, the growth of the community involves many such cycles, some occurring simultaneously, others consecutively, as the various species come into the habitat, settle into their niches, and are later dislodged.

But growth runs its course; it has an ending as well as a beginning. The final result of growth, as applied to the community, is termed the *climax* and may be regarded as corresponding to the adult phase in the life of the individual organism. The climax is reached when a complement of species appears which, through its control of climate and its ability to avoid unfavorable reactions on the habitat, can withstand indefinitely attempted invasion by foreign species. Of particular interest is the fact that for each area there is a characteristic climax phase. A given combination of organisms permits a most efficient utilization of the resources in a given habitat, and research has shown that this type of organization always tends to be produced in the area.

An interesting illustration of this occurred on a Scottish moor. Several pairs of black-headed gulls nested there and under the protection of the owner the gulls increased, in fifteen years, to approximately three thousand. By trampling and manuring the ground the gulls caused the heather to give way to a coarse grass. This, in turn, was displaced by rushes as the number of gulls increased, and this again by masses of docks. Grouse which had formerly occupied the area disappeared. While these changes were occurring pools of water were forming and attracting large numbers of teal. Thus the establishment of the gulls loosed a process of change which revolutionized the entire community. Protection of the gulls ended abruptly a few years later, however, and with the decline of the gull population the area returned to its earlier state of a heather moor.[46] Shelford's research in North-Central Indiana demonstrated that the beech-maple formation was the typical climax for that area. Although development began with cottonwood on the sand ridges, ragweed on floodplains, shadbush on clay banks, and water lilies in the ponds, the climax

---

[46] Elton, *Animal Ecology*, 24.

in every case was the same. The several lines of development, or seres, converged and culminated in a beech-maple-dominated community.[47]

Man's Place in the Biotic Community.—Man, like every other living creature, is inextricably involved in the web of life. Association with diverse species is a necessary condition of all life. This seems to be as true at present as at any time in the past. Nothing in the rising tide of civilization has altered the fact of man's dependence on the organic as well as on the inorganic elements of the environment. The multiplication of human wants and of techniques for their satisfaction, which has been such a prominent feature of man's recent past, have served to implicate man more thoroughly than ever in the natural environment. Modern man uses a far greater variety of plant and animal materials, to say nothing of mineral materials, than were used by any people of earlier times. Thus wherever found man is an integral part of a biotic community.

Nevertheless, man differs from other life forms in that his role with reference to associated species is not prescribed, within such narrow limits at least, by his anatomical and physiological structure. While many lower forms of life are found in different niches in different parts of the world, they exhibit nothing comparable to the variability of role displayed by man. The human species occupies no definite niche in nature's ecological hierarchy, as is evidenced in the relative lack of restrictions on the food habits of man. Man is omnivorous; while he may live almost wholly on either vegetable or animal foods at certain times and places, he generally prefers a combination of these two forms of diet. Moreover, the range in size of food objects is virtually unlimited. No organism is too large for him to eat. At the same time he is able to subsist on tiny vegetable objects such as seeds without an excessive expenditure of energy. Furthermore his tools and techniques of food preparation make edible a vast variety of organic materials inedible in their natural state. No other form of life has access to such a diverse assortment of food objects, and no other species has occupied such a diversity of roles.

Largely through his versatility in relating himself to other organisms, man is found in every major type of habitat which the land surface of the earth presents. His position in the various environments, however, reveals striking contrasts. In certain parts of the world today we find human beings, much the same as other organisms, almost completely dependent upon the materials and conditions of the

---

[47] Cf. Clements and Shelford, *op. cit.*, 231.

immediate environment. In other parts of the world, and frequently not far removed from areas of primitive occupance, we find men living in great cities in which all features of the natural environment have been so extensively modified and refashioned that they appear to be purely human phenomena.

Indeed one might classify the human populations of the world today on the basis of the degree of control acquired over the natural environment. A classification of this sort would reveal an ascending order of dominance beginning with the most primitive food collectors, such as certain of the native tribes of Australia, and progressing through the various hunting, pastoral, agricultural, and industrial levels to the highly industrial organization of Western European peoples. Such a classificatory scheme would present human life on a scale of increasing density and complexity of interhuman relationships with each advancing step in man's control over his physical and biotic environment. The several levels thus described would not, of course, stand out as discrete modes of life; human habitation cannot with accuracy be referred to in such simple language as food-collection, hunting, pastoral, agricultural, and so forth. Within each of these generalized categories there is a wide range of difference in human organization and control Moreover, the categories are not mutually exclusive. Many human groups are at one and the same time food-collectors, hunters, and agriculturalists. It is also true that some preliterate peoples can live more numerously in certain types of habitat than can modern civilized man, e.g., the Eskimos within the Arctic Circle.

Instead of a horizontal classification of the contemporary peoples of the world one might, like anthropologists and historians, view human life from a vertical or time perspective and attempt to determine temporal stages in man's dominance over his environment. In their efforts to discover an evolutionary sequence in human development anthropologists usually disregard the changes in specific habitats and peoples and consider human life as a whole. Taking as their criterion some material or artifact generally employed by man in adjustment to environment, they have divided human development into a number of great temporal stages, such as the stone, the bronze, and the iron age. Historians, with their narrower time perspective and more detailed knowledge, attempt to determine stages of industrial development representative of steps in man's increasing dominance over nature. Gras, for example, proposes a six-fold classification based upon modes of exploiting the natural environment. Human development thus has passed through a series of stages of economic organization, namely, collectional, hunting, pastoral, village, town, and metropolitan, each economy having emerged from the preceding one.[48] But the attempts of scholars to classify stages of human development "have rarely been felicitous. The reality is too fluid to be compressed within neat boundaries of genus and species. Types overlap and melt into each other; identity of form conceals difference of fact." [49]

Yet notwithstanding the difficulties involved in endeavoring to distinguish forms and stages of human development the fact stands out that man, in the course of his sojourn on this planet, has advanced from a relatively low position in the world of life to one of commanding dominance. He has gained "dominion over the fish of the sea, and over the fowl of the air, and over every living thing that moveth upon the earth" (Genesis 1:28). Nevertheless man's dominance is far from complete; there is considerable support for Allee's assertion that ours is actually an "age of insects" rather than an "age of man." [50] Certainly it is obvious that man's controlling influence is not uniformly distributed throughout the human species. Nor has leadership in dominance been an enduring prerogative of any particular group of men. The rise and fall of peoples, nations, and civilizations is a conspicuous fact of human history.

What is the explanation of man's rise in the animal kingdom; of the wide disparities existing between different human groups; of the shifting character of human dominance? These questions constitute some of the most important problems confronting students of human behavior. It is generally conceded that the answers are to be sought in the exceptional versatility or adaptive power inherent in the human organism, particularly as manifested in inventions and the accumulation of inventions to form culture.

It is usually accepted as axiomatic that the possession of culture is one of the great factors differentiating man from other forms of life. Indeed the ability to experiment with behavior and to retain workable patterns of action is so marked in man and, by comparison, so restricted in other species that many students have come to regard man as an entirely unique form of life. Such reasoning has furnished the logical basis for separating man from the rest of life as a distinct subject for study. In support of this view it is pointed out that human behavior unfolds ontogenetically while the behavior of other life forms is phylogenetic in origin. This position, however, is not substantiated entirely by available evidence.[51] The development of appropriate

---

[48] *An Introduction to Economic History* (New York, 1922).

[49] R. N. Tawney, *Land and Labour in China* (New York, 1932), 111-12.

[50] *The Social Life of Animals*, 241.

[51] Cf. Otto Klineberg, *Social Psychology* (New York, 1940), chap. ii, "Animal Social Psychology."

responses to the environment and their transmission to succeeding generations seems to be characteristic of life in general rather than of any particular species. The origin of human behavior, like that of lesser organisms, lies far back in the history of the species. As Klineberg states, "the more reasonable position appears to be one which finds the same continuity in animal and human social behavior as has been demonstrated in animal and human morphology." [52] It seems more appropriate, in other words, to draw such a distinction on a quantitative rather than a qualitative basis; man possesses the culture-producing capacity in a greater degree than any other species of life.

The superiority of man as a culture-builder, however, should not be minimized. No other organism compares favorably with man in this respect. The progress of lower forms of life in the elaboration of their behavior processes has moved at an imperceptible pace. But man in the brief space of approximately fifteen thousand years—a negligible interval from the standpoint of geological time—has advanced his culture from a very rudimentary state to one of inestimable complexity. The fact that this has been accomplished in the absence of any corresponding biological changes in the human organism constitutes a feat unique in the organic world.

For the greater part of man's existence upon the earth he has occupied a position in the organic world which differed in no significant respect from that of any other large mammal. Most of the details of prehistoric human life lie in obscurity, but contemporary collectional economy peoples offer what is probably a close parallel to man in his early state. [53] The problems of such peoples, their techniques for meeting them, and their relations with other life forms do not distinguish man significantly from other animals. In all such instances food presents the major problem; and the entire life of the group revolves about the ceaseless quest for nourishment. The food-getting procedures are essentially foraging and grubbing. Domestication and cultivation are almost completely lacking among collectional economy peoples. Their techniques of storage and transportation are so undeveloped as to limit them to the local food supply which in turn holds their numbers rigorously in check. Because of the nature of their enterprise, division of labor is necessarily simple and there is little time or reason for the development of ceremony or institutions. In short, the outstanding feature of their adjustment to environment is the element of deference:

---

[52] *Ibid.*, 26.
[53] Examples are the Semang of the Malay Peninsula, the Andaman Islanders, the Veddahs of Ceylon, the Shoshone of the North American basin-plateau area, the tribes of Central Australia, etc.

collectors defer to climatic change through movement, to attack by enemies through escape, to food shortage through death.

Where technology is simple and crude, as in the case of collectors and gatherers, man's relations with other organisms are close and familiar. The interaction, represented in the competition for food and shelter and again in the mutual assistance of the food cycle in which man is himself a food object as often as not, is direct and unremitting. That there is also a mental interchange is scarcely to be questioned, though it is impossible to estimate its importance. It is entirely plausible, as many scholars have suggested, that man's earliest inventions were borrowings from his animal associates. "The bears," says O. T. Mason, "were the first cave-dwellers; the beavers are old-time lumberers; the foxes excavated earth before there were men; the squirrels hid away food for the future, and so did many birds, and the last named were also excellent architects and nest-builders; the hawks taught man to catch fish; the spiders and caterpillars to spin; the hornet to make paper; and the cray-fish to work in clay." [54] It is likely, too, that many of man's food preferences were gained under the tutelage of animals. The Hottentots have been observed to look only for roots and tubers that are eaten by baboons and other animals.[55] The beginnings of agriculture may well have been suggested by animal behavior. It is well known, for instance, that squirrels are important planters of trees.[56] Furthermore, in the intimate give and take of the natural life community, preliterate man does not draw a sharp distinction between himself and the rest of life—that is a privilege which civilized man of the Western World assumes. Anthropomorphism is the prevailing habit of preliterate mind. Thus nature seems to furnish not only the materials for human life but also the patterns for their use. But unlike the creatures from which many of these first methods of action were possibly obtained, man has applied the techniques to a variety of new uses, elaborated them where possible to achieve greater efficiency, and combined them in various ways forming more complex schemes of action.

Each acquisition of a new technique or a new use for an old technique, regardless of the source of its origin, alters man's relations with the organisms about him and changes his position in the biotic community. The discovery of a new food, for instance, creates a whole complex of new relationships between man and the animate world.

[54] "Technogeography, or the Relation of the Earth to the Industries of Mankind," *American Anthropologist,* VII (April, 1894), 144.

[55] F. Ratzel, *History of Mankind* (London, 1896), Vol. I, 76.

[56] Cf. C. F. Korstian, "Factors Controlling the Germination and Early Survival in Oaks," *Yale School of Forestry Bulletin,* XIX (1927), 35.

Not only does it bring him into a direct relationship with the organism in question but also into competitive relations with all species that habitually prey upon that organism. A signal achievement, such as the discovery of how to control fire, effects far-reaching changes. With that innovation man tremendously enlarged the number of organisms that could be used for food, secured a potent weapon for defense against marauding beasts of the forest, liberated himself from the confines of semitropical habitat, and obtained an indispensable aid in the manufacture of pottery, knives, axes, and other tools with which further to enhance his control over nature. There is no need to multiply examples. It is easily understood that there can be no important modification of man's technical behavior without repercussions on the organization of the community.[57] And that these manifold effects have all fitted into a general trend toward man's increasing control over the environment is a commonplace among students of human culture. The history of invention is in effect a narrative of man's ascent in the biotic community from the status of a mere influent to that of the dominant.[58]

The emergence of man as a dominant species, however, did not occur until after the beginning of the iron age. In fact, not until the development of steel could man successfully challenge the age-old dominance of the forest trees. With the steel axe he felled the trees and availed himself of the space essential to the establishment of a man-dominated community. Long before this time he had begun the extermination of his mammalian competitors, the elephant, the man-eating tiger, the wolf, the bison, and others. The invention of the rifle hastened the process and in the end only remnants of these species were left in remote and inaccessible parts of the world. The steel plow supplemented the axe in holding the forests in check and became the determining factor in man's gaining a lasting control over vegetation. Finally, the steamship, the railway, the automobile, the airplane, and mechanical communication have released him from dependence upon local resources, making it possible for him to share in the products of distant areas.

Thus the development of human dominance through the agency of culture involves a reconstruction of the biotic community. Instead

---

[57] It is significant to note that among the inventions judged by modern scholars to be of first importance in the career of mankind upon the earth those pertaining to the procurement, preparation, and preservation of food are in the majority. A representative list includes the following: control of fire; use of seeds; pottery; writing; weights and measures; the germ theory; tinned foods. ("Inventions and Discoveries," *Encyclopaedia Britannica* (14th ed.), XII, 545-46.)

[58] See J. H. Breasted, *The Conquest of Civilization* (New York, 1926).

of accommodating his activities, as do primitive peoples, to the natural
life association, civilized man regulates the biotic community in accordance with his needs. He determines within the limitations of the
physical environment the kinds and abundance of life forms that compose the community. In some habitats many if not all the native
species are driven out and alien ones are introduced under the protection of man's practices of cultivation and domestication. When
Europeans came to North America, for example, they brought wheat,
oats, garden plants of various kinds, and innumerable flowering plants.
The apple, pear, cherry, grape, and other fruits were also imported.
The native fauna was displaced by animals of foreign origin, such as
the cow, horse, pig, sheep; crop pests too made their appearance, the
corn-borer, Hessian fly, cabbage butterfly, English sparrow, etc. Additional recruits brought to the reorganized community were man's
own parasites—the cockroach, housefly, bedbug, house mouse, and
others.[59] Moreover civilized man's control reaches down into the
subterranean depths of the habitat: through the selection of seeds and
the use of fertilizer the composition of the soil population is determined. Not content often with the original biological character of the
plants and animals used for food and other purposes, modern man
changes them through controlled breeding and selection.

A simplified conception of the organization of the man-dominated
community may be gained from Figure 2. The food objects are gathered together in the center under the protective custody of human
dominance indicated by the ring. The presence of various crop and
animal pests inside the ring suggests the fact that man's dominance
is not complete. Outside the ring are the animals which man has
expelled from the habitat and which do not come directly under his
dominance. Their presence, however, is a reminder that the community established by man is a temporary arrangement, lasting only
so long as man remains and exerts his dominance. With a relaxation
of human control these species would immediately rush in to drive
out the domesticated life and repossess the area. It is known that
when a field is left fallow for a brief period the land becomes inhabited
by wild life in a series of successional stages which restore the natural
climax association. What was formerly a prairie, for example, will
again become a prairie, and what once was a forested area will return
once more to the original type of forest. Man's interference with the
natural life community is analogous to a wound in the flesh. In both

---

[59] V. E. Shelford, "The Physical Environment," *Handbook of Psychology,* ed.
Carl Murchison, 571-72.

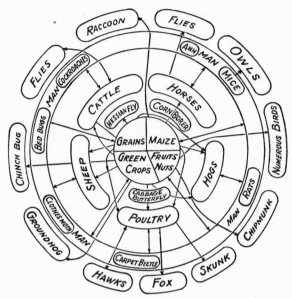

FIG. 2.—The man-dominated biotic community. (From Victor E. Shelford, "The Physical Environment," in *A Handbook of Social Psychology,* ed. C. Murchison [Worcester, Mass.: Clark University Press, 1935], 571. Used by permission.)

cases nature tends to restore the original condition. The revolution which man's dominance works in the biotic community may be appreciated by comparing Figures 1 and 2.

The particular life association found in a man-dominated community will depend upon two sets of factors: (1) the conditions of the physical environment—climate and soil; (2) the habits and desires of the human occupants. In regard to the first point it is obvious that every organism cannot be made to live in every type of environment, at least not without radical and usually impractical adjustments of the environment to the requirements of the organism. Oranges, for example, cannot be grown in the Arctic Circle, nor can wheat be successfully cultivated in tropical rain-forest areas. On the other hand, the actual kinds of plants and animals cultivated in a given area are within the range of natural possibilities supplemented by the extant technical arts. In regions where human populations depend on the products of their own activities the selection of cultivated plants and animals is determined by local life requirements as dictated by biological and cultural needs. In an exchange economy, however, the population of a region does not depend on its own products for the satisfaction of its needs; and the selection of plants and animals for cultivation in such areas is determined largely by their relative values in monetary exchange. Accordingly, in modern times, the nature of the biotic community is subject to rapid change and usually represents a high degree of specialization. One area, for example, may raise cotton almost exclusively, another wheat, or sugar, or fruit.

Human life, however, especially since the beginning of the nineteenth century and the recent tremendous strides in cultural advancement, requires more than organic material for maintenance. To an increasing extent civilized peoples have come to use inorganic materials in meeting life requirements. This is evidenced not merely in the increasing use of minerals in the manufacture of bigger and more elaborate tools, but also in the development of synthetic products which serve as substitutes for organic materials. According to Enid Charles, an important aspect of cultural evolution is the fact that man has constantly shifted "his dependence on other organisms to a lower level in the chain of energetic processes which link him to the soil and atmosphere." [60] The development of artificial silk shifted man's dependence from the animal to the green plant level. A century ago the primary means of illumination was animal fats; fats were later displaced by petroleum products; and today electric energy, obtained from water power, is in common use as a means of artificial light. Animal power is everywhere giving way to mechanical power. But a counter trend should not be overlooked. Man is also beginning to turn away from certain inorganic materials as the easily accessible natural resources near exhaustion. Witness the current use of plastics made from plants, soya beans, etc., as substitutes for the customary metals.[61]

Nevertheless, man's growing use of inorganic materials has progressed far. One of the principal manifestations of this tendency is the extensive use of such materials in the construction of an environment peculiar to himself, composed of concrete highways, buildings of glass, steel, concrete, etc. The supreme expression of this, of course, is the modern city wherein man has virtually isolated himself from the natural environment. Indeed, almost the only element of geography with which urban man is familiar is space—even climate is transmuted into weather in cities. Fraternization with living members of other species is for the city dweller largely a matter of keeping pets or suffering from disease. There is little question that the city is the fullest expression of human dominance.

---

[60] Charles, *The Twilight of Parenthood* (New York, 1934), 5.
[61] See National Resources Committee, *Technological Trends and National Policy* (Washington, D. C., 1937), 97-145, for a recent discussion of these trends.

Summary.—All forms of life are interrelated, a fact which gives to the whole of animate nature the appearance of a huge web of connections. Two general classes of relationships contain all the many interdependences that compose the web of life, namely, symbiosis and commensalism. The first of these is a mutually supplementary relationship that occurs between unlike forms of life. Symbiosis is expressed in the food-enemy relationship and in the various direct and indirect collaborations of a less sanguinary character. Commensalism is that relationship which arises among like organisms, organisms that make similar demands on the environment. Competition and combination are both expressions of the commensalistic relations. Although plant and animal ecologists tend to regard species as the units of these relationships, the emphasis here is placed on functional rather than morphological similarities and differences.

When the web of life is viewed in a particular time and place it reveals a form or structure which is referred to as the biotic community. This term applies to the organization of relationships among all organisms occupying a given place at a given time. The specific combination of inorganic conditions to which organisms are compelled to adapt their behavior is called the habitat, and it is as a consequence of their adaptive efforts that the biotic community takes form. A symbiotic association of diverse plants constitutes the basic structural feature of the community; it determines, through the food supply it offers and the breeding places it makes available, the animal population of the habitat. A second niche is that of the herbivore whose function it is to convert vegetable matter into animal matter. Carnivora of various types occupy third and subsequent niches in the community hierarchy, some of which feed directly on herbivora, while others subsist on smaller carnivorous animals. There are also numerous interstitial functions which further complicate community organization. The niche of key importance is that of the dominant which is occupied by the organism, usually the tallest plant, that by its activities controls the habitat and thus the conditions under which all related organisms live. Niches are linked together in food chains which from the standpoint of the numbers involved present the aspect of a pyramid. At the base are the smallest, the most numerous, and the most rapidly reproducing organisms. Each higher stratum is filled by larger, fewer, and slower-reproducing forms of life. Although there is a tendency toward balance in the number relations among interdependent organisms, equilibrium is never fully achieved. The biotic community is constantly in flux. In principle the biotic community is like an organism at least in that all the parts are essential to the whole and a disturbance arising at one point in the structure is quickly felt in all other sectors. Change and development of the community tend to occur in an orderly process termed succession. That is, the community grows through a series of stages that culminate in a climax stage at which relations are stabilized. A catastrophe, however, may destroy the rather delicate equilibrium and thus initiate a new succession of changes.

Man is also involved in the web of life. His niche, however, has been a changing one. In the simplest of human modes of life man's role in the biotic community is much like that of other large animals; he lives in close association with other life forms and is a food object as well as predator. But every advance in technology enhances his control over the habitat and raises his position higher on the scale of dominance. With the development of mechanical sources of power man emerged as a true dominant.

SUPPLEMENTARY REFERENCES

ALLEE, W. C. "Cooperation Among Animals," *American Journal of Sociology,* XXXVIII (November, 1931), 386-98.
BAKER, J. "Symbiosis: Prolegomenon to the Study of Ecology," Part II, *Science Progress,* XXV (January, 1931), 435-48.
CORT, W. W. "Human Factors in Parasite Ecology," *The American Naturalist,* LXXVI (March-April, 1942), 113-28.
HUXLEY, J. S. *Animal Ecology.* London: Sidgwick & Jackson, 1927.
McDOUGALL, W. B. *Plant Ecology.* Philadelphia: Lea and Febiger, 1926.

Chapter 4

HUMAN ECOLOGY

Relation to General Ecology.—We have attempted in the preceding chapters to show how the ecologist conceives the world of life as a subject for investigation. Our aim has been to outline the theoretical framework not of any special subdivision of the field but of ecology in general. We have sought to emphasize that ecology is a point of view which embraces life as a whole as well as particular populations of living things. All this, of course, has been preliminary to a statement of the nature of human ecology. Human ecology represents a specialization within the broader field of ecology and can be comprehended only when viewed against the background of the parent discipline. Before proceeding with our discussion let us summarize briefly what has been said by way of defining ecology as a general point of view.[1]

Implicit in the foregoing discussion has been the conception of ecology as the study of both the form and the development of organization in populations of living things. Ecology begins, as we have seen, with the problem of how growing, multiplying beings maintain themselves in a constantly changing but ever restricted environment. It proceeds, in other words, with the conception of life as a continuous struggle for adjustment of organisms to environment, a struggle initiated and continued essentially by the differential modes of change of these two components of the life process. In the ecological view, however, life is not an individual but an aggregate phenomenon. Hence the underlying assumption of ecology is that adjustment to environment is a mutual, in fact a communal, function. The adjustment of a population to its physical world occurs not through the independent actions of many individuals but through the coordination and organization of individual actions to form a single functional unit.

The inevitable crowding of organisms upon limited resources produces a complex interaction of organism with organism and of organism with environment in the course of which individuals adjust

---

[1] The content of this chapter is reproduced, with modifications, from Amos H. Hawley, "Ecology and Human Ecology," *Social Forces*, XXIII (May, 1944), 398-405.

to one another in ways conducive to a more effective utilization of the habitat. In consequence there arises among the organisms occupying a given habitat an equilibrium of relationships which approximates a closed system; that is, the aggregate assumes the characteristics of an organic unit as each type of life accommodates its behavior to that of every other. The community, as the ecologist is wont to call the pattern of symbiotic and commensalistic relations that develops in a population, is in the nature of a collective response to the habitat; it constitutes the adjustment of organism to environment.

The subject of ecological enquiry is therefore the community, the form and development of which are studied with particular reference to the limiting and supporting factors of the environment.[2] Ecology, in other words, is a study of the morphology of collective life in both its static and its dynamic aspects. It attempts to determine the nature of community structure in general, the types of communities that appear in different habitats, and the specific sequence of change in community development.

The unit of observation, it should be emphasized, is not the individual but the aggregate which is either organized or in process of becoming organized. The individual enters into ecological studies, on the theoretical side, as a postulate, and, on the practical side, as a unit of measurement. As something to be investigated in and of itself, however, the individual is subject matter for other disciplines. Ecology, as we have described it, then, is virtually synonymous with what plant ecologists call "synecology"—the study of the interrelations among organisms.[3] However, what plant ecologists term "autecology"—the study of the adaptations made by the individual organism throughout its life history [4]—is excluded from the conception as set

---

[2] This definition differs but slightly from others. For example: (1) Ecology is the science of "the correlations between all organisms living together in one and the same locality and their adaptations to their surroundings." (Ernest Haeckel, *History of Creation*, Vol. II, 354.) ; (2) "Ecology is the science of the relation of organisms to their surroundings, living as well as nonliving ; it is the science of the 'domestic economy' of plants and animals." (R. Hesse, W. C. Allee, and K. P. Schmidt, *Ecological Animal Geography*, 6.) ; (3) ". . . the essence of ecology lies in its giving the fullest possible value to the habitat as cause and the community as effect, the two constituting the basic phases of a unit process." (F. E. Clements and V. E. Shelford, *Bio-Ecology*, 30.) ; and (4) "The descriptive study of the interrelations between co-existing species, and, more generally, their environment, is the province of ecology." (A. J. Lotka, "Contact Points of Population Study with Related Branches of Science," *Proceedings of the American Philosophical Society*, LXXX (February, 1939), 611.)

It is of interest in this connection to note that Charles Elton, the eminent British ecologist, eschews formal definition of the subject, preferring to describe what the ecologist does and allowing the reader to formulate his own definition. ("Ecology, Animal," *Encyclopaedia Britannica* (14th ed.), VII, 915-16.)

[3] See Braun-Blanquet, *Plant Sociology*, 81.

[4] *Ibid.*

forth in these pages. To include this latter phase would appear to be
an unwarranted invasion of the fields of physiology and psychology,
disciplines which are much better equipped to deal with problems concerning the individual.

It is to be emphasized that ecology in all its applications necessarily
involves a sociological, not a biological, enquiry. The identification
of plant and animal ecology with botany and zoology in no way alters
this fact. If the study of behavior and particularly collective behavior
is biology, then it follows that all social science is biology laboring
under an assumed name. But it is not our desire to higgle over terms;
we wish merely to underscore the essentially sociological background
of human ecology.

As a Special Field of Study.—Human ecology, like plant and animal ecology, represents a special application of the general viewpoint
to a particular class of living things. It involves both a recognition
of the fundamental unity of animate nature and an awareness that
there is differentiation within that unity. Man, as we have seen, not
only occupies a niche in nature's web of life, he also develops among
his fellows an elaborate community of relations comparable in many
important respects to the more inclusive biotic community. In at
least one of its aspects the human community is an organization of organisms adjusted or in process of adjustment to a given unit of territory. Hence the rise of human ecology has meant a logical extension
of the system of thought and the techniques of investigation developed
in the study of the collective life of lower organisms to the study of
man. Human ecology may be defined, therefore, in terms that have
already been used, as the study of the form and the development of the
community in human population.

Ecology as applied to man differs in important respects from its
application to other forms of life or even to life as a whole. To reason
from "pismires to parliaments or from mice to men" would be to
commit a gross oversimplification. Man is an organism, to be sure,
and as such he has much in common with other forms of organic life.

But at the same time he is capable of an extraordinary degree of
flexibility and refinement in behavior. This is to be observed in man's
extensive control over his surroundings, as manifested in the degree
to which he modifies and reconstructs his environment through invention and the use of tools, and again in the complex cooperative
arrangements entered into with his fellowmen. Furthermore, man's
great facility for devising and accumulating methods of coping with
life situations is evidence of a dynamics in human behavior that is

without counterpart elsewhere in the animate world. It is this that constitutes man an object of special inquiry and makes possible a human as distinct from a general ecology.

Yet it is necessary to keep the phenomenon of human culture in proper perspective. When man by nature of his culture-producing capacity is regarded as an entirely unique type of organism the distinction has reached a point of overemphasis. Human behavior, in all its complexity, is but a further manifestation of the tremendous potential for adjustment inherent in organic life. Thus if we look upon culture as the totality of the habitual ways of acting that are general in a population and are transmitted from one generation to the next, there exist for human ecology no peculiar problems other than those involved in the fact of its complexity. The term simply denotes the prevailing techniques of adjustment by which a population maintains itself in its habitat. The elements of human culture are therefore identical in principle with the appetency of the bee for honey, the nest-building activities of birds, and the hunting habits of carnivora. To say that the latter are instinctive while the former are not is to beg the question. Ecology is not concerned with how habits are acquired— that is a psychological problem; it is interested rather in the functions they serve and the relationships they involve.

The definition of human ecology given here differs noticeably from earlier statements which seem to indicate a subordination of interest in functional relations to a concern with the spatial patterns in which such relations are expressed. For example, "Human ecology deals with the spatial aspects of the symbiotic relations of human beings and human institutions." [5] While such a statement possesses the merit of concreteness, it has had the unfortunate effect of permitting human ecology to be construed as the study of the distributive aspects of village and urban agglomerations. Much of the research carried on under the name "ecology" has consisted of compiling inventories of the observable characteristics of human settlement and of plotting the distributions of such findings on maps. Such a narrow interpretation of human ecology is incompatible with the fundamental logic of ecological theory and is not in accord with the subject as it is being developed in its other applications.

Its Place in Social Science.—The collective life of human beings, especially as it bears upon the habitat, is also the focus of interest of a number of other branches of social science, such as demography,

---

[5] R. D. McKenzie, "Human Ecology," *Encyclopedia of the Social Sciences*, V, 314.

human geography, economics, and sociology. It is because of the close convergence of interest of these several disciplines and the consequent danger of confusion as to the nature of their respective fields that we need to consider the place of human ecology among the social sciences.[6]

The simplest way of viewing the human community is as a statistical aggregate. A population may be regarded as a collection of discrete and definite units which as a whole possesses certain interrelated tendencies to change that lend themselves to mathematical analysis. This type of approach to the study of population has become known as demography.[7] In the words of Wolfe, demography is the "numerical analysis of the state and movement of human population inclusive of census enumeration and registration of vital processes . . ."[8] However, while the demographer takes an abstract view of population, it does not follow that he deals with population in general. Demographic analysis is usually limited to the study of the conditions of community life as revealed in birth, death, and migration statistics.[9]

The distinction between demography and human ecology is more or less apparent. Although both study the community, the one is concerned with vital processes in the communal population while the other is interested in the organization of the population constituting the community. Demography may be considered as a service discipline to the other branches of social science. Its data and findings are basic to every other social science because of their immediate descriptive value and, what is even more important, because of their use in suggesting problems for research in other disciplines.

The relation of man and his activities to the physical condition of the earth has long been a concern of geography. Human geography, however, which explicitly emphasizes the influence of the geographic environment on man, had its inception in systematic form in the latter part of the nineteenth century, with the publication of Friedrich Ratzel's *Anthropogeographie*.[10] This new emphasis was at first greatly exaggerated, as the result of Ellen Churchill Semple's English interpretation of Ratzel,[11] to mean a thoroughgoing environmental deter-

---

[6] See R. D. McKenzie, "The Field and Problems of Demography, Human Geography, and Human Ecology," chap. iv, in *The Fields and Methods of Sociology*, ed. L. L. Bernard (New York, 1934).
[7] Term first used by Achille Guillard, *Elements de statistique humaine ou demographic comparie* (Paris, 1855), XXVI.
[8] "Demography," *Encyclopedia of the Social Sciences*, V, 85-86.
[9] *New English Dictionary on Historical Principles*, Vol. III, 184.
[10] Two vols. (Stuttgart, 1882-91).
[11] *Influences of the Geographic Environment* (New York, 1911).

minism. But for the most part human geographers have adopted the more modest conception of their task as outlined by Paul Vidal de la Blache,[12] Jean Brunhes,[13] and others, namely, that of discovering in detail the manner and extent in which geographic factors influence human behavior. Confronted, however, with the indubitable fact that man characteristically responds to his physical environment in ways that are customary rather than mechanical, geographers have tended to invert the original form of the problem, thus making human geography the study of man's adaptations to his geographic environment. Barrows asserts that "geography is the science of human ecology." [14] Elaborating further, this author states: "Geographers will, I think, be wise to view this problem in general from the standpoint of man's adjustment to environment, rather than from that of environmental influence." [15] Not all human geographers [16] concur with Barrows although his viewpoint has found support among ecologists as well as geographers.[17]

The geographer, in point of fact, despite his increasing interest in human phenomena, has not been distracted from his initial preoccupation with the physical environment. Human geography simply involves carrying the analysis through to man.[18] Man, in a sense, is read into the field of study; since he occupies the earth's surface, he is a part of the natural landscape.[19] Accordingly, the geographer may concern himself with population, in which case he seeks correlations between population and other elements of the natural landscape. He describes the changing pattern of population distribution and explains it in terms of geographic factors. But man not only occupies the earth, he alters its form through his removal of forests, cultivation of fields,

---

[12] *Principles of Human Geography,* trans. C. F. Brigham (New York, 1926).

[13] *La geographie humaine* (3d ed.), 3 vols. (Paris, 1925).

[14] "Geography as Human Ecology," *Annals of the Association of American Geographers,* XIII (1922), 3.

[15] *Ibid.*

[16] "Geography as the study of responses or adjustments is in the stage of medieval alchemy, geography as the study of the mutual space relationships of phenomena on the face of the earth is a science." Preston E. James, *An Outline of Geography* (New York, 1935), ix.

[17] See C. Langdon White and George T. Renner, *Geography: An Introduction to Human Ecology* (New York, 1936) ; and Barrington Moore, "The Scope of Ecology," *Ecology,* I (January, 1920), 4.

[18] See Charles C. Colby, "The California Raisin Industry: A Study in Geographic Interpretation," *Annals of the Association of American Geographers,* XIV (1924), 49-108; and Robert B. Hall, "The Cities of Japan: Notes on Distribution and Inherited Forms," *ibid.,* XXIV (1934), 175-99.

[19] "The people on the land are in the geographer's province because they are on and of the land and the relative density of population is a matter of geographical concern." (Stanley Dodge, "World Distribution of Population: Preliminary Survey and Tentative Conclusions," *Papers of the Michigan Academy of Sciences, Arts and Letters,* XVIII (1932), 138.)

construction of buildings, roads, dams, and the like. Modifications of the physical landscape of this character form, in the German phrase, "cultural landscape." [20] This latter may itself, apart from population, be treated as an object of study by the cultural geographer who is interested in finding correlations between the cultural and the natural landscapes. The influence of geographic factors on man or man's adaptation to the geographic environment, as the case may be, is reflected in part in his distribution and in part in the changes he effects in the natural landscape.

Human ecology is therefore something different from human geography. Geography treats men and their activities in their visible aspects and so far as they may be regarded as distributed phenomena. It does not concern, except incidentally, the interrelations among men. Human ecology, which is also interested in the relations of man to his geographic environment, fastens its attention upon the human interdependences that develop in the action and reaction of a population to its habitat. In other words, while geography views the adjustment of man from the standpoint of modifications of the earth's surface, human ecology makes a detailed analysis of the process and organization of relations involved in adjustment to environment. This brings us to a second point of distinction between the two disciplines. Geography involves a description of things as they are at a point in time; its interest is in distribution rather than development. Ecology, on the other hand, is evolutionary.[21] It undertakes to describe the developmental process as well as the form of man's adjustment to his habitat. Human geography and human ecology thus constitute diverse approaches to the question of man's relation to environment; the one proceeds by way of environment, the other by way of organism.

The line of demarcation between economics and human ecology is somewhat less clear. Indeed, ecology has been described as but an extension of economics—if this term may be considered in a broader sense than implying a conscious economy—to the whole realm of life.[22] Such a statement is equally appropriate, though in a more limited sphere, of human ecology. Economics, which deals with those human interrelations that are mediated through a set of exchange values, does not include within its purview the whole of collective life.

---

[20] Carl Sauer indicates a distinction between human and cultural geographers. "The one group asserts directly its major interests in man; that is, in the relationship of man to his environment, usually in the sense of adaptation of man to physical environment. The other group . . . directs its attention to those elements of material culture that give character to area." ("Geography, Cultural," *Encyclopedia of the Social Sciences*, VI, 621.)

[21] Cf. Patrick W. Bryan, *Man's Adaptation of Nature* (New York, 1933), 8-10.

[22] Wells, Huxley, and Wells, *The Science of Life*, 961-62.

It does not, for instance, investigate the nonpecuniary aspects of economic relationships. Nor does it treat those subsidiary but contingent relationships which do not find expression in a pricing system, such as occur in the family and between nonprofit institutions.[23] Yet the community is fundamentally an economy and one which involves a far more intricate division of labor than that with which the economist ordinarily deals. It is in this conception of the community that human ecology represents an extension of economics beyond its nominal scope.

But it should not be supposed that human ecology is simply economics on a grand scale. Although the terms derive from a common origin, the disciplines differ both in problem and approach. Economics is concerned with the efficiency, as measured in units of cost, of the interrelations required in a given task of production, and with the changes in those producing relationships resulting from changes in costs. The point of view may be characterized as that of an entrepreneur planning and managing the production and sale of goods or services. This is in contrast to ecology in which attention is directed more to the form or pattern of human sustenance relations, the process of development of such patterns, and the factors that affect their development. The ecological viewpoint is that of individuals and groups seeking position in a developing system of relationships.

Human ecology emerged as and remains primarily a sociological concern. It deals with the central problem of sociology, that is, the development and organization of the community. Human ecology, however, does not pretend to exhaust that problem. The human community is more than just an organization of functional relationships and to that extent there are limitations to the scope of human ecology. Man's collective life involves, in greater or less degree, a psychological and a moral as well as a functional integration. But these, so far as they are distinguishable, should be regarded as complementing aspects of the same thing rather than as separate phases or segments of the community. Sustenance activities and relationships are inextricably interwoven with sentiments, value systems, and other ideational constructs. Human ecology is restricted in scope,

---

[23] Cf. Allyn Young's definition of economics in *Encyclopaedia Britannica* (14th ed.), VII, 925.

O. A. Taylor declares: "The three non-economic elements to be considered are (1) technology; (2) the power element, i e., the pursuit and use by members of society of coercive power to control the actions of other members and (as one use of power) exploit others for their own gain; and (3) the element of prevailing ethical attitudes." ("Economic Theory and Certain Non-Economic Elements in Social Life," *Explorations in Economics,* Essays in Honor of F. W. Taussig (New York, 1936), 381.)

then, not by any real or assumed qualitative differences in behavior but simply by the manner in which its problem is stated. The question of how men relate themselves to one another in order to live in their habitats yields a description of community structure in terms of its overt and measurable features. It does not provide explanations of all the many ramifications of human interrelationships, though it may serve as a fruitful source of hypotheses concerning those aspects of the community.

The definition of human ecology presented in this volume is not the only conception that is recognized.[24] It is one, however, which builds upon the contributions of plant and animal ecologists and seeks to follow the logical implications of general ecological theory. As such it leads to the investigation of a fundamental and otherwise neglected sociological problem. The remaining chapters outline that problem and review the existing knowledge relevant to it. That there are many gaps in that knowledge is a commentary on the youth of human ecology.

SUPPLEMENTARY REFERENCES

ALIHAN, M. *Social Ecology*. New York: Columbia University Press, 1939.
BARROWS, H. H. "Geography as Human Ecology," *Annals of the Association of American Geography*, XIII (1922), 1-14.
GETTYS, W. "Human Ecology and Social Theory," *Social Forces*, XVIII (1940), 469-76.
McKENZIE, R. D. "The Ecological Approach to the Study of the Human Community," in R. E. Park, E. W. Burgess, and R. D. McKenzie (eds.) *The City*. Chicago: University of Chicago Press, 1925.
———. "The Scope of Human Ecology," in E. W. Burgess (ed.), *The Urban Community*. Chicago: University of Chicago Press, 1926.
PARK, R. E. "Human Ecology," *American Journal of Sociology*, XLII (July, 1936), 1-15.
QUINN, J. A. "Human Ecology and Interactional Ecology," *American Sociological Review*, V (October, 1940), 713-22.

---

[24] See J. A. Quinn, "Topical Summary of Current Literature in Human Ecology," *American Journal of Sociology*, XLVI (September, 1940), 191-226.

PART II

THE HUMAN AGGREGATE

Chapter 5

INTRODUCTION

The most abstract way of viewing any social phenomenon is as an aggregate of biological units. Population therefore constitutes the common denominator of all the social sciences. Data describing the number and characteristics of the people involved in any social situation isolated for purposes of study serve as the point of departure for whatever analytical approach one chooses to take. This is no less true of human ecology than of any other social-scientific point of view.

The term *population* requires definition, for it has a precise meaning. According to Boulding, whose statement is generally accepted: "A population may be defined as an aggregate of disparate items, or individuals, each one of which conforms to a given definition, retains its identity with the passage of time, and exists only during a finite interval. An individual enters a population, or is 'born,' when it first conforms to the definition which identifies the population; it leaves the population or 'dies' when it ceases to conform with its definition." [1] In other words, population is essentially a quantitative concept. It is applied widely in statistical usage to denote aggregates of all kinds— of men, animals, plants, and observations and measures of all descriptions. So long as the aggregate in question conforms to the specifications stated by Boulding, it may legitimately be called a population.

The use of the indefinite instead of the definite article to define the application of the term population merits particular attention. Although its application may be unlimited (e.g., the universe of things), such a use is rare. More frequently than not use of the term involves certain distinctions, as among the classes of a classification. Each species of animal life, each color class or linguistic group of men is a population. There may be as many populations as there are classes identified for observation. The denotative limits of population are always indicated in the definition stated or implied in each specific use of the term. As applied to human beings, unless otherwise specified, population refers to a spatially delimited aggregate, such as the

---

[1] K. E. Boulding, "The Application of the Pure Theory of Population Change to the Theory of Capital," *Quarterly Journal of Economics* (August, 1934), 650.

population of Europe, of New England, or of New York City. It is
in this sense that we are interested in population.

When we speak of a group of individuals as a population, then, we
refer only to their existence as a spatially delimited aggregate of discrete units all of which have the physical properties of human beings.
The term conveys no information as to their mode of life, their interrelationships, or their language, tradition, hopes, fears, and so on.
Population is thus an abstraction, a fact which cannot be too strongly
emphasized. Failure to recognize that is a constant source of confusion. It leads, for example, to the attribution of causal power to
population, as though it were a thing completely detached from all the
ramifications of collective life.

A strictly populational analysis of a human social situation yields
a quantitative account of the number, composition, or distribution of
the participants, or of the rates of change in those respects. But not
only does it provide an inventory; the statistical account describes the
structure of differences in the characteristics of the aggregate or, if
movement has been the object of attention, the mechanics of change
in that structure. Demography, the name assigned to the quantitative
study of population,[2] of necessity proceeds as though the facts about
an aggregate form a closed universe. Stated differently, it is a descriptive rather than an explanatory discipline. The demographer can tell
how a population increases in size but not why it does so. Questions
the answers to which require other than population data cannot be
treated within the framework of demography. Such questions take
one into one or another of the spheres of social science.

Within its limitations, however, demography is of great value to
human ecology and social science in general. In the first place, quantitative descriptions of populations afford a direct and ready comparison which, when coupled with knowledge of the qualitative significance of numbers, reveals much about the communities being
studied. Secondly, the inventory of characteristics, particularly age
and sex, defines a biological structure to which the organization of
interrelationships either is or must be adapted. Demographic structure contains the possibilities and sets the limits of organized group
life. Again, demographic changes, such as changes in the rates of
birth, death, growth, and migration, have proved to be among the
most cogent indicators of social change. There is irrefutable evidence

---

[2] It is of interest to note that both the terms demography and statistics had similar
origins. Each emerged as a political concept to connote the collection and ordering of
facts of use in the administration of the state. For some time they were used interchangeably. (See Walter F. Willcox, *Studies in American Demography* (Ithaca,
1940), 491-510.)

in the shift of a population trend that a significant alteration has occurred somewhere in the mode of life of the aggregate.[3]

These considerations express in brief the nature of the human ecologist's interest in population. But in addition human ecology is concerned with developing and enhancing the qualitative significance of demographic data. Population is conceived as one of the principal permissive or limiting causes of social phenomena. Hence problems such as the implications of size, of biological structure, of rates of population change for the organization of relationships occupy a position of major importance in ecological work. Needless to say, perhaps, these problems have not been fully resolved; rather has progress toward their solution barely begun.

The chapters of this section are designed to set forth the features and problems of population that in the present state of knowledge seem relevant to an understanding of man's collective life. No attempt is made to present the intricacies of demographic method. The reader who wishes to pursue that matter intensively should consult the references cited.

Supplementary References

Byron, L. "Population and Culture," *Annals of the American Academy of Political and Social Science,* CLXII (1932), 185-97.

"Demography," *Encyclopedia of the Social Sciences.* New York: The Macmillan Co., 1931. Vol. V.

Gause, G. F. "Ecology of Population," *Quarterly Review of Biology,* VII (1932), 27-46.

Lotka, A. J. "Contact Points of Population Study with Related Branches of Science," *Proceedings of the American Philosophical Society,* LXXX (February, 1939).

Willcox, W. F. *Studies in American Demography.* Ithaca, N. Y.: Cornell University, 1940. Chap. i and Appendix i.

---

[3] Demographic changes are held by Willcox to be the most useful measures of progress. He mentions increase of size, decrease of death rate, increase in life expectancy, reduction of physical and cultural heterogeneity etc. (See *ibid.,* 5-21.)

Chapter 6

HABITAT AND POPULATION

Habitat

Human ecology is concerned with that population which comprises the human universe of day to day life. Such a population is territorially localized, having as the principal element in its definition the spatial boundaries of its locale. The place of occupance, moreover, poses the basic problem of adaptation. Presumably, therefore, such distinctive characteristics as a population may have are at least partly attributable to the peculiarities of its habitat.

The significance of place for both the identification and the study of population has long been apparent to social scientists. This has resulted in strenuous efforts to arrive at a most appropriate characterization of the human habitat. The attempt, in other words, has been to define the habitation area so as to contain all that is relevant for an understanding of collective life. Since the fruits of these efforts have become firmly established in the thought patterns and language of social science, it will be well for us to examine them rather closely. Two different views of the place of occupance have been developed: these are the natural area and the culture area conceptions. We shall consider each conception and the relation between the two.

The Natural Area.—The simplest conception of the territorial unit of habitation is as a natural area, a term introduced by Friedrich Ratzel. Any area physically delimited, by rivers, coast lines, mountains, or other such features so as to constitute a definite physiographic unit is a natural area.[1] Continental areas such as Australia and North America and insular areas such as Ireland, Luzon, and Madagascar clearly come within the meaning of this concept. Likewise subunits of continents may represent natural areas, e.g., the Inter-Mountain Basin of western North America, the plateau of Tibet, the Vistula Basin in northeastern Europe. The latter type of unit, in fact, most

---

[1] See Neven N. Fenneman, "Physiographic Boundaries Within the United States." *Annals of the Association of American Geographers,* IV (1914), 85 ff.

nearly represents the natural area as the term is ordinarily used. Not always, however, is the term natural area restricted to units described on the basis of physiographic features; it is often applied to areas of uniform climate, soil type, or vegetation, and to areas possessing a combination of these factors.

The geographer's conception of the region in most instances has as its basis the idea of a natural area.[2] That element is quite explicit in statements by A. J. Herbertson,[3] W. S. Tower,[4] and W. L. G. Joerg.[5] "A natural region may be defined as any portion of the earth's surface whose physical conditions are homogeneous." [6] Upon this conception of the region has developed a specialized branch of geography known as chorography—the scientific study of natural regions. Recently, however, geographers have tended to minimize the natural area aspect of the human region in favor of other criteria which we shall discuss later.

Still another application of the natural area conception may be mentioned. Originally the adjective "natural" was meant to exclude, as factors in determining natural areas, conditions introduced or effected by man. But after the term "natural" had become an integral part of the vocabulary of social science the natural area concept was broadened to include all physically distinct territorial units regardless of whether such units were created or conditioned by human activities. Thus natural areas have been recognized as unit parts of the physical structure of the city. In this sense, the natural area is an area of uniform physical type bounded by elongated buildings, railroad tracks, arterial thoroughfares, or other similar features.

The Culture Area.—A somewhat different approach to the description of the habitation unit exists in the concept culture area. Anthropologists are chiefly responsible for the development of this idea, but it should be observed that elements of the concept have from an early date been actively though implicitly present in the theories of many different social scientists. American anthropologists, more than any other group in this field of study, were attracted to the culture area concept and have succeeded in formulating it as a useful research tool and in giving it systematic presentation.

---

[2] It is implicit in the geographer's concept "fundament."

[3] "The Major Natural Regions: An Essay in Systematic Geography," *Geographic Journal*, XXV (1905), 300-12.

[4] "The Human Side of Systematic Geography," *Bulletin of the American Geographic Society*, XL (1908), 522 ff.

[5] "The Subdivision of North America into Natural Regions: A Preliminary Inquiry," *Annals of the Association of American Geographers*, IV (1914), 55-83.

[6] W. L. G. Joerg, *ibid.*

According to Clark Wissler, the culture area concept is based on the observation that culture is found in "patches" rather than distributed at random throughout the world's population.[7] Specifically, however, the idea was developed from the use of geographic distribution as a basis for the classification of museum collections.[8] At the outset the idea represented a somewhat arbitrarily drawn area of homogeneity with respect to culture. But close examination of the territorial spread of a given culture trait or complex [9] later revealed that the area as thus delimited was not uniformly homogeneous. The distribution of a given trait was found to be thicker in one part of the area and more sparse with distance from that center. It was possible then to plot zones of distribution arranged concentrically about a point, the series of zones describing a distribution gradient ranging from maximum frequency at the center to minimum frequency of occurrence at the margin. This pattern was rather clearly portrayed by the distribution of a curious type of prehistoric stone ornament in eastern North America and by the distribution of potsherds in the Rio Grande Valley.[10] It was also demonstrated, though with less distinctness, in the culture of the American Indian as represented by the distribution of ceramics, architecture, metal work, family organization, shamanism, mythology, and other evidences of culture traits.[11] "We are therefore justified in assuming," Wissler concludes, "that the true culture area is a succession of distribution zones encircling a nucleus and that this center is the point of dispersal from which trait complexes are diffused." [12]

---

[7] "The Culture-Area Concept in Social Anthropology," *American Journal of Sociology*, XXXII (May, 1927), 885.

[8] See A. A. Goldenweiser, "Cultural Anthropology," in *The History and Prospects of the Social Sciences*, ed. H. E. Barnes (New York, 1925), 244, fn. 72.

[9] The culture trait is defined by Wissler as the unit part of a culture—e.g., a technique, a mannerism, a concept; the culture complex is a constellation of traits related to a given activity. (*Man and Culture*, 50-52.)

[10] Wissler, *ibid.*, 58-61.

[11] Wissler, *The American Indian* (New York, 1917).

[12] *Man and Culture, op. cit.*, 63. This definition indicates that the culture area has a temporal as well as a spatial dimension. Support for this inference was found in the fact that the center of the area contained traits of recent origin and of ancient vintage, whereas each succeeding zone comprised relatively fewer new traits and proportionally more old traits. The radii of distribution apparently varied as the time (p. 62).

An illustration may be taken from Griffith Taylor, who observed that types of transportation in use around Sydney, Australia, display a zonal distribution in accordance with their ages. Flying to and from Sydney is the airplane, which touches only the center. In a zone extending some hundred miles about the center the automobile is the prevailing mode of transportation. Horse and wagon transportation predominates in a third zone, an area roughly one hundred to two hundred miles from the city's center. Beyond the third zone is a fourth in which the oxcart, common in Sydney in the nineteenth century, is the principal carrier. ("The Ecological Basis of Anthropology," *Ecology*, XV (July, 1934), 226.)

Described as a culture area the human habitat is essentially a diagrammatic construct rather than an actual portion of the physical landscape occupied by population. Some attempts have been made to conform the culture area to natural surface features, but the concept does not appear to have lost its formal character. In one of his more recent books Wissler states: "We have approached the culture area concept as an outgrowth or a crystallization of the geographical point of view, and consequently emphasized its geographical aspects, but the phenomenon upon which the culture area concept is based is not geographical, in the usual sense of the word, but is expressed in similarities in tribal cultures. It is only when the habitats of tribes having similar cultures are plotted upon a map that the geographical aspect of the situation appears." [13] Nevertheless, habitat defined in cultural terms has proved an important leavening in the simpler natural area conception. It has served to direct attention, in the delineation of habitats, to the human use factor and also to the fact of change. That influence is reflected in the changing conception of the region.

Application of this concept to areas of human settlement has not been very extensive. Wissler indicated ten distinct culture areas in aboriginal North America and five tentative areas in South America.[14] Herskovits made a preliminary subdivision of Africa on the same basis,[15] following his analysis with an intensive study of one area in East Africa.[16] Beyond this, however, the work of identifying the culture areas of the preliterate world has not been carried. Moreover, until quite recently, no systematic attempt to test the concept in the civilized world had been made. Since 1930 a number of studies have appeared in which the central problem is the determination of contemporary culture areas. One of these will be sufficient to indicate the adaptation of the concept to the modern situation.

A. R. Mangus delineated rural culture areas in the United States by means of substantially the same technique as that employed by anthropologists.[17] Instead of dealing with specific culture traits, however, various quantitative indexes of culture were used. Thirteen cri-

---

[13] Wissler, *An Introduction to Social Anthropology* (New York: Henry Holt & Co., 1929), 349.

[14] *The American Indian*, 218, 245. In this connection see also O. T. Mason, "Influence of Environment on Human Industries or Arts," *Smithsonian Institution, Annual Reports, 1895* (Washington, D. C., 1896), 639-665.

[15] "A Preliminary Consideration of the Culture Areas of Africa," *American Anthropologist*, XXVI (1924), 50-63.

[16] "The Cattle Complex in East Africa," *American Anthropologist*, XXVII (1926).

[17] *Rural Regions of the United States*, Works Projects Administration, Division of Research (Washington, D. C., 1940).

teria of local culture, expressed as ratios, by counties, were selected. Examples of these criteria are: a rural-farm plane of living index; a rural-nonfarm plane of living index; a rural-farm population fertility index; per cent of farm tenancy; type of nonfarm industry; etc.[18] Proceeding with twenty tentative types of farming areas, as a working basis, the counties in each area were analyzed with respect to their similarities of culture indexes and were regrouped in subunits of homogeneous clusters of counties. Through a grouping of subunits and a series of boundary readjustments the thirty-four culture areas, shown in Figure 3, were obtained. Mangus's areas differ in at least one respect from the concept set forth by Wissler: centers are not distinguished from peripheries, hence there is no measure of the distribution of culture within an area. This is characteristic of efforts to determine culture areas in modern life.[19]

Correlation of Natural and Culture Areas.—There is some question as to how adequately either conception of area defines the human habitat. Indeed, this issue has often been raised as a criticism of both natural and culture areas. Presumably this question may be answered by testing the degree of coincidence of the two. There have been few such attempts, however. Rather we have an assortment of opinions and assumptions dominating most of the literature, with the few empirical studies appearing in recent years. A review of the different viewpoints will enable us to explore the relationship between natural and culture areas.

The anthropogeographers were among the first to emphasize an intimate relationship between the geographic environment and man's mode of life.[20] They carried their interpretations to the extreme of environmental determinism and consequently are remembered primarily for that phase of their work. The physical environment, they claimed, controlled the physiological functioning of the human body, the choice of occupations, the consumption habits, the content of the mind, and all the many and kaleidoscopic systems of human behavior —political, religious, philosophical, scientific, and so on. If these were not the products of the immediate physical setting, they were contributions of habitats previously occupied. Semple declares: "It is not difficult to see, back of the astronomy and mathematics and hydraulics

---

[18] *Ibid.*, 79-80, 87.
[19] Cf. Howard W. Green, "Culture Areas in the City of Cleveland," *American Journal of Sociology*, XXXVIII (November, 1932), 356-67.
[20] See E. C. Semple, *Influence of the Geographic Environment* (New York, 1911), 1-60, and F. Ratzel, "Studies in Political Areas," *American Journal of Sociology*, III (November, 1897), 279-313 and III (January, 1898), 449-63.

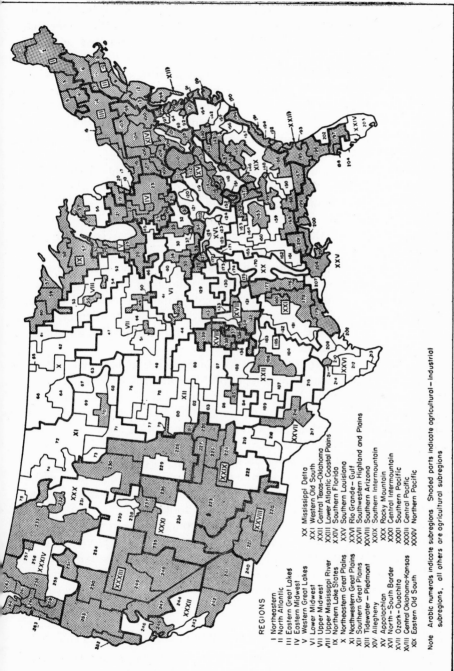

REGIONS

I Northeastern	XX Mississippi Delta
II North Atlantic	XXI Western Old South
III Eastern Great Lakes	XXII Central Texas-Oklahoma
IV Western Great Lakes	XXIII Lower Atlantic Coastal Plains
V Eastern Midwest	XXIV Southern Florida
VI Western Midwest	XXV Southern Louisiana
VII Lower Midwest	XXVI Rio Grande – Gulf
VIII Upper Midwest	XXVII Southwestern Highland and Plains
IX Upper Mississippi River	XXVIII Southern Arizona
X Northern Lake States	XXIX Southern Intermountain
XI Northeastern Great Plains	XXX Rocky Mountain
XII Northwestern Great Plains	XXXI Central Intermountain
XIII Southern Great Plains	XXXII Southern Pacific
XIII Tidewater – Piedmont	XXXIII Central Pacific
XIV Allegheny	XXXIV Eastern Old South
XV Appalachian	XXXV Northern Pacific
XVI North – South Border	
XVII Ozark – Ouachita	
XVIII Central Oklahoma-Kansas	
XIX Eastern Old South	

Note   Arabic numerals indicate subregions   Shaded parts indicate agricultural – industrial
        subregions,   all others are agricultural subregions

FIG. 3.—Rural culture areas of the United States.   (From A. R. Mangus, *Rural Regions of the United States*, WPA, [Washington, D. C., 1940], p. 4.)

of Egypt, the far sweep of the rain-laden monsoons against the mountains of Abyssinia and the creeping of the tawny Nile flood over that river-born oasis." [21] Thus the correlation of the cultural with the physiographical area was regarded as all but complete.

Anthropogeographers placed too great a burden on the "principle of parsimony," as students in other fields, including geography, were quick to point out. Numerous instances were brought to light in which a given resource was used differently by different people, or in which two or more diverse culture patterns co-existed in a single natural area. The reindeer, for example, is hunted as a game animal in certain parts of the world, in others it is used to supply milk, and in still other places is used solely as a beast of burden. Lowie's much quoted illustration of the Navajo and Hopi Indian tribes was particularly damaging to the deterministic position.[22] These tribes, though occupying the same physiographic area in Arizona, display markedly different cultures. The Navajo are a pastoral people, live in conical earth-covered huts, and practice polygamy, while the Hopi are agriculturalists, builders of terraced sandstone dwellings, and are monogamous in marriage. Human geographers, sociologists, and others participated in the marshaling of evidence contradictory to geographic determinism, and in the end anthropogeography was rather thoroughly discredited.

For the geographer the question of association between cultural and geographical phenomena is involved in the task of identifying regions. It may almost be said that the state of the regional conception at any one time reflects the knowledge that has been attained, or at least the agreement that has been reached, regarding the correlation of what men do with the character of the place in which they do it. Geographers have not been alone in attempting to determine a most appropriate definition of region : the problem represents a point at which all social sciences converge. The region, as R. B. Hall has asserted, is one of the most widely used of research tools.[23]

Physical geographers are inclined to conceive the region as a natural area. It is implied that an area homogeneous in physiographic, climatic, or soil features will also be homogeneous in human use and related activities. In some instances the implication seems to involve determinism, in others merely correlation. A logical difficulty in this

[21] Semple, op. cit., 23.
[22] Culture and Ethnology (New York, 1917), 62-65. See also C. D. Forde, Habitat, Economy, and Society (London, 1934), 374.
[23] "The Geographic Region: A Résumé," Annals of the Association of American Geographers, XXV (1935), 122.

theory is revealed in the failure of physical geographers to agree on the proper criteria for the delineation of natural regions. Regions mapped on the basis of one set of criteria cut across those obtained by another.[24] Moreover, since there is such a lack of correlation among the criteria themselves, it follows that regions are large or small depending on the number of criteria employed. It is hardly to be expected that the culture "correlate" will accommodate itself to the regional map of each and every geographer. This state of affairs has led some students to the conclusion that there are no regions per se, that the region at best is simply a conceptual device for dealing with specific problems, having to be defined anew for each problem.

Since the substitution of Vidal de la Blache's *possibilisme* for the determinism of Ratzel and Semple, the trend has been away from the physio-geographical conception of the human region. Jean Brunhes, an eminent student of Vidal de la Blache, regarded the region as a human use area. Describing the task of the geographer as the study of man's modification of the surface of the earth, Brunhes listed six classes of "essential facts" to be considered: (1) houses and (2) roads —facts of the unproductive occupation of the soil; (3) cultivated fields and (4) domesticated animals—facts of plant and animal conquest; (5) exploitation of minerals and (6) devastation in plant and animal life—facts of destructive economy.[25] These in part at least have been recognized in subsequent regional studies, though the tendency has been to combine them with certain physical criteria for purposes of delimiting regions. R. B. Hall, for example, suggests as the irreducible minimum for regional identification four classes of criteria: (1) surface features; (2) vegetation; (3) climate; and (4) Brunhes' six fundamental human facts.[26] But Hall takes a more radical position than many of his fellow geographers, and in this respect he is regarded as marking the culmination of the trend away from the natural region concept.[27] "One might hazard the opinion at this point," Hall remarks, "that a great deal of value might come from approaching the region through the medium of culture rather than through the orthodox approach of surface configuration." [28] Whether or not this suggestion is acceptable to geographers generally, it is true that the

---

[24] Cf. R. H. Whitbeck, "Facts and Fiction in Geography by Natural Regions," *Journal of Geography*, XXII (1923), 87 ff; and National Resources Committee, *Regional Factors in National Planning and Development* (Washington, D.C., 1935), 152.

[25] *Human Geography*, trans. I. C. LeCompte (Chicago, 1920), 48-52.

[26] *Op. cit.*, 128.

[27] H. W. Odum and H. E. Moore, *American Regionalism* (New York, 1938), 299.

[28] *Op. cit.*, 129.

region has become established as a human use area. A recent survey of opinion would seem to show that geographers prefer the human use rather than the natural region conception.[29] Woofter's definition of the region, therefore, may be taken as representative of the prevailing view. A region is "an area within which the combination of environmental and demographic factors has created a homogeneity of economic and social structure." [30]

In actual fact, human geographers have not adopted a categorical position regarding the correlation of human activities with physical geographical factors. Definitions of the human region in terms of both cultural and natural features do not necessarily imply a correlation; they are simply attempts to fill the practical need for delineation of the human habitat. The relationship nevertheless remains a subject for investigation and constitutes, now as in the past, one of the important problems of geographical study.

Returning to the work of anthropologists, so long as the culture area remained for them merely a classificatory tool the geographic element in the concept was principally a matter of place names. The mapping of areas, however, required precise boundaries and consequently it became necessary to give fuller attention to the specific features of the territory over which a given culture was distributed. In *The American Indian*,[31] Wissler noted certain very general geographic correlations, such as food supply and altitude; the relation of culture to geography, however, was incidental to his primary task of describing the areal pattern of culture in the Western Hemisphere. It was recognized more fully in later studies that culture areas are seldom symmetrical—their centers are not geometric centers and their boundaries are irregular depending on the disposition of surface features which affect the spread of culture. Thus Kroeber revised Wissler's original fifteen culture areas, adjusting their boundaries to natural barriers, e.g., topographic and climatic features.[32] Wissler himself later examined the relationship in greater detail.[33] Thus the culture area has gradually come to involve a segment of land as well as a type of culture having certain linear and temporal dimensions. But this transformation is not complete and, except for the work of Kroeber, very little attention is being given to the correlation.

[29] National Resources Committee, *op. cit.*, 145-49.
[30] Cited in *ibid.*, 142.
[31] Chap. i and pp. 368-72.
[32] Kroeber, *Anthropology* (New York, 1923), 337.
[33] Wissler, *The Relation of Nature to Man in Aboriginal America* (New York, 1926).

Kroeber's study of the relation of culture to natural areas in aboriginal North America[34] is the most intensive that has been undertaken to date. The continent is divided into six major culture areas which from the standpoint of historical development are presumed to be more or less self-contained and these, in turn, are subdivided into some eighty-odd minor culture areas representing variations within the major units. The relations of these to natural vegetation areas (as identified by different authorities) are studied, the correlation being observed by means of the superimposition of maps. The investigation is repeated with physiographic areas. In brief, the results of this painstaking research point to a fairly close association of native cultures with floristic and physiographic factors. Important differences in the degree of association are noted, however. In the far western part of the continent, especially the northwest, the correlation is quite close. East of the Mississippi River the association is much less distinct. It is probable that this discrepancy is a function of the more highly differentiated physical landscape and plant cover in the west and the relatively greater population mobility which is known to have occurred in the east. For understandable reasons, no tests of significance of differences were applied by Kroeber.

Sociologists, who have also concerned themselves with the relation of cultural to physical factors, have confronted the problem in the course of their studies of urban phenomena. A few sociologists, such as Geddes, Branford, LePlay, and Giddings, have dealt with this relationship in its regional aspects, though for the most part their approaches differ in no important respect from those of human geographers. Mukerjee, in his *Regional Sociology,* presents a general ecological analysis which also parallels closely the work of human geographers. The regional concept likewise is uppermost in the previously cited work by Odum and Moore. The distinctive contribution of the sociologist, as was said, lies elsewhere—namely, in the results of urban research.

Studies of distributions of social phenomena in the city have led to an adaptation of the natural area idea to the description of patterns. The natural area, in its sociological use, is an area of more or less uniform physical composition, particularly in regard to type, congestion, and degree of deterioration of buildings : sometimes such factors as location, altitude, and street pattern are also included. Usually, however, the natural area conception as applied to the city entails more than an area delimited simply on the basis of stationary physical

[34] *Cultural and Natural Areas of Native North America* (Berkeley, California, 1939).

characteristics. It comprises a particular kind of population with respect to social heritage, occupation, interests, or other distinguishing cultural possessions.[35] Indeed, sociologists have often relied more heavily on the latter set of facts than on the former. Nevertheless, there is implicit in the conception a close correlation of cultural with physical factors. Nor is this merely presumptive; a large number of studies have demonstrated the relationship.

In an early study, McKenzie developed the conception of natural areas in the city and indicated the correlation of various behavior patterns—e.g., population mobility, dependency, delinquency—with physical areas in Columbus, Ohio.[36] There followed a number of monographic studies which appeared to substantiate McKenzie's observations, such as those in Chicago by Thrasher,[37] Wirth,[38] and H. Zorbaugh.[39] Of much greater importance from a quantitative standpoint, however, are studies by Shaw,[40], Faris and Dunham,[41] Hoyt,[42] and Bowers.[43] In these investigations delinquency rates, mental disease rates, racial composition, birth rates, and other attributes of the population are shown to be closely associated with physical features of the city.

Thus it appears that there is a tendency for human behavior to reflect in one way or another the physical characteristics of the area in which it occurs. This is no more than might be expected. Man lives close to the ground and must of necessity relate his activities to his physical milieu. It does not follow, however, that habitat factors are the sole determinants of behavior: the weight of evidence forces the conclusion that the physical environment exerts but a permissive and limiting influence. And even that influence differs with the extent to which man has advanced his technology. Populations possessing very simple tools and techniques are confined to local habitats to the details of which they are acutely sensitive. But with the development of technology, especially that pertaining to transportation and communi-

---

[35] Cf. R. E. Park, "The City: Suggestions for the Investigation of Human Behavior in the Urban Environment," in *The City*, ed. R. E. Park, E. W. Burgess, and R. D. McKenzie (Chicago, 1925), 1-46; and H. W. Zorbaugh, "The Natural Areas of the City," in *The Urban Community*, ed. R. E. Park (Chicago, 1926), 219-29.

[36] "The Neighborhood: A Study of Local Life in the City of Columbus, Ohio," *American Journal of Sociology*, XXVII (1921-22), 145-68, 344-63, 486-508, 588-610, and 780-899.

[37] *The Gang* (Chicago, 1927).

[38] *The Ghetto* (Chicago, 1928).

[39] *The Goldcoast and the Slum* (Chicago, 1929).

[40] *Delinquency Areas* (Chicago, 1929).

[41] *Mental Disorders in Urban Areas* (Chicago, 1939).

[42] *The Structure and Growth of Residential Neighborhoods in American Cities*, Federal Housing Administration (Washington, D.C., 1939).

[43] "Ecological Patterning of Rochester, New York," *American Sociological Review*, IV (April, 1939), 180-89.

cation, man participates in a progressively wider habitat and the limitations of the immediate locale drop away.[44] Hence we find, in the modern era as never before, populations occupying radically different natural areas but with similar consuming and occupational habits. Of this more will be said in a later chapter.

As it has turned out, however, most of our knowledge about population is cast in territorial units that approximate the culture area conception more closely than the natural area conception. These, to be more specific, are the political or administrative areas into which the world has been subdivided. The political area, though bounded arbitrarily in many instances, is readily determined and therefore is the most convenient unit in which to observe population. Furthermore, the occupants of the political area are usually sufficiently organized to constitute a more or less distinct population. In fact, were it not for their political organization, it is unlikely that the people would be induced to take inventories of their numbers and characteristics.

To a very large extent our knowledge of areas has advanced with our knowledge of their occupants. Habitat and inhabitant are different facets of the same prism. Knowledge of human population, like all other knowledge, has accumulated in an exponential progression. A very brief review of this trend and its present stage is instructive both in respect to the influencing factors and in regard to some of the difficulties under which science still labors.

THE DEVELOPMENT OF INTEREST IN POPULATION: THE CENSUS

There is no point, says Carr-Saunders, before which we know nothing about population and after which we have complete knowledge.[45] Starting from vague beginnings, the growth of interest in population has been gradual and cumulative. Virtually all human groups have had at least a crude appreciation of the relation between numbers and welfare, and therefore have shown a concern for population size. Early evidences of this are to be found, for example, in the numerous Biblical references to population. The same interest is widely exhibited by contemporary preliterate peoples. Formal enumerations are known to have occurred sporadically in many different places. The records of some of these are still extant. Charlemagne's Breviary, for example, compiled in the latter part of the eighth century, lists all males of military age in the empire. The English Domesday Book was prepared in 1086 to determine the fiscal rights of the king. It enumerates

---

[44] See Chapter 9 for a fuller discussion of this point.
[45] *World Population* (Oxford, 1936), 10. See also chap. i for an extended treatment of the development of census activity.

all the taxable households of that date. A series of enumerations was begun in the colony of New France (Canada) in 1665 and was continued until 1754. The Japanese, between 1721 and 1846, also carried out periodic counts of their population. These two series constitute our earliest extended records of population. But most early enumerations were inspired by some sort of expediency and for that reason were incomplete. They usually dealt with persons eligible for military service or with those subject to taxation.[46]

The practice of taking a complete count at regular intervals of all people in a given area, which is the modern connotation of the term census, is of rather recent origin. It is commonly dated from the beginning of the Swedish census, in 1749. After that date there was a lapse of some forty years before the census spread to other areas. Then, in 1790, the United States census was established and subsequently became a model which was copied by many other nations. The ensuing years brought a rapid diffusion of the census across Europe and into Asia and South America.[47] Nevertheless, even at this late date, there are large areas in the world in which there is nothing resembling a modern census. The populations of most of Africa, of China, and of many other parts of Asia and Oceania have never been counted systematically. Kuczynski estimates that only about three fifths of the world's population is regularly enumerated.[48] Hence, while it is generally agreed that the population of the world at present is approximately two billion, that estimate probably contains a 10 per cent error.

The development of the census is incidental to the rise of an industrial-exchange economy and its political counterpart in the national state. The enormous multiplication of administrative problems resulting from the great growth in the size and complexity of aggregates, the accelerating rate of change with the consequent dubious character of the future, and the centralization of economic and political control created an almost insatiable need for accurate information about the characteristics of population. Thus the census emerged as an indispensable tool for the administration not only of economic and political affairs but also of activities in all phases of collective life, educational, religious, and so on. The same context is favorable, indeed essential, to the development of census-taking on yet another score. In few

---

[46] The series in New France is an exception; it obtained complete coverage of the population.

[47] A partial chronology of the development of the modern census is: England, 1801; France, 1801; Ireland, 1821; Denmark, 1834; Belgium, 1846; Spain, 1857; Italy, 1861; Portugal, 1864; Germany, 1871; Canada, 1871; India, 1872; Russia, 1897; Egypt, 1897; Japan, 1898; Turkey, 1927; and Java, 1930.

[48] *Population Movements* (Oxford, 1936), 4.

other instances are relationships sufficiently secularized and the general level of sophistication sufficiently high to permit, as a matter of routine, an impersonal inquiry into the private affairs of individuals. Premature efforts to introduce a comprehensive census produce strenuous and often violent resistance. When the bill for a British census was introduced into Parliament in 1753, a member declared, "I did not believe that there had been any set of men, or, indeed, any individual of the human species as presumptuous and abandoned as to make the proposal we have just heard." [49] Such a reaction has frequently been encountered by imperial nations in their attempts to enumerate the native population in their colonial acquisitions. Nor is that kind of response entirely eliminated in modern civilized nations. There are spheres of privacy, differing from place to place, which still resist the importunities of the census taker. But as interdependences develop and their ramifications become more generally understood, a population is increasingly receptive to the census.

A very pronounced vertical as well as horizontal or territorial expansion of the census has occurred since its inception. The items reported in the early counts were few in number, limited for the most part to the number, age, and sex of the population. In succeeding enumerations, however, the number of details obtained about each individual has steadily increased. The number of questions on the United States census schedule, for example, has multiplied from three, in 1790, to fifteen, in 1940. In addition to the latter, which were asked of each person, ten more questions were asked of a sample group of individuals. Thus the most recent enumeration secured information on such matters as family and marital status, nationality origin, mobility, employment status, occupation, income, fertility of women, and other subjects. Moreover, the census has been extended to institutions and has embraced a progressively larger sector of the institutional order. It provides information in great detail on agriculture, industry, business, religious bodies, governmental units, and many other formally organized aspects of society. In short, the census publication contains an exhaustive descriptive account of contemporary life and may be counted among the most significant documents in our literature. [50]

Although the elaboration of the census has been very general in all countries that have adopted the practice of taking regular enumer-

---

[49] Mantoux, *The Industrial Revolution in the Eighteenth Century*, 350 n.

[50] Until the middle of the nineteenth century the decennial census publications in the United States never exceeded one small volume. In contrast, the 1940 census comprises some 60 volumes containing over 40,000 pages of printed matter, mostly statistical tables.

ations, international comparisons are limited nevertheless to but a few population characteristics. This is due to many factors. The fact that the various nations are at different stages in their development of census procedure is responsible for differences in the completeness of coverage and in the accuracy of results. There are also differences in the dates of enumeration, in the selection of characteristics for enumeration, and in the definitions employed. Different conceptions of how population should be enumerated alone constitute a discrepancy of major import. The census in the United States is a *de jure* census —that is, people are enumerated as of their legal residence or "usual place of abode." But most other censuses are *de facto;* they enumerate people where they happen to be at a given moment. This lack of standardization of procedures makes the existing knowledge about population in that part of the world where it is most highly developed much less useful than it could be.

Despite the large variety of details reported periodically by a modern census, the items of widest popular appeal are those concerning the size of population and the rate of increase or decrease of size. "The most frequent inquiries for population data which come to the [United States] Census Bureau are those calling for the total population of specified areas on specified dates." [51] In our number-conscious era the relative size and rate of change of population are symbols of progress. This is indicated even in census terminology: an increase of number in an area is referred to as a "gain," a decrease as a "loss." Fortunately, it is with respect to size of population that censuses are most accurate and most comparable one with another.

The Distribution of Population

The population of the world is very unevenly distributed over its surface, as may be seen in Figure 4. An area equivalent to about one fourth of the 55 million square miles of land space on the earth holds approximately 90 per cent of the total population. The remaining 10 per cent is very thinly scattered over the other 42 million square miles of land, most of which is too arid and cold for agriculture. Three large blocks of population may be identified. One is that of eastern and southern Asia, including China, Japan, and India, which contains over half the world's total population. These 1,100 million people occupy 10 per cent of the world's land area, or about 5 million square miles. A second large segment is the population of Europe. There

[51] Leon E. Truesdell, "Value of the Population Census for Research," *Annals of the American Academy of Political and Social Science,* CLXXXVIII (November, 1936), 329.

ı fourth of all population, 500 million, occupies an area which amounts to roughly 6 per cent of all land. The third largest concentration of population, equal to one tenth of the total, or 200 million, is found in the Great Lakes and Atlantic coastal areas of North and South America.

These are very rough delineations of the areas of concentration. Within each of these territories the population is very unevenly spread. Four fifths of the population of China, for example, live within one third of the land area. Three quarters of the population of India reside within about two fifths of the territory. Even in the islands of Japan proper the population is crowded into approximately 20 per cent of the land area.

Professor Fawcett, the English geographer, has delineated the major areas of concentration in the English-speaking countries. His computations show that 58 per cent of the population of Great Britain (1931) lives in about one fifth of the land area of the country—a zone extending diagonally from the southeast to the northwest including the London and Manchester territories; that 43 per cent of the population of Canada lives within a narrow strip of land extending along the St. Lawrence and the northern shores of Lakes Ontario and Erie, which comprises less than 1 per cent of the total land area of the Dominion; two fifths of Australia's population are residents of two metropolitan districts—Sydney-New Castle and Melbourne, whose combined areas represent less than one tenth of 1 per cent of the total area of the continent.[52] The population of the United States presents equally pronounced concentration features. The 1940 census showed that 48 per cent of the total population of the country was concentrated in 140 metropolitan districts, the aggregate area of which was only 1.5 per cent of the total area of the country.

The conventional method of measuring the distribution of population is in terms of density, or population per square mile. In Table 1 are shown approximate densities for the world and the major continental areas. Asia and Europe stand out as areas of exceptional densities, while the remaining continents have densities well below the average for the world as a whole Also noteworthy is the fact that the concentration of population in Europe relative to the land space is almost three times that in Asia. This would seem to belie the widespread impression of extreme congestion in Asia. The ratios in Table 1, however, are rather crude. Moreover, the density ratio must be interpreted with considerable care.

---

[52] "Areas of Concentration of Population in the English-Speaking Countries," *Population*, Vol. I (November, 1934), 4-13.

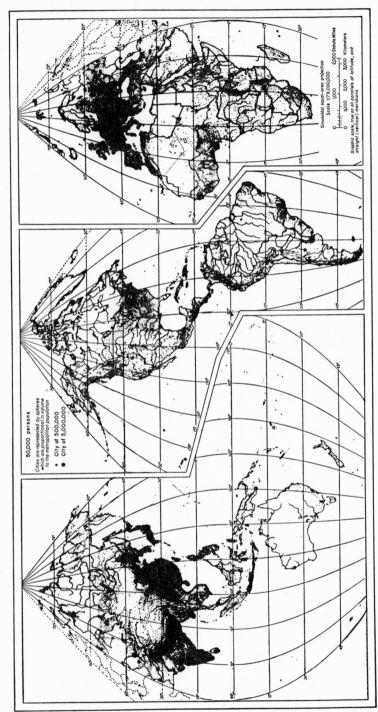

FIG. 4.—Distribution of world population. (From *Atlas of World Maps*, Army Service Forces Manual M 101, 1943, p. 8.)

TABLE 1

POPULATION DENSITY, BY CONTINENTS, 1935

Continent	Square miles of land (000,000's) *	Population (000,000's) †	Population per sq. mi.
Total	56.6‡	1,995	35.2
Asia	17.0	1,045	61.5
Europe	3.7	528	170.0
America	16.7	264	15.8
Africa	11.0	148	13.4
Oceania	3.3	10	3.0

* From *Encyclopaedia Britannica* (14th ed.), XVIII, 230.
† W. F. Willcox, *Studies in American Demography*, 45.
‡ Includes 4.9 million square miles of Arctic and Antarctic land.

It is well known, for example, that land and agricultural productivity are not the same thing. Many continents contain vast barren spaces which have little or no value for the production of food. When this fact is taken into account by computing refined density ratios using only the amount of arable land, a somewhat different picture emerges. The crude and refined comparisons are shown in Table 2 for a few selected areas. Egypt, with an unimpressive crude density of 37 per square mile, actually has over a thousand persons per square mile of agriculturally productive land. The disparities between crude and refined measures of density are only slightly less striking in the other countries listed.

TABLE 2

POPULATION DENSITIES IN SELECTED COUNTRIES, 1930

Country	Population per square mile	
	all land	arable land
Sweden	34	428
Egypt	37	1,047
United States	46	221
Spain	107	369
France	190	483
Italy	326	790
Germany	332	811
China	504	1,767
Belgium	653	1,710
Switzerland	242	2,111
Japan	444	2,853
Netherlands	543	2,249
England & Wales	669	2,265

A further qualification that should be recognized in observing such a series of distribution measures is that the density ratios are not all comparable. Density in Egypt and China represents a situation different from density in western Europe and America, for the relationship of population to land is different in each case. A relatively self-sufficient agricultural population, such as those in the two eastern countries, lives on a single plane, so to speak; increases in density can occur only with reduction in the amount of space and hence of sustenance materials available to each individual. But in western industrialized countries population lives on many planes, to continue the figure; that is, settlement is extended vertically as well as horizontally. In order for this to happen the area from which sustenance materials are assembled must be greatly enlarged. The high densities in Europe reflect a dependence on worldwide rather than simply local resources. Thus while the density ratio serves as a rough measure of "population pressure" on resources, it does not follow that "pressure" is greatest in Switzerland, the Netherlands, Japan, and England and Wales.

An inspection of a population distribution map, such as Figure 4, reveals the phenomenon of density gradients. Density is very high at certain points and declines with distance away from these points. This may be seen in all areas of the world. Density gradients, however, are based on different kinds of places in different areas. Throughout most of Asia and other areas of predominantly agricultural settlement, soil fertility is the decisive factor in determining the distribution of population. Densities are greatest in the river valleys and deltas. In China, for example, the bulk of the population is concentrated along the lower reaches of the Hwang Ho and Yangtze Rivers. Likewise, in India the fertile land adjoining the Ganges and the Indus Rivers contains most of the population; the interior regions of India are very sparsely settled. But the tendency for density to vary with soil fertility is evident in all countries. The flood plains of the Po, the Rhine, the Rhone, the Mississippi, and other great rivers are thickly settled as compared with adjacent lands.

In industrialized nations, however, peak densities occur at points of maximum accessibility with respect to interregional exchange. It is at those points that huge metropolitan cities appear. The thirty-seven cities in the world with populations of one million or more contain over eighty million people, or about 4 per cent of all population, and a minute proportion of the total amount of land.[53] Whereas a density of 2,000 per square mile is near the upper limit of possibility

53 W. S. Thompson, *Population Problems* (New York, 1942), 312.

in agricultural areas, densities exceeding several times that figure are not uncommon in large urban places. The number of persons per square mile tends to decline rapidly, though somewhat irregularly, with distance away from those points of heightened activity. As may be seen in Figure 5, the densities of political subdivisions lying on a straight line from Dayton, Ohio, to Columbus, Ohio, fall sharply to a low point approximately 25 miles from Dayton, where a new gradient based on an intervening city is encountered. Beyond that city a steep

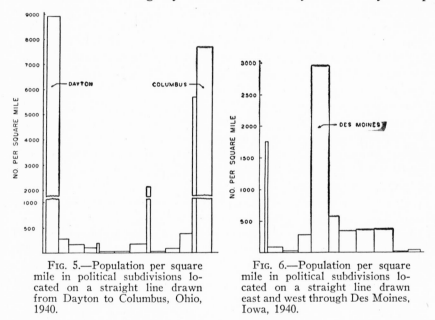

FIG. 5.—Population per square mile in political subdivisions located on a straight line drawn from Dayton to Columbus, Ohio, 1940.

FIG. 6.—Population per square mile in political subdivisions located on a straight line drawn east and west through Des Moines, Iowa, 1940.

gradient rises to Columbus. Figure 6 shows the demographic topography along an east-west line drawn through Des Moines, Iowa. The gradient pattern of distribution is clearly visible on each side of the city. By plotting numerous gradients about a city and drawing a line connecting the points at which they intersect with gradients based on adjacent cities it is possible to reach an approximate identification of the significant population unit. This is roughly the method employed by the United States Bureau of the Census in the delineation of metropolitan districts.

The two kinds of locations at which maximum densities are found —on fertile lands and at city sites—occur in the same regions in many parts of the world. Shanghai, with well over 3,000,000 inhabitants, is situated on the Si Kiang; and Cairo is located on the flood plain of the Nile. This coincidence exists in numerous other instances. It is due, in part, to the fact that the water which carries alluvium and is so essential for irrigation also often creates a high degree of accessibility. But in regions of relatively simple technology the concurrence is not merely a matter of juxtaposition. In such areas large cities can only appear in or near rich agricultural zones. It would otherwise be impossible to supply their population. Technological improvement, however, permits nonagricultural or urban populations to live at greater distances from their sources of supply. Hence in areas served by efficient transportation and communication facilities cities may locate with little or no reference to soil fertility.

The rise of cities is largely responsible for the geographic concentration of population, particularly in Europe, America, and other areas settled by people of European origin. That development, following from the rapid advance of mechanical technology, has involved a large-scale withdrawal of population from agricultural settlement and its concentration in dense agglomerations at selected points on the margins of regions. The various definitions of "city" or "urban place" in use in different countries make difficult the comparison of proportions living in cities. Nevertheless, some indication of the extent of the urban-rural distribution in different places may be given. England, which has progressed farthest in the direction of urbanization, has approximately 80 per cent of its population living in places of 2,000 or more people. In Belgium and the Netherlands the proportions living in such places exceeds 70 per cent. The figures for Germany, Australia, and Switzerland range from 60 to 65 per cent. And in the United States, France, and Canada they are above 50 per cent. By contrast, the proportion of India's population living in places of 2,000 or more is but 10 per cent, while in China it probably does not exceed 22 per cent.

The growth of urban population, moreover, is a continuing process. It progresses with each additional application of mechanical technology to agriculture. What its ultimate limits are is a matter for conjecture. But that the process will take hold of the remaining predominantly agricultural areas of the world can hardly be doubted. The tendency to urban concentration in Asia, Africa, and South America is already well marked. Their population distributions will become increasingly distorted with the passage of time.

The Significance of Distribution

Population distribution as measured by the density ratio is a rough gauge of two aspects of settlement: (1) the physical spacing of individuals, or their accessibility to one another, and (2) the adaptation of population to land or, as this is sometimes phrased, population pressure. Since the latter is treated at length in Chapter 9, nothing further concerning it need be said here. There are several considerations regarding density as a measure of spacing, however, which should be noted in passing.

It has already been pointed out that the density ratio is an average and thus may conceal great variation. The larger the territorial unit for which a ratio of population to land is computed, the less reliable is its descriptive value for any segment of the total area. Although density in the United States is approximately 47 per square mile, the range is from less than 1, in Nevada, to 25,000 in New York City. This limitation should be familiar to anyone who has had experience with averages.

The distribution of population in space has much to do with the kinds of collective activities that are possible in various localities. To illustrate this, let us assume that the 1,995 million people on the earth were evenly distributed over the 56 million square miles of land. That would produce an average density of 35 per square mile. Assuming further that three miles (walking distance) is the radius of local travel, a density of 35 would place each individual within easy access of 979 other individuals. The aggregate of 980 persons would then tend to become the effective population unit and the variety and complexity of cooperative arrangements that could be developed would be limited to relatively simple devices. If, however, the radius of convenient movement should be increased to 10 miles as a result of technological improvement, while the density remained the same at 35 per square mile, then the scope of interindividual accessibility would be raised to 10,990 individuals. An aggregate of that size would obviously permit a much more elaborate organizational structure.

Needless to say, a density of 35 per square mile is not unusual. In fact, it is well above the average for many parts of the world. A density of approximately one per square mile, such as characterizes many continental interiors and the tropical rain-forest areas, would mean, under conditions of uniform distribution, that a three-mile radius would encompass only 28 persons. A ten-mile radius would contain 314 persons. In such circumstances, even though relatively efficient transportation facilities were at hand, collective life would necessarily be confined to a comparatively simple level. Actually, of course, population is seldom evenly distributed over the land. Preliterate people, in whose areas densities are lowest, are usually bunched in aggregates of a few hundred individuals each. Hence they are able to enjoy a more efficient group organization than would be possible with uniform distribution. The nucleated settlement pattern is found in all areas regardless of level of technological achievement.

The massing of population in cities has tremendously increased the potential size of the social aggregate. The average density of the 92 cities of 100,000 population or more in the United States, in 1940, was 8665. On this basis a circle with a three-mile radius would contain 242,600 persons, and a ten-mile radius would embrace 2,720,800 individuals. Never before was it possible for an individual human being to come into physical contact in an hour's time, whether by walking or by riding a wheeled vehicle, with so many other individuals. And never before have the problems of organization, on the one hand, and of adjustment to the land, on the other hand, been so numerous and so difficult of solution.

Summary

Since the population concept, as used by human ecology, involves a territorially delimited aggregate, interests turn to the question of what constitutes the most appropriate territorial unit. The "natural area," or area of uniform physical characteristics, has been suggested for this purpose. So also has the "culture area," the area of relatively homogeneous culture traits. Attempts to observe the relation between the two concepts have revealed evidences of a correlation. But, inasmuch as studies of the relationship between natural and culture areas have been confined largely to preliterate groups, the results are inconclusive for civilized populations. Indications are that highly efficient transportation and communication reduce the bounds of natural areas to comparative insignificance so far as culture characteristics are concerned. In any event, knowledge about population has developed primarily with reference to political territories which resemble culture areas more nearly than natural areas. The development of interest in and knowledge about population has progressed with the economic and political organization of areas; and has been expressed in the emergence of the census. Because of the recency and irregular spread of the practice of census-taking, interregional and international comparisons are difficult and in some respects impossible.

The outstanding feature of population distribution over the earth is its unevenness. In general, the points of concentration are zones of fertile soil, as in nonindustrial areas, and locations of easy accessibility, as in industrial areas. Population density grades downward with distance from both types of places. The growth of cities has produced unusually dense concentrations, particularly in the western parts of the world, though the same tendency has already begun to manifest itself elsewhere. The density ratio is, among other things, a rough measure of the frequency and variety of interhuman contacts. When considered in connection with the kind of facility for movement that is in use, density is an index of the potential complexity of group organization.

SUPPLEMENTARY REFERENCES

DAWSON, C. A. "Population Areas and Physiographic Regions in Canada," *American Journal of Sociology,* XXXIII (July, 1927), 43-56.

MUKERJEE, R. *Regional Sociology.* New York: Century Co., 1926.

REDFIELD, ROBERT. "The Regional Aspect of Culture," *Publication of the American Sociological Society,* XXIII (December, 1929), 33-41.

THOMPSON, W. S., and WHELPTON, P. K. "Changes in Regional and Urban Patterns of Population Growth," *American Sociological Review,* V (December, 1940), 921-29.

Chapter 7

POPULATION GROWTH

Variations in numbers, whether in the direction of increase or decrease, constitute an important means by which population maintains an adaptation to environment. Changes in numbers or changes in the rate of increase or decrease are not only one of the most accessible but also one of the most sensitive indexes of fundamental social change. It is largely for this reason that population growth and its opposite have significance for human ecology. The implications extend further, however. Change in numbers alters the potentialities for organization in a population, opening up new possibilities and imposing different limitations. The student of collective life should at least be familiar with the mechanics of population growth. It is that with which this chapter is concerned.

The Tendency to Increase.—Man possesses a tremendous capacity for multiplication. Human fecundity—that is, the maximum potential number of babies that may be had during the childbearing period —has never been accurately measured. But it has been estimated that a healthy woman is capable of giving birth to 30 or more children in her 35 years of fertility. Actually, however, such reproductivity is seldom, if ever, realized. Fecundity is impaired by many contingencies such as personal accidents, inappropriate or insufficient diet, and various injurious practices. It is curtailed further by numerous customs which differ from place to place. Thus the average number of babies born per woman in any population is well below 30, though it may vary over a considerable range.[1] Then there is also the ever present fact of mortality, which takes a particularly heavy toll of infants. Despite these considerations, man is capable of rapid increase. He has many times demonstrated his ability more than to double his numbers within a generation.

---

[1] S. B. de Aberle found the average number of pregnancies for Pueblo women of completed fertility to be 9.4. ("Frequency of Pregnancies and Birth Intervals among Pueblo Indians," *American Journal of Physical Anthropology,* XVI (July-September, 1931), 63-80.

It is of more than passing interest, therefore, that growth of human population appears to be the exception rather than the rule. The modal tendency seems to have been toward stability throughout most of man's existence on earth. Let us consider the size of world population. In 1650, the earliest date for which anyone is willing to venture an estimate, the number of people on earth was about 470 millions.[2] Even if that figure were in error by as much as 100 per cent, it would not represent a very impressive accomplishment. Man has been on the earth for no less than 15,000 years. There must have been many long intervals of stable population in the millennia prior to 1650.

That this is highly probable is suggested by available data on the growth tendencies of various populations living under relatively constant life conditions. Such conditions prevailed in Japan during the period from 1650 to 1865, known as the Tokugawa Era. As an instrument of the rigid control exercised over the entire area during that period, a census was taken every six to eight years after 1721. Although the enumerations consistently excluded certain segments of the population, the results indicate that numbers seldom deviated more than four per cent from the 26.5 millions counted in 1726.[3] Ta Chen, on the basis of less detailed evidence, concludes that the population of China has not changed appreciably since 1850.[4] Numerous anthropological reports of preliterate groups occupying islands and isolated mainland habitats present evidence of population stability.[5] Speaking of Europe, Kuczynski declares, "We have no reason to assume that the population in 1700 was any larger than in 1600, or that the population in 1600 was much larger than in 1300." [6]

Thus the growth of world population since 1650 is a remarkable event in human experience. As may be observed in Table 3, the population of the world has quadrupled in the 285 years ending in 1935. In Asia the increase has been somewhat less than 300 per cent while in Europe the increase has exceeded 400 per cent. European population, moreover, has supplied most of the increase shown for Africa, the Americas, and Oceania. The total increase of European population, if all the scattered populations of European stock are included in the count, is actually near 700 per cent.

---

[2] W. F. Willcox, *Studies in American Demography* (Ithaca, N. Y., 1940), 45.
[3] Ryoichi Ishii, *Population Pressure and Economic Life in Japan* (Chicago, 1937), 5-16.
[4] Ta Chen, *Population in Modern China* (Chicago, 1946), 4-5.
[5] See A. M. Carr-Saunders, *The Population Problem* (Oxford, 1922), 213 ff; and Clark Wissler, *Man and Culture* (New York, 1923), 343.
[6] R. R. Kuczynski, *Population Movements* (Oxford, 1936), 23.

TABLE 3

ESTIMATED POPULATION OF THE WORLD AND ITS SUBDIVISIONS, 1650-1935.*

Area	Population (in millions)					
	1650	1750	1800	1850	1900	1935
Total..................	470	694	919	1,091	1,571	1,995
Asia......................	260	441	600	664	879	1,045
Europe....................	100	140	188	266	401	528
Africa....................	100	100	100	100	141	148
North and Central America.....	} 8	} 6	15	39	106	178
South America..............		} 5	14	20	38	86
Oceania...................	2	2	2	2	6	10

* From W. F. Willcox, *Studies in American Demography* (Ithaca, N. Y., 1940), 45.

Of course, growth is but one alternative to stability of numbers. A second alternative, population decline, has occurred many times in the experience of mankind. The native occupants of Tasmania have become extinct; the numbers of Andaman islanders, Yucatan natives, and many other preliterate groups have dwindled to a fraction of their former size, and the population of contemporary Ireland is less than half as large as it was in the middle of the nineteenth century. Many of the instances of depopulation of which we have record are the results of invasions by foreign peoples. Wherever Europeans expanded their empires they dislodged native peoples from their territories and forced them into new modes of life with almost universally disastrous consequences. Inadvertently the white man transmitted his diseases to native peoples in whom there were no protective immunities. Presumably population decline has been induced in this fashion in many places for which there are no available accounts. Occasionally, however, an inappropriate use of resources culminates in declining populations. This clearly is what lies behind the shrinkage of numbers in Ireland.

Intergroup contact does not always result in a decline of the native population; it sometimes has the opposite effect, especially if the native population is large enough to absorb the shock of the revolution in its mode of life. European invasions have in many instances initiated rapid growth in previously stable populations. This applies to Egypt, India, Japan, and Java, for example. The general result has been that the population of the non-European world has more than doubled, in the last century and a half. Japan's population increased from 32 million in 1870 to about 70 million at the present time. The population of India grew from 254 million in 1881 to 365 million in 1931, a gain of approximately 45 per cent. The population of Egypt has shown equally rapid growth, while that of Java, with its much longer period of contact with the West, has increased over 800 per cent from 1815 to 1930.[7]

The Measurement of Growth.—Population growth may come about in several ways. Natural increase, or the excess of births over deaths, is the fundamental growth process. There is no other way for the population of the world as a whole to increase. A second means of growth is through net migration, the excess of in-migrants over out-migrants. Net migration may be a factor only in the growth of population in local areas, and always occurs at the expense of populations in other areas. The populations of continents, islands, and fixed geographic regions may grow both from natural increase and from net migration. But the numbers of people occupying areas with elastic boundaries, such as politically defined territories and functionally delimited areas, may grow through these two means and, in addition, through annexation or consolidation of occupied areas. These modes of growth are, in reverse fashion, the modes of decline.

Excluding, for purposes of discussion, the factors of migration and annexation, population increase or decrease is a function of the ratio of births to deaths. This is commonly expressed as a rate of natural increase and it may have a positive or a negative value. The rate of natural increase, which is nothing more than the difference between the crude birth rate and the crude death rate, expresses the annual excess of births over deaths per 1,000 of the total population. Rates of natural increase are shown for selected countries in column 3 of Table 4. All countries but two had natural increases in 1936, while these two, Austria and France, had natural decreases.

Although these data are accurate measures of the rates of increase for the particular year, they are inaccurate as indications of growth tendencies. Nor are they closely comparable with one another. Deficiencies such as these result from the fact that no account is taken in the calculations of the influence of other variables. Age composition is a factor of universal incidence which directly affects the number of children born and the number of persons dying in any time period. Other things remaining equal, a population with an exceptionally large number of young adults has a high crude birth rate and a low crude death rate, whereas where there are relatively few persons in the in-

---

[7] Briz Narain, *The Population of India* (Lahore, 1925) ; W. Cleland, *The Population Problem of Egypt* (Baltimore, 1936),

TABLE 4

MEASURES OF POPULATION GROWTH FOR SELECTED COUNTRIES, 1936

Country	Crude birth rate	Crude death rate	Natural increase	Net reproduction rate *
	1	2	3	4
New Zealand............	16.6	8.7	7.9	1.00†
Australia...............	17.1	9.4	7.7	0.96*
Netherlands.............	20.2	8.7	11.5	1.12†
Norway................	14.8	10.3	4.5	0.75
Denmark...............	17.8	11.0	6.8	0.90*
Sweden................	14.2	12.0	2.2	0.72*
Germany...............	19.0	11.8	7.2	0.90**
Canada................	20.0	9.7	10.3	1.30
England and Wales.......	14.8	12.1	2.7	0.76§
United States...........	16.7	11.5	5.2	0.95
Austria................	13.1	13.2	−0.1	0.64
France.................	15.0	15.3	−0.3	0.88
Finland................	18.1	13.1	5.0	0.96
Italy..................	22.4	13.7	8.7	1.18#
Bulgaria...............	25.6	14.1	11.5	1.19‡
Portugal...............	28.3	16.4	11.5	1.29
Hungary...............	20.4	14.3	6.1	1.01#
Poland................	26.2	14.2	12.0	1.11‖
Chile..................	34.6	25.3	9.3	1.30**
Japan.................	29.9	17.5	12.4	1.57

Source: *International Vital Statistics.   Summary Vital Statistics*—Special Reports, Vol. 9, No. 36, 1940.
* 1935
† 1937
‡ 1933-1936
§ 1934-1936
‖ 1934
1933
** 1930-1932

termediate years the crude birth rate is low and the crude death rate is high.   To obtain a more accurate and comparable measure of growth tendency, therefore, birth and death frequencies must be weighted with a standard age composition.[8]

The effects of such a procedure are shown in Table 5.[9]   Intrinsic rates are the total rates in a stable age composition which would result from an indefinite continuance of the age specific birth and death rates of the given year.   Comparison of the intrinsic and crude rates of

---

[8] The age composition of the population of England and Wales, in 1901, has been adopted as the standard for international comparisons.

[9] This is not illustrative of the conventional standardization procedure.   For a description of the conventional method see *Vital Statistics Rates in the United States, 1900-1940* (Washington, D.C., 1943), 66 ff.

natural increase shows a large disparity. The crude rates range from 35 to 100 per cent above what would have been the case had there been no distortions of age composition. Furthermore, year-to-year changes in age composition invalidate any comparison among crude rates. But none of the difference among intrinsic rates may be attributed to differences in age composition.

TABLE 5

CRUDE AND INTRINSIC RATES OF BIRTH, DEATH, AND NATURAL
INCREASE, UNITED STATES, 1940-45 *

Year	Crude Rates†			Intrinsic Rates		
	Natural Increase	Birth	Death	Natural Increase	Birth	Death
1945........	9.5	20.7	11.2	4.9‡	17.4‡	12.5‡
1944........	10.3	21.5	11.2	5.8	18.1	12.2
1943........	11.9	22.9	11.0	7.8	19.5	11.7
1942........	11.9	22.3	10.4	6.5	18.6	12.1
1941........	9.7	20.3	10.6	2.7	16.6	13.9
1940........	8.6	19.4	10.8	0.9	15.7	14.8

* Adapted from *Population, Special Reports,* Series P-47, No. 2, Bureau of the Census: Washington, D.C., March 27, 1947, Table 1.
† Crude rates based on estimates of total population including men overseas. Military deaths included.
‡ Based on provisional mortality data.

A widely used method for measuring growth tendency is the net reproduction rate. Although it is calculated only for the female portion of the population, the net reproduction rate is a standardized measure, that is, it reflects only the influence of age specific fertility and mortality rates. It measures the number of female children a newly born female will have if subject to the current age specific rates of birth and death.[10] The net reproduction rate thus measures the growth tendency on a per-generation basis. Returning to Table 4, the data in column 4 show the extent to which the several populations are replacing themselves.[11] For example, while New Zealand, in 1936, had a natural increase of 7.9 per 1,000 population, its population was reproducing and dying at rates which in the long run would maintain a stationary population. Evidently New Zealand had a concentration

---

[10] See R. R. Kuczynski, *The Measurement of Population Growth* (New York, 1936), 205-29 for the procedure used in calculating the net reproduction rate.
[11] P. K. Whelpton has demonstrated that the net reproduction rate tends to overstate the replacement rate especially in periods of rising marriage rates. ("Reproduction Rates Adjusted for Age, Parity, Fecundity, and Marriage," *Journal of the American Statistical Association,* XLI (December, 1946), 501-16.)

of its numbers in the young adult years. Similar though more extreme discrepancies in a number of other countries are shown in Table 4. Only a few, and those mainly in southern and eastern Europe, have net reproductive rates that exceed replacement needs. That of Japan would permit a doubling of the population in two generations.

The Growth Pattern.—The available data, all of which pertain to the modern phase of man's history on the earth, indicate that population growth follows a typical pattern. According to Raymond Pearl, that pattern describes an S-shaped curve.[12] Starting from a condition of stability of numbers, population grows, very slowly at first, then at a rapidly accelerating rate, and finally slowly once more, eventually ceasing as a new equilibrium is established. Pearl was able to demonstrate this pattern in many different populations, though he was not successful in his attempts to explain the observed regularity.[13] His failure in this respect was due in part to the fact that he dealt only with gross numbers in a given area at successive intervals.

When growth is analyzed with reference to the movements of death and birth rates, the S-shaped pattern is considerably illuminated. A generalized description of the movements of vital rates involved in growth is presented in Figure 7. It will be observed that growth begins with a decline of the death rate, while the birth rate remains, for a time, at its early level. The widening gap between the two rates means an increasing excess of births over deaths. After a more or less extended delay the birth rate begins to fall, thus reducing the annual excess of births. And as the birth rate seeks the level of the death rate, growth gradually subsides and tends to stop completely.

This generalized growth cycle has been observed in one or another of its stages in many populations about the earth. The death rate in northwestern Europe, which was approximately 33 per 1,000 in 1700, passed into a long-run decline shortly after 1750. But the birth rate continued at its high level, of about 35 per 1,000, for another 100 years. Around 1850 the birth rate began to fall and it gathered a downward momentum through the remainder of the nineteenth and early part of the twentieth centuries.[14] After an extraordinary increase of 600 to 700 per cent between 1750 and 1930, the population of northwestern Europe is now at the end of its growth cycle. North American, New Zealand, and Australian populations also appear to be in the final growth phase. In southern and eastern Europe and in Japan

---

[12] *The Biology of Population Growth* (New York, 1930), 26-44.

[13] Margaret Sanger (ed.), *Proceedings of the World Population Conference* (London, 1927), 22-58.

[14] A. M. Carr-Saunders, *World Population* (Oxford, 1936), 59 ff.

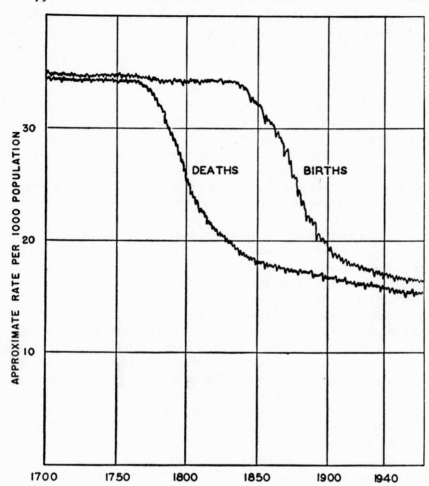

Fig. 7.—Approximate trends of death and birth rates in western Europe, 1700 to 1940.

and India the birth rate has but recently begun its decline and the populations of those areas continue to grow rapidly. In a few places, such as Puerto Rico, Java, and Asiatic Russia, the death rate has been falling for some years but the birth rate remains unchanged at its high level. There are found the world's fastest growing populations. China's is the largest population which has not recently entered upon the growth cycle.[15] Although there are no satisfactory data for the pre-modern period, it seems entirely probable that the same growth

---

[15] Ta Chen, *op. cit.,* 3.

pattern has unfolded wherever a relatively permanent increase of population has taken place.[16]

The Decline of the Death Rate.—Change in mortality rates such as are involved in the growth cycle is a part of the general readjustment of population to a new mode of life. The incidence of death fluctuates in close relationship to changes in the abundance and availability of food and other essential materials. Although insanitation and disease operate somewhat independently of the supply of sustenance materials, their contribution to mortality rises or falls with variations in diet and shelter. In any case, the supply of sustenance materials, insanitation, disease, and other factors that may be peculiar to specific locations constitute general mortality risks to which an entire population is exposed.

General mortality risks, however, have a differential effect, especially as among age categories. The very young and the very old are acutely susceptible to their influence, while the ages from roughly 10 to 50 years are to some degree resistant. But reductions of general mortality risks produce the greatest declines in death rates in the youngest age groups. Whereas the death rate in the Western world during the past two centuries fell from about 33 per 1,000 to 11 or 12 per 1,000, infant mortality declined from several hundred per 1,000 to around 40 or less per 1,000. The advanced ages, on the other hand, have contributed to mortality decline in inverse relation to their magnitude. This may be observed for a brief period in the United States in Table 6. Age specific death rates declined between 1900-1902 and 1930-1939 by about 66 per cent in the first year of life, 50 per cent at age 20, 33 per cent at age 45, and 4 per cent at age 70.

Likewise most of the gain in life expectancy, or average future lifetime, occurs through the saving of life in the earliest years of life. In Table 6 it is apparent that after a 25 per cent increase in life expectancy at birth, the increases at later ages for males are almost negligible. Females have experienced some significant gains in the advanced ages. But in general after a person achieved age 45 he could not expect any more added years of life in 1940 than he could have expected 30 years earlier.

Changes in life expectancy have profound, though inadequately explored, implications for a population. For instance, a life expectancy of 30 years at birth means that 100,000 persons may expect an aggregate of 3,000,000 man-years of life. Such life expectancies are not improbable: the estimated figure for the United States in 1800 is 30

---

[16] See *ibid.*, 4-5.

TABLE 6

Year	At birth		Age 20		Age 45		Age 70	
	Male	Female	Male	Female	Male	Female	Male	Female
Age specific death rate								
1900–02†....	133.5	110.6	5.9	5.5	12.6	10.6	58.9	53.7
1919–21‡....	80.5	63.9	4.3	4.3	9.3	8.1	54.6	50.2
1929–31.....	62.3	49.6	3.2	2.8	9.3	7.0	58.0	48.7
1930–39.....	57.0	45.0	2.7	2.2	8.6	6.3	56.3	45.8
Average future lifetime								
1900–02†....	48.2	51.1	42.2	43.8	24.2	25.5	9.0	9.6
1919–21‡....	56.3	58.5	45.6	46.5	26.0	27.0	9.5	9.9
1929–31.....	59.1	62.7	46.0	48.5	25.3	27.4	9.2	10.0
1930–39.....	60.6	64.5	46.8	49.7	25.5	28.0	9.3	10.2

* From Bureau of the Census, *United States Life Tables,* 1930-1939 (Preliminary),
(Washington, D.C., 1941).
† For the original registration States.
‡ For the registration States of 1920.

years; and India in 1939 had a life expectancy of 27 years. But where
the life expectancy is 64 years, as in the United States in 1939-1941,
100,000 persons may account for a total of 6,400,000 man-years of
life, more than double that derivable from a mean after lifetime of 30
years. In other words, a population with the higher life expectancy
realizes more man-years of life in one generation than a population
with the lower figure can obtain in two generations. Furthermore,
the figure of 6,400,000 man-years is obtained with but one period of
childhood rather than two. In childhood the individual is primarily
a consumer; his producing role is of relatively small consequence. A
population with a high life expectancy, then, is both biologically and
functionally a more efficient population. An interesting question is
to what extent added years of life displace potential births. No satisfactory answer to this question is available at present, however.

Sooner or later the fall of the death rate and the increase of life
expectancy must come to an end. Although man's potential life span
is estimated at 100 years, it is doubtful that life expectancy will ever
rise much above 75 years. There is evidence at present that death
rates, in the United States and most other parts of the western world,
are near the minimum in view of the present mode of life. In fact, the

crude death rate in this country in 1940, which was 10.8 per 1,000, is abnormally low. It reflects among other things a favorable age composition. If age specific rates remain the same through the following 20 years, the death rate will rise to 13.6 by 1960 as a result of the aging of the population.[17] Upward adjustments of the total death rate may be even more radical in places such as Australia and New Zealand, which have crude rates around 9 per 1,000. Presumably, however, a new cycle of change in mode of life will bring about a new decline of mortality. Any such decline must be very limited. For if every member of a population lived to be 100 years of age, there would still be a total death rate of 10 per 1,000. The lower the death rate, the less opportunity there is for subsequent decline.

Decline of the Birth Rate.—The downward movement of the birth rate, which is responsible for the decreasing rate of population increase in the late phase of the growth cycle, is itself a complex phenomenon. Nor is there a simple explanation of birth rate decline. Factors such as a rising standard of living, economic insecurity, emancipation of women from household tasks, the invention and spread of contraceptive devices, etc., are at best merely correlated variables; they are effects of the same causation that brought about declining rates of reproduction. These and other changes that might be mentioned may be traced to the general reorganization of population involved in the rise of cities and the abandonment of local self-sufficiency.

Where the family is the exclusive producing unit, its principal tools and source of power are its members. The family's strength as a producing enterprise therefore varies with its size. Under such conditions the compulsion to reproduction is powerful. Children are an economic imperative. Among agriculturalists the world over the promise of fertility is an important factor in the selection of mates for sons.

But when production is transferred to extra-familial units which employ mechanical tools and sources of power, the function of reproduction loses much of its former significance. Family welfare hinges not on family size, but on the stamina, skill, or fortitude of the worker in a wage job. Of course a large family might prosper from having many members gainfully employed. The loss of the producing function, however, reduces the need for adults to remain together in a family unit. They may drift apart in pursuit of employment opportunities. But whether together or apart their total income is the same.

---

[17] *Vital Statistics Rates in the United States, 1900-1940* (Washington, D. C., 1943), 64.

Hence children are not a necessity; in fact, they represent an unnecessary burden on the family budget. Even though the desire for children may be strong, it encounters competition from alternative interests.

Thus a declining family size accompanies the transition from a subsistence to an industrial-exchange economy. In the United States, for example, the median size of household unit or family was 5.7 persons in 1790 and 3.8 persons in 1940.[18] While part of the decline is due to a diminishing tendency for adult children to remain with their parents and part to fewer domestic servants living in the households of their employers, most of it can be charged to the falling birth rate. In the same period the crude birth rate fell from an annual average of about 35 per 1,000 to approximately 18 per 1,000, or by about 50 per cent.

When the birth rate decline is examined more closely it is found that most of the reduction has come about through the elimination of high birth order children. This is shown in Table 7. In the 20-year

TABLE 7

STANDARDIZED * BIRTH RATES PER 1,000 AT AGES 10 TO 54 FOR NATIVE WHITE FEMALES, BY BIRTH ORDER OF CHILD, UNITED STATES, 1920-1940 †

Year	Order of Child at Birth							
	All orders	First	Second	Third	Fourth	Fifth	Sixth and Seventh	Eighth and over
1940..........	50.7	19.4	13.1	7.0	3.9	2.4	2.7	2.2
1930..........	55.0	17.6	12.5	8.0	5.3	3.6	4.4	3.6
1920..........	64.9	20.4	14.0	9.6	6.5	4.5	5.5	4.4

* Standardized on the basis of the age distribution of total females of ages 10 to 54 in the United States in 1940.

† From *Statistical Bulletin,* Metropolitan Life Insurance Company, 25 (November, 1944), 5.

period first and second order birth rates declined by negligible amounts. Each higher birth order rate shows a progressively larger decline, reaching a 50 per cent decrease in the sixth and higher birth orders. It is quite probable that first born children occur as frequently today as ever in the past, and that second born children occur but slightly less frequently.

Another and highly important manifestation of differentials in birth rate decline appears in relation to social-economic differences.

---

[18] Paul C. Glick, "Family Trends in the United States," *American Sociological Review,* VII (August, 1942), 505.

This seems to take the form of a cycle which, at least in the recent historic period, involves three distinguishable phases. In the first phase social-economic classes have either the same birth rate or rates that vary directly with class position. Available evidence for Europe prior to 1850 suggests that births occurred in all classes at about the same rates.[19] This seems to be true also of contemporary China and India.[20] The direct correlation of birth rates with social-economic position in

TABLE 8

MEASURES OF FERTILITY IN A SAMPLE OF THE URBAN WHITE POPULATION, BY SOCIAL-ECONOMIC GROUP, UNITED STATES, 1935 *

Social-economic group	Standardized fertility rate†		Net Reproduction Rate
	Nuptial	General	
Family income			
$3000 & over................	84.6	31.1	.42
2000–3000................	84.8	41.6	.55
1500–2000................	93.0	48.4	.63
1000–1500................	102.5	60.5	.75
Under 1000................	132.9	83.1	.96
Education of women			
College...................	96.9	39.1	.52
High school...............	102.5	53.7	.68
7th or 8th grade...........	117.5	71.0	.86
Less than 7th grade........	130.7	82.9	.97
Total....................	108.9	56.8	.70

* Adapted from B. D. Karpines and C. V. Kiser, "The Differential Fertility and Potential Rates of Growth of Various Income and Educational Classes of Urban Population in the United States," *Milbank Memorial Fund Quarterly,* XVII (October, 1939), 376.
† Standardized on the basis of the white female population, 15-44 years of age, in the United States, in 1930.

pre-industrial populations is probable, but the fertility data at our disposal are too crude to permit a confirmation.[21] Although family size tends to be directly associated with class position in such populations, it is evident that differential death rates are largely responsible for family size variations.

---

[19] J. Rumney, "The Problem of Differential Fertility," *Population,* II (November, 1935), 9.
[20] J. L. Buck, *Land Utilization in China* (Chicago, 1937), 385; and B. K. Sarkar, "The Trend of Indian Birth Rates," *Indian Journal of Economics* (July, 1934), 60.
[21] J. L. Buck's data indicate that the direct association of birth rates and social-economic status obtains in China. (*Op. cit.*)

Starting from a situation of uniformity of birth rate among social-economic classes, or possibly of direct correlation with class position, birth rate decline introduces a second phase. Apparently the influences producing the curtailment of reproduction operate first and most effectively on the highest social-economic groups and with diminishing effectiveness on each lower stratum. Thus the amount of decrease in the birth rate varies with class position. Figure 8 shows the differ-

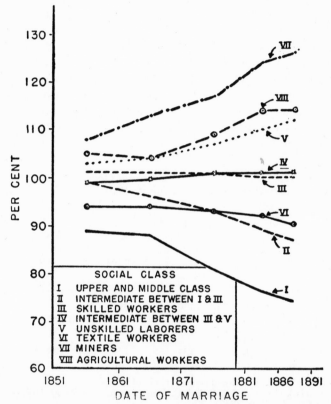

Fig. 8.—Movements of fertility rates of socio-economic groups, England and Wales, 1851-91. (From F. W. Notestein, "Class Differences in Fertility," *Annals Amer. Act. Pol. Soc. Sci.,* CLXXXVIII [November, 1936], 27. Used by permission of the publisher.)

entiation of social-economic groups that took place in England and Wales between 1851 and 1891.[22] Presumably it is this kind of change that produced the well-known inverse pattern of birth rate differentials

---

[22] In Figure 8 the fertility of women of each class is expressed as a percentage of the fertility rate of married women of all classes. The rates are standardized for duration of marriage.

which prevails in many places at present. This pattern is illustrated in Table 8 for two criteria of social-economic differences, income and education. Variables such as occupation and race are associated in like manner with measures of fertility. A similar pattern of differences has appeared in all industrialized populations.

The inverse pattern of association between fertility and social-economic groups seems, however, to be but a transitional phase in the general decline of the birth rate. A third and final phase of the cycle, characterized by a direct correlation of the two variables, is developing in many populations of the Western world. The movements involved in the emergence of this phase appear to be as follows : the birth rates among the highest social-economic groups, since they are the first to begin their declines, run their downward courses and reach their minimums relatively early. Declines in the lower groups start later and continue after the declines have virtually ceased in the higher groups, though eventually leveling off at minimums below those of

TABLE 9

STANDARDIZED * FERTILITY RATES OF FOUR OCCUPATIONAL GROUPS, BY INCOME, STOCKHOLM, 1919-1922 †

Income (Kronor)	Manufacturing Industry		Trade and Commerce	Arts and Professions	Total
	Manual Workers	Technicians, Supervisors, Clerical			
Under 4,000......	111	104	110	110	110
4,000– 6,000....	109	120	115	112	112
6,000–10,000....	105	125	131	127	125
10,000 & over....	—	152	154	154	154
Total........	110	124	124	123	

* Standardized for age and marriage periods of wives.
† From Karl A. Edin and Edward P. Hutchinson, *Studies of Differential Fertility in Sweden* (London, 1935), 59.

the higher groups. Thus the social-economic groups change their positions relative to one another on the fertility scale and assume a positive relationship with fertility rates. This pattern of differentials has already developed rather fully in Stockholm, as the data in Table 9 indicate. It may be observed that occupational differences are either negligible or inconsistent. But in all occupational groups excepting manual workers in manufacturing fertility varies directly with income. The tendency for a direct association of fertility and social-economic status to appear has been noted also in England [23] and in the United States.[24]

Figure 9 offers a schematic illustration of the cycle we have been describing. The letters A, B, and C represent high, middle, and low social-economic groups, respectively, and the subscripts 1, 2, and 3 represent the size rank of the birth rate for each class. It is assumed for purposes of illustration that a direct correlation obtained in the earliest period shown.

Migration and Growth.—The contribution of migration to the growth of regional and local populations presents a difficult problem of measurement. Perhaps that is why the matter has been the subject of lively debate. According to Francis Walker, onetime director of the United States census, "Foreign immigration into this country has, from the time it first assumed large proportions, amounted not to a re-enforcement of our population, but to a replacement of native by foreign stock." [25] This conclusion was based on observations of increases in net immigration paralleling declines in the rate of increase of the resident population. That both might have been effects of a third factor did not occur to Walker. It is possible, however, that there may be an element of truth in the conclusion he stated, especially if applied to a static society. But where there is expansion and development no such conclusion could be supported without due allowance having been made for the rate of development and the trend of the replacement prior to the beginning of immigration. These requisites apply particularly to the United States in the nineteenth century, with which Walker was specially concerned.

An estimate of the amounts of growth of the United States population arising from natural increase and from net immigration is set forth in Table 10. The contribution from migration is substantial in all decades, and at one point, the 1880-1890 decade, more than a third of the total growth is chargeable to net immigration. Growth from migration results not only from the absolute number of migrants added but also from the reproducing power they possess. And since migrants are usually concentrated in the young adult ages, the increment

[23] J. W. Innes, "Class Birth Rates in England and Wales, 1921-1931," *Milbank Memorial Fund Quarterly*, XIX (January, 1941), 1-25.
[24] Clyde V. Kiser, "Birth Rates and Socio-Economic Attributes in 1935," *Milbank Memorial Fund Quarterly*, XVII (April, 1939), 1-24. A more recent observation of the same tendency is made in P. K. Whelpton and Clyde V. Kiser, "Social and Psychological Factors Affecting Fertility: I. Differential Fertility among 41,498 White Couples in Indianapolis," *Milbank Memorial Fund Quarterly*, XXI (July, 1943), 24-27.
[25] "Immigration and Degradation," *Forum*, XI (August, 1891), 639-42.

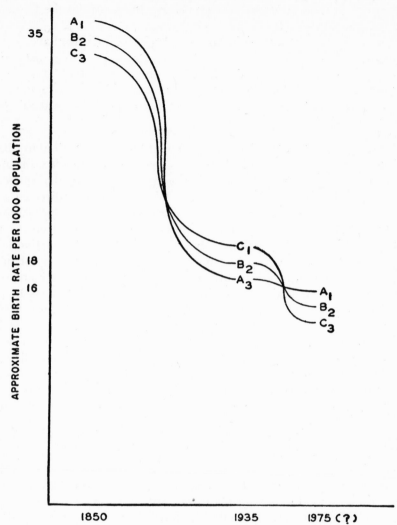

FIG. 9.—The changing pattern of birth rate differentials.

resulting from their natural increase may be considerable. Unfortunately Table 10 does not distinguish between natural increase of the native population and natural increase of the migrant population.

The effect of net emigration on the size of the losing population is perhaps even more difficult to ascertain. It is well known that various peasant peoples maintain stable populations through expelling surplus members of the generation succeeding to control of the farms. The Irish experience since the 1850's also indicates that emigration may

TABLE 10

POPULATION, AMOUNT OF INCREASE, AND ESTIMATED NATURAL INCREASE
AND NET IMMIGRATION, UNITED STATES, 1770-1940 *

Year	Population (adjusted)	Amount of Increase	Natural Increase	Net Immigration
1770............	2,215	—	—	—
1780............	2,810	586	566	20
1790............	3,964	1,163	1,123	40
1800............	5,363	1,399	1,349	50
1810............	7,270	1,907	1,845	62
1820............	9,673	2,403	2,332	71
1830............	12,921	3,248	3,125	123
1840............	17,154	4,233	3,740	493
1850............	23,260	6,106	4,686	1,420
1860............	31,502	8,242	5,684	2,558
1870............	39,915	8,413	6,339	2,074
1880............	50,262	10,347	7,767	2,580
1890............	63,056	12,794	7,830	4,964
1900............	76,129	13,073	9,384	3,689
1910............	92,422	16,293	10,050	6,243
1920............	106,424	14,002	11,777	2,225
1930............	123,191	16,767	13,432	3,335
1940............	131,775	8,584	8,630	— 46

* From Victor S. Van Szeliski, "Population Growth Due to Immigration and
Natural Increase," *Human Biology,* VIII (February, 1936), 27.

play a significant part in population decline, though no separation of
the effects of increased mortality and the rising age of marriage has
been made.[26] Instances in which net emigration significantly affects
the size of population are usually found to involve small aggregates.

Emigration from large populations seldom removes important proportions from parent groups within short time intervals. Evidently
simple physical difficulties, as encountered in transporting and reset-
tling emigrants, impose severe limitations on the numbers that can
be moved in a week, a month, or even a year.[27] High growth rates in
countries that at the same time have had large excesses of emigrants
over immigrants, such as Italy and Poland, suggest that the places
vacated by migrants are quickly filled by persons who otherwise would

---

[26] The population of Eire declined from 6,548,000 in 1840 to 2,992,034 in 1939.

[27] The Red Cross Commission sent to investigate famine conditions in China, in
1928-1929, observed: "It is estimated that if all the ships in the world now engaged
in passenger traffic on the seven seas were withdrawn from their usual routes and
were devoted solely to transporting Chinese from their native land to other countries,
they could not keep up with the growth of population." (Cited by H. P. Fairchild,
People: The Quantity and Quality of Population (New York, Henry Holt & Co.,
1939), 233.)

have died or would not have been born. Migration seems to have no more than a momentary effect on the replacement power of a population, and that solely through altering the proportion of reproducers. At most the effect of net out movement is to slow the growth rate or to hasten the decline of numbers. For it to have a more lasting effect, whether in large populations or in small, the exodus must be cataclysmic and must be accompanied by radical readjustment measures.

The Significance of Size.—"Mere numbers are important. . . . There are some thoughts which will not come to men who are not tightly packed," observed F. W. Maitland when studying the history of the English borough.[28] It is a matter of common knowledge that as the size of the social aggregate increases the behavior of its members changes. This is implied in the adage: "Two's company, but three's a crowd." The possibilities in a crowd of three are not so great, however, as in a crowd of 300 or of 3,000.[29] But we have little precise knowledge of the relation between size of population and organization. Apparently the relation has been so taken for granted that it has not been thought worthy of careful investigation. Yet size of population is doubtlessly one of the most important limiting factors in man's collective life.

Population size imposes limits on both the extent of specialization and the number of different activities that may be carried on simultaneously. Specialization presupposes a sufficient number of users of the given service to support a concentration of effort on its production. As Adam Smith put it:

There are some sorts of industry, even of the lowest kind, which can be carried on nowhere but in a great town. A porter, for example, can find employment and subsistence in no other place. A village is by much too narrow a sphere for him; even an ordinary market town is scarce large enough to afford him constant occupation.[30]

In a small population the degree of specialization of activity is necessarily slight. On the other hand, every increment in size increases the extent to which specialization may be developed. That this is also affected by variation in heterogeneity with size is entirely probable.

---

[28] *Township and Borough,* Ford Lectures, Oxford University (Cambridge, 1898), 24.

[29] According to Simmel, "To every definite number of elements there correspond . . . a specific sociological form, a characteristic organization, and a definite degree of firmness of texture." (N. J. Spykman, *The Social Theory of Georg Simmel* (Chicago, 1925), 129.) See also Louis Wirth, "Urbanism as a Way of Life," *American Journal of Sociology,* XLIV (July, 1938), 1-24.

[30] *The Wealth of Nations* (New York: The Modern Library, 1931), 17.

The range and diversity of individual abilities may be expected to widen with population increase. Hence large populations not only offer greater opportunity for intensive specialization than do small populations, they also may be expected to contain greater assortments of potential specialists.

The complexity of organization structure that may be developed in a group is determined in large part by the availability of the requisite personnel. Obviously a population of a few score cannot staff an establishment such as a modern mass-producing factory. Nor can it support a great variety of continuous activities. Its technology as well as its organization is restricted to what can be manufactured and operated by relatively few individuals. The increase of manpower that results from population growth permits, though it does not compel, the adoption of more complicated and efficient processes, and to the extent that it does so the number and diversity of concurrent activities may also be increased.

Population Forecasting.—Knowledge of the future population of an area is of the utmost importance to the effective planning of the collective affairs of the occupants, even though the relation between size and organizational features has not been fully explored and measured. But forecasting is by no means an easy undertaking. This is one of the many phases of demographic study in which it becomes apparent that population cannot be detached from the totality of social life and treated as a thing apart.

Various techniques for forecasting population have been tried and most have proved deficient. Among the simpler methods are the so-called arithmetic and geometric projections. The first assumes the continuation through successive equal intervals of time of the amount of growth observed in a base period. The second differs only in that the increment employed is a constant percentage rather than a constant amount. In both instances the usefulness of the method is limited to very short-run projections—i.e., ten years or less; the more extended the projection, the greater is the error likely to be. The arithmetic method, by failing to take into account the cumulative nature of growth, understates future population. On the other hand, the geometric method neglects to consider the effect of increases in the total population on growth rate with the result that it consistently tends to overstate future population.

Another and more elaborate technique of projection is that which employs the logistic curve developed by Raymond Pearl.[31] According

---

[31] *Op. cit.*

to that procedure, knowledge of how far a population has advanced along its S-shaped growth curve is all that is needed in order to anticipate how big it will be at given dates in the future. A simple projection of the curve in keeping with the logistic formula is all that is required. The principal difficulty with this technique is found in the uncertainty as to when one growth curve may be expected to end and a new one to begin. This is relatively easy to determine after the fact, but no basis for doing so before the fact other than simple guesswork has been suggested. Furthermore, there is some evidence that the logistic curve overestimates future population in progressively larger amounts.[32]

The net reproduction rate represents another means of forecasting population. It tells what the growth tendency contained in the specific fertility and mortality rates is on a per generation basis, assuming no change in the rates. But in leaving migration out of account it falls short of a useful instrument for purposes of forecasting, except in rare cases where there is no in or out migration. As a matter of fact, the net reproduction rate was designed for other uses.

The most satisfactory forecasting procedure thus far devised is that put forth by P. K. Whelpton and W. S. Thompson and which, for want of a better label, may be called the analytic method. This consists in advancing various hypotheses based on different combinations of assumptions regarding future trends in fertility, mortality, and net migration. By applying the assumed trends to a population with a given size and composition it is possible to obtain for any future date a figure that is as accurate as the assumptions are reliable. After this is done for a number of combinations of assumptions one may select the hypothetical future population which best accords with his interpretation of subsequent developments in technology, medical practice, politics, and other features of organization that affect the growth of population. In Table 11 are shown four hypotheses regarding future population in the United States. These are examples: many other hypothetical populations may be constructed. The so-called medium forecast—that shown in the first column—is currently accepted as being the most probable. Like any other, however, it is only as reliable as the assumptions upon which it is based.

The risk of error in forecasting varies inversely with the size of the territorial unit concerned, or, more properly, with the degree to which the area approximates the universe of interdependence. Trends in the population of a large area tend to be much more stable than in

[32] R. Pearl, L. J. Reed, and J. F. Kish, "The Logistic Curve and the Census Count of 1940," *Science*, XCII (November, 1940), 486-88.

the population of a small area.   That is largely because the smaller the population the greater may be the rate of change occasioned by migration.   This is partly a matter of simple proportional arithmetic and partly one of a probable predominance of short over long distance migration.   Moreover, the population of a small area is apt to be relatively more specialized in function than is a larger one, and its potential variability is therefore correspondingly greater.   Changes in the market for a local product, relocations of industrial plants across the boundaries of the small area, technological improvements that alter

TABLE 11

FORECASTS OF THE POPULATION BASED ON DIFFERENT SETS OF
ASSUMPTIONS, UNITED STATES, 1945-1975 *

Year	Medium fertility Medium mortality No immigration	Medium fertility Medium mortality Net immigration 100,000 yearly	Low fertility High mortality No immigration	High fertility Low mortality No immigration
1945....	139,621	139,621	139,621	139,621
1950....	145,460	145,959	144,922	146,087
1955....	149,840	150,911	147,990	152,017
1960....	153,375	155,075	149,827	157,609
1965....	156,692	159,055	151,047	163,446
1970....	159,847	162,888	151,627	169,612
1975....	162,337	166,069	151,090	175,750

* P. K. Whelpton, *Forecasts of the Population of the United States, 1945-1975,* Bureau of the Census (Washington, D. C., 1947), 76-97.

the number of job opportunities in the locale, and other such changes may have radical import for the small area but may exert no appreciable effect on the total economy.   This is dramatically illustrated by the rise and fall of boom settlements ; but even though such fluctuations may occur more gradually, they may be the same in principle.   In effect, no satisfactory method of forecasting the population of the small area can be developed until a reliable technique of projecting the trend of job opportunities is made available.   The analytic procedure offers the only useful approach to the problem.

Summary.—Although man possesses a tremendous capacity for increasing his numbers, population growth appears to be the exception rather than the rule in human history.   Available evidence suggests that the quadrupling of world population during the past 280 years is an extraordinary event.   The means of growth include natural increase, net migration, and annexation, depending on the size and character of the area in question.   Natural increase, which is the difference between crude birth and death rates, is a useful though rough measure of growth from vital processes. More refined measures are derived by controlling the distorting effects of age composition differentials.

The movements of birth and death rates involved in natural increase describe a pattern that is highly recurrent. Growth begins with a decline in the death rate while the birth rate remains at its high level. The increasing excess of births over deaths continues until the birth rate begins to fall, after which the excess of births declines and eventually returns to zero. All known instances of growth based on vital processes either have followed or are following this pattern, though the time between the flections in the two curves may vary greatly.

The decline of mortality, due largely to increases in the abundance of sustenance materials, tends to be greatest in the earliest ages of life and least in the more advanced ages. Fertility decline, on the other hand, appears to result from changes in the organization of society, changes that curtail the functional role of the family. The fall of the birth rate accompanying changes in social structure has been most pronounced among high birth orders. Rates of first and second order births have not changed appreciably. Another important differential in birth rate decline is social-economic position. It is probable that the present inverse relation of fertility with social-economic position is a transitional phase in the downward movement of the rate.

The effect of migration on growth is difficult to measure. Yet, contrary to early arguments, migration does contribute to the growth rate of a population in the receiving area both directly through addition of migrants and indirectly through the reproduction of migrants. There is less certainty, however, that net emigration significantly affects growth rates except perhaps in very short intervals of time. Although there are no satisfactory data on the matter, it seems probable that emigrants are replaced by persons who might otherwise have died.

The rather obvious importance of population size indicates the desirability for practical purposes of forecasting the future population. While various simple techniques of forecasting have been used, they are for the most part of meager value. The most satisfactory of the methods currently in use is that which makes specific assumptions about trends in fertility, mortality, and net migration and applies these assumed trends to an existing age and sex composition. The task of forecasting becomes vastly more difficult in the small area, owing to its greater potential variability. No adequate method for use in small areas has been developed.

SUPPLEMENTARY REFERENCES

DUBLIN, LOUIS I. and LOTKA, ALFRED J. *Length of Life.* New York: The Ronald Press Co., 1949.

GLASS, D. U. *The Struggle for Population.* Oxford: Clarendon Press, 1936.

PEARSON, S. VERE. *The Growth and Distribution of Population.* New York: John Wiley & Sons, 1935.

SWEENEY, J. SHIRLEY. *The Natural Increase of Mankind.* Baltimore: Williams & Wilkins Co., 1926.

WHELPTON, P. K. "On the Rapidity of the Decline in the Birth Rate," *Journal of the American Statistical Association,* XXIX (September, 1934).

Chapter 8

THE COMPOSITION OF POPULATION

We have dealt with human populations thus far as though they were aggregates of homogeneous units. And in a number of respects such a treatment is appropriate, for all men are alike in that they are members of the same species. Nevertheless, there are important differences among the components of any aggregate, differences which play a part in giving the aggregate a distinctive character. No full understanding of distribution, growth, or any other aspect of population may be had without references to the differentiation that obtains within the aggregates of mankind.

The kinds of differences found within populations are legion. These are differences of age and sex, of nativity and race, of religion, occupation, income, marital status, education, health, and so on. The array of characteristics with reference to which individuals are differentiated varies among populations in accordance with their past experiences and the circumstances under which they live. Racial differences, for example, may exist in one aggregate but be entirely lacking in another. Furthermore, of the many variables that are identifiable in a given population there are usually some that have no significance; that is, they are irrelevant to the functional organization of the aggregate. This is generally true of such characteristics as hair and eye color, but it may also apply to religion, nativity, and other traits. Thus with few exceptions what constitute noteworthy elements of composition must be determined separately for each population.

Two important exceptions to this rule are age and sex. These occur universally, though there are local variations in their functional expressions. Everywhere they form a basic biological structure upon which functional organization is built. The treatment of composition in this chapter therefore will be restricted to age and sex characteristics.

The Population Pyramid.—The age and sex composition of population is conventionally portrayed by means of a graphic device known as the population pyramid. This may be illustrated with the concept of the stationary population, shown in Figure 10. A moment's inspection will reveal that Figure 10 is composed of two bar diagrams, one for males, the other for females, placed back to back. Each bar of the resulting pyramid represents an age group ranging from youngest at the bottom to the oldest at the top. Since it is constructed on a percentage basis, each half-bar indicates the per cent that the respective age-sex group is of the total population. Hence the pyramid provides an instantaneous description of the age and sex composition of the population for which it is prepared.

The rather neat pyramidal shape of Figure 10 is the expected result of the continuous operation over a relatively long period of time,

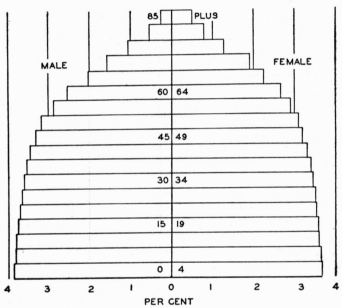

FIG. 10.—Stationary population of the United States, 1939-41.

e.g., three generations, of identical birth and death rates and assuming no migration. This is what is meant by a stationary population: a population that is neither increasing nor decreasing. Under these conditions each higher bar is reduced in size by the amount of mortality in the age group represented by the bar immediately below it.

Close scrutiny of the male and female portions of each bar in Figure 10 will reveal a different numerical relation between the sexes in each age group. Males are born in larger numbers than are females and they die at higher rates. At birth the ratio of males to females in the United States in 1939-1941 was 106 to 100. But in the stationary population the male excess is eliminated by age 50, at which the sex ratio is 100 males per 100 females, and at successively higher ages males fall into a progressively smaller minority. At ages 75-79 there are but 77 males for every 100 females. The total sex ratio for the population shown in Figure 10 is 98 males per 100 females. These differences are shown more clearly in Table 12.

TABLE 12

PERCENTAGE DISTRIBUTION BY AGE-SEX GROUPS AND SEX RATIOS,
UNITED STATES LIFE TABLE POPULATION, 1939–41 *

Age	Sex		Males per 100 females
	Male	Female	
Total.........	49.6	50.4	98.1
0–4..............	3.8	3.7	104.7
5–9..............	3.8	3.6	104.6
10–14............	3.7	3.6	104.5
15–19............	3.7	3.6	104.2
20–24............	3.7	3.5	103.9
25–29............	3.6	3.5	103.6
30–34............	3.5	3.5	103.3
35–39............	3.5	3.4	102.9
40–44............	3.4	3.3	102.5
45–49............	3.3	3.2	101.0
50–54............	3.1	3.1	99.1
55–59............	2.8	2.9	96.2
60–64............	2.5	2.7	92.4
65–69............	2.0	2.3	87.9
70–74............	1.6	1.9	82.6
75–79............	1.0	1.3	76.7
80–84............	0.6	0.8	70.0
85 and over........	0.2	0.5	60.7

* Adapted from Tables 2 and 3. Sixteenth Census of the United States, *United States Life Tables and Actuarial Tables, 1939–41* (Washington, D. C., 1946), 28-31.

Needless to say, the age and sex composition we have been discussing is that of a constructed or conceptual population. Such a population does not actually exist in the United States, nor has it ever existed since the settlement of this country by Europeans. It is unlikely, in fact, that the age and sex distribution of a stationary population has occurred among any people of European extraction since the beginning of the nineteenth century. But this is not to say that a stationary population has never existed. On the contrary, it is highly probable that the age-sex compositions of many isolated or nonindustrial peoples have varied closely about the pattern of a stationary population. Evidence of lack of growth or decline over prolonged periods in such instances suggests this probability. Unfortunately, the data needed to test the hypothesis are not available.

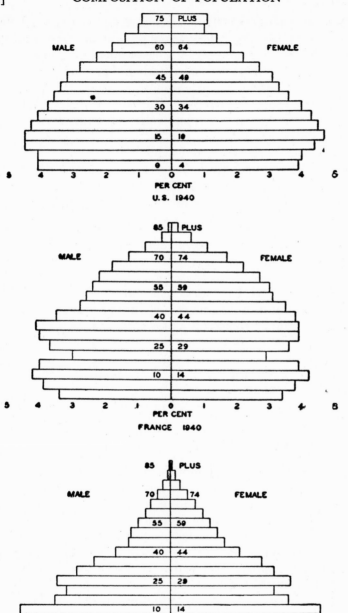

FIG. 11.—Age and sex compositions of the populations of the United States, France, and the Union of Soviet Socialist Republics, 1940.

The pyramids in Figure 11 describe some types of deviations from the stationary population. The age and sex composition in the United States, in 1940, is characterized by a heavy concentration in the years of early adulthood. This is representative of an "aging population." France, in 1940, had an "older" population than that of the United States, as is evident in the narrower base and the bulge in the higher age groups. A marked deficiency of males in the advanced ages is also noticeable. Soviet Russia, on the other hand, had a "young" population. The large proportions in the childhood years and the relatively small proportions in the higher ages make for a low average age. It is probable that the irregularities in the lower section of the pyramid are the result of errors in enumeration.

Composition and Natural Increase.—A factor of major importance in producing irregularities of composition is the phenomenon of change in size, or, more precisely, change in the rate of change of size. This is because the additions to or losses from a population are persons with selected characteristics. Natural increase, for example, is rigorously selective with respect to age: it adds only persons of zero age to an aggregate. Hence growth due to an excess of births over deaths enlarges the infant category first and only with the passing of time are its effects carried over the entire age range. A growing population's pyramid, such as that of Soviet Russia, in Figure 11, typically has a broad base. And if the rate of natural increase remains constant, the age composition will retain its pattern indefinitely. But where the rate of natural increase is rising the base grows progressively broader, for each year a larger number of infants is added to the population. Whether this is happening in Soviet Russia cannot be determined from a single pyramid; the age distribution for a series of years is needed for such a conclusion to be drawn.

On the other hand, where there is a declining rate of natural increase each succeeding cohort of infants is smaller than the preceding one. The persistence of such a tendency causes the base of the pyramid to narrow and the sides to steepen. Eventually the excess of births over deaths may fall so low that new infant groups are too small to replace the next older groups. In that event, age composition loses its pyramidal shape and acquires an outline resembling a top. Such a pattern has appeared in the United States and in France, as illustrated in Figure 11. Age distributions of this type cannot be maintained permanently by vital processes alone; they represent a transitional stage in the shift to a lower growth rate. Ultimately, assuming the attainment of some kind of equilibrium in the ratio of births to deaths, the large numbers of people in the advanced ages will die out of the population and the distribution of ages will regain its pyramidal form.   In the meantime the average age of the population rises rapidly.

The aging process, incident to a declining growth rate, is described in Table 13.   The median age of the United States total population has advanced from 21.4 years, in 1890, to 28.9 years, in 1940, an in-

TABLE 13

MEDIAN AGE OF POPULATION BY SEX, UNITED STATES, 1890–1940 *

Census Year	Total	Male	Female
1940.............	28.9	29.0	28.9
1930.............	26.4	26.7	26.1
1920.............	25.2	25.8	24.7
1910.............	24.0	24.6	23.5
1900.............	22.9	23.3	22.4
1890.............	21.4	21.8	21.0

* United States Bureau of the Census, Release P-5, No. 1, Jan. 1941.

crease of approximately 33 per cent.   Of interest is the discrepancy between male and female ages.   That difference is due to the preponderance of males in the population resulting from foreign immigration in past years.   With no further net immigration the average age of males will drop below the female average age, as males die at higher rates than females.

The increase of the proportion in the advanced ages is, in fact, general over western Europe.   This may be observed in Table 14.   In-

TABLE 14

PERSONS 60 YEARS OF AGE AND OVER PER 1,000 TOTAL POPULATION IN SELECTED WESTERN EUROPEAN NATIONS, 1850-1947 *

Nation	1850	1900	1947
Belgium	89	95	156
Denmark	82	99	131
England	72	75	152
France	101	124	160
Germany	70	78	138
Norway	88	109	137
Switzerland	79	93	142
The Netherlands	77	92	116

* Alfred Sauvy, "Social and Economic Consequences of the Aging of Western European Populations," *Population Studies,* II (June, 1948), 115.

creases in the ratios of persons 60 years of age and over to the total population range from 50 per cent to over 100 per cent for the nations represented.

Age composition provides a rough index of the growth phase in which a population is at the moment. Where the proportions in the youngest ages are very large the population is doubtless in the phase of rapid growth. But where the numbers in the youngest ages show evidences of decline, it is likely that the population has passed its period of maximum growth. And a high proportion of aged indicates that the population is near the end of its growth cycle. All this, of course, assumes no migration. Thus the United States's population is approaching a cessation of growth. So also are the populations of England and Wales, Austria, and Sweden, as indicated by their age compositions in Table 15. The same tendency prevails in most northern and western European countries. Referring again to Table 15, it appears that Italy and Poland have recently entered upon periods of

TABLE 15

PERCENTAGE AGE DISTRIBUTION OF SELECTED EUROPEAN POPULATIONS, 1940 *

Age	England and Wales	Austria	Sweden	Italy	Poland	Yugo-slavia
Total........	100.0	100.0	100.0	100.0	100.0	100.0
0–9.............	13.6	13.4	13.5	19.1	20.7	24.1
10–19...........	15.3	16.2	15.5	18.9	20.5	21.3
20–29...........	16.1	14.1	17.1	16.2	16.6	15.3
30–39...........	16.0	17.0	16.2	14.5	16.2	14.8
40–49...........	13.4	13.9	13.3	11.2	10.7	9.9
50–59...........	11.6	11.5	10.7	9.0	7.3	7.4
60–69...........	8.6	8.6	7.7	6.5	4.9	4.6
70 and over.......	5.4	5.3	6.0	4.6	3.1	2.6

* F. W. Notestein, et al., The Future Population of Europe and the Soviet Union (Geneva, 1944), Appendix IV.

declining growth rates, though other factors may have been responsible for depressing the proportion in their 0-9-year age groups. Yugoslavia's population is representative of many, including those of Greece, Romania, Spain, Albania, Soviet Russia, and Japan, that are increasing at high rates. Such an age composition results from vital rates that operated in industrialized nations 75 to 100 years ago. Figure 12 reveals a close similarity of patterns between the age structure of the United States, in 1870, and of Japan, in 1935.

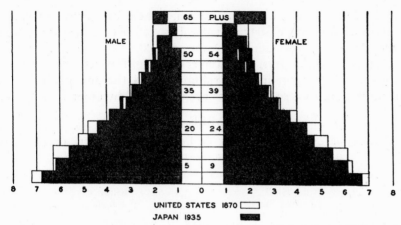

FIG. 12.—Age and sex composition of population in United States, 1870, and in Japan, 1935.

Thus far little has been said about sex distribution and natural increase. The fact of the matter is that the numerical relation between the sexes is not greatly affected by natural increase variations. Males and females are born in almost constant proportions and the existing age-sex specific death rates distribute them in a more or less uniform pattern. Slight variations in sex composition are produced by changes in mortality rates inasmuch as males are more susceptible to mortality risks. In general a population with a high death rate tends to have a larger proportion of females than a population with a low death rate. The differences, however, are not great.

Composition and Migration.—Growth from migration exerts a different influence on composition. Since migrants are usually in the ages of young adulthood, they enlarge the proportions in the inter-mediate ages and the proportions in the other ages are reduced accord-ingly. The subsequent effects of migration on growth are transmitted downward along the age scale through the reproduction of migrants and upward along the age scale as a result of the aging of migrants. Migration also alters sex composition. Males and females are seldom attracted to a given place, and at any one time, in equal proportions. For the most part, long-distance migration weights the balance in favor of males, whereas short-distance migration adds a larger number of females than of males to the receiving population.

Of the national populations we have discussed only those of the United States and, to a lesser extent, France have been significantly affected by migration. The disproportionate numbers in the adult ages in those populations are due partly to declining rates of natural increase and partly to net immigration. The consequences of migration are shown more clearly in Table 16. In the urban population the relatively large proportions between ages 20 and 60 years suggest a substantial net in-migration. Conversely, the relatively small proportions in that age range in the rural farm population imply a heavy net out-migration. These inferences are confirmed by other information.

TABLE 16

PERCENTAGE AGE DISTRIBUTION OF POPULATION, BY TYPE OF PLACE, UNITED STATES, 1940 *

Age	Total United States	Urban	Rural non-farm	Rural farm
Total.......	100.0	100.0	100.0	100.0
0–9............	16.1	13.5	18.4	20.4
10–19..........	18.3	16.6	18.5	22.3
20–29..........	17.2	18.1	17.1	15.2
30–39..........	15.0	16.3	14.9	11.8
40–49..........	13.0	14.3	11.7	10.9
50–59..........	9.9	10.6	8.9	9.3
60–69..........	6.5	6.6	6.3	6.4
70 and over......	4.0	4.0	4.4	3.7

* Sixteenth Census of the United States, *Population, United States Summary* (Washington, D. C., 1943), Table 7.

Perhaps it has already become evident that the interpretation of composition data relative to sources of growth involves a considerable risk of error. Declining rate of natural increase and migration may produce nearly identical effects on age structure. It is entirely possible for changes in natural increase rates alone to result in age structures such as those of the United States and France, or even those of the United States urban and rural farm populations. To distinguish the effects of the two sources of growth requires,[1] in most instances, the use of additional data. The sex distribution, however, often provides a clue as to the source of growth. In Table 17 are presented sex ratios for the same populations described in Table 16. The sex distribution from 0 to 30 years of age in the total United States population is about what is expected solely from the operation of fertility and mortality rates. But the large proportions of males above age 30

[1] For example, with the annual age specific fertility and mortality rates that have operated during the lifetime of the existing population it is possible to construct the age structures expected on the basis of vital phenomena above. Similar data for migrants together with the annual amount of net migration may be used to the same end.

TABLE 17

MALES PER 100 FEMALES BY AGE AND TYPE OF PLACE, UNITED STATES, 1940 *

Age	Total United States	Urban	Rural non-farm	Rural farm
Total.......	100.7	95.5	103.6	111.6
0–9............	103.1	102.7	103.2	103.5
10–19..........	101.6	97.4	101.2	109.8
20–29..........	96.5	89.6	98.5	117.7
30–39..........	98.4	94.2	105.4	106.0
40–49..........	102.5	99.1	110.8	106.2
50–59..........	106.7	101.6	110.2	119.0
60–69..........	101.2	90.4	103.6	132.7
70 and over.....	92.9	79.1	99.2	132.0

* Sixteenth Census of the United States, *Population, United States Summary* (Washington, D. C., 1943), Table 7.

could hardly have been produced by natural processes. They are, in fact, survivors from the large scale overseas migration that terminated in 1924. The urban population, on the other hand, shows a deficiency of males, especially between ages 10 to 40 years, that exceeds the probable effects of natural processes. It reflects the preponderance of females in the migration to cities. Again, the exceptionally large numbers of males in the advanced ages in both the rural non-farm and the rural farm populations are clearly consequences of migration. They are due mainly to the urbanward movement of females.

Composition and the Settlement Process.—The extent to which the settlement of an area has been stabilized and has become permanent is reflected in the composition of its population. Normally migration to an area newly opened for settlement is made up predominantly of young unattached males. In time females and family members follow the initial migrants, thus rounding out the complement of sex and age groups. The settlement in Hawaii of numerous foreign ethnic groups has provided many repetitions of this process. Some of these are described in Figure 13.

The Filipino population, of 1920, and the Korean, of 1910, show extreme distortions on the male sides of the pyramids and in the youthful ages. The structures could only have resulted from a highly selective migration influence. In this instance that influence was exerted by a program of systematic labor recruitment to supply the needs of Hawaii's rapidly expanding economy. The sequence of migration of the several groups may be estimated by noting the positions on the age scale of the excess male proportions. Thus it is evident that the

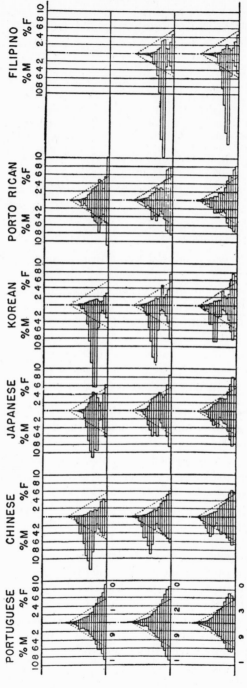

Fig. 13.—Age and sex compositions of selected ethnic groups, Hawaii, 1910-30. (From Andrew W. Lind, *An Island Community* [The University of Chicago Press: Chicago, 1938], Figure 11. Used by permission of the publisher.)

Portuguese and Chinese came first and were followed by Japanese, Koreans, Puerto Ricans, and Filipinos, in that order. A complicating factor in any such interpretation, however, is the degree of selectivity that has been exercised in the migration. Although it appears that the Portuguese preceded the Chinese in Hawaii, they actually came later.[2] The migration of Portuguese included wives and children, while the stream of Chinese migration was composed almost entirely of young males. The Puerto Rican migration was also rather unselective.

Evidence of the maturation of settlement is present in Figure 13 in the formation of symmetrical pyramids beneath the distorted age groups in each population. By 1930 the Chinese had almost achieved a balanced age and sex distribution. The Japanese and Koreans were also well along the way to that end. In population of this type average age continues to rise and reaches an abnormally high figure as the early migrants move into the most advanced ages. Average age declines somewhat, however, with the removal by death of the large numbers of old males.

Essentially the same process of change in composition has been observed by Clark and Roberts to accompany the establishment of settlement in the state of Kansas.[3] That state forms a rectangle in the very center of the United States. By dividing the area of Kansas into approximate thirds with lines running from north to south, three subregions are identified. Settlement began at the eastern border of the state about the middle of the nineteenth century and spread westward across the state. Hence subregion I is the oldest in point of occupancy, while subregion III was the last to be settled. Table 18 describes the age composition of the population in the three subregions. It is clearly apparent that the oldest population is found in the area of first settlement, subregion I, and that age declines in subregion II and again in subregion III. Moreover, males are older than females; that is, there are more males in the 65-year and over group than females and fewer males than females in the under 20 years of age group. While the age difference between the sexes exists in all subregions, it is smallest in the oldest subregion and greatest in the most recently settled subregion. In other words, the expected pattern of age and sex distribution is nearer attainment in the area of first settlement.

It is not assumed of course that every region of settlement will show identical demographic changes in its maturation. The beginning

---

[2] Andrew Lind, *An Island Community* (Chicago, 1938), 123-34.
[3] C. D. Clark and Roy L. Roberts, *People of Kansas: A Demographic and Sociological Study* (Topeka, 1936).

TABLE 18

NUMBER OF PERSONS, BY AGE, PER 1000 TOTAL POPULATION
IN THE SUBREGIONS OF KANSAS, 1930 *

Age	Total			Male			Female		
	Sub-region I	Sub-region II	Sub-region III	Sub-region I	Sub-region II	Sub-region III	Sub-region I	Sub-region II	Sub-region III
Total...	1000	1000	1000	1000	1000	1000	1000	1000	1000
Under 20....	363	380	434	361	379	423	364	382	448
20–64.......	561	552	513	562	551	521	562	552	503
65 & over....	76	68	53	77	70	56	74	66	49

* Adapted from Clark and Roberts, *People of Kansas: A Demographic and Sociological Study* (Topeka, 1936), 106.

stages of settlement are usually associated with the exploitation of natural resources of the region and the character of the resources is an important factor in the selection of the first immigrants to the area. An agricultural development, such as occurred in Kansas, will tend to select a preponderance of married couples and will therefore in the early stage show high proportions of small children and young adults. A logging or mining development, however, will select unattached male adults mainly and very small proportions of women and children. But in any case, if settlement is permanent, the age and sex distribution will acquire the pattern implicit in the prevailing fertility and mortality rates. That will require a longer period of time when the proportion of females in the migrant stream has remained small.

Composition and War.—Various historical incidents may likewise affect the demographic structure of an aggregate. Conspicuous among these is war. Since large scale military operations involve a segregation of the sexes and a disruption of family life, the birth rate of a population engaged in war falls abruptly. The deficiencies of children in ages 2 to 6 years in France and England and Wales, and in ages 5 to 10 years in Germany, as shown in Figure 14, may thus be explained. Some compensation for the war-time losses of births occurs, however, through a momentary rise of the birth rate after the war as a result of the reunion of the sexes. That is visible in the large numbers under two years of age, especially in France and England and Wales. The slight depressions in the curves for France and Germany around age 50 are probably due to birth losses incurred in the Franco-Prussian war of 1870. War also increases male mor-

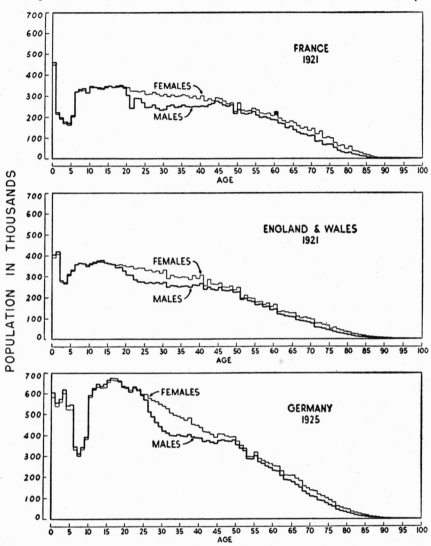

POPULATION IN THOUSANDS

FIG. 14.—Age distribution, by sex, of population in France, England and Wales, and Germany at first post World War I census. (From "The Cumulative Effect of Successive Wars on Age Composition of Populations," *Statistical Bulletin,* Metropolitan Life Insurance Company, Vol. 21 [April, 1940], 4. Used by permission of the publisher.)

tality and thereby lowers the ratio of males to females. Figure 14 shows large excesses of females between ages 20 and 45 for all three populations. Such distortions remain in the composition until the generations affected die out of the population.

Composition in Cities.—City populations differ considerably in their demographic structure. As may be seen in Table 19, age distribution varies consistently with size. The larger the city the smaller is both the proportion of children and the proportion of aged individuals. Sex composition likewise varies with city size. It may be

TABLE 19

PERCENTAGE DISTRIBUTION BY AGE, BY SIZE OF CITY, UNITED STATES, 1930 *

Size of City	Total	0–4	5–19	20–29	30–44	45–64	65 and over
500,000 and over......	100.0	7.7	25.0	19.3	25.7	17.9	4.3
100,000–500,000.......	100.0	7.8	25.4	18.7	24.4	18.5	5.1
25,000–100,000........	100.0	8.2	26.5	18.1	23.5	18.3	5.3
2,500–25,000..........	100.0	8.7	28.2	16.9	22.0	18.2	6.0

* National Resources Committee, *Population Statistics, 3. Urban Data* (Washington, D. C., 1937), 15.

observed in Table 20 that females are relatively more numerous in the larger places. These data strongly suggest that cities of different sizes are functionally different. The assumption underlying this inference is that every distinctive function requires a particular combination of age and sex.

Size is but one among a number of variables. Composition may also differ among cities of a given size. The comparison of age and sex distribution of Detroit and Los Angeles, each with a population of about one and a half million, is shown in Figure 15. The very

TABLE 20

MALES PER 100 FEMALES BY AGE, BY SIZE OF CITY, UNITED STATES, 1930 *

Size of City	Total	0–4	5–19	20–29	30–44	45–64	65 and over
500,000 and over......	100	103	99	95	107	104	85
100,000–500,000.......	96	103	96	88	99	100	83
25,000–100,000........	97	103	97	90	101	101	86
2,500–25,000..........	97	103	98	90	99	101	89

* National Resources Committee, *Population Statistics, 3. Urban Data* (Washington, D. C., 1937), 17-18.

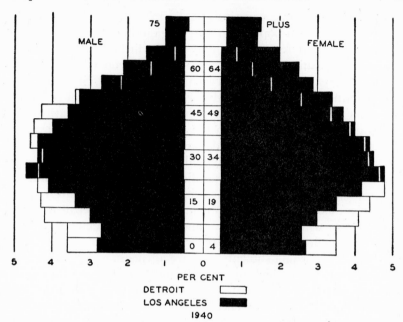

Fig. 15.—Age and sex composition of population in Detroit and Los Angeles, 1940.

pronounced difference is a result of the peculiar functional development of each city. Los Angeles' older population is a consequence of the migration there of aged persons, chiefly women, for purposes of retirement. The role of that city as a refuge for the old is of several decades' standing. A new phase in the migration to Los Angeles began, however, with its rapid rise as an industrial center and is evident in the large proportion of persons from 20 to 40 years of age. On the other hand, Detroit's age composition shows the effects of rapid population growth through migration during the 1920's. That is indicated by the large proportions up to age 50 and by the small proportions in higher ages. The sex distribution is also noteworthy. As a general rule females are numerically dominant in cities and that clearly applies to Los Angeles in which, in 1940, there were 96 males per 100 females. But the general rule does not apply to Detroit, wherein the sex ratio is 103. Detroit is typical in this respect of heavy industry cities.

Composition as a Limiting Factor.—We have pointed out that the age and sex distribution of a population reflects the major events experienced by the generations living at the moment of observation. There is a second and equally important, though much less fully explored, implication of demographic structure. That is, the composition of any given time constitutes a limiting factor on the kinds of collective activities a population may engage in. If, for example, an aggregate contains fewer than nine able-bodied males, it is unlikely that a baseball team will appear there; or if the proportion of individuals over 65 years of age is very small, the probability that an old peoples' home will be established is rather remote. In effect, the organization of relationships in a population is an adaptation to its demographic structure. And to the extent that the organization is differentiated, the adaptation to demographic features must be precise.

Unfortunately, our knowledge about this association is rather crude. In the first place, the specific demographic requirements of the various forms of collective activity are very inadequately known. No problem exists, of course, in connection with baseball teams and other units in which the numbers and kinds of participants are constitutionally defined. But units of organization such as manufacturing and retailing establishments, welfare agencies, etc., present a difficult problem, one in which only preliminary investigations have been made. Assuming this important deficiency to be corrected, another serious problem is promptly encountered: namely, what are the limits of tolerance within which demographic variations may occur without changing the form of organization? To illustrate, the average number of children of a given age necessary to secure the continuous operation of a factory producing a certain type of toy may be readily determined, but the effects on the character of the factory of increases or decreases in the number of children of that age remain to be measured. A related question concerns how large the population of children must be to include the requisite number of users of the toys produced by the factory. Such problems as these obviously require the control of certain other variables. Despite the inadequacies of knowledge about the limiting effects of demographic structure, it is possible to point to many probable consequences of composition.

The most generalized influence of age and sex composition on population organization derives from the pattern of consumer habits it represents. The total structure of industrial and service functions is necessarily accommodated to the complex of wants and thus indirectly to the population's composition. It is for this reason that the aging of population, such as is occurring in this country, is expected to have widespread repercussions in the economy. Instead of the present emphasis placed on the production of children's clothes, foods, toys, medicines, facilities, and services of various kinds, the economy will have to orient itself to the consumer requirements of a progressively older population. That may mean fewer detached residences and more apartments, fewer services to families and more personal services, fewer recreational facilities of the participant type and more of the vicarious sort, etc.[4] In any event, some redistribution and reorganization of industrial activity are indicated.

The decline in the number of children might alter the pattern of consumer expenditures in another respect. It promises to leave a larger proportion of the worker's expendable income for the satisfaction of his individual wants. This, as W. B. Reddaway suggests, may result in an increased demand for and production of luxury and semiluxury goods.[5] For a large part of the so-called "necessities" consumed by a population is chargeable directly to the nurture of children. Pursuing his reasoning further, Reddaway adds that an industry devoted largely to the production of luxury goods would be subject to the fluctuations of fashion and fad and therefore would be highly unstable. That, in turn, might discourage heavy capital outlays for individual plants and perhaps a loss of the economies of large scale production.[6] An obvious weakness in this kind of speculation lies in the uncertain distinction between necessary and luxury goods. What is a luxury at one time may be a necessity at another. Both are normative concepts.

An alternative to the increased emphasis on personal satisfactions in a relatively old population is a greater rate of saving. An inducement to more saving might arise from the small number of progeny on whom the worker could rely for old age security or for supplementation of publicly financed security programs. Thus it is conceivable that an old population would make available a large volume of funds for capital investment. If so, the lag in industrial expansion anticipated by Alvin Hansen [7] as a result of declining growth rate might be overcome through the aging of the population.

A more definite implication of composition for the economy derives from the labor force it contains. Age, of course, is but one of many factors that affect the size of the labor force; nevertheless, since it constitutes a general limiting condition, age may be used as an index of potential labor power. In a "young" population the proportion of the total that is within the most productive ages—e.g., 20 to 65 years —is relatively small. Although such a population is usually experi-

---

[4] For an interesting discussion of the medical aspects of aging see Louis I. Dublin, "Statistical and Social Implications in the Problem of Our Aging Population," *University of Pennsylvania Bicentennial Conference.*

[5] *The Economics of a Declining Population* (London, 1939), 94-95.

[6] *Ibid.*

[7] *Hearings Before the Temporary National Economic Committee,* p. 9, "Savings and Investment," (Washington, D. C., 1940), 3497-3518.

encing rapid growth and may therefore expect substantial absolute increases in its labor force, the burden of dependents or persons not in the labor force it must carry will remain large. From the standpoint of numbers alone, a "young" population has less productive capacity than an "older" population of equal size. In the latter the proportion of individuals in the nonproducing ages is small. The aging process distributes a progressively larger proportion of the total in the years of productive activity. Table 21 describes the trend at work in the United States. As the rate of growth declines, the number of individuals 20 to 65 years of age per 1,000 of the total population rises from 536, or slightly more than one half of all people, in 1910, to over three fifths of the total, or 611, in the year 1970. Continuation of the

TABLE 21

Total Population and Persons 20-64 Years of Age and 15-19 Years of Age per 1,000 Total Population, United States, 1910-2000 *

Year	Total Population (000's omitted)	Persons 20-64 years of age per 1,000 total population	Persons 15-19 years of age per 1,000 total population
1910	91,972	536	99
1920	105,711	546	89
1930	122,775	558	94
1940	131,669	588	94
1950	145,460	593	73
1960	153,375	591	90
1970	159,847	611	73
1980	163,877	605	71
1990	164,585	603	71
2000	163,312	610	66

* Figures for 1950 to 2000 are based on the "medium" estimate. See Bureau of the Census, *Population—Special Reports*, Series P-46, No. 7 (September 15,1946).

aging process, beyond 1970, however, will reduce somewhat the number in the producing ages and increase the number of dependents in the late years of life. Thus O. E. Baker is of the opinion that "A stationary population is probably the most desirable condition, for one reason because a larger proportion of the population is in the productive age group—20 to 60 or 15 to 65 years of age—than in an increasing or decreasing population." [8]

Table 21 also points to another feature of the labor force in an aging population which under certain conditions might be an advantage and under other conditions might be a disadvantage. That

[8] "Significance of Population Trends to American Agriculture," *The Milbank Memorial Fund Quarterly*, XV (April, 1937), 122.

is the declining number of new entrants into the labor market. The last column of the table shows that the proportion of persons 15 to 19 years of age, and who enter the labor force in the five years following each census date, falls from 99 per 1,000 total population, in 1910, to 73, in 1970, and to 66, in 2000. In a stable economy the problem of absorbing new workers would be lessened with each passing year. But while the decreasing numbers of new job applicants might contribute to the preservation of stability, it could foster excessive stability. The result might be to check further expansion of the economy, especially of the sort that would require large numbers of additional workers.

It is sometimes argued that an aging labor force grows increasingly rigid or less adaptable. Therefore new industries and technological changes are discouraged and the economy is threatened with stultification. This position patently involves an assumption about the physiological and psychological concomitants of age for which there is little supporting knowledge. Superficially, however, the suggestion has merit. Old persons do not readily acquire new skills, whatever may be the reasons for their inertia. Furthermore, agility and stamina seem also to decline with age. Experience likewise has shown that it is much more difficult to effect a territorial redistribution of old people than of young people. It would appear that old people, in fact, do constitute a rather inflexible labor force. Perhaps subsequent research in problems of age will yield methods of maintaining adaptability with the advance of age.

A given age composition defines the potential, if not the actual, clienteles of virtually all specialized service functions. This is easiest to demonstrate in connection with educational systems because of the rather precise age grading practiced in such institutions. The number of children from ages 6 to 14 regulates to a large extent the number of teachers and the amount of plant and equipment needed for elementary education. Hence a decline in the number of elementary school age children, as was happening in this country up to 1940, may either result in a contraction of the elementary school system or invite a change of educational procedures.[9] Since 1940 there have been several radical fluctuations in the annual number of births and those changes doubtless will necessitate adjustments and readjustments as the suc-

---

[9] For extended discussions of this problem see: W. G. Carr, "Population Trends and the School Building Program," *American School and University* (1939) ; O. E. Harvey, "Enrollment Trends and Population Shifts," *Elementary School Journal,* XXXVIII (May, 1938) ; "The Decline in Elementary School Enrollments and Problems of School Organization," *Elementary School Journal,* XXXIX (October, 1938).

cessive age groups pass through the school system. Perhaps it is needless to point out that what is true on a national scale in this respect may not apply to a local area within the larger unit. Irregularities of distribution may compensate for low reproductive ratios in some localities and aggravate the decline in number of school age children in other localities.

The specializations of many other service units in a community limit their activities to rather specific age, sex, or age-sex groups. This is true of juvenile courts, pediatricians, beauty shops, homes for the aged, women's exchanges, specialty retail stores of all kinds, boy and girl scouts, etc. Such units in the degree to which they are specialized are highly sensitive to changes in age and sex composition.

Summary.—The reference point in all discussions of age and sex composition is the stationary population concept, an abstraction defined as a population in which births and deaths are equal and the age distribution is that of the life table. Although such a population is doubtless approximated in societies that have been static for long periods of time, it is not to be found where change is at work.

Knowledge about composition has two broad uses in ecological work. In the first place, it is useful as an evidence of past events in the career of the population. Composition reflects changes in growth trends, the sources of growth, and the circumstances attending the settlement of the population in its habitat. Considerable caution must be exercised, however, in the effort to identify the effects of different possible events, inasmuch as similar effects may result from unlike occurrences.

Secondly, composition data are useful in assessing the limits of possibility in the organization of population. But this utility remains to be developed. Much research is needed in the relation of various forms of collective activity to population. Nevertheless, it is evident that changes in age and sex distribution have profound implications for the economy and for many specific service agencies.

SUPPLEMENTARY REFERENCES

RUCH, F. L. "The Differential Decline of Learning Ability in the Aged as a Possible Explanation of Their Conservatism," *Journal of Social Psychology,* V (August, 1934), 329-37.
THOMPSON, W. S., and WHELPTON, P. K. *Population Trends in the United States.* New York: McGraw-Hill Book Co., 1933.
TIBBITTS, CLARK (ed.). *Living in the Later Years.* Ann Arbor, Mich.: University of Michigan Press, 1949.
YERUSHALMY, I. "The Age-Sex Composition of the Population Resulting from Natality and Mortality Conditions," *Milbank Memorial Fund Quarterly,* XXI (January, 1943), 37-62.

Chapter 9

POPULATION BALANCE

A study of the mechanics of population growth provokes a number of important questions. What initiates growth, and what are the limiting factors? How much population can an area contain? These and other questions that might be raised take the discussion out of the realm of description and into that of explanation. They involve an exploration of the cause and effect relations between population and its environing conditions. And it is in attempting to deal with such questions that we encounter the ecological problem, namely, the explanation of how populations of men maintain themselves in particular areas.

The relationship of population to its habitat is generally conceived as a problem of balance. This concept, *balance,* like many other terms in common usage, has many applications. Its most general connotation is that of a quantitative relationship between two interacting factors, as, for example, the balance of objects on a scale, the balance of receipts and payments, the balance of imports and exports, and the like. The term is also used to refer to more complex equilibria, as when we speak of a balanced diet, which involves various proportions of different food elements required to maintain an organism at a given level of efficiency. The same usage is employed in the phrase "balance of nature," denoting a more or less stable quantitative relationship among interdependent species.

As applied to human populations the concept balance concerns the ratio of numbers to the opportunities for living. Man is no different from other organisms in that at any given time the supply of available materials and the existing conditions will support only a limited number of individuals. This, coupled with his tremendous power of multiplication, creates for man an ever-present problem of maintaining an adaptation to his habitat. Stated broadly in this fashion the problem of balance is unquestionably the most important issue confronting mankind whether in its preliterate or its civilized phases, in small aggregates or in large.

Theories of Population Balance.—Thomas Malthus, in 1798, set forth what is now regarded as the classic statement of the problem of population balance.[1] He viewed the problem as involving essentially a relationship between numbers and the food supply. Thus Malthus reasoned that in any area the resources of which had been brought into full use the food supply could only be increased arithmetically, that is, by addition of new units of territory. But population, if unrestricted, could multiply in a geometric progression. The invariable tendency, therefore, is for numbers to outrun subsistence. As population size approaches the maximum possible for the area, however, certain checks on growth come into play. These include lethal or positive checks, such as war, crime, and disease, and preventive checks, notably vice, which lower the birth rate.[2] Hence balance tends inevitably to be struck at the subsistence level, a point at which the available food is just sufficient to maintain the population at a minimum level of work efficiency.

However harsh and dismal may be the picture of man's estate on earth painted by Malthus, his statement is descriptive of the life situations of most populations of the world in the past and in many at present. Man's dependence on the resources and conditions of the physical and biotic environment is a fundamental fact of his existence. And for the large majority of mankind the opportunities for life are closely restricted. At the same time, so great is its growth potential that human life seems constantly to be thrusting against the limits that hem it in. Man's tendency to multiply up to the maximum carrying capacity of the land is superficially evident in many parts of the world.

Uncritical acceptance of the Malthusian interpretation and of the empirical evidence supporting it has led to a naïve view of population balance which may be characterized as the organism-food, or heads-bushels, conception.[3] That conception proposes, in effect, that the number of human beings may be directly compared with the number of acres or units of whatever resources are necessary to survival to

---

[1] T. R. Malthus, *Essay on the Principle of Population as It Affects the Future of Society* (1798).

[2] In later editions of his work Malthus, in response to criticism, added "moral restraint" as another preventive check. By "moral restraint" he meant sexual continence. Thus he admitted the possibility of individuals regulating reproduction in their own self-interest. While this check does not affect the descriptive value of his theory, it does destroy the biological imperative Malthus tried to establish.

[3] This view is still encountered in many quarters, particularly in the writings of biologists who attempt to speak authoritatively on matters of social science. It has had its most recent restatement in William Vogt's *Road to Survival* (New York, 1948).

determine whether population size is or is not appropriate. But the implied assumption that some absolute standard of per capita need exists has still to be demonstrated. A simple ratio of organisms to units of a resource or resources, moreover, would be legitimate only if each individual with his own energy supplied all his requirements and produced no surplus. This is nowhere the case. Living creatures confront the external world and the sustenance problems it presents as members of functional organizations, and in no other way.

The population-carrying capacity of land is only partially determined by resources, climate, and other physical conditions. It is also affected by the manner in which the population is organized to use the resources. Thus populations living in terms of a hunting and fishing economy cannot on the average be so numerous as populations practicing a pastoral mode of life. The latter is a more intensive utilization of land than is the former. Wiechel, who classified all peoples of the world, arrived at the following density ranges for different types of economies: [4]

Persons per square mile	Type of economy
1-8	Hunting and fishing
8-26	Pastoral and forestry
26-64	Beginnings of agriculture
64-192	Agriculture
192-256	Beginnings of industry and trade
256-381	Agriculture and industry
381 and over	Industry predominates.

Although these data are quite general, they show clearly the effect of group organization on the number of persons who may live in an area. Parenthetically, they throw considerable doubt on the concept of "free land" which has often been employed to justify the overrunning of the territory of a simpler people. It is more than likely, in the historic period at any rate, that all lands have been populated to capacity in view of the particular modes of life of their occupants.

The naïve conception of the relation of population to resources is actually a misconstruction of Malthus' reasoning. He explicitly indicated, in the later editions of his work, that the "state of the arts," or the extent of technological development, is a qualifying factor in every situation. Thus, as he put it, in any given state of the arts, assuming that the existing resources have been developed to the point of diminishing returns, subsistence can only be increased arithmetically. Without such a qualification Malthus could not have defended what he regarded as a universal population law.

---

[4] Cited by M. S. Jefferson, "The Anthropography of Some Great Cities," *American Geographical Society Bulletin,* XLI (1909), 543.

Yet Malthus erred in his oversimplification of the problem. His assumption of a "given state of the arts," by which he delimited the universe of the population problem in each instance, was never set aside so that organization or culture might be treated as a variable. In fact, Malthus seemed to lack a full appreciation of the possibilities of social change, even though he lived in the midst of the most revolutionary epoch the world has known. The rigid logic of his reasoning caused him to look upon population problems as having their causes and solutions within particular areas. It is just on this point that history has shown Malthus' theory to be deficient.

That the organization factor may be a significant variable in the welfare of population was first pointed out by Karl Marx in his critique of modern capitalism.[5] According to Marx, in a capitalist-industrial society overpopulation has no necessary relation to the supply of resources. Rather is it a consequence of the progress of capital accumulation which involves not only a quantitative but also a qualitative change in the composition of capital. The proportion devoted to the financing of buildings, tools, and other means of increasing productivity grows increasingly larger, while the proportion of the total capital fund available for the employment of labor is progressively reduced. Although this trend is offset by the emergence of new industries, the effect is temporary, and the major trend inevitably reasserts itself. In Marx's view technological displacement of laborers from employment is an essential characteristic of capitalist economy. He concludes: "The laboring population therefore produces, along with the accumulation of capital produced by it, the means by which itself is made relatively superfluous, is turned into a relative surplus population; and it does this to an always increasing extent."[6]

What is important in Marx's statement is its implication rather than the specific content of his argument. Indeed his illustration of how laborers render themselves redundant is defective in several respects and is an incomplete description of the development of capitalist-industrial economy. Nevertheless, he called attention to the dynamics of organization as a source of disequilibrium and showed one way in which that factor might operate. We may generalize Marx's point of view, in other words, to state that any disturbance in the organization of a population may produce some excess numbers. Thus overpopulation becomes a relative condition; it is relative to whatever necessary factor in the collective life of a people is too scarce for all to share.

---

[5] *Capital* (New York: The Modern Library, 1936), 689 ff.
[6] *Ibid.*, 692.

Variables in Population Balance.—Our examination of the theories of Malthus and Marx indicates that there are three general variable factors involved in the level of living of every human group. The factors are: (1) population size; (2) amount of subsistence materials or resources; and (3) organization of the population. Any given level of living is a function of the particular combination formed by the three variables at the moment. Population size may be regarded as a dependent variable, while the amount of resources and the organizational structure may be treated as independent variables. This is an arbitrary categorization of the factors which is useful only for the purposes of analysis. For though it is clear that the amount of resources is independent of both remaining factors, organizational structure is not actually independent of population size. We shall have occasion to observe this fact more closely in a later connection.

Inasmuch as the amount of resources and the organization of population are independent of one another as well as of population size, they do not vary together. That is, the amount of resources may vary with no change in organization, and, conversely, organization may change without a corresponding change in resources. And, since the size of population that can be maintained in an area is contingent on both the amount of subsistence and its organization, disequilibrium results from change in either or both of the factors. In practice, however, it is found that variations in one of the independent factors is accompanied by stability in the other. Hence there are two different kinds of problems of population balance, different as to causation and as to their modes of resolution.

The Balance of Numbers and Resources.—To a very widespread extent the population problem is substantially as Malthus stated it. The primary concern, in other words, is with the equation of size and the supply of subsistence materials. That has been the case since time immemorial, as is indicated by the numerous references to such a problem in the folklore or literature of virtually every human group. Preliterate peoples the world over, as well as the peasant groups of contemporary Asia, are currently preoccupied with the relation of numbers to resources.

Characteristic of all situations in which the population problem may be so stated is a high degree of isolation and stability of organization. The pattern of work relations in such a group is defined early by use and wont, and having become fixed in the habits of the group, it is transmitted as a whole from one generation to another with little or no modification. Isolation excludes external influences that might disturb the status quo. The inertia of habit, rationalized as tradition, reinforces the rigidity fostered by seclusion. Thus there is a tendency to reject, or at least to be suspicious of, improvements of techniques and cooperative arrangements should they be presented. The innovator is looked upon as a threat to the tried and tested ways of doing things. The attitudes of most isolated peoples, as Ralph Linton has phrased them, seem to be that it is better to have all routine tasks done passably well than to incur the risk of total failure by seeking to have a few things done exceptionally well.[7] Of the three factors that are determinative of the level of living of population, then, group organization tends under conditions of isolation to be constant. No variations in organization as a means of adjusting to changes of numbers can be expected.

Not only is the organization of an isolated group static, it seldom provides a very effectual control over the habitat. Insulation from frequent intergroup meetings leaves the population with a rudimentary technology. Producing techniques are usually too crude to yield much in the way of a surplus product. Hence the nomadic existence of most preliterate peoples. Even if there were a surplus, as indeed there is occasionally in the lives of the simplest of peoples, the methods of storage are often inadequate for the preservation of a large quantity of material for a time of need. Moreover, an accumulation of any kind of material creates a necessity for its transportation. Food, because of its bulk, places a particularly heavy burden on transport facilities. But the techniques of transportation of an isolated group are no more efficient than its other methods. Although transport facilities may be adequate for assembling materials from a local habitat, they rarely are sufficient for the importation of surpluses that might be available in adjacent areas. The area immediately accessible to such a population is in fact very small. The maximum scope is measured by the radial distance that may be traversed in a half-day's journey from the village site. That, where walking is the principal means of travel and carriage, may be as much as fifteen miles.[8] By pursuing a nomadic existence, however, a group can supplement the resources of one locality with those of other areas which it occupies in succeeding seasons. In any case, the isolated population lives in a narrow universe, and within the close confines of that universe it must work out the solutions to virtually all its sustenance problems.

---

[7] *The Study of Man* (New York, 1936), 129.
[8] But the radius of the zone within which most daily activities take place seldom exceeds five miles.

A technology so simple exposes a population to the effects of radical environmental fluctuations. It has but a nominal protection against variations in climate such as drought, flood, and shortening of the growing season, invasions by pests and predators on the food supply, and other untoward events in the habitat. The local physical and biotic environment is thus for the group with a stable organization a highly variable factor. And the group has no other recourse than to vary its numbers in accordance with environmental variations.

The adjustment of population size to changes in the supply of sustenance materials occurs automatically, for the most part, through variations in the death rate. Mortality rises steeply in years of adversity and falls just as abruptly in periods of plenty. Although data on vital phenomena in isolated groups are very fragmentary, the death rate for a given population seems to range about an average annual figure of approximately 40 per 1,000. Rates of more than 100 per 1,000 have been known to occur, as have also rates of less than 25 per 1,000. In general, however, isolated populations live close to the brink of catastrophe at all times. That is indicated by their high average death rates and life expectancies of about 30 years or less. The margin of safety is sometimes so small that a decline of but a few inches in the annual rainfall or the loss of a few days from the normal growing season is sufficient to produce widespread suffering and loss of life.

The incidence of famine is high in such areas. Mallory reports a study of China which reveals that between 108 B.C. and 1911 A.D. there were 1,828 famines, almost one per year in one province or another.[9] According to W. S. Thompson, famine frequencies of that magnitude have been experienced in many places about the world.[10] Even where actual famine conditions may not be present, the prevalence of undernourishment may be such as to make the population an easy prey to epidemic diseases. Jenness' characterization of living conditions among the plains Indians of Canada could be applied to numerous populations.

Famine conditions, and the hardships and accidents incidental to a migratory existence devoted to hunting and fishing, must have shortened the average span of life and caused a high rate of mortality among all classes of the population, adults and children alike. The infant death rate was appalling, partly through ignorance of some of the most elementary principles in child welfare, partly also through lack of proper food. The total absence of milk, except what

---

[9] W. H. Mallory, *China: Land of Famine* (New York, 1926), 1.
[10] "Human Populations," in *A Handbook of Social Psychology*, ed. Carl Murchison (Worcester, Mass., 1935), 57.

the mother herself could provide, and the absence of cereals among all but the agricultural tribes, lengthened the period of lactation, because no infant under the age of three years could assimilate a diet solely of meat and fish. . . . The hardships of the never-ending food quest fell heaviest on the weaklings, who were often deliberately abandoned when they could no longer keep pace with the wanderings of the main tribe.[11]

Population pressure on resources tends to be maintained by a continuously high rate of reproduction. The women of an isolated group are almost constantly pregnant, though both the prenatal and postnatal losses are so great that relatively few progeny reach adulthood. Nevertheless, the wellspring of life is such that there is always a potential population ready to absorb whatever margin of excess food a good crop year may produce. Unless its numbers have been too thoroughly decimated, a group therefore may quickly recover the losses suffered during a period of shortage. The impact of rising mortality is greatest on the very young and the very old, and least on persons in the reproducing ages.

Although the high fertility rates of isolated groups may be attributed in part to ignorance, they also have an understandable functional basis. Because of the simple technology possessed by such groups, their manpower requirements are relatively great. It is for that reason that all able-bodied members, including children, women, and the aged, are pressed into service in the primary sustenance activities. The larger the size of population the more effectively and the more quickly may essential tasks be accomplished. In an agricultural economy the size of population tends to be governed by the work load peaks which come in the planting and in the harvesting seasons. There must be enough workers to complete the planting of crops early in the growing season and, again, to get in the harvest before it is damaged by rain or frost. This usually means that throughout the remainder of the year there is underemployment or, what amounts to the same thing, overpopulation. The isolated population therefore is confronted with a difficult problem: it can produce only enough to support a small population, yet it must have a relatively large number of workers on hand to assure the accomplishment of the tasks that have to be done.

The control of numbers, however, is seldom if ever left to chance. Every organized population observes a variety of practices that bear directly on the control of size. These may be divided into two groups: those that guard against exceeding the upper limit of size; and those

[11] Diamond Jenness, *The Indians of Canada,* National Museum of Canada, Bulletin 65 (Ottawa, 1932), 51-52.

that prevent numbers from falling below the lower size limit. The collective welfare is contingent upon size being kept within the limits of maximum and minimum. Too large a population may result in extinction as a consequence of debilitation and epidemic disease. On the other hand, too small a population makes impossible the manning of essential functions and this also threatens the group with extinction.[12]

Practices which restrict the size of group include the elimination of unwanted members through infanticide and patricide, sexual controls of all kinds, rules prohibiting the remarriage of widows, and, most important of all, emigration. Infanticide is very generally practiced. "A Tikopian family," says Rivers, "is usually limited to four children, any in excess of this number being killed by burying them alive in the house or just outside it. . . ."[13] Jenness observed that "as late as 1916, during a rather severe winter, five Eskimo mothers around the western end of Coronation Gulf, where the total population did not exceed four hundred, destroyed their babies within an hour of delivery."[14] Such examples could be cited at great length. It is of interest that infanticide is practiced most frequently on females, thus striking directly at the source of population. Although by no means so general a practice, the elimination of aged members occurs in many societies. A nomadic group may simply leave the old by the wayside to die of starvation or to be eaten by animals. In other instances patricide is accomplished with greater ceremony. The son may dispose of his parents as a filial duty. In this as in many other forms of population control the sanctions which surround the act may obscure its significant function. Until the interference of the British, the Hindu widow was cremated alive on the funeral pile of her husband in a rite known as *suttee*. In India today, as in many other places, widows are not eligible for remarriage, especially if they have given birth to a child.

Emigration is perhaps the most effective immediate means of disposing of surplus numbers, since it may be applied to any proportion of the group. Certainly it is ecologically the most significant, for through repeated emigrations human population has succeeded in scattering itself over the earth. In a crisis a too numerous group splits in a fission-like manner and throws off a segment to settle elsewhere. According to Vidal de la Blache, the surplus members are banished to

---

[12] Neither Malthus nor Marx gave thought to the lower size limits of population. They thought of poverty as resulting only from too many people.

[13] W. H. R. Rivers, *The History of Melanesian Society* (Cambridge, 1914), Vol. I, 313.

[14] *Loc. cit.,* 52.

a distant location so that they cannot infringe upon the domain of the parent group.[15] From many populations occupying fertile regions have issued numerous colonies of this sort. Such a process cannot continue indefinitely to the equal benefit of all. Once the most available or the best lands are occupied, subsequent colonies must come into conflict with earlier ones or they must drift into hazardous environments. Both alternatives have frequently taken place. A. C. Haddon has charted the wavelike migration out of south central Asia and into Africa, for example, indicating how each succeeding group has pressed earlier occupants further to the south and west.[16] Settlement in a hostile environment is well illustrated by the development of some twenty villages on the outer crater of the still active volcano Aso-son on the island of Kyushu, Japan. From the new crater in the center rises a column of sulphurous vapor, a reminder to the villagers of the extreme to which they have been driven.[17]

Emigration is sometimes a continuous flow rather than a periodic outpouring of surplus population. Settled agricultural groups in many instances have adapted the practice of expelling most of the members of the young generation at the time of succession. From its progeny a family selects a son to inherit the farm and a daughter to whom a dowry is to be given and the others are expected to remove themselves from the household.[18] The dispossessed tend to settle the available lands; but after the land is fully occupied they have no choice other than to drift away.

It is to be noted that the checks to growth may or may not be fully employed as the occasion warrants. In periods of stress the elimination of surplus members occurs frequently, sexual controls are more stringently enforced, and emigration involves large numbers. But when the crisis is passed the controls are partially relaxed, though never entirely, for the threat of overpopulation is ever present.

Groups that observe restrictive folkways carry on at the same time one or more of various practices that encourage and maintain the flow of new members into the population. Behavior patterns of this order include informal compulsions to marry and reproduce, multiple marriage, concubinage, adoption, slavery, and, when all else fails, the merging of groups.

---

[15] *Principles of Human Geography,* trans. Millicent T. Bingham (New York, 1926), 58.
[16] *The Wanderings of Peoples* (Cambridge, 1919), 51-73.
[17] J. E. Orchard, "The Pressure of Population in Japan," *Geographical Review,* (July, 1928).
[18] C. Arensburg, *The Irish Countryman* (New York, 1937), 80 ff; and Horace Miner, *Saint-Denis* (Chicago, 1939), 80 ff.

In virtually all groups it is expected that the child will eventually marry and have children. Celibacy is rarely accorded formal recognition and is often stigmatized as unbecoming to a mature adult. Agricultural peoples impose particularly severe sanctions on celibacy for all who remain within the group. The necessity of securing a continuity of operations on the farm lands is such that marriage is a familial rather than an individual concern. And in some instances marriage is arranged prior to puberty. The compulsion to reproduction is equally strong. It is common for a new wife to receive a very tentative acceptance in her husband's family until after having given birth to a child. With that achievement she gives proof of her ability to contribute to the population requirement of the group and the continuity of the family line. Barrenness is perhaps the most widely recognized ground for dissolution of the marriage union even in the modern period.

On occasion circumstances interfere with the marriage of all group members. A deficiency of women, resulting from excessive female infanticide, leaves some men without mates. Or a shortage of men, perhaps as a consequence of military mortality, may mean that a corresponding number of women will have to forego marriage. It is probable, though not established, that such conditions give rise to multiple marriage.[19] However that may be, it is clear that multiple marriage when it involves a plurality of wives, as is usually the case, is an effective means of augmenting the increase of population. Some groups, such as the Mormons, deliberately adopted the practice for that purpose, but in most cases the extent of group awareness of the effects of polygyny is undetermined.

Adoption is a very generally practiced means of compensating for failures of reproduction to supply the new group members required. The loss of a child at birth or the failure to have a son occasions a resort to adoption. Many of the American Indian tribes, however, felt it necessary to replace lost members regardless of how the loss was incurred. Individuals of the same age and sex were sought to replace the deceased.[20] Some tribal groups, the Wyandots for example, went to war to secure candidates for adoption.[21] Slavery, though it lacks the trappings of kinship, is a comparable method of supplementing the size of a group. Unlike adoption, it does not involve any reciprocal obligations.

---

[19] Cf. Robert H. Lowie, *An Introduction to Cultural Anthropology* (New York, 1934), 243, 245.

[20] W. I. Thomas, *Primitive Behavior* (New York, 1937), 145-46.

[21] W. E. Connelly, *The Wyandot Folk-Lore* (Topeka, Kan., 1899), 237.

The most drastic of measures for dealing with the threat of under-population is the merging of groups. Such a step requires that many traditional behavior patterns be relinquished by each group and that many radical readjustments be made. Yet when numbers are reduced to a size below the minimum needed to carry on a given mode of life, merging may be the only alternative to death. The Andaman Islanders, whose numbers were seriously depleted by the spread of syphilis from a European penal colony located on the Islands, re-grouped in fewer units.[22] The ravages of smallpox and influenza have produced a similar response on the part of the Taperape Indians in central Brazil. The number of villages, each with approximately 200 members, was reduced from five, in 1890, to one, in 1939.[23]

From this discussion it is possible to draw several conclusions. First, where the organizational factor is stable, as in isolated situa-tions, the environmental or resource factor is dynamic; for the former provides relatively slight control over the latter. Second, under such conditions population size tends to vary directly with fluctuations in the available supply of subsistence materials, there being no alterna-tive means of compensating for deficiencies in the food supply. Third, in these circumstances population problems must be resolved within the local area, since isolation limits the opportunity of securing as-sistance from without. This conforms to the requirements of Mal-thus' theory. And finally, the relation of numbers to resources is in all instances contingent upon the character of organization.

The Balance of Numbers with Organization.—The dissolution of local group isolation, brought about by the development of modern forms of transportation and communication, makes the Malthusian interpretation of population problems decreasingly useful. Popula-tions acquire a different orientation to their habitats and are subjected to a new kind of dynamics. The spread and multiplication of inter-group relations, in other words, change the variability of the factors involved in the level of living of a population. This calls for a revised conception of the problem of balance, a conception in which, as it turns out, the elements of Malthus' theory are comparatively unimportant.

The development of extended and manifold intergroup relations together with the technological improvement generated thereby has steadily diminished the limiting influence of the local physical and biotic environment. Each population, to the extent that it is involved

---

[22] A. R. Radcliffe-Brown, *The Andaman Islanders* (Cambridge, 1933), 19.
[23] Charles Wagley, "The Effects of Depopulation upon Social Organization as Illustrated by the Taperape Indians," *Transactions of the New York Academy of Science,* Series 2, Vol. 3 (November, 1940), 12 ff.

in the network of interrelationships, is emancipated from the confines of its locale, the restriction of a more or less fixed variety and supply of materials, and the decisive effects of local climate. Efficient transportation facilities and exchange arrangements give it access to the resources of the total area over which relations extend. A crop failure or the depletion of a local resource means not starvation and wastage but simply that the population must turn to another source of supply. In fact, a population living in such a context assembles its food supply from numerous regions and utilizes a large assortment of other materials, some of which are brought from the remotest corners of the earth. So far has the influence of the immediate environs been neutralized that there are large populations—i.e., those occupying cities—whose only interest in the land upon which they reside is in the space it affords.

This is not to say that famine and malnutrition are completely eliminated from the modern scene. The great famine in the Russian Ukraine, in 1932 and 1933, took hundreds of thousands of lives. How much mortality occurred in Europe as a result of food shortages in the years immediately following World War II may never accurately be known, but it was doubtless enormous. There may be malnutrition in the midst of plenty. In the United States, during the depression years of the 1930's, the number of undernourished individuals was estimated to be in excess of one hundred thousand.[24] In no instance, however, are such conditions due to exhaustion of resources, climatic events, or even an actual lack of food. Political expediency lay behind the Russian famine: it was deliberately encouraged in order to force the collectivization of peasant farmers. The more recent European famine is a product of the confusion brought on by the war; the maldistribution of workers, the breakdown of transportation systems, and monetary inflation were the specific factors responsible. Likewise the malnutrition in the United States has its basis in low earnings due to market conditions.

Along with the emergence of an extensive territorial division of labor has gone a growing abundance of resources. According to C. O. Sauer, "What has happened is that all the major physical resources of the world have been brought into use, resource by resource and area by area, at first slowly, then with a rush until only minor possibilities remain of the discovery of great additional centers or forms of

---

[24] F. Lorimer, E. Winston, and L. K. Kiser, *Foundations of American Population Policy* (New York, 1940), 92. According to a report cited by these authors, 3,400 deaths due to pellagra were registered in 1934.

raw materials." [25] This, however, reckons without further techno-logical advances. Yet, leaving the future out of account, the world at the moment has access to a superabundance of materials. With huge agricultural areas unused in the western United States and Canada, in central Australia, in South Africa and in many other places, there is more food-producing capacity than is currently needed. The re-serves of coal, oil, iron, and other metals are likewise great.[26] That these may be exhausted someday is beside the point. The important fact is that a plentitude of raw materials is known to exist and the machinery for producing and fabricating the materials and distribut-ing the finished products is developed and available for use.

In short, the resource factor, having been stabilized at a high level of abundance by the development of an elaborate territorial divi-sion of labor, may be regarded as a constant or at least a neutral element in the well-being of a population. It plays little or no part in regulating the size of populations. There continue to occur, of course, changes in the population-carrying capacities of local areas. But these changes, with few exceptions, are due to shifts other than in climate, soil fertility, or the reserves of mineral resources. The significant variations are those which occur in the organization of populations.

With the development of the territorial division of labor each local-ized population becomes more sensitive to what is taking place in other populations and in the relations between populations than to events in the local natural environment. This tendency is the more marked where specialization is greatest. The phenomenon is particularly clear in areas of extractive industry.

Under the pressure of the expanding rubber industry (in Malaya), rice cultivation has been pressed very much into the background. Despite the fact that rice is the principal article of diet for the vast bulk of the Malayan peoples, it occupies only some 765,000 acres as compared with the 3,280,000 planted with rubber, and the 610,000 acres of coconuts, the greater part of which con-sists of small holdings. Since the arrival of the depression in Malaya, the several administrations have made somewhat halfhearted efforts to encourage cultivation at the expense of the spreading rubber tree, but no very considerable results have been achieved, primarily because of the greater profitability of rubber. There can be no doubt that a dangerous number of the Malayan eggs have been placed in the rubber and tin baskets, making the country almost wholly dependent on economic conditions elsewhere and particularly on the

---

[25] "The Prospect for Redistribution of Population," in Isaiah Bowman (ed.), *The Limits of Land Settlement* (New York, 1937), 8.
[26] Cf. E. W. Zimmerman, *World Resources and Industries* (New York, 1933), 429 ff.

prosperity of a few industries in the United States. This danger the depression all too vigorously demonstrated. . . . At the present day only 40 per cent of the rice which is consumed in Malaya is produced in the country, the bulk of it in the less developed unfederated States of the north, and the remaining 60 per cent is imported from Siam, India, and elsewhere.[27]

One need not go so far afield for this evidence. The farmer, who is commonly regarded as most thoroughly committed to the natural environment, is in the modern world increasingly preoccupied with considerations of costs, prices, credit, and the like. As E. G. Nourse has said: "The farmer's role as financier is fast gaining ground on his role as skillful husbandman."[28] What he plants and how much acreage is devoted to each crop tend to be determined by his anticipations of the market situation at the time of harvest. In this respect the farmer does not differ significantly from any other entrepreneur.

In fact, the very phenomena which have neutralized the influences of the local environment have introduced an unprecedented changeability into the organized life of man. Intensive specialization exposes a population to numerous disturbances arising from many different sources, most of them originating from beyond the dominion of its control. Intercommunity and interregional competition, rapid technological advances, and the vagaries of market fluctuations make for a more or less chronic instability of organization. "We have substituted," says Zimmerman, "the dangers of long-distance transportation, of a tear in the gossamer fabric which makes up the system of world-wide communication, of disturbances in the political equilibrium, of financial breakdowns, of strikes and lockouts, etc., for dangers which beset the primitive farmer, such as hail, drought, locusts, floods, etc."[29]

For illustration of this variability we have only to review recent experiences. During the early 1930's in the United States, the excess or unemployed portion of the labor force was variously estimated at from 6 to 12 million workers. A decade later, during which time the total population had increased by almost 10 per cent, there was a critical shortage of workers and a supplemental labor force was being imported from foreign areas. In small areas the expansions and contractions may be notably radical.

---

[27] Rupert Emerson, *Malaysia: A Study in Direct and Indirect Rule* (New York, 1937), 41-42. Copyright 1937 by The Bureau of National Research of Harvard University and Radcliffe College. Used by permission of The Macmillan Company.
[28] "Some Economic and Social Accompaniments of the Mechanization of Agriculture," *American Economic Review*, XX (March, 1930), Supplement, 125.
[29] E. W. Zimmerman, *World Resources and Industries* (New York, Harper & Bros., 1933.)

Mark Twain's Virginia City on the Comstock lode rose over night from nothing to several thousand souls. The population of Storey County, Nevada, in which the Comstock lode lies, increased to 16,000 at the census of 1880. In 1930, the census enumerator recorded 667 souls left to guard a camp that in its time had produced nearly 400 million dollars in gold and silver. In 1877 the site of Leadville, Colorado, was occupied by a village of 200 people. Three years later the population had increased to 14,820, and at the last census it had fallen again to 3,771. Cripple Creek, in the palmy days, claimed 45,000 inhabitants, and even the unimpressionable census taker recorded 29,002 people in Teller County, of which it is the center, in the year 1900. By 1930, the official count for Teller County had fallen to 4,141, and the depression revival of gold mining had brought it up to perhaps 7,500 today (1936).[30]

Such changes do not necessarily imply an exhaustion of resources. Experience in the Michigan copper mining industry makes this apparent. Until 1910 the Michigan mines supplied most of the world's marketed copper. After that date activity at the mines rapidly declined, despite the fact that the Michigan ores, the metallic content of which ranges above 90 per cent, are still the richest deposits known to exist. The industry's demise may be charged to two related developments. First, as the shafts deepened the cost of the product increased and the mines encountered increasing competition from producers in Montana, South America, and Rhodesia.[31] A pound of Rhodesian copper, for example, could be laid down in London for less than half the cost of production of Michigan copper. Secondly, the perfection of cheap refining processes brought many low-grade ores into the market. It became possible for the 1 to 4 per cent metallic content ores of Arizona, Nevada, New Mexico, and Utah, though far removed from the principal consuming centers, to undersell Michigan copper. As a result, an estimated 5,000 copper miners and their families were converted into a surplus population in the Michigan mining counties.[32]

This illustration is unique only for its simplicity. The elements of the problem observed in Michigan are of the same order in nearly all instances of disequilibrium in an industrial-exchange society. Although the impoverishment of the cotton farmer in southeastern United States may be attributed in part to soil depletion, much more important factors are the competition emanating from superior producing areas, notably southwestern United States, and the substitution of rayon for cotton. Agriculturalists generally are faced with

---

[30] Carter Goodrich, et al., Migration and Economic Opportunity (Philadelphia, University of Pennsylvania Press, 1936), 271.
[31] Ibid., 434.
[32] Ibid., 186.

declining opportunity for employment. Many of agriculture's traditional tasks have been absorbed by mechanical industry as a consequence of technological change. "The slaughter of livestock, the canning of produce, the preparation of hides, grains, and syrup have all been taken over by industry." [33] Deep inroads have also been made in the raw-material-producing function of agriculture, as in the substitution of "coal tar dyes for indigo and madder root, gasoline for oats, rayon for cotton, etc." [34] Add to such changes the rapid increases in productivity per worker in agriculture [35] and the inelastic market for food products, and the surplus population in agricultural areas in the United States, estimated in 1936 at 2.5 million,[36] is understandable.

A somewhat different situation obtains in the countries of southern and eastern Europe. There the surplus population in agriculture is also high, ranging up to 78 per cent in some localities, as shown in Table 22. But instead of resulting from increases in agricultural productivity and the absorption of agricultural tasks by mechanical industry, as in the United States, the excesses seem to be due to a combination of rapid population growth and a lagging industrial development.[37] The majority of agriculturalists in southern and eastern Europe engage in cash-crop farming. Through this means largely the level of living has risen sufficiently to permit substantial declines in death rates. Yet birth rates remain high. The surplus numbers from high rates of natural increase, however, are not drawn off to cities within the respective countries. Nor have they the opportunity to move across national boundaries. Since most neighboring countries have a similar problem, they are in no position to offer relief.

It would be erroneous to assume that disturbances of relationships affect only raw-material-producing populations. Groups that derive their livelihoods from manufacturing and commerce are just as subject to such changes. Thus technological improvements have all but eliminated the functions of blacksmithing and wheelwrighting, carriage making, cooperage, custom making of shoes and men's clothing, and many another handicraft industry. The transference of skills from human hands to machine processes creates at least temporary

[33] Rupert B. Vance, *Research Memorandum on Population Redistribution Within the United States,* Social Science Research Council Bulletin 42 (New York, 1938), 58.

[34] *Ibid.*

[35] See Mordecai Ezeckiel, "Population and Unemployment," *Annals of the American Academy of Political and Social Science,* CLXXXVIII (Nov. 1936), 232.

[36] Goodrich, *et al., op. cit.,* 400.

[37] Wilbert E. Moore, *Economic Demography of Eastern and Southern Europe* (League of Nations: Geneva, 1945), 122 ff.

TABLE 22

ACTUAL, EXPECTED, AND ESTIMATED SURPLUS AGRICULTURAL POPULATIONS, SOUTHERN AND EASTERN EUROPEAN NATIONS, 1930 *

Country	Population dependent on agriculture (000's omitted)	Agriculture Net production in crop units† (000's omitted)	Expected agricultural population‡ (000's omitted)	Surplus population	
				Number§ (000's omitted)	Per cent
Albania........	800	7,464	178	622	77.7
Bulgaria........	4,038	82,394	1,921	2,167	53.0
Czechoslovakia..	4,812	216,125	5,038	−226	−4.7
Estonia.........	626	26,755	624	2	0.4
Greece.........	2,829	60,265	1,405	1,424	50.3
Hungary........	4,472	148,898	3,471	1,001	22.4
Italy...........	17,953	561,726	13,094	4,859	27.1
Latvia..........	1,036	49,285	1,149	−113	−10.9
Lithuania.......	1,657	51,713	1,205	452	27.3
Poland.........	19,347	404,339	9,425	9,922	51.3
Portugal........	2,954	67,269	1,568	1,386	46.9
Roumania......	13,069	272,318	6,348	6,721	51.4
Spain..........	11,864	448,199	10,448	1,417	11.9
Yugoslavia......	10,629	175,752	4,097	6,532	61.5

* Wilbert E. Moore, op. cit., 63-64.
† For a definition of crop unit, see Moore, 30-31.
‡ The data in this column are derived by dividing the figures for agriculture net production by 42.9, the European average per capita value of agricultural production, expressed in crop units.
§ Derived by subtracting the expected population from the population dependent on agriculture.

unemployment and among older workers unemployment is apt to be permanent. Labor power as well as skill has been displaced by the process of technological change. According to Weintraub, of every 100 men employed in manufacturing in 1920, increased productivity had eliminated 32 by 1929, but 27 of these had been absorbed by the increased volume of production. Five of every 100 were permanently displaced from manufacturing.[38]

Industrial failures and relocations may leave whole populations stranded with little or no source of income. The gradual liquidation of the Amoskeag textile mills, located in Manchester, New Hampshire, left nearly two-thirds of the total working force of the city of 75,000 population unemployed.[39] Competition from southern textile mills

---

[38] "The Displacement of Workers through Increases in Efficiency and Their Absorption in Industries, 1930-31," Quarterly Journal of the American Statistical Association, XXVII (December, 1932), 383-400, cited by Rupert Vance, op. cit., 63.
[39] Daniel Creamer and C. W. Coulter, Labor and the Shut-Down of the Amoskeag Textile Mills, Work Projects Administration, 1939, 82.

has produced similar effects in Fall River, Lowell, and many other New England textile producing centers. The removal of rubber goods manufacturing plants from New Haven and Hartford, Connecticut, likewise left relatively large surplus populations in those cities.[40] In other instances populations deriving their livings from retail and service activities have had their economic bases destroyed by relocations of transportation routes. The opposition of people in New York and Boston to the proposed development of the St. Lawrence River waterway has its basis in the probable loss of markets to middle western centers. The examples of this sort that might be cited are legion.

It should be evident from the foregoing discussion that the kind of problem experienced by a group involved in a highly developed territorial division of labor is one of occupational rather than territorial overpopulation. The difficulty is seldom a local shortage of materials: most of the materials used are obtained from distant sources. The shortage is of jobs or opportunities to participate in the local and hence the interregional economy. Contrary to Malthus, population problems do not have their causes and their solutions within their respective local areas. Both the cause and the solution may originate thousands of miles away in a central office, a diplomatic conference, a competitor's policies, or an inventor's newest innovation.

Unemployment rather than the death rate is the gauge of overpopulation. In fact, death rates may vary but slightly between areas of relatively great unemployment and other areas with a minimum unemployment or between alternating periods of employment and unemployment in a given area. The only biological response that is noticeable, if it may be called that, is a variation in the birth rate. As may be seen in Table 23, death rates remained fairly constant through the years of depression and prosperity in the United States, while birth rates fluctuated between wide extremes. Birth rate changes of this sort are functions of changes in marriage rates. In periods of economic stress young people withhold from marriage, causing the crude birth rate to fall precipitously. With a return of prosperity and employment the frequency of marriage increases rapidly, and the birth rate follows the same course, though lagging nine to fourteen months behind.

Readjustments to disequilibrium are effected primarily, however, through mobility. Population tends to distribute itself in relation to job opportunities, evacuating areas of diminishing opportunities and

---

[40] Ewan Clague and W. J. Couper, *After the Shutdown* (New Haven, 1934).

TABLE 23

CRUDE DEATH AND BIRTH RATES, UNITED STATES TOTAL
POPULATION, 1926-1945 *

Year	Crude death rate	Crude birth rate
1945	10.6†	19.6†
1944	10.6‡	20.2‡
1943	10.9‡	21.5‡
1942	10.4‡	20.9‡
1941	10.5‡	18.9‡
1940	11.1	17.9
1939	11.1	17.8
1938	11.0	17.6
1937	11.5	17.1
1936	11.7	16.7
1935	11.3	16.9
1934	11.4	17.2
1933	11.3	16.6
1932	11.3	17.4
1931	11.4	18.0
1930	11.5	18.9
1929	12.4	18.8
1928	12.5	19.7
1927	11.9	20.5
1926	12.9	20.5

* U. S. Bureau of the Census, *Vital Statistics Rates in the United States, 1900-1940* (Washington, D. C., 1943), 175, 666-67.

† "Births and Deaths by Specified Race, United States, Each Division and State, 1945," *Vital Statistics—Special Reports,* 27 (August 20, 1947).

‡ "Summary of Natality and Mortality, Statistics, United States, 1944," *Vital Statistics—Special Reports,* 25 (March 27, 1946).

gravitating to areas of increasing opportunities. The whole rural to urban movement has been of this character. So also has the general westward movement that populated the new world. The Americas served as the dumping grounds of Europe's surplus population. Migration is a continuous aspect of the functioning of every population involved in an elaborate territorial division of labor. Industrial-exchange economy is premised on the free mobility of labor.

The balance between population and jobs is a much more definite and determinable thing than the balance between numbers and resources in an isolated situation. The best adjustment is basically a mathematical problem and once computed it becomes evident that there is but little room for the absorption of excess numbers. Nevertheless, migration is far from being an efficient corrective for disequilibrium. Migration flows irregularly and often in the wrong direction. Numerous restraining influences operate to deter potential migrants.[41] Experience with uncontrolled migration indicates that it may have a significant ameliorative effect only where comparatively small populations are concerned. In populations numbering several tens of millions and more the disposal through migration of the surplus proves to be a cumbersome and slow process. Long before the feat is accomplished the crises may either have passed or have deepened into catastrophe.

But the mobility that alleviates disequilibrium involves materials, tools, and capital, as well as people. Whereas men constitute a bulky and expensive type of cargo, these other agents of production are transported at low cost. But since their movements are much less spectacular than are the migrations of men, they attract comparatively slight attention. Yet, if the truth were known, it is likely that human migration would be found to form a smaller proportion of the total volume of all types of movement today than ever before in the past. A vast amount of potential migration is anticipated and prevented by redistributions of the nonhuman factors. On the other hand, every large scale migration is preceded by movements of capital.

There is actually no known upper limit to the number of people that can live in any given area. With unrestricted access to sources of capital funds, markets, and resource deposits, a population may increase to a great density and yet enjoy a high level of living. Switzerland, The Netherlands, and England and Wales, the highest level of living areas of Europe, have population densities in excess of 2,200 persons per square mile of arable land. Indeed many of our large cities have average densities of 25,000 or more persons per square mile, and in some of their sectors the density figure surpasses 100,000. It is obvious, of course, that such densities could not in the present stage of technology be universal. Large sparsely populated areas are needed for extensive agriculture. There are many other parts of the world that are poorly located from the standpoint of participation in interregional relationships. Yet for all areas of the world the nearest approach to an absolute limitation on population size is the cost of supplying the population relative to the exchange value it can create with its labor power. And that is a constantly changing factor.

In this connection it is interesting to note some of the recent experiences of industrial nations that have attempted to colonize their overseas empires. Colonization in the twentieth century, even for nations whose leaders have most loudly proclaimed a need for "lebensraum," has been a consistent failure. The Germans prior to World

---

[41] For an extensive discussion of resistances to migration, see Chap. 17.

War I never had more than 20,000 of their nationals in their African holdings and a large proportion of those were managers and technicians. Employing heavy subsidies the Italians succeeded in establishing only about 57,000 colonists in Libya, Eritrea, and Abyssinia. The Japanese, who also found it necessary to subsidize the movement to Manchukuo, had little to show for their efforts. Most of the few thousand Japanese who settled in that richly endowed area did so under the duress of a semimilitary discipline. Even the British, who during the eighteenth and nineteenth centuries displayed such a remarkable pioneering zeal, seem to have lost interest in the settlement of frontiers. Although the Canadian, Australian, and South African governments extend attractive financial inducements to British settlers, very few take advantage of the opportunities. Apparently it is not land as such that is needed by the peoples who claim to be overpopulated.[42] As a matter of fact, industrialism is everywhere accompanied by a withdrawal from the land and a concentration of population in cities. What is needed, to reiterate a point made earlier, is free participation in world markets.

Japan, prior to World War II, provides a convenient illustration of this fact. The population of Japan, which doubled in the 50 years following 1880, attaining a figure of 64 million in 1930, gave every indication at that time of adding another 20 million in the next 40 years. Notwithstanding the rapid growth, there was no overpopulation in the territorial sense in the 1930's. The level of living had increased as fast as the population.[43] Yet Japan may be said to have had a population problem, though it was a problem of the future rather than the present. The difficulty facing the Japanese was that of absorbing into the economy an expected annual increment of half a million workers.[44] This might not have been a serious problem had not Japan's economy shown signs of stagnation. Having come late to the competition for world markets, the Japanese found themselves hemmed in by tariff and other forms of trade barriers. The United States market was almost completely closed to Japanese goods. The British system of empire preferences severely hampered Japan in the Indian and South Asiatic markets. And the Western nations were firmly established in China. Economic strictures imposed from with-

---

42 An intriguing paradox is the claims during the 1930's of Germany, Italy, and Japan to overpopulation, on the one hand, and the simultaneous domestic policies in each of the countries to stimulate the birth rate, on the other hand.

43 E. F. Penrose, *Population Theories and Their Application, with Special Reference to Japan* (Stanford University, 1934), 123; and R. Ishii, *Population Pressure and Economic Life in Japan* (Chicago, 1937), 161 ff.

44 Ishii, *op. cit.*, 138-39.

out, therefore, held forth the prospect of increasing stress within the Japanese organization.

Optimum Population.—Whenever the problem of equilibrium enters into practical concerns it tends to become a question of optimum population. By optimum population is meant that population size which yields the best quality of life. The concept seems to have had its origins in observations of plant and animal populations. Beginning with a perception of the fundamental interdependence among living things, on the one hand, and with numerous observations of the disastrous effects of overcrowding, on the other hand, the general ecologist arrives at a statement of the role of the population factor in collective life in terms of optimum theory. The optimum, for any species of life, is simply the number above and below which the chances for the survival of the species in a given area are considerably lessened, the number without which necessary forms of behavior cannot be maintained.[45]

But the use of survival as the criterion of the optimum, though relevant to species of lower forms of life at least from the standpoint of their utility to man, is hardly satisfactory in respect to human populations. What constitutes the optimum or best condition of human life is a question fraught with controversy. There may be as many conceptions of optimum as there are significant cultural differences. Religious and military enthusiasts are apt to favor sheer power, which means maximum numbers. The Indian scholar, R. Mukerjee, interestingly enough, thinks of the optimum as measured by survival or longevity.[46] Many different economic criteria have been suggested.[47] And one competent student writes at length on a welfare optimum.[48] A second problem almost as difficult as that of getting agreement on the appropriate criterion or criteria is the problem of finding a quantitative measure of the optimum quality so that an equation can be written. If there are a number of criteria, the necessity of giving each its proper weight further complicates the problem.

----

[45] Charles Elton, *Animal Ecology,* 113; W. C. Allee, *The Social Life of Animals,* 31, 50.

[46] "On the Criterion of Optimum Population," *American Journal of Sociology,* XL (November, 1934), 344-49.

[47] A. M. Carr-Saunders, *The Population Problem* (Oxford, 1922), 200-203; Lionel Robbins, "The Optimum Theory of Population," in *London Essays in Economics in Honor of Edwin Cannan,* ed. T. E. Gregory and Hugh Dalton (London, 1927), 103-37; A. B. Wolfe, "The Theory of Optimum Population," *Annals American Academy of Political and Social Science,* CLXXXVIII (November, 1936), 250-59; Omar Pancoast, Jr., *Occupational Mobility* (New York, 1941), 20.

[48] E. F. Penrose, *op. cit.*

Since economic criteria of the optimum receive the widest attention, we may use one such view to illustrate the complexities of the problem. A. B. Wolfe defines the matter as follows: "The optimum size of population will be that which furnishes the labor supply which, fully utilized, is necessary to operate the total resources of land, materials, and instrumental capital at the point of least (labor) cost per unit of product or income." [49] This statement rests on a number of assumptions. It assumes a given state of the arts and constant resources of land and raw materials. There is also the assumption "that the distribution of the product, the marketing organization, and the monetary system are such that the total output of the productive process running continuously at full capacity is constantly and fully taken off the market for consumption." [50] The "given state of the arts," if interpreted broadly, includes not only tools and mechanical processes, but the composition and organization of the labor force and the entire institutional order that has any bearing on the character of the labor force. The definition of an economic optimum, in other words, requires a number of very inclusive assumptions concerning the structure and functioning of society.

The pursuit of the optimum, however, is an administrative and engineering function. That is, it takes place, if at all, in a practical rather than an academic setting. That being the case, all the assumed constants promptly become variables. Thus it turns out that many factors other than population size influence per capita productivity, including the way capital is distributed, the size of the labor force relative to the size of population, the habits and customs regulating entrance into and tenure of gainful employment, the transportation and communication system, consuming habits, in fact, virtually every phase of organized life. Population size becomes but one among numerous factors and perhaps not the most important one in determining the optimum condition.

In the light of these observations the task of devising and implementing a policy to achieve the optimum condition assumes an enormous magnitude. The necessary knowledge as to the relative importance of each factor and the interactions between factors is simply not at hand. Many of the research techniques required to produce that knowledge have yet to be developed. Optimum population, one is forced to conclude, is not a practical possibility at the present time. It it, however, the ultimate goal of all social discovery.

[49] *Op. cit.*, 246.
[50] *Ibid.*, 247.

Summary.—The adjustment of numbers to the opportunities for living, commonly referred to in the term population balance, is the ecological problem in its broadest aspect. Thomas Malthus is credited with offering the first systematic statement of that problem. His naturalistic theory, while descriptive of the relationship of population to resources in many parts of the world, was too rigidly conceived to deal adequately with the fact of change. Apparently it was this that led Malthus to the position, which has proved to be his major error, that population problems necessarily have their causes and their solutions within specific local areas. That the dynamics of organization may be a cause of disequilibrium was pointed out by Karl Marx. Thus it seems that the level of living of any population is a function of three variables: (1) population size; (2) resource abundance; and (3) organization of the population.

Under conditions of isolation and self-sufficiency organization tends to be a constant and the amount of resource materials tends to be highly variable. The group therefore is faced with the necessity of adjusting its size to the fluctuations in the habitat. Adjustment occurs mainly through rises and falls of the death rate. On the other hand, where there is extensive interdependence among spatially separated aggregates, the resource factor is stabilized through the medium of exchange and variability passes to the organization factor. The problem of adjustment or equilibrium becomes one of relating numbers to the job opportunities locally available. And mobility takes the place of mortality as the means whereby adjustment is maintained, mobility not only of people but of all agents of production.

When the maintenance of equilibrium becomes a matter of administrative policy, it gives rise to the question of optimum population —i.e., that population size which makes possible the best quality of life. This raises two related problems. First, what is the best quality of life to be sought? Secondly, to what extent is size of population a sufficient determinant of the many variables that influence the quality of life achieved? Since it is not possible to answer these questions at the present time, the optimum population is an unattainable goal.

Supplementary References

Cleland, Wendell. *The Population Problem in Egypt: A Study of Population Trends and Conditions in Modern Egypt.* Lancaster, Pa.: Science Press, 1936.
Demographic Studies of Selected Areas of Rapid Growth. Proceedings of the Round Table on Population Problems. Twenty-Second Annual Conference of the Milbank Memorial Fund, April 12-13, 1944. New York: Milbank Memorial Fund, 1944.
Field, James A. *Essays on Population.* Chicago: The University of Chicago Press, Chicago, 1931. Chap. i.

McAtee, M. L. "The Malthusian Principle in Nature," *The Scientific Monthly,* XLII (May, 1936), 444-56.

Robbins, Lionel. *London Essays in Economics: In Honor of Edwin Cannan.* London: G. Routledge, 1927.

Speier, Hans and Kohler, Alfred (ed.). *War in Our Time.* New York: W. W. Norton, 1939. 105-31.

Webb, Walter E. *The Great Plains.* Boston: Ginn and Co., 1931.

PART III
ECOLOGICAL ORGANIZATION

Chapter 10

INTRODUCTION

It has been pointed out that collective rather than solitary living prevails in most, if not all, species of organisms. So general is this fact that earlier students sought its basis in a "gregarious instinct." But no such fiction is needed to account for collective life; it is simply that organisms either live together or they don't live. Yet there are wide differences in the extent to which the members of various species engage in a collective life. Apparently the less specialized is the biological equipment of the organism the greater is the compulsion to interdependence. Certainly man, the least specialized of all organisms, exhibits the most pronounced tendency to develop and maintain cooperative relations with his fellows. More than that, interdependence is the inescapable and fundamental aspect of human existence. Such, at any rate, is the elementary assumption of social science generally and of human ecology in particular. Ecology seeks to discover and describe the pattern or patterns that human organization assumes. Since organization is a key concept in ecological discussion, an examination of its meaning and uses is in order.

Organization, as already indicated, represents an expansion of the idea of organism, and is used to describe a variety of phenomena in which numbers of differentiated and more or less discrete objects exist together in such a way as to constitute larger units or wholes. Such units are not usually regarded as organizations, however, unless they are active in the performance of one or more functions. Thus a rock, although it is a distinguishable unit composed of a number of different minerals, is not commonly considered an organization [1] since it performs no apparent function. An automobile, however, may appropriately be described as an organization: it is an assemblage of differentiated parts and serves the function of transportation. In fact it is only by virtue of the integration of its specific parts that an automobile is capable of fulfilling this particular function. A group of cooperating organisms constitutes, perhaps, an even better example of the exact meaning of organization. The family, for instance, is a unit made up

---

[1] The rock, however, possesses a structure—a term more appropriate to use when no function is involved or when we refer simply to the distribution of the parts comprising a whole apart from the function performed.

of diverse individuals, e.g., young and old, male and female, who co-operate to achieve survival, an end that would otherwise not be possible of realization. By organization, then, we mean an arrangement of differentiated parts suited to the performance of a given function or set of functions. The term implies the interdependence of dynamic individuals whose varied activities are coordinated in a single functional system.

In order to bring this discussion into a more meaningful relation with our central problem, let us consider organization in a somewhat different light. It is evident that the concept has to do with the relation of an aggregate of individuals to something outside or beyond the individuals themselves, something which is necessary to, or at least utilized by, the individuals in question. This, we may note, is the same relationship with which we have been concerned in our consideration of adaptation. In short, organization is an adaptive technique; adaptation may be said to be its essential function. Thus organization may be taken to mean the relating of individuals to one another in such a way as to increase the efficiency of their actions. This is by no means a narrow or specialized definition. All human behavior manifests a tendency toward economy of effort through the dovetailing of activities and the development of division of labor. Even a type of activity so far removed from sustenance matters as sport displays this tendency. A baseball team, for example, is a little economy in itself. The players are disposed about the field in positions in which each is most skilled, and the several specialized functions are coordinated by the team captain. Without this organization the game would go forward slowly and awkwardly, if at all. All but the most transitory human groupings embody the same principle, though the complexity of organization varies considerably in different groups.

Ecological organization is the broad and general term used to refer to the complex of functional interrelationships by which men live. Admittedly there is a trace of tautology in the term, for we are inclined to draw a rather close parallel in the meanings of ecological and organization. Nevertheless, organization is a concept so generic that without the adjective there might be some confusion as to the ecologists' subject matter.

This definition of ecological organization brings us into conflict with earlier definitions in which the term was used to denote the spatial arrangement of population and functions.[2] Although that interpreta-

---

[2] Cf. R. D. McKenzie, "Ecology, Human," *Encyclopedia of the Social Sciences,* V, 314.

tion undoubtedly had certain merits in the early phase of ecological work, it now seems to be a misplacement of emphasis. Any significance that may attach to spatial distributions is found in their index value relative to patterns of relationships. Presumably the study of the former is a means of getting at the latter, though there have been few attempts to demonstrate the correlation. In any case, the primary focus of ecological attention is logically the organization of functional relationships. Space, and time as well, are dimensions in which ecological organization may be observed and measured.

Ecological organization thus considered is closely allied with what is ordinarily referred to as economic organization. In fact, the former term includes most of the content of the latter's meaning and more besides: it is a more inclusive concept. Economic organization, after the fashion of the discipline of economics, is normally understood to apply to those activities and the relationships they involve that are amenable to cost analysis.[3] But interrelationships among human beings possess many aspects which are noneconomic in this special sense, and which therefore are not generally considered as elements of economic organization. For example, the mutual aid manifested within the household or kinship group, the functions rendered by various nonprofit agencies, the influence exercised by various non-producing associations, these and other features of collective life may be of vital importance to the mode of life and yet have no direct representation in the price system. Ecological organization pertains to the total fabric of dependences that exist within a population.

In view of the general similarity of the concepts ecological and economic organization there may be some tendency to conclude, along with Dr. Walter Firey,[4] that human ecology assumes human behavior to be wholly rational. If rational were to mean intelligible, that would be true. But if rational is allowed to mean deliberate and calculated, then such an inference would be patently false. Ecologists are as fully aware of the force of habit and sentiment as anybody else. As a matter of fact, however, the issue of rationality versus irrationality does not concern us. Human ecology studies the structure of organized activity without respect to the motivations or attitudes of the acting agents. Its aim is to develop a description of the morphology or form of collective life under varying external conditions. With its problem stated in that manner the irrelevance of the psychological properties of individuals is self-evident.

---

[3] Walton Hamilton defines economic organization very broadly, giving it essentially the same connotation that we here give to ecological organization. ("Organization, Economic," *Encyclopedia of the Social Sciences,* XI, 484-85.)

[4] *Land Use in Central Boston* (Cambridge, Mass., 1947), chap. i.

A more familiar term, and one that is widely used in ecological literature, is *community*. For our purposes community has essentially the same meaning as ecological organization, the one difference being that the former is applied to a relatively small unit of territory whereas the latter may extend over an area of indefinite scope. Formally defined, community refers to the structure of relationships through which a localized population provides its daily requirements. In some instances the bounds of ecological organization and of community are coterminous, in others ecological organization extends well beyond the limits of a single community embracing two, three, or any number of communities. The chief advantage in dealing with the community is in that it offers a relatively small and convenient unit for investigation. It is, in fact, the least reducible universe within which ecological phenomena may be adequately observed. There is also the further fact, as will later be brought out, that the elaboration and extension of ecological organization proceeds from a community center and always has such a center as its focal point. The community, then, is the basic unit of ecological investigation.

Human ecology makes no attempt, however, to exhaust the possibilities of community analysis. It is concerned mainly with the structural features of functional organization and with how these change in response to changes in external conditions. This leaves untouched the psychological counterparts of symbiosis and commensalism. Attitudes, sentiments, motivations, and the like are omitted from consideration not because they are unimportant, but because the assumptions and point of view of human ecology are not adapted to their treatment. On the other hand, the results of ecological research provide a framework, i.e., knowledge of community structure, which should prove useful to psychological study.

Many of these preliminary remarks should become clearer in the following chapters. The content of the present section represents an attempt to identify the conditions and the nature of organization in the human community. We use the word *attempt* deliberately, for there are large gaps in the existing knowledge of these matters. Where possible the gaps are filled by inference supported by illustrative data, but in some instances it has even been impossible to find satisfactory illustrative material. As will quickly become apparent, community structure is in need of a much greater amount of research than it has received to date.

SUPPLEMENTARY REFERENCES

"Community," *Encyclopedia of the Social Sciences,* IV. New York: The Macmillan Co., 1931, 102-05.

HOLLINGSHEAD, A. B. "Human Ecology and the Social Sciences," in R. E. Park (ed.) *An Outline of the Principles of Sociology.* New York: Barnes and Noble, Inc., 1939.

PARK, R. E. "The Urban Community as a Spatial Pattern and a Moral Order," in E. W. Burgess (ed.) *The Urban Community.* Chicago: The University of Chicago Press, 1925. B-18.

Chapter 11

DIFFERENTIATION AND ORGANIZATION

Population, we have seen, responds to the various conditions of environment through differentiation and organization. It is in this way that any given aggregate passes from a mere polyp-like formation into a community and in the transition achieves adaptation to its habitat. The human community, like the more inclusive biotic community, is an organization of differences and similarities. Unlike the biotic community, however, ecological organization among human beings rests less on purely biologically determined traits and thus achieves much greater complexity of form.

Bases of Differentiation.—In simplest terms, the collective life of a human group is founded upon individual abilities, whether native or acquired, and upon local territorial conditions. Individual abilities are, in a direct sense, the raw materials of collective life. This was alluded to earlier in connection with the possible effects of a changing age and sex composition upon the functioning of a population. Local territorial circumstances, i.e., the habitat, pose the major problems of life and at the same time offer materials and other conditions which assist in meeting them. The differentia which lie at the basis of population organization, therefore, may be considered as of two kinds: physio-psychological and territorial. These, it should be noted, do not in themselves create the interdependence of the community population. They are rather the elements with which an organization is built.

Physio-Psychological Differentiation.—It is an axiom of social science that individuals are the primary sources of action and consequently the bearers of behavior traits. It is equally axiomatic that no two individuals are identical. Differentiation in the human aggregate then is at least partly a matter of diversity among the associated individuals.

The physical basis of individual differences is to be found in the mechanics of human genetics and heterosexual reproduction.[1] Indi-

---

[1] The range of individual differences in a population has recently been subjected to quantitative measurement and the findings, while not fully descriptive, are noteworthy. In a thousand adults the range of variation in anatomical, physiological,

vidual potentialities, according to present theory, reside in sub-microscopic particles known as genes, of which there is an undetermined number. Each individual possesses a gene composition which sets certain limitations upon the development of his organic structure and behavior. In reproduction the gene compositions of both parents are merged in the offspring, thus making it virtually impossible for the child to be identical with either parent. Identical individuals must have identical gene compositions, and the probability that a mating pair will be so equipped is infinitesimal. The only proximate possibility for identity of hereditary constitution, aside from remote chance, lies in plural births resulting from a subdivision of a single fertilized cell. The progeny from a subdivided cell are theoretically identical and in fact they are remarkably alike in many measurable characteristics. Nevertheless, they may exhibit important differences. One of a pair of identical twins may be left-handed and the other right-handed, or one may be larger and stronger than the other. They may also develop differences of intelligence and personality.[2] The Dionne quintuplets, who are identical progeny (by pairs), display numerous differences in anger control, sociability, intelligence, etc.[3] This merely serves to emphasize the well-known fact that the human individual acquires through heredity a very general potentiality which may be developed in an indefinite number of ways. The degree to which the behavior of the individual is predetermined in the organism or acquired through interaction with environment remains an open question. Whatever may be the final resolution of this problem, it is unlikely that it will alter the generally accepted conclusion that human behavior represents a synthesis of the two sets of influences.[4]

Despite the great range of individual diversity a few simple distinctions are widely used in the distribution of functions. Sex and age differences, for example, serve universally as bases of functional differentiation in the human aggregate. Everywhere, from the most simply to the most complexly organized groups, the sex dichotomy

---

and psychological traits is a little over 100 per cent. Standardized ratios of the highest to the lowest in each rank-order series are as follows: bodily temperature, 1.03:1; linear measurements of body, 1.30:1; measures of metabolic rates, 1.59:1; measures of body circumference, 1.52:1; measures of physiological function, 2.07:1; measures of motor coordination and speed of movement, 2.23:1; measures of body weight, 2.33:1; and measures of perceptual and intellectual abilities, 2.58:1. (Murphy, Murphy, and Newcomb, *Experimental Social Psychology* [New York, 1931], 771-72.)

[2] G. G. Tallman, "A Comparative Study of Identical and Non-Identical Twins with Respect to Intelligence Resemblances," *Twenty-Seventh Yearbook National Society for the Study of Education* (1928), Pt. I, 83-86.

[3] Wm. E. Blatz, *The Five Sisters* (New York, 1938).

[4] For an authoritative discussion of this problem see H. S. Jennings, *The Biological Basis of Human Nature* (New York, 1935).

is mirrored in the distribution of functions and privileges and is reflected in even the most minute details of collective life. In contrast to sex, which divides the group into two segments, age introduces a different stratification, the number of strata varying from one group to another. Age distinctions appear in connection with numerous activities, the members of one age category being segregated from those of another. Racial heterogeneity, wherever it occurs, forms a third generally recognized basis for the division of labor. Different racial groups tend to differ in the functions they perform and are usually set apart, too, by various prescriptions and other marks of distinction. So consistent are all peoples in the observance of these several differentials that it might seem to the superficial observer that collective life is biologically determined. But such a conclusion is far from the truth.

That the universal sex division of functions and privileges derives from inherent differences in ability and disposition finds presumptive support in the many anatomical differences that exist between male and female. In addition to differences in primary sexual characteristics, males are on the average taller and heavier than females; they have longer legs and arms, though proportionally shorter trunks; the male skull is somewhat larger than that of the female; and there are innumerable other differences in skin texture, hairiness of the body, size of teeth, etc. But so far as psychological potentialities are concerned all such differences appear to be superficial. Important psychological differences do arise in connection with unequal rates of maturation in male and female; but these seem to be transitory, lasting only during the period from puberty to maturity. Modern techniques of testing intelligence, aptitude, motor skill, sensory activity, and other similar psychological capacities yield, when all other things are held constant, no results that explain sexual differences in behavior on the basis of biological differences.[5] This is borne out by the great variations in sex division of labor that exist among different peoples. Agriculture in many preliterate groups, such as the Ifugao and the Melanesians, is woman's work; among most peasant peoples in Europe only men engage in agriculture; whereas both men and women are agriculturalists among the Samoans and Maori. Again, the trading function is restricted to the men of the Arapesh, to the women of the Dahomey, while among the Manus men and women share this function. In most instances men perform the heavy tasks, leaving the

[5] Catharine Cox Miles, "Sex in Social Psychology," in *A Handbook of Social Psychology,* ed. Carl Murchison, (Worcester, Mass., 1935) 683-748.

lighter chores for women, but many of the American Indian groups assigned the toilsome labor to women and men concentrated upon hunting and warfare. In modern society we have seen women take over men's work with alacrity, especially in war times.

No one has been able to observe the succession of events by which sex division of labor is brought about, but from a comparative study of various human groups it appears that the phenomenon may be the result of the respective roles of male and female in reproduction. The male's freedom of action is unaffected by participation in reproduction, whereas for the female, pregnancy and postpregnancy are periods of relative disability in which her movements are hampered and more or less closely circumscribed. The utter necessity for some form of division of tasks, therefore, finds a convenient basis in the heterosexuality of the species. Everywhere the general tendency is for men to assume those tasks that take the individual far afield or that require great strength and endurance; and for women to engage in the functions that may be accomplished closer to the domicile and that involve a smaller degree of strength. Men are typically the warriors, herdsmen, traders, and providers of raw materials. Women are usually the processors or fabricators; they are responsible for the weaving, pottery-making, preparation of foods, and care of children. That there are many variations in these respects scarcely needs to be argued.

Though there appears to be this indirect physiological basis for sex differentiation the particular distinctions observed in a group are, for the most part, customary rather than necessary. It is not by necessity that the men of the New Zealand Maori are restricted to the catching of certain species of fish and the women to different species, that Murngin men dominate the religious rituals while their women are either excluded entirely or play subsidiary roles, or, as in modern society, that women are subject to one moral code and men to another and less restricting one. It may be fairly assumed that all such distinctions were once of functional significance in that they were important elements in the adaptation of the group to its habitat. Once established, however, patterns of behavior acquire an inertia that carries them beyond the period of their usefulness. Cataclysmic shifts in life conditions are often required to eliminate an accumulation of outworn and inappropriate ways of acting.

Every group has experiences and problems different from those of other groups which may modify the distribution of functions in numerous and subtle ways. Important among such experiences is the fact of change in life conditions. Radical alteration in the conditions of life usually introduces equally profound revision in the existing differentiation. This occurred among the Iroquois when the federal government finally succeeded in breaking their military power. The males had been warriors and had looked with disdain upon agriculture which was woman's work. But with the reduction of their military power the principal reason for their neglect of agriculture disappeared and men took to the fields.[6] Similarly, the gradual contraction of the hunting area claimed by the Yuman tribes, in southern California, as a result of the relentless expansion of white settlement was accompanied by a shift from a matriarchal to a patriarchal form of family organization.[7] How many such changes and what related influences entered into any existing sex differentiation, it is impossible to say.

Age, however, is undoubtedly a physiological factor of first importance in determining what the individual is capable of doing. Its effects are direct and more or less obvious. At birth the individual can engage in only random and incoherent activity; as he matures the individual gains increasing control over his responses, development reaching its peak in 30 or 35 years; thereafter the individual lapses gradually into senescence and ultimate inutility. The rise and decline of the individual as a responsible functioning entity is paralleled, on the one hand, by anatomical changes, external as well as internal; and, on the other hand, by related changes in psychological processes, in alertness, interest, and general social responsiveness.[8] The universality of age differentiation, then, may be regarded in its generality as an outgrowth of physiological conditions.

The fact that age is a continuously changing quality of the organism is important in several respects. In the first place, age may be subdivided into an indefinite number of grades, ranging from a very few, e.g., young, middle-aged, and old, to twenty, thirty, or as many as may prove useful. Secondly, as already suggested, the continuous variation of age makes possible a relatively close adaptation of age-grading to the problems and requirements of life in a given habitat. It permits a distribution of functions in fair correspondence with the respective capacities of the individuals composing a population. Age is thus responsible for a much greater heterogeneity and a more precise adaptation than is the simple sex dichotomy. The Incas of Peru recognized ten distinct age grades:

---

[6] Arthur C. Parker, *Iroquois Uses of Maize and Other Food Plants,* New York State Museum Bulletin 44 (New York, 1910), 24.

[7] Julian H. Steward, "Ecological Aspects of Southwestern Society," *Anthropos,* XXXII (1937), 87-104.

[8] See Walter R. Miles, "Age in Human Society," in Carl Murchison, *op. cit.,* 596-682.

1. *Punuc rucu* (old man sleeping), 60 years and upward.
2. *Chaupi rucu* (half old), 50-60 years. Doing light work.
3. *Puvic* (able bodied), 25-50 years. Tribute payer and head of family.
4. *Yna huayna* (almost a youth), 20-25 years. Worker.
5. *Coca palla* (coca picker), 16-20 years. Worker.
6. *Pucllac huamra,* 8-16 years. Light worker.
7. *Tarta raquizic* (bread receiver), 6-8 years.
8. *Macta puric,* under six years.
9. *Saya huamrac,* able to stand.
10. *Mosoc caparic,* baby in arms.[9]

Among the South Andamanese who, according to Thomas, had no numeral higher than two, twenty-three age grades were in effect.[10] The natives of New Guinea, in the vicinity of Bartle Bay, consider all persons born within each successive two-year interval as members of a given age grade. "Thus, in a community where the oldest man is seventy years of age, there may be as many as thirty-five *kimta* (age-grades)." [11]

Differentiation on the basis of age is also prominent in modern civilized populations. Virtually every phase of collective life—every institution—involves a system of age grades implicit, if not explicit, in its functioning. Producing institutions hire and fire with respect to age and consider age, at least in point of service, in the determination of wage increases and promotions. Civil institutions recognize a more formal series of age grades. Offenders less than seventeen years of age are remanded to the juvenile courts, while those over seventeen are tried in the regular criminal courts; at twenty-one years a person achieves full legal status including the right to vote; at thirty he is eligible to hold almost any political office, except that of President of the United States, which requires an age of thirty-five. The schools embody a highly detailed age grading beginning with the "preschool" period and continuing with one-year intervals well into maturity. Age gradations appear in articles produced for consumption, in a variety of recreational facilities, in church activities, in the manners and customs of every family, neighborhood, and region.

The functional differentiation of races, though it proceeds from physiological differences, rests almost wholly upon superficial criteria so far as inherent capacities are concerned. So-called races are rarely

[9] C. R. Markham, *The Incas of Peru* (London, 1910), 161-62.
[10] W. I. Thomas, *Primitive Behavior* (New York, 1937), 358.
[11] W. H. R. Rivers, *Social Organization* (New York, 1929), 136.

genuine biological entities in the sense of being genetically homogeneous. In every instance, except for relatively brief intervals in their life histories, human groups are subject to the infusion of alien blood through interbreeding. Consequently any given set of racial characteristics is scattered diffusely through an ever-increasing population and is possessed by individuals in varying degrees of completeness. Race, in other words, is a statistical conception, however informal may have been the mental processes by which the concept was reached. The meaning that such a conception may have for inherent capability is on the surface obscure. Direct investigation of the relationship is necessary and has been extensively pursued. The research literature on the significance of racial differences is too abundant to review here;[12] but the uniform conclusion from every reliable study is that all racial groups are of equal psychological potentiality.

In certain instances, race, as a physiological quality, has direct behavior implications. This is noted especially in connection with acquired immunities to local diseases, which develop from prolonged exposure to given infections. The possession of an immunity may give one group superiority over another in the settlement of an area. There seems little question that this factor has influenced the division of labor between Europeans and natives in tropical areas. The superior technology of Europeans has enabled them to invade the tropics, but European settlement in these areas has been restricted to traders, technicians, and managers; and even these must be replaced at intervals of two or three years. White colonization of the tropics has been singularly unsuccessful, perhaps largely because of the inability of Europeans to modify their habits to suit the conditions, but also because of the lethal effects of malaria, yellow fever, etc., diseases to which the natives are relatively immune. It also may be true that a dark skin offers more protection from the intense rays of the sun than does a light skin. Thus the relationship of white employer and native laborer, established in the first invasion of tropical areas by Europeans, has persisted down to the present and is general throughout the tropics. On the other hand, European diseases have been almost as important as European technology in subduing the aboriginal peoples of the world.[13]

---

[12] For comprehensive summaries see T. R. Garth, *Race Psychology* (New York, 1931) ; and Otto Klineberg, *Race Differences* (New York, 1934).

[13] For the most part, white man's diseases have fought for him his battles with aboriginal peoples. The Portuguese, however, are reported to have eliminated many villages of native peoples in Brazil by planting smallpox germs from the clothing of a victim of this disease. (Donald Pierson, *Negroes in Brazil* [Chicago, 1942], 6.)

For the most part race is confused with culture. Race characteristics, as well as sex and age characteristics, have high visibility and
when they are found in association with peculiar behavior traits, it
is often reasoned that the one causes the other. It appears that this
inference has been historically a basic conception in the practice of
slavery. An alien individual could be reduced to a slave's status because he was believed to be less than "human," as was evidenced by
his strange behavior which, like his physical appearance, was relatively unchangeable. Even when alien peoples possess no noticeable
physiological differences their behavior peculiarities in mode of dress,
food habits, language, etc., may elicit the racial response from the
native population. Behavior is a quality as objective and distinguishing as is color or physiognomy. Thus we hear native Americans
speaking of the "French race," the "Italian race," or the "English
race." The significance of observable physiological distinctions, of
course, is that they permit a perpetuation of race differentiation,
whereas behavior distinctions may be lost with the passing of two or
three generations. In some instances behavior differences are preserved through the establishment of a rigid system of controls, as in
the caste structure of India.[14] In any event, there is a tendency in
every multiracial population toward the development of a racial division of labor which is secured by various practices premised upon the
presumed immutability of racially "determined" behavior traits.[15]
That the assumptions underlying race differentiation are fictitious
does not limit their effectiveness.

⋅ Among preliterate peoples race differentiation usually appears in
the form of territorial or regional differentiation and will be discussed
later in this chapter. In populations living under the dominion of
Western civilization, which are ordinarily large enough to comprise
many members of different races, race differentiation is a well-marked
phenomenon. This is particularly true in areas such as Hawaii and
Malaya, where the economic development rapidly overreached the
size of the native population, necessitating a large-scale immigration
of labor.[16] This is also true in South Africa. The typical Boer household is composed of a number of different races: "the governess is a
German; the cook is a Half-cast, partly Boer and partly the descendant

---

[14] It is of interest that certain Hindu castes which lack visible racial markings
substitute artificial differentia, such as insignia painted on the foreheads, peculiar
modes of hair-cutting, or distinctive dress.

[15] Brazil, in which there appears to be no race-caste structure such as exists in
the United States, is nevertheless no exception to the general tendency regarding the
development of a racial division of labor. (Cf. Donald Pierson, *op. cit.*, chap. vii.)

[16] See R. D. McKenzie, "Cultural and Racial Differences as Bases of Human
Symbiosis," in *Social Attitudes,* ed. Kimball Young (New York, 1931), 136-65.

of the old slaves; the housemaid is a Half-cast, partly Hottentot, and whose father was perhaps an English soldier; the little nurse girl is a pure Hottentot; and the boy who cleans the boots and waits, a Kaffir; and the groom is a Basuto." [17]   In the United States, the Negroes are laborers and domestic servants; Orientals are truck gardeners, dairy farmers, domestic servants and are engaged in various other service occupations; Jews tend to be primarily a service population, while Gentile whites are distributed over the whole range of occupations.

We have been dealing with only the more obvious and general aspects of physio-psychological differentiation. This has led us to speak in terms of categories of individuals but it should be stated that this form of differentiation is always fundamentally a differentiation between individuals. Sex, age, and race characteristics as considered here are merely rough indexes of individual differences. Every such category is, potentially if not manifestly, heterogeneous. It happens that the distinctive qualities of each individual have proved extremely difficult to describe in precise terms. Only now are geneticists and psychologists beginning to make substantial progress in this field. It will suffice to call attention to the well-known fact that every individual is the locus of an indefinite variety of peculiarities in gene structure, physical constitution, health, experiential background, habits of perception, interests, occupation, etc. Unfortunately, the amount of intercorrelation among these characteristics is very incompletely known, but it is clear that individuals may be alike in one or more of them and yet differ radically in others. The range of variation in any randomly selected aggregate is at least as extensive as the size of the aggregate.

Territorial Differentiation.—The materials and conditions essential to the maintenance of human life are very unevenly distributed over the surface of the earth, there being no two areas exactly alike. Thus the fact that human beings occupy a multitude of widely different habitats is an important factor in human differentiation. Each habitat not only permits but to a certain extent necessitates a distinctive mode of life. Special problems and opportunities occasioned by the presence of certain materials, plant and animal life, climatic conditions, topography, etc., favor the development of certain habits and techniques to the exclusion of others. In the degree to which the isolation of a unit of territory is complete the occupants acquire a set of responses peculiar to themselves. Consequently as populations settle into adaptations with their respective habitats there arises a cultural differentiation

---

[17] Olive Schreiner, *Thoughts on South Africa* (London, 1923), 59.

which tends to be as extensive as the variety of places occupied. It is largely in this manner that the Eskimo has become distinct from the Hindu, Occidentals distinct from Orientals, mountain folk such as the Scotch distinct from the plains-dwelling English, English different from German, German from French, and so on.

It is of interest to observe that the circumstances which lead to a cultural differentiation of population are essentially the same as those which produce racial differentiation. The widespread distribution of population causes each group to become isolated, in greater or less degree, from every other—a basic condition in the development of both locally held physical traits and locally held behavior traits. Seclusion makes for a relatively intense give and take in which ways of acting that are adapted to the area displace those that are not, with the result that each local group develops a distinctive culture. Similarly, through prolonged inbreeding fostered by isolation, a limited number of physical characteristics become more and more general in the group with successive generations as the gene composition of each individual approximates that of every other. The racial differentiation of mankind in a very real sense is a product of territorial differentiation. Although race is a biological term and culture is a term devoid of biological content, there is no practical or significant difference between so-called racial and cultural groups. The terms *race* and *culture* simply refer to different aspects of the same thing. Each is a consequence of territorial isolation and each tends to lose its identity as external influences multiply and the protective isolation is dissipated.

Territorial differentiation is undoubtedly a prior condition to the particular race division of labor that appears in any population. The complete unfamiliarity of African Negroes with Western civilization caused them to be readily amenable to slavery in the new world. Moreover, their protracted experience as plantation laborers is at least partially responsible for the Negroes' remaining an agricultural population long after their emancipation. A free immigrant population may exert more selectivity in a new area than may a subjugated group; even so, however, it will be guided by the habits acquired in the homeland. It is no accident, therefore, that Greeks predominate in the Florida sponge industry, that Italians are so numerous in the California wine industry, that Scandinavian immigrants settle in the northernmost sections of the United States, or that immigrants from Britain settle primarily in cities. There are other factors to be considered in explaining the occupational and regional selection of a migrant population, but the influence of pre-established habit appears to be unmistakable.

Differentiation and Population Increase.—Differentiation is a variable condition of mankind, shifting and altering with the passage of time and displaying permutations in one place that are not to be found in another. Several factors influence the degree and kind of differentiation that exists in an aggregate at any one time, though the relative importance of each has never been accurately assessed. One of the most generally significant variables, however, is population size, whether considered from the standpoint of absolute number or of relative number, i.e., density. Population increase bears directly upon differentiation in both its physio-psychological and its territorial aspects.

The range of individual differences is limited only by the size of the population. Accordingly in an aggregate of two individuals physio-psychological differentiation is at a minimum, and as the population becomes more numerous, whether through reproduction or immigration, differentiation proceeds apace. But it is to be noted that all differences present in a population may not be relevant to the prevailing mode of life. Thus certain individual potentialities are allowed expression while others are suppressed. Every human group behaves selectively in this respect. It may be assumed that the functional differentiation in a group is always somewhat less than the intrinsic differentiation.

But whether we are speaking of functional or intrinsic difference, the size of the group appears to be, within certain limits, the principal controlling factor. Age and sex differences, we pointed out, are observed in all groups regardless of size. In the smallest human groups these differentia take precedence over all others. It is probable, of course, that in a small group, such as a family, they represent fairly reliably the respective abilities of the several members, though the forms of expression those abilities take will be regulated in the interest of the group. In larger groups there are usually more individuals than there are differences of sex and age so that such criteria are no longer sufficiently discriminating, yet the whole population may be compressed into a set of sex and age categories for each of which there are standardized ways of acting. This is true of a great many preliterate groups which include up to fifty or sixty persons. Groups above this size may recognize a greater diversity but without relinquishing any control over the kinds of individual abilities that are to be given expression. The reason for the more or less rigorous control exercised by such groups is not hard to find. A small self-sufficient group cannot tolerate a wanton display of individuality. It is confronted with a number of pressing sustenance problems which have to be dealt with day by day and which require all available individuals. At the other extreme are the large metropolitan centers in which the opportunities for individual expression are at a maximum. Compounded of innumerable differences, the great city places a premium upon individuality, especially during its period of growth. Nevertheless, even so there will be found certain restraints; order is essential and hence there is selection of types of individuals or individual abilities.

It is also through increase that population becomes differentiated on a territorial basis. The continued growth of population in an area, if unchecked, results in overpopulation and a crisis in the life of the group. If no corresponding improvement in technology is forthcoming, the most practicable immediate solution of excessive pressure of number on resources is found in the migration of a segment of the aggregate to a new area of settlement. This response to overpopulation is widely practiced by all forms of life and apparently has been followed by man since his emergence as a distinct species. Alternate overpopulation and group fission is presumably the process by which mankind was distributed over the habitable world.

According to ancient legend, the followers and the flocks of Abraham and Lot grew so numerous that strife arose between them. Finally Abraham suggested to Lot: "Is not the whole land before thee? If thou wilt take the left hand, then I will go to the right; or if thou depart to the right hand, then I will go to the left." [18] Similar accounts are to be found in the literature of all ancient peoples. Thus may be understood the myth of the Promised Land.

In all parts of the world, continental and insular, in modern times as well as in antiquity, the swarming of surplus populations has occurred again and again. The early Greeks found outlet for their excess numbers in numerous settlements established along the shores of the Mediterranean Sea and its tributaries. To Italy flowed a stream of these migrants forming colonies up and down the length of the peninsula. Somewhat later this became an area from which further expansion proceeded as the Italians, largely under the direction of the Romans, sent out colonies to the Iberian Peninsula on the west and into Gaul on the north. Not until the insurgence of the Barbarians had reached its full power in the fourth and fifth centuries was an end brought to the spread of Italian population over Europe.

The outpouring from Central Asia flowed to the east and south as well as to the west, into China and India. The so-called period of the Great Migrations, during which the major part of these move-

---

[18] Genesis 13:9.

ments took place, is long past, but the relocation of segments of population is continuing in many out of the way parts of the world. In 1871, the British, when they were penetrating the interior of India to organize the Central Provinces, were surprised to learn that the agricultural occupation of those districts dated only from the latter part of the sixteenth century [19] when Mongolians began the settlement as a way of disposing of excess population. Now, however, agricultural settlement of the Central Provinces is continuing mainly from the congested sections of India itself. This phenomenon has been observed by Barton on the island of Luzon. When Silipanese, a branch of the Ifugao people, reached the limit of the cultivable rice-land area in their valley they began to overflow their habitat, migrating into the foothills and adjoining valleys. At the time of Barton's observation some three hundred individuals were leaving the home area every year.[20]

The history of European settlement in the Western Hemisphere is replete with instances of the same character. Emigration from Europe for the most part was an expression of overpopulation, resulting from either an excessive growth of population or a catastrophic reduction in the food supply, such as the Irish potato famine of 1845. From the early colonies established in America there were frequent separations in which bands of dissatisfied individuals moved off to settle new lands. This movement reached a crescendo as population surged over the Appalachians after the Revolutionary War and again after the Civil War. There is not space to describe here the settlement of the West, or the expansion of population in Canada and South America. Nor are we able to discuss the numerous relocations of population of the contemporary period. It is clear, however, that group fission and migration are universal responses to overpopulation.

Thus is human population brought into intimate contact with the great diversity of the earth's surface, the inevitable consequence of which is differentiation. A colonial population may retain its familiar techniques and customs for a period perhaps because of ignorance of other ways of acting or through frequent reaffirmation of traditional values and occasional pilgrimages to the homeland. In time, however, often after much suffering and wastage, the population settles into a mode of life adapted to the new habitat. As a result of relative isolation and unique problems many old patterns of behavior atrophy—a few being preserved in various symbolic references—to be

[19] Paul Vidal de la Blache, *Principles of Human Geography*, trans. C. F. Brigham, 69-70.
[20] R. F. Barton, "Ifugao Economics," *University of California Publications in American Archaeology and Ethnology*, XV (April, 1922), 420-21.

replaced by new and more appropriate ones. Thus does territorial differentiation develop.

Organization and Population Increase.—Organization necessarily presupposes differentiation. Only when divergent though mutually complementary units are articulated in some sort of system of working relationships may we properly use the term *organization*. Furthermore, the more complex the organization the more extensive and minute must be the differentiation among the parts involved. But is the converse true? Does it follow, in other words, that the degree of differentiation determines the nature or form of organization—that increase in the size of the aggregate, which produces differentiation, is inevitably accompanied by a corresponding growth of interdependence and organization?

According to Herbert Spencer, the evolution of the human community and of human organization in general typifies the operation of a universal evolutionary process. Briefly stated, this process involves a transition from a state of incoherent homogeneity, in which all the parts can perform one another's functions, to one of coherent heterogeneity, in which each unit is so specialized that no other can perform its functions correctly if at all. The driving force back of this sweeping biological principle is multiplication or increase of size. "In societies, as in living bodies, increase of mass is habitually accompanied by increase of structure." [21] "The advance of organization which thus follows the advance of aggregation, alike in individual organisms and in social organisms, conforms in both cases to the same general law: differentiation proceeds from the more general to the more special." [22]   In comparative ethnological materials Spencer found what was for him an adequate demonstration of his thesis: the complexity or organization varied with the size of the residence group. Thus the development of human organization is viewed as an inevitable consequence of population growth and differentiation.

It is not clear from Spencer's theory, however, why the great growth of Oriental populations carried organization no further than a handicraft and domestic industry stage, whereas Occidental populations, with fewer numbers, have achieved a much greater complexity of organization. Nor are we given any explanation of the extended time lag between the early territorial distribution and differentiation of man and the relatively recent rapid growth of interdependence among spa-

---

[21] Herbert Spencer, *The Principles of Sociology,* Vol. 1 (New York, Appleton-Century-Crofts, Inc., 1921), 471.
[22] *Ibid.,* 475.

tially separated groups. Apparently Spencer failed to consider at least one important qualification which was later supplied by Emil Durkheim, who otherwise adhered rather closely to the conception stated by Spencer.[23]

In Durkheim's view there exists a distinction between physical density and what he chose to call "social density." The former, of course, refers to the ratio of population to land area, while the latter pertains to the frequency of contacts and interchanges among the members of a population. Thus an aggregate might have a high physical density but a very low social density, i.e., a population might be closely packed in an area without possessing either the habits or the facilities for general intracommunication. Such segmented populations, to use Durkheim's term, are to be found in the rich alluvial plains of the Yangtze, Ganges, and Indus Rivers. On the other hand, a sparsely settled population such as we have in North America may have a very high social density. Although physical density in the United States is among the lowest for major land areas movements and contacts among units of the population occur with a frequency that is unequalled elsewhere.

Now, as we have seen, increase in physical density, though instrumental in producing differentiation, is not in itself sufficient to stimulate growth of organization. There is little to be gained from differentiation in the way of cooperation if the units remain isolated from one another. Such was the state of affairs in the human world before the expansion of trade. Cooperation requires that individuals and groups have access to one another's special abilities and products. Only as population increase multiplies the frequency and variety of meetings between elements of population does it lead directly to the development of organization. Thus organization is fostered primarily by the increase of social density. This, to be sure, depends somewhat on the proximity of individuals to one another, and up to a certain point increase in physical density is paralleled by an increase in social density. Beyond that point there may be no further increase in social density without the introduction of additional factors.

Let us use a homely illustration. The addition of each new member to a family furthers the complexity of the domestic situation in several elementary respects. It increases the number of familial relationships, adds variety to the composition of the family and hence to the experiences of each member, and multiplies the problems of ad-

[23] George Simpson, *Emil Durkheim on the Division of Labor in Society* (New York, 1933), 256-63.

ministration and control.[24] At the same time, the enlargement of the family makes possible a more elaborate division of labor and the conduct of more extensive enterprises in recreation, religion, etc., as well as in sustenance matters. This has been experienced by most persons, whether they hail from subsistence farms or modern urban regions.

If we were able to observe the course of development of a preliterate group, or, lacking that, if we had sufficient knowledge of preliterate peoples to enable us to compare the structures of residence groups arranged in order of size from smallest to largest, we would undoubtedly observe the same phenomenon—each increment in size is accompanied by an advance in the complexity of organization. Unfortunately, only the latter of these opportunities for observation is open to us and that so incompletely as to yield but a very rough picture. Nevertheless, the available knowledge is instructive. Among the Semang, the Andamanders, the Paiute, and other peoples, who live in groups of twenty to thirty persons, organization is cast almost exclusively in terms of age and sex differences. Within his age and sex category each individual is a jack-of-all-trades and consequently organization exhibits a minimal simplicity. In larger groups, ranging roughly from fifty to one hundred, greater differentiation appears in the form of a chieftain and perhaps also a shaman or priest. In groups of this size such specialized functions are generally on a part-time basis, the individual assuming the distinctive role only as the need arises. When the local group numbers as many as two hundred individuals, as with the Maori, Comanche, and Hopi, specialized birdcatchers, bow-makers, canoe-builders, and potterers appear, who, though they do not practice their specialties continuously, are recognized as having unusual skills and thus assume leadership in such functions. On occasion, too, the political functions of the chief are shared by one or more subordinates. Groups that range above five hundred, represented by Masai, Kwakiutl, and many Polynesian groups, often display a well-marked caste structure composed of noblemen, commoners, and slaves, each caste having a fixed set of functions. Within the castes there may be, in addition to age and sex distinctions, further though less explicit subdivisions based on special abilities.

[24] James Bossard has declared a law of family interaction. "With the addition of each person to a family or primary group, the number of persons increases in the simplest arithmetical progression in whole numbers; while the number of personal interrelationships within the group increases in the order of triangular numbers." Letting x equal the number of personal interrelationships, and y the number of persons, the law is as follows: $x = \dfrac{y^2 - y}{2}$. ("The Law of Family Interaction," *American Journal of Sociology*, L (January, 1945), 293.

Actually, however, settlement units seldom attain great size among preliterate peoples. Wissler indicates that groups of over five hundred are the exception rather than the rule, the average size being about two hundred and fifty.[25] Consequently, the range of differentiation in a preliterate group is necessarily restricted and the degree of organization attainable is correspondingly limited. The conditions favorable to the development of specialization are lacking. The mode of life seldom involves techniques that are so elaborate as to require the services of a full-time specialist; moreover the number in the group is too small to maintain an individual in the continuous pursuit of a specialty. Preliterate peoples are thus caught in something of a vicious circle. The techniques possessed for exploiting the habitat are inadequate to yield more than a limited amount of food and other materials. As a result, the number that may be supported in the area over which the group is able to operate is held at the most to a few hundred. The small size of the group, in turn, reacts upon the technology to prevent or at least seriously hamper its improvement. The narrow range of differences in a small population and the infrequent occurrence of exceptional individuals is a primary restraint upon the invention and new ideas. Of even greater importance is the fact that a small number of individuals cannot man a complex technology. Every cooperative activity presupposes a certain number of individuals as well as certain kinds of materials and habitat conditions.[26]

It is not to be supposed, of course, that local groups in the preliterate world occupy tight compartments between which there is no interchange. Isolation is never more than a relative condition. Virtually every residence unit is linked with others in some sort of symbiotic federation. The tribe, for example, based principally on blood relationship, is a more inclusive unit which functions periodically in various ways to supplement the efforts of the constituent local groups. The Blackfoot tribes, having a total population of approximately ten thousand at one time in their history, were each composed of a number of more or less self-contained bands each of which included several families and possessed a territory of its own. Throughout most of the year the band was the unit of life, but in the summer months the bands came together in tribal gatherings for mass buffalo drives which required a larger population and higher degree of organization than

---

25 *An Introduction to Social Anthropology*, 33-36.

26 Wissler explains the tendency for preliterate groups to specialize on one or two foods on the basis of small numbers. "Such specialization is natural because more or less elaborate techniques are required in food production and small tribes cannot carry on many such techniques simultaneously." (*Ibid.*, 58.)

was possible in a single band. In some instances the tribe may serve as a trading union,[27] but usually trade proceeds between groups occupying adjoining areas whether or not they are affiliated in a tribe. The Hopi were the focus of an extensive network of trading relationships among the Navajo, Zuni, Havasupai, Paiute, and numerous other tribes.[28] Nor was this unique, for in the mounds of Ohio and Tennessee were found "obsidian from the Rocky Mountain region; pipestone from the great red pipestone quarries of Minnesota and Wisconsin, stealite and mica from the Appalachians, copper from the region of the Great Lakes and elsewhere, shells from the Gulf of Mexico and the Atlantic, dentalium and abalone shells from the Pacific Coast, and now and then artifacts which at least hint at some remote contact with Mexican Indian culture."[29] Nevertheless, trading activities were restricted for the most part to incidental and luxury items and may be regarded as of secondary importance in the life of those local groups. Complete dependence cannot be placed on trade as the source of a primary material such as food when transportation is slow and distances are great. Isolation, though never complete, hems in the preliterate group and forces it to become self-sufficient with respect to the greater part of its needs.

Thus when the isolated local group reaches a certain size, varying with the character of its mode of life, instead of further organization, a fragmentation of the group occurs with one or more segments moving out to settle in new areas. When overpopulation develops abruptly, as in the event of a cataclysmic environmental change, there may be a neat division of the group, one part remaining in the area and the other emigrating. But population pressure may develop until it becomes a constant threat to group welfare, necessitating an annual exodus of families. In any case, the growth of organization as a consequence of population increase occurs within narrow limits in preliterate society.

In order that organization may progress with population growth beyond the limits set by a few hundred there must be an increase in the social density or, specifically, an increase in the frequency and range of interhuman contacts. This can be achieved only through the facilitation of movement. The term *movement* is used here in a broad sense to include all forms of transportation through space, whether of

[27] Cf. Margaret Mead (ed.), *Cooperation and Competition Among Primitive Peoples* (New York, 1937), chap. i, "The Arapesh of New Guinea."
[28] Melville J. Herskovits, *The Economic Life of Primitive Peoples* (New York, 1940), 173.
[29] Wm. E. Myer, *Indian Traits of the Southwest,* 42d. Annual Report, Bureau of American Ethnology (Washington, D.C., 1928), 736-37.

individuals, materials, or ideas as such. In the beginning movement was simply a matter of individual locomotion. Life under such conditions was characterized by fixity of materials and products and instability of human settlement. But man has since called to his aid various secondary agencies for movement such as vehicles of one kind or another and many other devices including the telegraph, the telephone, and the radio. It has thus become possible to achieve a fixity of settlement without loss of mobility. In a very large degree the history of the growth of human organization is a record of the development and perfection of the facilities for movement.

The most elementary basis for human movement is found in those conditions of the habitat that serve as natural avenues for travel. Mountain passes, valley floors, level beaches, streams, and coastal waters have at all times been the paths of least resistance along which population has flowed. This explains in part why coastal regions and river valleys have always been the most densely settled areas. The spread of population is channelized by such avenues. Movement and interaction are greatest, however, where routes and especially different kinds of routes converge, as on a plain, at the confluence of rivers, or where a stream empties into the sea. It is not surprising that such locations become the foci of extensive systems of interrelations. But favorable topographic conditions are by no means the only factors that facilitate movement. Technological innovations, as we are well aware, may have tremendous significance for mobility and the frequency of intergroup contacts. Nevertheless, it is quite likely that natural avenues initiated the earliest movements and opened up the ways and means for improving facilities for further mobility. Moreover, the smaller the resistance offered by a passageway the simpler, and hence the more feasible, may be the technological advance required to increase the ease and efficiency of transportation. This would seem to constitute one of the great advantages of streams and bodies of water. The effortless flow of a stream is vastly superior to the burden of human carriage; and the construction of a crude raft is far simpler than the domestication of a beast of burden. Overland movement is difficult and tedious and any large scale transportation of men and their possessions requires, as a minimum, a vehicle, power to move the vehicle, and a substantial roadway upon which it may be moved. All these but the vehicle are provided by nature in water transportation.

Hence, as Adam Smith pointed out, it is usually along the water courses that organization develops most rapidly. Here rather than inland are movement and intercommunication freest. Among preliterate peoples, coastal tribes are far more active than forest- or mountain-dwelling tribes. Often such groups develop far-flung interdependences with remote peoples, a notable example being the Malays in Oceania. The great civilizations of the past and the present sprang into existence and flourished along the water's edge. Early Egyptian civilization would undoubtedly have been impossible without the long thoroughfare of the Nile which gave comparatively easy access to all sections of its fertile valley and, at the same time, an outlet to the external world. Similarly, the rise of Hellenic civilization must be viewed against the background of Mediterranean relief. The highly indented coastline of the Greek Peninsula permitted an intense interaction among widely different groups occupying the many sheltered valleys and isolated coastal plains—an interaction which broadened in scope as the expanding population of Greece spread over the island-dotted Aegean Sea and to the mainland shores round about. In contrast to these examples are the interiors of Africa and Asia where organization has lagged at the preliterate level and also the interiors of Europe and America, which only recently have become populated and organized.

Every improvement in transportation and communication has further reduced the barrier that distance presents and has broadened the scope of interdependence. The tendency from the earliest advances in navigation to the most recent developments in air travel and radio communication has been toward an enlargement of the social units in which men live without corresponding increases in the physical density of settlement. At the same time, the number of relationships in which the individual is involved, the variety of materials and ideas accessible to him, and the tempo of daily life have been increased many times over. Thus the organization in terms of which modern civilized man lives is a vast and extremely ramified network of relationships with its physical counterpart in a maze of routes of travel and lines of communication.

Competition.—It is generally taken for granted that functional differentiation and organization are due to competition. "If 'all the world's a stage,'" wrote C. H. Cooley, "this is a process that distributes the parts among the players." [30] Walton Hamilton adds: "Competition is the term in social theory which associates the fact of struggle with the function of order. It is the key word in an account, real, abstract, or fictitious, of how rivalry for prestige and income, for

[30] "Personal Competition," in *Sociological Theory and Social Research*, ed. R. C. Angell (New York, 1930), 164.

power and wealth, comes to promote organization." [31] This indeed is a very plausible hypothesis. Hence it is not a little strange that the concept has received almost no direct investigation. Since that is the case, our analysis of competition must be cast in theoretical terms.

For purposes of simplification let us think of competition as involving a sequence of stages. The initial stage appears whenever the number of individuals or units with similar demands, or rather the aggregate demand they represent, exceeds the supply of that which is sought whether it be food, raw materials, markets, occupational positions, or positions in any type of social system. The actions of all on the common supply gives rise to a reciprocal relation between each unit and all others, if only from the fact that what one gets reduces by that amount what the others can obtain. The competitive relationships, in other words, may be entirely indirect, though among human beings it is seldom exclusively of that character. Nevertheless, without the element of indirection, that is, unless units affect one another through affecting a common limited supply, competition does not exist.

A second stage is one of increasing homogeneity among the competitors. The singularity of the supply and the given character of environmental factors impose standard conditions of competition which call forth more or less uniform responses from all units engaged in the relationship. Presumably it is in this stage that the first threats of elimination from access to the supply are felt, which, if true, constitute an added impetus to the adoption of the most appropriate forms of behavior, i. e., those practices which yield the largest returns. Thus all plumbers sooner or later turn to the same kinds of tools and techniques; medical practitioners seek to attain the same knowledge, skills, and mannerisms; and strivers after prestige cultivate the same acquaintances and sources of power. Likewise grocery stores move toward similar modes of displaying goods, similar prices, and similar services; while colleges are inclined to identity of curriculums, of degrees offered, of alumni associations, and of athletic activities.

In the third stage the pressure of congestion begins to operate selectively, eliminating the weakest competitiors. Weakness may reflect lack of physical strength, incompetence, inadequate capital, unfavorable location, and the like, depending on the nature of the competitive situation. Elimination may be expected to continue until the combined demand of the surviving competitors no longer exceeds the supply of the thing demanded. This marks the end of competition. It

---

[31] "Competition," *Encyclopedia of the Social Sciences,* IV, 141.

may be renewed, however, should there be either further population increase or a depletion of the supply below what is required to sustain the demands of the survivors. But the point to be made here is that competition is a self-resolving relationship.

But the usual interpretation of competition implies a fourth stage in which differentiation and organization occur. That differentiation follows close upon the resolution of competition seems entirely probable. The deposed competitors may scatter to other areas which offer different opportunities and call forth different adaptations. The result is a territorial differentiation. Or they may remain in the home area and develop special abilities which will permit them to make oblique attacks on the supply. That is, they take up ancillary roles in which they become dependent on but noncompetitive with those who have gained command over the supply. For example, farm operators who are eliminated from the competition for an agricultural market, assuming they stay in the vicinity, may become entrepreneurs of commercial establishments, craftsmen, farm laborers, or domestic servants. In time competition may arise among commercial entrepreneurs, resulting in the elimination of some contenders for that function, and these, in turn, may either develop new occupations or enter into competition for other existing occupational positions. In this manner, according to the popular presumption, competition differentiates and multiplies functions, thereby producing a more or less elaborate division of labor.

It is important to note, however, that in any such development the effects of competition are mingled with those of other factors. The particular combination of intrinsic capabilities that is represented in a given population, granted the difficulty of identifying and measuring these, has a bearing on the types of functional specialties that are apt to appear among the units excluded from direct access to a supply. Likewise population size, as we have seen, constitutes a limitation upon the extent to which functional differentiation may be carried. Size fixes, as it were, the opportunities for specialization and also determines the complexity of structure that can be supported by the group. Again, the state of efficiency of the transportation and communication facilities affects the degree to which spatially separated activities may be interrelated. This applies particularly to the probability that territorial differentiation will result in a territorial division of labor. In other words, although competition seems to act as a force that initiates differentiation, it does not determine the subsequent functional specialization nor is it responsible for the linking together of different functions to form an organization.

Summary.—Functional differentiation is based upon physio-psychological differences and territorial or habitat differences. Although individual characteristics, as determined by the combination of genetic and environmental influences, vary to such an extent that identical individuals rarely occur, the universal traits of age and sex everywhere serve as primary bases for the distribution of functions. Differences of race, though not found in every population, are similarly utilized wherever they appear. These differentia, however, are very rough indexes of differences in abilities and may be exclusively used only in the simplest of situations. In any case, functions are distributed within a population with reference to real or assumed individual abilities. Territorial differentiation applies to aggregates instead of to individuals. It arises from the divergent influence of local peculiarities of environment to which each spatially separated population is subject. Accordingly the mode of life of every settlement group becomes more or less distinguished from that of every other localized population.

The extent of differentiation in a population is contingent to a large degree upon its size. Size determines the range of physio-psychological variation and also the extent of territorial scatter. Increase in number produces a corresponding increase in the number of intrinsic differences in the population, though not necessarily a corresponding increase in the functional differentiation. Contrary to Herbert Spencer, functional differentiation varies with the size only up to a certain point when other things remain constant. Increase beyond that point merely results in emigration of added numbers to other areas. For functional differentiation and organization to keep pace with population increase there must be improvements in the facilities for movement and communication. As Durkheim observed, organization is more closely associated with "social density," i.e., the frequency of contacts and exchanges, than with physical density.

Competition, commonly regarded as the principal cause of functional differentiation and organization, seems rather to be but one among several influential factors. Competition begins when the number of individuals with similar demands exceeds the supply of that which is in demand, and ends when, as a result of the elimination of some contestants, demand is brought into balance with supply. If differentiation follows the conclusion of competition, it is in no small degree an effect of population size and the facilities for mobility.

SUPPLEMENTARY REFERENCES

GRIERSON, P. J. HAMILTON. *The Silent Trade: A Contribution to the Early History of Human Intercourse.* Edinburgh: Wm. Green & Sons, 1903.

KOLLMORGEN, W. M. *The German Settlement in Cullman County, Alabama: An Agricultural Island in the Cotton Belt.* United States Department of Agriculture, Bureau of Agricultural Economics. Washington, D. C.: 1941.

MASON, OTIS T. "Primitive Travel and Transportation," *United States National Museum Annual Report for 1894.* Washington, D. C.: Government Printing Office, 1896, 237-593.

MCGEE, W. J. "The Relation of Institutions to Environment," *Smithsonian Institution Annual Report (1894-95)*, 701-11.

SIMMEL, GEORGE. "The Number of Members as Determining the Sociological Form of the Group," *American Journal of Sociology*, VIII (July and September, 1902), 1-46, 158-96.

Chapter 12

COMMUNITY STRUCTURE

The Meaning of Structure.—The interdependence that develops in a population may be simple or complex and may assume any one of a great variety of specific expressions, depending on the manner in which the conditions favorable to the growth of organization have presented themselves. Despite the large range of variability, the human community retains a sufficient consistency of pattern in different times and places to permit its ready identification as such. It is to this generalized pattern or structure that we address our attention in this chapter.

The term *structure* connotes some sort of orderly arrangement of discrete or at any rate distinguishable parts. As applied to the community, structure relates to all the essential functions and their interrelations by which a local population maintains itself. That mechanism may be regarded as existing independently of the particular individuals living at any one time. Generation may succeed generation and individual may replace individual without disrupting the pattern of interdependences that constitutes the community. When we speak of community structure, then, we refer not to the attributes of individuals but to a property of the aggregate. Two tasks are involved in a structural analysis of the community. First, it is necessary to identify the kinds of parts that make up the whole. The second step is to ascertain the configuration or pattern of the whole, i.e., the relative numbers of different kinds of parts and their interrelationships. The first of these tasks is dealt with in the early part of this chapter, and the second in the last part.

The Individual as Unit.—If we think of the community as simply an aggregation of human beings, individuals constitute the basic units. The individual organism is a discrete entity, hence it meets the minimum specification for statistical treatment. The individual organism is also a distinct physiological unit capable of independent locomotion. It is the individual that makes demands on the resources of the habitat and that supplies the energy for the fulfillment of those demands. In other words, the individual is the primary producing and consuming agent. Thus it is possible to conceive of collective life as an effect of the individuals who happen to be associated.

From the standpoint of the actual business of living, however, the individual is a unit in but an atomistic sense. As with an organ of the body, he has no existence apart from a larger whole. From birth to death the individual lives in relationship with those about him: he is the product of a union of male and female; he owes his survival to the protective care of others during the early years of his life; and he never ceases to require the support and cooperation of his fellows. Biological discreteness should not be mistaken for independence.

To be sure, the importance of the individual may vary considerably at different times and places. In relatively isolated, self-sufficient populations, where the universe of life is small and there is little specialization, one individual is much like another and all are uniformly subordinated to the group. But as the sphere of life is expanded and the aggregate becomes highly differentiated, the individual acquires a distinction and a measure of freedom that indicate a certain degree of ascendancy over the groups of which he is a member.[1] Nevertheless, individuals cannot overcome the fact of their dependence. They may shift from dependence on a small number of kinsmen and neighbors to dependence on a large number of widely scattered strangers but without altering the basic situation. Man is inexorably dependent.

If the effective unit of the community is not the individual, it then must be some combination of individuals. This conclusion calls for an analysis of combinations with reference to the kinds of relations involved and the factors bearing upon combination. It also requires a classification of combinations. But before proceeding with this let us examine briefly the history of thought on the nature of group unity.

Theories of Social Unity.—Two conceptions of the nature of social unity have vied with one another throughout the past hundred and fifty years. Auguste Comte, one of the foremost social philosophers of the nineteenth century and often acclaimed the "father of sociology," contended that the essential unifying factor in the collective life of man is "consensus."[2] By that term he referred to common habits, beliefs, and traditions. In other words, men are held together, according to Comte, by their common interests and possessions. He did

---

[1] Such a transition was recognized in the United States, in 1850, when in the reorganization of the official census the individual replaced the household as the unit of enumeration.

[2] *Positive Philosophy,* trans. Harriet Martineau (New York, 1854). Vol. II, 140-48.

not deny the presence of other bases of unity, but he did insist upon the primary importance of "consensus."

Writing somewhat later and under the influence of a different set of circumstances, Herbert Spencer looked upon collective life as basically a division of labor.[3] Differentiation, which in his view characterizes all higher forms of life, necessitates mutual supplementation. Hence the human group and, in fact, society in its entirety is analogous to an organism: it is an organization of specialized functioning parts each of which is essential to the survival of the whole. Unlike Comte, then, Spencer held that the basis of social unity was to be found in the interdependence of unlike parts.

The two conceptions of group integration—"consensus," and differentiation and interdependence—presented by Comte and Spencer as alternative possibilities, were brought together by Emile Durkheim in a single theoretical formulation.[4] In Durkheim's thought the two types of integration occupied different positions in an evolutionary sequence. In very small, isolated, and usually preliterate population groups "consensus," or, as he termed it, "mechanical solidarity," prevails. Group members are held together by their likenesses from which they derive mutual support. Unity is of the order of simple cohesion. But with increases in the social density "mechanical solidarity" is superseded by "organic solidarity." That is, differentiation develops and interdependence involves specialists to an increasing extent. Unity in the large, mobile, and civilized population, therefore, is that of the division of labor, rather than that of "consensus."

Still another application of the two principles of group unity is found in the works of Ferdinand Tönnies.[5] Instead of a differential distribution in time, Tönnies placed them differently in space. The individual, according to this author, is born into a small, homogeneous, and intimate group (Gemeinschaft) in which interrelations are personal and based on common interests. As the individual matures, however, he moves out into a larger universe of interrelations characterized by impersonality and functional specialization (Gesellschaft). The small local group is united by "consensus," to use Comte's term; surrounding it is the larger society which derives its unity from differentiation and interdependence.

---

[3] *Principles of Sociology* (New York, 1888). Vol. I, Pt. II, chap. i.

[4] George Simpson, *Emile Durkheim on the Division of Labor in Society* (New York, 1933).

[5] *Fundamental Concepts of Sociology: Gemeinschaft und Gesellschaft,* trans. Charles P. Loomis (New York, 1940). Tönnies looked upon the two concepts, Gemeinschaft and Gesellschaft, as ideal types and there is some indication in his writings that, instead of polar concepts, they constitute two segments of a single continuum.

All the conceptions that have been discussed simplify the nature of social integration to a point of excess. Simplification is indeed an objective as well as a procedure in scientific work, but it should not be achieved at the expense of completeness. The relationship in which men are held together seems to be more than just "consensus" or the mere division of labor; nor does it seem to be one of these at a given time or place and the other at a different time or place. Social unity is considerably more complex than has been suggested thus far. A further step in the trend of thought from Comte through Tönnies is supplied from the theoretical position of ecology.

It appears, in fact, that the collective life of man, as of all other organisms, revolves simultaneously about two axes, one of which is symbiotic, the other commensalistic. The former pertains to the interdependence of unlike forms, i.e., units of dissimilar functions; the latter to the co-action of like forms, i.e., units of similar functions.[6] The two types of relationship are found in all organized populations. Each represents a peculiar and complementary integrative force and together, therefore, they constitute the basis of community cohesion. The community is thus a symbiotic-commensalistic phenomenon.

But this statement, simple as it is, carries implications having extensive ramification. Symbiosis, for example, does not exist uniformly among all individuals in the communal aggregate, and among those who are so connected the relation may occur in varying degrees of directness. The community presents the aspect of a cluster of symbiotic groupings through which are mediated the relations of individuals to the population at large. Likewise, commensalism is not at all times constant throughout the community. It appears mainly among individuals of similar functions. And, since functional differentiation is a fundamental characteristic of the community, commensalism tends to occur disjunctively in each functional category.[7] From the standpoint of this relationship, the community may be conceived as a series of layers or strata. We have here but a preliminary view of the tangled fabric of relations that is the community. Nevertheless, it suggests the kinds of units in terms of which collective life is organized.

Communal Units.—It is evident that two distinguishable forms of groupings develop from the two relationships. The symbiotic relation is the basis of what may be called a *corporate* group. Such a group

---

[6] A similar conception, though developed within a social psychological context, is stated by George H. Mead, *Mind, Self and Society* (Chicago, 1934), 258-59, 261.

[7] See, for example, J. E. Cairnes' discussion of noncompeting groups in *Some Leading Principles of Political Economy* (New York, 1874), 66 ff., and E. Durkheim, *op. cit.*, 267.

is internally differentiated and symbiotically integrated; it constitutes an organ of the larger communal organism. The commensalistic relation gives rise to a *categoric* group, an association of functionally homogeneous individuals.[8] Every such segment of the communal aggregate is or is capable of becoming a categoric group. The community, then, may be regarded as a congeries of corporate and categoric groups. It is not to be assumed, however, that the two types of groups are mutually exclusive; rather they interpenetrate one another at numerous points. Corporate groups combine portions of different categoric groups; for example, in the family different sex and age categories are represented and the business enterprise includes representatives of many different occupational categories. On the other hand, categoric groups cut through the corporate groups embracing all individuals who exercise similar demands on and make similar contributions to the community. Thus janitors, entrepreneurs, and specialists of all other kinds, though they may constitute categoric groupings, are distributed in a large number of different corporate units. Hence every individual may be thought of as standing at one or more intersections of the symbiotic and commensalistic axes. Every role he occupies in a corporate group qualifies him for membership in an appropriate categoric unit.

It is to be emphasized that the categoric grouping or unit is something other than just a category. The latter is a statistical concept applicable to all individuals that have similar characteristics. But when like individuals attain a formal and more or less permanent pattern of co-action which gives them unit character they constitute a categoric unit. How the transition from category to categoric unit is made is not our concern at the moment.

Corporate and categoric groupings are further distinguished by their functions.[9] Because of the internal organization peculiar to each type of unit, it assumes a unique functional position in communal structure. As an organization of specialists the corporate unit is able to engage in elaborate and aggressive programs of action. Thus it is essentially a producing unit: it is the responsible agency for the production of goods and services. The dynamics of the community, as manifested both in its day to day operation and in change in response

---

[8] Corporate and categoric groups are analogous to Braun-Blanquet's "dependent unions" and "commensal unions." (*Plant Sociology*, trans. George D. Fuller and Henry S. Conrad (New York, 1932), 5-17.)

[9] The term *function* is used in two senses in this chapter, the general and the specific. In this paragraph we are concerned with the general functions of types of units. However, each unit within a class carries on a particular activity—that is its specific function.

to altered conditions, are traceable mainly to the corporate units. In contrast, the categoric group, by virtue of its homogeneous membership, is capable of only the simplest kind of collective activity. Its activity is evident in the aggregate of parallel reactions of its members to a threat to their common position. The power that can be developed by numbers acting in unison is the basis of unity in the categoric group. This type of group, then, is characteristically reactive, and its function is to conserve or protect what is necessary to the welfare of its members. Categoric groups are to a large extent responsible for whatever rigidity a community possesses.

This is an appropriate place for a brief consideration of the role of competition in community structure. That relationship constitutes a condition very important to the rise of categoric units. Competition fosters and in fact accentuates individuality. Hence, if uncontrolled, it exposes the individuals who perform a given function to greater risks than are necessary. Conversely, joint action to meet a common threat requires a reduction of competition and ultimately, if the threat is continuous or if other hazards are to be anticipated, competition must be brought under control. In effect, the emergence of a categoric unit invariably produces a control of competition. This takes the form of rules of procedure, parceling out of territory, definition of the common interest, and other similar devices. With control accomplished the members are mobilized to meet recurring crises. It is important to note that categoric units develop among active or potential competitors. This is but a way of saying that individuals with the most in common are at the same time most apt to enter into competitive relations.

It is evident on the surface that corporate and categoric are generic concepts. Each term applies to a variety of groupings which differ in certain minor respects. The corporate grouping is manifested in familial, associational, and territorial forms; while the categoric type of grouping appears as age and sex groups, occupational groups, social classes, and the like.[10] An examination of representatives of each subtype will aid in clarifying the nature of communal units.

Familial Corporate Unit.—The family constitutes a universal expression of corporate organization. By *family* we mean a relatively small association of individuals, differing in age and sex, who, as a result of their close physical association in a common residence and their mutually sustaining activities, form a distinguishable entity or unit within a larger aggregate.

---

10 These are not intended as classifications.

There is general agreement among competent students that the family is the most fundamental type of grouping in the realm of human association. Its primacy results from a combination of biological circumstances, such as the physiological differentiation of sex, maternal glandular conditions which persist for some months after childbirth, and the prolonged immaturity and dependency of offspring. The last-named factor is doubtless the most significant in accounting for the existence of the family. Indeed, the union of parents and progeny is essential among all animals whose offspring pass through a more or less lengthy period of postnatal maturation. Without an arrangement of this kind, the survival of the species would be hazardous in the extreme, if not impossible. The family, then, is fundamentally a subsistence group, its essential activities being the feeding, protecting, and nurturing of offspring.

The relationship of parent to child, though it is the basic and determining feature of the family, is seldom found in its simplest form. Responsibility for children carries numerous ramifications, even under the most rudimentary conditions of human life, and these operate to draw into the family additional individuals and to complicate its subsistence function.[11] Rarely are there fewer than two adults involved in the relationship with children. A single adult, the mother for example, may be able to provide all the sustenance materials required by the children and herself and may even possess the requisite knowledge and skill for training sons and daughters. But her efforts are rendered more effective if supplemented by those of another adult, preferably a male who, because of his superior strength, freedom of movement, and different experience, is able to make a distinctive contribution both to the nurturing of children and to the maintenance of the female. In a great many instances, however, the family includes a number of adults such as grown children, brothers and sisters of the parents, various other relatives, and occasionally selected nonrelatives. The accumulation of members, at least up to a certain point differing with related conditions, makes possible a greater subdivision of tasks and therefore a more efficient performance of the subsistence function. In short, gathered about the pivotal parental relation is a number of relationships which serve the needs of adults as well as of children.

The biological and sentimental bonds in the family are usually emphasized at the expense of the symbiotic. Of course the family is commonly a genetic aggregate, all the members being blood relatives.

---

[11] See Audrey Richards, *Hunger and Work in a Savage Tribe* (London, 1932), 38-47, for an analysis of the implications of the nutritive relation between mother and child as observed among the Bantu.

But there are many exceptions to this rule. Adoption, the conferring of full family membership upon a nonrelative, is a common practice. Although in our own society adoption is occasional, in others it is much more frequent as among the Andaman and other South Pacific island groups where, it is said, one rarely finds children living with their biological parents.[12] Blood brotherhood and various other types of "kinship equivalents" are widely recognized, especially by preliterate peoples. The inclusion of nonrelatives in the household, with or without ceremonial sanctions, is in fact so general that it raises serious doubts as to the necessity of a biological basis. It may be that the accident of proximity among blood relatives led such persons to form symbiotic unions more readily than nonrelatives. The only other practical significance of blood relationship would seem to be to serve as a rationalization of the sentiments that arise in the course of prolonged and intimate association under one roof. An ancient Japanese adage —"A stranger at hand is better than a relative afar"—appears to express the attitude of most peoples.

Thus the parent-child relationship is susceptible to indefinite elaboration, as is evident in the wide variety of family forms that have been observed in different times and places. There are differences in size and the number of generations represented, in the concentration of authority and the status of the subordinate members, in the temporal continuity and the mode of reckoning lineage, and in a multitude of lesser matters. It is not our task to review in detail the many family types that have been discovered,[13] but some indication of the range of possibility may be given. These unions may vary from the "joint family," including fifty or more members and as many as five generations, to the "small family," with around five members and no more than three generations. It may be patriarchal, matriarchal, avuncular, equalitarian, etc., in each of which the numbers may be arranged in various patterns of work relationships. The consanguineous family, which may be patrilineal or matrilineal, is continuous through time, whereas the conjugal family, in which lineage is calculated from both parents, breaks up and reforms in each generation. Classifications such as these, and others that might be mentioned, are not mutually exclusive. For example, the "joint family" is usually patriarchal, consanguineous, and patrilineal, although it is often matri-

---

12 W. I. Thomas, *Primitive Behavior,* 140 ff.
13 See R. Briffault, *The Mothers* (London, 1927) ; E. Westermarck, *The History of Human Marriage* (5th ed., London, 1921) ; L. H. Morgan, *Systems of Consanguinity and Affinity of the Human Family,* Smithsonian Contributions to Knowledge, Vol. XVII, Art. II (Washington, D. C.) ; and R. H. Lowie, *Primitive Society* (New York, 1920).

archal and matrilineal. Each feature may be used as a basis of classification and a somewhat different distribution of families would be
obtained in each case.

Unfortunately, anthropologists have neglected to inform us of the
functional significance of most of the traits used in family classifications.[14] Just what bearing patrilineage or the avunculate may have
on the way a community operates is not made clear. Only two types
—the consanguineous and the conjugal families—seem to have un-
disputed functional significance. Hence we shall return to them in
later discussion.

Associational Corporate Unit.—In contrast to the family, which is
oriented toward the broad problem of subsistence in its entirety, the
associational unit is limited to the performance of a particular service
or set of services, such as the making of a certain tool, the distribution
of manufactured products, the maintenance of law and order, or the
provision of education. Corporate units of this type, therefore, can
never stand alone; they must always be complemented either by
the family or by other associational units. Consequently it is only
in relatively complex communities that associational units may be
observed.

Specialization of function presupposes what in economic parlance
is called a market, i.e., the existence of a uniform requirement in a
population which, by virtue either of concentrated settlement or possession of efficient communication facilities, is able to express its
wants. Accordingly associational units appear only when and where
such a condition obtains and disappear when for any reason the "market" is dissipated. In the modern form of business enterprise this is
clear enough. A striking illustration is to be had in the cycle of growth
and decline of population in so-called "boom towns" and the corresponding appearance and disappearance of retail and service agencies.
Dependence on a "market," however, is also true of nonpecuniary
enterprises, such as hospitals, schools, churches, etc. Although the
profit stimulus generally does not operate in units of this character,
they nevertheless cannot continue functioning unless income is equal
to or greater than expenditures, unless, in other words, there is at
hand a minimum supporting population. Schools cease to operate because of a declining number of children, churches dissolve for lack of
adherents, and governments collapse when their constituents lose con-
fidence in them.

[14] A notable exception is Lewis H. Morgan, *Ancient Society* (Chicago, 1909),
393-94.

Dependence on a "market" thus makes for a kind of instability which is not ordinarily encountered in the family unit. One of the most important of the many implications of the element of risk attendant upon specialization is the emphasis thereby placed on efficiency in the performance of functions. This finds expression in numerous ways, but most noticeably in the high degree of selectivity of personnel constituting the associational unit. The demands upon the component individuals tend to be precise and exacting; and only those with skills and abilities which contribute directly and most effectively to the particular function succeed in gaining a niche in the unit. Moreover the personnel is never permanent. Individuals pass into and out of the associational unit as the need for them waxes and wanes. Modifications in the function to be performed, as well as in the size of the supporting population, also affect variations in the personnel. The deterioration of skill or the loss of agility may cause one individual to be replaced by another.

The membership of the associational unit is, therefore, seldom if ever representative of the general population from which it is drawn. It may be composed entirely of individuals of one sex, or it may combine varying proportions of both sexes. Likewise certain age groups usually predominate and others such as the very young and the old may not be represented at all. The unit's function may be that of serving the needs of dependents, as in the case of welfare agencies, but the organization includes only employable individuals. The associational unit is also atypical in respect to its occupational composition. The division of labor in a manufacturing enterprise, for example, includes no place for a preacher, a teacher, or an obstetrician, just as a church has no niches in its functional organization for printers, railroad engineers, entomologists, etc. In short, the associational unit is an extra-familial grouping. It cuts across family lines, drawing together in a symbiotic union occupationally differentiated individuals without reference to kinship affiliations.

Territorial Corporate Unit.—A territorially localized organization of familial and associational units which functions as a whole in the performance of one or more specialized services constitutes a territorial unit. Such units begin to take form whenever trade or interdependence of any kind springs up between spatially separated aggregates. But not until interrelations are developed to the extent that no one of the aggregates involved is able to maintain itself without the aid of the others can it be said that communal units of this type exist. The populations affected, though previously each may have been a community in itself, thus become unit parts in a more extended and inclusive community.

The conception of the territorial unit clearly envisages a situation in which transportation and communication facilities are so far developed that vital interdependences may be maintained over relatively great distances on a daily or at most a weekly basis. Territorial units in effect are phenomena of the contemporary Western world. Yet units of this character have been observed in rudimentary form among a number of preliterate peoples. Trading unions, in which the local residence group or village is the unit of participation, occur in a number of places. A striking illustration is found in East Africa where a number of villages were united in relationships of interdependence under the domination of the Masai. To each village group is allocated a certain function, such as shepherding cattle, manufacturing implements, etc., while from their villages the Masai performed administrative and policing functions.[15]

But the city, and particularly the modern city, is the consummate example of the territorial unit. The role of the city, its *raison d'être,* is to function as a service center. Cities arise with the separation of certain activities from primary production and their concentration at points where they may be most satisfactorily conducted from the standpoint of the largest number of persons. The city's population is always, therefore, a dependent group. A continuous exchange of goods and services with the villages and towns round about is necessary to the very existence of a city. The emasculation of Vienna through depriving it of much of its hinterland, by the peace of St. Germain, is cogent evidence of the city's dependence.[16] A city in fact is but one among a number of territorial units which together by virtue of their interrelationships form a community.

Categoric Units.—In our discussion of differentiation [17] we noted that the full array of individual peculiarities present in a residence group never gains expression. Rather are individuals distributed in a limited number of categories, classes, or strata, each of which is homogeneous in itself and readily distinguishable from all others. Although individual differences lie at the basis of the categorization or stratification that appears in local populations, it is the existence of categories which is the striking and in fact the significant manifestation of differentiation.

---

[15] Richard Thurnwald, *Black and White in East Africa* (London, 1935).

[16] C.-E. A. Winslow, "Vienna," *Science,* Vol. LV (April 7, 1922), 363-64; "Dying Metropolis," *Living Age* (January, 1920), 198-200.

[17] Chapter 11.

The sorting of individuals into categories may conceivably follow any one or more of an unlimited number of principles. Individuals may be classified as to hair color, stature, food preference, clothing design, religious belief, etc. As a matter of fact many similar criteria are actually employed in various human groups. Age and sex everywhere serve as bases for the subdivision of population. Wealth, place of residence, occupation, race, and many other differentia, are also widely used to the same end. But while numerous ways of designating human categories are practiced, all may be reduced to a common denominator. Whether they be called age grades, sex groupings, castes, classes, socio-economic groups, or what not, all are functionally differentiated segments of the whole. Each is an "occupational" division in which are classed all individuals who habitually perform the same or very similar functions. Any other terms used to designate or identify existing categories either pertain to convenient reference points for the ascription of function, e.g., age, sex, race, or are indexes of functions regularly discharged, e.g., wealth, place of residence, etc.

A universal basis for the predominance of occupational over other possible types of categorization exists in the inevitable preoccupation of men with gaining a livelihood from and otherwise maintaining themselves in their several habitats. Individual attributes which receive the first and the greatest emphasis are those which directly affect the success of sustenance-producing activities. The same factor, of course, is important in understanding the manifestations of human differentiation in categories rather than as ungrouped heterogeneity. Not all individual aptitudes and abilities are equally pertinent to the requirements of a group living under given conditions. In fact, in every situation there tends to be a limited number of tasks the performance of which is imperative and which command the attention of the entire group. Accordingly individuals are pressed into relatively few more or less standard activities and these serve as bases for the emergence of categoric units.

The number of occupational differences in a communal aggregate determines in a general way the number of categoric units that may appear. It should be noted, however, that the occupation concept is often construed too narrowly. The usual census tabulation of occupations includes only the "respectable" activities, even though illicit or criminal occupations may constitute permanent and integral functions in the community. There likewise is a tendency to overlook occupations that do not command a wage. Housewives and unpaid family workers of all kinds are excluded from occupational lists or classifications. The term *occupation* is used here synonymously with sustenance-producing activity.

Many occupational divisions in a community may exist only as potential categoric units. These are the occupations that have encountered no threat which would endanger the sustenance base of their members. Family workers and domestic service workers in general are of this type. In some instances the occupation has been undermined but the sustenance position of the individuals concerned has remained the same or has even improved. Domestic service workers, for example, have tended to desert that occupation for more lucrative employments.

Categoric units emerge only in those occupations that have been confronted by challenges which, if unattended, might impair or eliminate the sustenance base of the individuals involved. These are usually the most highly skilled occupations which are often so specialized that the individuals committed to them cannot readily shift to other occupations. The medieval guild and the modern professional association are illustrative of highly developed categoric units. In such units the reaction to threats often assumes a sharply defined and rather complex pattern. It includes a set of rules which govern admission, performance, and retirement from the occupation. The paraphernalia of control may be further embellished by ritual and symbolism. Through these and other devices the occupational group builds a defensive wall about its niche in the division of labor.

Although categoric units based on occupation are the most stable and significant units of that type in the community structure, the phenomenon of grouping with reference to common interest (i.e., common function or requirement) occurs in almost limitless variety. It seems that any characteristic shared by two or more persons, however minute or tenuous it may be, is a potential basis for a commensalistic or categoric grouping. Cliques, clubs, "societies," neighborhood associations, and the like, are all representative of the categoric reaction.[18] In a large city the instances of such groupings may defy enumeration. Many groupings of this kind doubtless are transitory; others may endure for generations. But in all instances their activities tend to be alike in principle: they are protective and conservative.

---

[18] An important question concerning such groupings is: To what extent are they units of the community? The test, no doubt, is the degree to which they affect the functioning of the community as a whole. This may be difficult to determine. What is at issue here, of course, is the matter of relevance, clearly one of the most crucial problems in social science. It hinges, in this case, upon the clarity and demonstrability of the definition of communal unit. That, in turn, requires a great deal more exploratory research than community structure has received to date.

Now while it is possible to distinguish corporate and categoric units, both symbiotic and commensalistic relations are or tend to be present in every human grouping. The members of a corporate unit are alike in the common fact of membership. Moreover the functions of all, however diversified they may be, have a like effect in maintaining the organization upon which all depend. But that commonality, vital as it is, serves as basis of categoric behavior only when the corporate unit is threatened with extinction or with radical change. Then the differentiated members tend to coalesce in a united action to protect the common possession. An attack upon a family, for example, brings forth a common defensive response. That effect is more dramatically portrayed when an entire community or nation is confronted with a crisis. Internal conflicts and differences are set aside as the entire population rises to meet the threat. After the threat is removed the group resumes its corporate form. The commensalistic aspect of the corporate unit, in other words, seems to be intermittent, appearing and disappearing as crises arise and subside.

The categoric unit, on the other hand, often develops within itself a corporate structure. That seems to occur whenever the unit undertakes a positive program of action whether it be to gain control of crucial conditions in anticipation of future threats or to expand and develop the common interest. Differentiation occurs and a small corps of specialists emerges to carry out the action program. It is thus that categoric units gain permanence. Many labor unions appear to have developed in this fashion. They begin as simple mass reactions, acquire a program and a staff of officers, and become permanent. The same process may be traced for most religious sects. In any case, whatever the process may be, a large number of categoric units are comprised of a mass of undifferentiated members and a small nucleus of specialists.[19]

In the light of these observations, the definitions of corporate and categoric units require some modification. The corporate unit is a grouping the relations in which are primarily rather than exclusively symbiotic. And the categoric unit is a grouping the internal relations of which are basically though not exclusively commensalistic. It may be that what we have described as units are more appropriately viewed as patterns of relationships which develop to implement their respective functions. Thus an aggregate seeking to engage in a producing activity assumes a corporate form. The same aggregate, how-

---

[19] An interesting problem in this connection concerns the tendency of the corps of specialists, the corporate nucleus, to detach itself from a specific body of members and to offer its service to a market.

ever, may find it necessary to perform a conserving function, in which case it takes on a categoric form. This is clearly a matter that is in need of further investigation. But for present purposes it makes little difference whether the groupings are discrete things or shifting patterns, as systems of relationships which constitute unit parts of the community.

The community, in fact, should be regarded both as a symbiotic and as a commensalistic phenomenon. Its twofold basis of integration is found, as we have pointed out, in its being composed of corporate and categoric units, but also in the interunit relationships that necessarily develop. All components of the community are enmeshed in one way or another in a symbiotic fabric. Likewise all components have that fabric as a common interest; their diverse functions contribute to the maintenance of the whole without which each would find survival difficult.

Interunit Relations.—The relations in which individuals are linked together to form communal units occur also as between such units. Every unit is or tends to be a junction of symbiotic and commensalistic relations involving other units.

The corporate unit, in the degree to which it is specialized in function, presupposes other and differently specialized corporate units. Where the family concentrates its efforts on the nurturing of children to the exclusion of producing activities, it must obtain needed materials and services from other sources such as factories, stores, schools, churches, etc. Nor is any factory, store, school, or church capable of independent existence.

While the specialized corporate unit requires supplementation by functionally diverse units of similar type, it may also derive support from units of like specialization. Corporate units tend to form categoric combinations whenever the strength of number is needed to deal with a common danger. Families of the same general type combine in a social class; grocers, barbers, manufacturers of automobiles, etc., enter into "associations" of their particular kind; churches join together in denominations; schools affiliate; and so on throughout the gamut of unit differences.

Interunit relationships likewise develop among categoric units. Such units, of course, are involved, by their nature, in symbiotic relations with one another. But that relation is not a result of the formation of categoric units; rather it is due directly to the specialization of functions in the community. It appears unlikely that a commensalistic union can exert a positive influence on the development of symbiosis. The formation of categoric groupings, however, makes possible an extension of the commensalistic relation. Thus fairly similar categoric units may combine in larger categoric groupings. Labor unions, for example, form federations of unions; various retailer groups join in "chambers of commerce"; church denominations establish federations of churches; and so on. Supraunits of this sort may be assumed to have the same function as their components, though they are adapted to a wider universe and to a more general type of problem.

A hierarchy of power relations emerges among differentiated units. Two consequences of differentiation contribute to that result. In the first place, inequality is an inevitable accompaniment of functional differentiation. Certain functions are by their nature more influential than others; they are strategically placed in the division of labor and thus impinge directly upon a larger number of other functions. The functions performed by specialized corporate units, in effect, are distributed on a scale of dominance or control. Secondly, mutual supplementation through functional differentiation necessitates a centralization of control. To insure the regular operation of the system there must be a sufficient governing and coordinating power vested in some one function. It is possible that an organization might function for a period without a coordinating agency, but only at great risk. Minor dislocations and frictions could accumulate rapidly into chaos.

Dominance attaches to the unit that controls the conditions necessary to the functioning of other units. Ordinarily that means controlling the flow of sustenance into the community. Any alteration of the sustenance flow requires immediate readjustment on the part of all other units. Such influence may be exercised directly or indirectly through control over the allocation of space to different activities, the determination of who shall be employed, the regulation of credit, the censoring of news and information reaching the community, and in many other ways. In other words, the dominant function need not be a specialized coordinating function to have that effect. Both dominance and coordination may operate informally, that is, simply through other units seeking to accommodate their functions to the activities of the unit carrying on the strategic function.

Dominance, as we have suggested, is a matter of degree. All corporate units in the community exercise some degree of influence or control. Thus what has been said of the dominant unit, or rather the most dominant, applies in lesser degrees to all other corporate units. The influence a unit is capable of exerting depends on the extent to which its function regulates the conditions under which other units must work. We shall use the term *subdominant* to refer to subordinate corporate units, reserving the term *dominant* for the unit or units that exercise the maximum influence.

Corporate units may maintain or even enhance their dominance by entering into categoric groupings. Units of the dominant type respond in this fashion whenever their position is threatened by change. Such collusion may operate as price fixing or as various restraints of trade. Through such methods change may be long delayed. Subdominants also frequently resort to categoric groupings by which they achieve a force well out of proportion to the importance of their specific function in the division of labor. The familiar "boycott" is a potent instrument of the categoric grouping. Churches have been known to coerce large corporations through the means of the "boycott."

Examples of Community Structure.—The variety of structures exhibited by different communities is too great to be adequately treated here. More than that, however, knowledge about community structure is altogether too undeveloped to permit a satisfactory description of even one type. Our analysis therefore must be confined to the more salient features of structure, omitting much that is doubtless essential to a full understanding of community organization. Presumably subsequent research will fill in the gaps in our description.

Two general types of communities may be recognized, the independent and the dependent. As with most dichotomies, this classification is a first approximation to an adequate description of differences. Independent and dependent classes of communities should be thought of as comprising two parts of a continuum which measures degree of independence. If complete independence is represented on a scale by −1, and complete dependence by +1, then all communities which fall below an indistinct "midpoint"—the 0-point—comprise the independent class, and all that fall above the 0-point make up the dependent class. Differences between communities, in other words, are conceived as quantitative rather than qualitative in character. Furthermore, it is entirely probable that polar types on the scale of independence are nowhere to be found. Complete independence may occur from time to time, but only under extraordinary circumstances. On the other hand, complete dependence of a community is illogical, for the very concept of community implies a separate identity. The classification of communities employed here, then, is not in terms of polar or ideal types, but is based on ranges on a hypothetical scale.

The Independent Community.—As the name indicates, the independent community is a self-sufficient entity, that is, it produces most of the goods and services it consumes. Associated with this characteristic are a number of other distinctive attributes including isolation, small population, simple technology, and marked stability. Community independence is a consequence of the interconnected effects of these several attributes. Isolation makes self-sufficiency mandatory, and once established self-sufficiency preserves isolation. The exclusion of disturbing influences from without promotes stability in all phases of collective life. Technological development, for example, is highly improbable: if it occurs at all, it does so at an imperceptible pace. Moreover, as was noted earlier, simple technology and population size are locked in a vicious circle. Meager techniques cannot support many persons on the resources at hand, and a small number of persons, in turn, cannot staff a complex set of techniques. This provides further support to isolation and self-sufficiency. Communities of this sort are characteristic of virtually all preliterate societies. They also are typical of peasant life in Europe and Asia. Examples may be found, too, in some of the more remote sections of contemporary North America.

The structure of the independent community is simple. Corporate and categoric units are limited in number and variety. The family or household group is the principal form of corporate organization. In some instances, as among the Shoshone Indians,[20] the community is hardly more than a categoric grouping of families, there being little or no interfamilial symbiosis. Occasions of such extreme simplicity are rather infrequent. Some degree of specialization of function which is available to the entire population usually occurs in the independent community. But specialization tends to develop as among families rather than individuals. That is, a few familial units may carry on, in addition to the typical round of domestic activities, special functions for the entire communal aggregate, such as trading, fishing, blacksmithing, housebuilding, etc. Seldom does a familial unit derive all its sustenance from a special function. So complete a reliance on specialization occurs only in the very large community. For the most part, the independent community is incapable of supporting a sufficient number of persons to maintain full-time specialists. It is for this reason, too, that associational corporate units are rarely found in such a community.

The familial unit in most instances is consanguineous in organization; that is, it includes only blood relatives or their equivalents, and

---

[20] J. L. Steward, *Basin-Plateau Aboriginal Sociopolitical Groups*. Smithsonian Institution, Bureau of American Ethnology Bulletin 120 (Washington, D.C., 1938).

excludes marriage partners. This sort of unit continues without interruption through the generations. The individual is always identified with a particular family, there being no opportunity to escape into another. Thus the consanguineous family is a compact and durable unit. It is an effective, if not the most efficient, way of maintaining the discipline required to deal with a precarious life situation.

Age and sex are the principal and almost the exclusive bases of categoric groupings in the independent community. Age and sex distinctions, of course, denote occupational distinctions: virtually every occupation is identified with an age grade and with a sex category. A few functions may be selective within a sex-age group, notably that of the warrior, but in most instances each sex-age group is occupationally homogeneous. In many independent communities miscellaneous categoric groupings appear particularly among the adult males, such as secret societies of one sort or another. These, however, are restricted to age grades usually and are in most instances based upon occupational distinctions.

Where the main source of sustenance is in the extraction of materials from the land, as is universally true of the independent community, dominance tends to be concentrated in the units directly engaged in extractive industry. In communities in which hunting or the grazing of animals is the basic industry there is seldom a significant differentiation among familial units.[21] Such as there is arises as between an administrative or ruling family and all other families. The adult males of ruling families are presumably expert hunters, warriors, or herdsmen who can therefore give counsel and direction to mass endeavors. The important differentiation exists within the familial unit. There the adult male performs the coordinating and directing function, though among some peoples this functional position is held only by the old man of the household. Dominance tends to be diffused among the heads of family units who generally consolidate and protect their positions through the formation of a categoric unit.

But in the settled agricultural community, which is the most common type of independent community, family differentiation is often pronounced. Apart from the farm families there may be artisan families of various specializations who are either landless or who work small holdings when not engaged in their special functions. Under such conditions dominance resides with the farm families, for the maintenance of the community is contingent upon their activities. Whatever surplus wealth is available for the support of the services of the

[21] Exceptions occur in very large pastoral communities such as the Torguts as described by W. L. River, *The Torgut* (New York, 1939).

artisans is produced by the agriculturalists. The latter, moreover, are capable of relatively greater self-sufficiency. Hence the specialized functions tend to be ancillary and subsidiary to the agricultural function. In the medieval village community the cotters, as the artisan families were known, occupied as a group an inferior functional position, though there were also gradations within the cotter class. Since their functions were of incidental importance, they had very little influence on collective affairs.

The gradient of influence not only runs vertically through the several functions, but also horizontally within a functional category. Within the farm family class dominance is associated with the size of the farm. The larger the farm holding, the stronger is the sustenance position of the family, and the greater is its influence on the amount of sustenance available to the community as a whole. In fact, in the agricultural village community, the amount of land in the possession of the family enters into the dominance position of every unit including the artisan families. The extent to which a family relies on the "sale" of nonagricultural services varies inversely with the size of its land holding. At the bottom of the dominance hierarchy are the landless who are utterly dependent on exchange of services for sustenance materials.

The structure of the independent community, then, may be described as a collection of slightly differentiated corporate units threaded through with a small number of biologically identified categoric units. Because of the very moderate specialization, there is but a nominal centralization of control. Control rather is held diffusely by the head of each familial unit.

The Dependent Community.—The dependent community, by definition, is not self-sufficient. It obtains its sustenance materials through exchange with other communities. What it has to offer in exchange is usually gained through intensive specialization in extractive, manufacturing, or service industry. Isolation is obviously contrary to the requisites for exchange; as the latter increases, the former must be reduced. Dependence exposes the community to the effects of events that occur anywhere within the scope of intercommunity relations. The probability that change will occur is therefore vastly greater than in the independent community. This is evident in the diffusion and change of techniques that takes place in dependent communities. The limitations of local population size tend to be eliminated, for numbers in the local population are complemented by numbers in other communities with which relations are established. Technological change, however, permits population increase which in turn makes possible further elaboration of technology. The size of the dependent community may range between wide extremes and the complexity of structure may likewise vary extensively. In general, the characteristics of the dependent community are opposite to those of the independent community. That, of course, is attributable to the assumption of a continuum upon which the classification is based.

The structure of the dependent community is built of a large number and diversity of corporate units. So great is the impetus to specialization that virtually every specific function seems inclined to appear in a separate corporate unit. Familial units, though present in even larger numbers than in the independent community, are complemented by numerous associational units. The dependent community seems to require a different organization of the familial unit from that found in the independent community. The limitations of size and resources and the informal mode of functioning of the consanguineous family disqualify it for extensive possession of the producing role in a context of intricate interdependence. A household group could hardly supply the peculiar personnel requirements of highly specialized functions, assemble huge volumes of operating capital, carry on numerous exchanges within a large and heterogeneous population, or maintain extensive intercommunity relations. Hence where the producing function imposes such responsibilities the associational unit tends to displace the familial unit in production, and a smaller and more flexible family organization is appropriate. The conjugal type of family is adapted to a more restricted function and also to the dynamics of community change and development. Its small size and reformation in each generation give it a high degree of mobility both spatially and in accommodating to changes in requirements imposed upon the family from without.

Although the producing function of the conjugal family is much reduced as compared with the consanguineous family, it is by no means negligible. The family in the dependent community retains a large part of the responsibility for the nurturing of progeny, though to be sure that service is shared with a number of associational units. The family also carries on a number of important supporting services to its members. It maintains a residence unit, performs the final step in the preparation of food for consumption, repairs and launders clothing, provides a variety of opportunities for recreation, and administers many community rules and regulations. From the standpoint of the community the family may be regarded as having two general functions. It fosters conditions which favor the orderly and productive behavior of individuals, and, secondly, it serves as an agency for the final step in the distribution of consumer goods to individuals.

Associational units range from small and simple organizations such as represented by the division of labor in a neighborhood church or corner grocery store to gigantic corporate enterprises employing hundreds of thousands of workers. Their functions and degree of specialization vary over a comparable range. The general store, or its more sophisticated form as a drug store, contrasts sharply with the establishment that manufactures a tool to make a tool that turns out a single part for an automobile, or locomotive, or steam ship. All the functions of associational units were formerly, in principle at least, functions of familial units. The usurpation has progressed far. Along with the more familiar functions of manufacturing, distribution, education, religion, government, etc., associational units have assumed many intimate functions of the family. The care of the aged, the dependent, and the infirm, the resolution of domestic strife, the disciplining of children, and many another such activity has emerged as a function of one or more extra-familial unit.

It is impossible at present to state in simple terms a generalized pattern in which corporate units arrange themselves. Their number and their interrelations are too many for any such attempt to be more than an arbitrary suggestion. A brief description of the array of units in a moderate-sized community will have to serve our purpose at the moment.

A dependent community in the United States today, having about 20,000 people and including a central city of 10,000 population, contains approximately 5,500 familial units. These are served by roughly 430 retail and personal service units which supply materials and assistance ranging from food and clothing to shoe-shining and the performance of household chores. Domestic functions are also complemented by some 7 to 10 schools, 20 to 30 churches, 1 or 2 newspapers, 3 or 4 banks, a dozen or more medical and legal services. A large part of the income upon which these many units subsist is derived from 15 to 20 manufacturing units and 2,000 farm units. Superimposed upon these units are 20 or more local government units, some of which provide up to 30 distinct services. Nor do these 6,000-odd corporate units comprise the full range of symbiosis. For while they may provide all the day to day requirements of the communal aggregate, they do so through many and devious connections with units located elsewhere.

Let us assume that the principal producing function of this community is the manufacture of farm machinery. The manufacturing establishment, which is either partly or wholly owned by a concern located in another state, obtains its machine tools from a neighboring community and its steel and other materials from processing establishments scattered widely over the country. A railroad, the operations of which are governed from offices situated in a distant metropolis, transports the materials; State and Federal governments prevent interference with the shipments; and the local government protects the materials and the plant in which they are fabricated from theft or damage. The organization of workers in the local manufacturing establishment, dependent for its productivity upon the uninterrupted functioning of the entire community, assembles the materials into finished products which are then transported, again under government protection, to wholesalers in scores of cities in agricultural regions. With the aid of credit, advertising, and local transportation agencies wholesalers redistribute the products once more to hundreds of retailers and thence the products finally reach the farm units. The income to the community in which the farm equipment is manufactured is used to import hundreds of commodities produced elsewhere and to facilitate intramural exchanges of services. The Federal government supplies a dependable medium of exchange which permits raw material producers, manufacturer, railroads, wholesalers, retailers, local service units, and the ultimate consumer to act in an organized manner without being under a single administrative authority. Government also enforces contracts so that at each step in the sequence of exchanges there is assurance of continuity of relationship.[22]

Running through the welter of corporate units are numerous categoric units. As in the independent community, age and sex categories are present as operating units; they are, however, relatively unimportant. The occupational differentiation within each such category tends to be so great that characteristics of these categories have little or no value as means of identifying specific functions. Occupation itself, rather than a secondary trait, is the main basis of grouping. The potential number of categoric units based directly upon occupations may be counted in the thousands.[23] But whatever may be the limits of possibility, the number of actual categoric units is usually much less.

---

[22] This illustration is adapted from National Resources Committee, *The Structure of the American Economy, Part I, Basic Characteristics* (Washington, D. C., 1939), 96.

[23] The *Alphabetical Index of Occupations,* of the United States Bureau of the Census, lists approximately twenty-five thousand different occupational designations. These include many duplications. The number of occupations for many purposes is reduced to 207, and these are further grouped in nine so-called social-economic categories, viz., professional; proprietor, manager and official; farm owners and operators; clerical; skilled; semiskilled; farm laborers; domestic servants; other laborers.

Still, conditions in the dependent community favor the emergence of categoric units to an extent not realized in the independent community. Continuous movement and change sooner or later produce threats of varying seriousness to all occupational divisions. In any event, the number of categoric units based on occupation is sufficiently great to make their listing difficult.

There are, moreover, myriads of categoric groupings that are but indirectly connected with occupational divisions, many of which seem to have no occupational connection whatever. The heterogeneity of the population, the high degree of mobility, and the diversity of meetings and exchanges provide opportunity for almost any conceivable type of common interest grouping. Surveys have indicated that the frequency of units of this sort may range from one for every 165 adult members of the population in small villages [24] to one per 48 of the adult population in an urban community of about 20,000.[25] These are crude figures, however, for they include some units that are corporate in form. Nevertheless, they suggest something of the extent to which the grouping tendency operates.[26]

It is commonly assumed that government occupies the dominant position. Government holds the police power through which it exercises many regulatory functions. Yet its dominance is not without qualification. The domain of local government is circumscribed by narrowly drawn boundaries which in a dependent community is a serious limitation on its power. Furthermore, government, especially in the United States, plays a passive part in the sustenance flow to the community. In effect government shares and is in competition for the dominant position with associational units whose functions enable them to exert a decisive influence on the community's sustenance supply.[27] Unrestrained by the bounds of local government, business and industrial units may exercise control over the sustenance process long before it reaches the particular community. Their power derives largely from the fact that they are the mediators of the community's external relations. The segmentation of local governments is a curious anomaly in a context of manifold and intimate intercommunity

[24] Edmund de S. Brunner and J. H. Kolb, *Rural Social Trends* (New York, 1933), 102, 244.

[25] Frederick A. Bushee, "Social Organizations in a Small City," *American Journal of Sociology,* II (November, 1945), 217.

[26] Mirra Komarovsky has demonstrated that membership in voluntary associations, i.e., categoric units, varies directly with occupation and income. "The Voluntary Associations of Urban Dwellers," *American Sociological Review,* XI (December, 1946), 686-98.

[27] This competition is analyzed, though as it concerns the Federal government, in an interesting essay by Walton Hamilton, *The Pattern of Competition* (New York, 1940), 53-82.

exchange relations. How powerful associational units may exploit that situation to subvert the authority of local governments is too well known to require discussion here.

The position of co-dominant may be occupied by units with different specific functions in different communities. Where the community derives the major part of its livelihood from the extraction of minerals the mining company tends to be the government's competitor for control of the community. By varying the tempo of its operations the mining company may affect activities in every phase of collective life. It also exercises a commanding influence through hiring policies, wage payments, property ownership, and in some instances by participation in politics and direct pressures on other units. Likewise, in communities that rely primarily on manufacturing, the manufacturing unit or units occupy the strategic position. Or in communities that specialize in distribution and marketing, commercial units are dominant.[28] That such units may be controlled by financial agencies or central offices situated in other communities in no way minimizes their influence in the communities of their location. Specialization in the local economy concentrates dominance in one or a few units. But what control might conceivably be lost in diversification is often salvaged through the creation of categoric groupings of business units. The Chamber of Commerce or the manufacturer's association may prove just as effective a co-dominant as a single unit.

Whereas dominant units in the dependent community acquire their power largely from their control over intercommunity relations, units that are engaged mainly in serving the day to day needs of the resident population occupy subdominant positions. Retail and personal service establishments, recreational units, churches, schools, etc., have relatively little influence over the major source of sustenance of the community, and of these the nonpecuniary service units doubtless have the least influence. The individual familial unit stands lowest in the scale of dominance. With few exceptions, the family exerts a very minute control over employment opportunity and income received, over the commodities and services available for its purchase, and over the processes of government. The training its children receive is removed from the family's control. Even the religious services it receives are adapted to the generalized requirement of an aggregate of families.

---

[28] Paul Landis, in his *Three Iron Mining Towns* (Ann Arbor, 1938), describes the shifting of control from mining corporations to local business as the iron resources approached depletion.

Although the individual family's ability to affect the conditions essential to the operation of other units in the community is limited, a combination of families is capable of tremendous influence. Categoric units involving entire families may appear as various kinds of pressure groups, as for example the neighborhood association for the protection of property. Perhaps the most generally discussed categoric grouping of familial units, and in some respects one of the most indefinite, is the so-called social class.

A social class is normally composed of families whose heads hold similar functional positions in the community. The income and other amenities obtained from that occupation or occupations measure its attractiveness and place its representatives on a scale of respect or prestige. The function of the social class seems to be to secure an occupational position for a restricted group. One set of devices by which this may be accomplished includes father to son transmission of functions and prohibition or at least a control of intermarriages. Thus the family lends itself conveniently to the protection of position in the community. The social inheritance of occupations and the restriction of intermarriage are prime evidences of social class, and the rigor with which those customs are practiced indicates the extent to which classes have been formalized.

Similarity of occupation is not an entirely sufficient evidence of functional uniformity. Within a given occupational division there are among the members differences of degree of establishment, of success, and of participation in the occupation. These variations are measured, roughly at least, by education and income which therefore serve as additional bases of class formation. Where classes are most highly formalized there is usually homogeneity in all evidences of functional position. That is, the members of each class have the same occupation, income, and kind of training or educational attainment. Conversely, where evidences of functional position are not coordinate, such that individuals engaged in the same occupation have different incomes and different education, classes are probably either nonexistent or incipient. Apparently it is for this reason that classes in a large American community are very indistinct, if indeed they are present at all.

The scope of the social class may be confined to a single occupational category, as represented by the subcastes of India, or it may comprise two or more occupational divisions, such as found in most parts of the Western world. Apparently the wider scope results from extreme differentiation and the fact that the similarities among certain functions are more important than their differences. The many professional occupations, for example, have similar rewards, similar requirements for admission, and similar conditions of work. It is likewise with proprietary, skilled, and unskilled occupations. Each such broad occupational group may therefore constitute a social class.

Summary.—In view of man's inescapable dependence on his fellows it appears that the effective unit of the community is not the individual but some combination of individuals. The combinations that constitute effective communal units develop from two prevalent types of relationships: symbiosis and commensalism. Communal units based on the symbiotic relationship are called corporate units; those based on the commensalistic relationship are identified as categoric units. The corporate unit, by virtue of its organization, performs a producing function. The categoric unit, on the other hand, is capable of serving only the function of protection or conservation. Several types of corporate units are distinguishable, namely, the familial, associational, and territorial. The principal categoric units are occupational in character, though the same principle of organization gives rise to cliques, clubs, and common interest associations of many types. Symbiosis and commensalism, however, may appear in the same grouping on different occasions. Thus the corporate unit may function, particularly when its unity is threatened, as a categoric unit. And the categoric unit may develop a corps of specialists—a symbiotic nucleus within the mass of commensals. In fact, what have been described as groupings or units might more appropriately be regarded as patterns of relationships. Subsequent research will probably provide a basis for resolving that uncertainty.

Symbiosis and commensalism occur as between units as well as between individuals. Corporate units, as a consequence of their specialization, are symbiotically related to one another. Furthermore, corporate units of the same type often form categoric combinations. Categoric units, particularly those based on occupations, are symbionts in a division of labor. They likewise may coalesce in larger categoric combinations. An important aspect of interunit relationship is that of dominance. Inequality of function differentiates the power exercised by each unit which, together with the necessity for coordination, is responsible for the emergence of a dominant unit. The function of dominance is usually exercised by the unit that controls the conditions necessary to the activities of other units. Categoric groupings of units tend to enhance or preserve a dominant position.

Communities may be classified as independent or dependent, in accordance with the extent of their self-sufficiency. The independent community is highly self-sufficient, isolated, small in population, and possessed of a simple technology.   It has few units of either type.   The familial corporate unit is most prevalent and is usually consanguine-ous.   Age and sex are the principal bases of categoric units.   Since the differentiation of units is slight, there is relatively little centralization of control : control is diffused more or less equally among family heads.   The dependent community is involved in a network of intercommu-nity exchange relations, may have a very large population, and exists where technology is rather far advanced.   Its organization comprises a large number of diverse corporate and categoric units.   The cen-tralization of control is pronounced, though it tends to be shared by government, which holds the police power, and by those other asso-ciational corporate units which regulate the flow of sustenance into the community.   Rivalry for dominance arises from categoric com-binations of lesser corporate units, e.g., the social class.

SUPPLEMENTARY REFERENCES

ANDERSON, ELIN L. *We Americans: A Study of Cleavage in an American City.* Cambridge: Harvard University Press, 1937.
ANGELL, R. C. *The Integration of American Society.* New York: McGraw-Hill Book Co., 1941.
MACIVER, ROBERT M. *Community.* New York: The Macmillan Co., 1920.
PARK, ROBERT E. "Symbiosis and Socialization: A Frame of Reference for the Study of Society," *American Journal of Sociology,* XLV (July, 1939), 1-25.
REDFIELD, R. (ed.). *Levels of Integration in Biological and Social Systems. Biologi-cal Symposia,* VIII. Lancaster, Pa.: Jaques Cattell Press, 1942.
ROBINSON, E. A. G. *The Structure of Competitive Industry.* London: Cambridge University Press, 1931.

Chapter 13

SPATIAL ASPECT OF ECOLOGICAL ORGANIZATION

The Settlement Pattern.—If we were in a position to take an over-all view of human settlement, we should doubtless be impressed by its uneven distribution. The most striking feature probably would be the clusters of population with sparsely settled interstitial areas. The size of these clusters, ranging from tiny groupings to huge agglomerations, would be seen to vary in different parts of the world. In some sections small groupings would predominate while in others, large concentrations would be proportionately more numerous. Where small clusters prevail their spacing is fairly uniform but where large groupings predominate there is a marked irregularity in pattern. For, gathered about the large concentrations, like satellites hovering about a planet, are numerous smaller groupings, their distance from the principal agglomeration seeming to vary inversely with their size. The number and variety of these satellites also appear to bear a close relation to size of the main center.

Continuing the aerial view, we note that the many settlement clusters appear to be enmeshed in a network of roadways. The larger the settlement the more numerous are its ties with other settlements and the thicker is the web of linkages about it. Some of the routes of travel, being wider and further extended, are obviously more important than others. These reach out from major agglomerations linking together in radial chains the lesser satellite clusters. Branch routes reach into the interstitial areas between radiating thoroughfares, becoming more numerous as we approach the larger settlements.

Thus we discern that the pattern of human settlement in its spatial arrangement resembles that of the wheel, or rather a series of wheels, with the essential features of center, spokes, and rims. Villages, towns, and cities are centers from which radiate like spokes the transportation routes. These, terminating more or less abruptly, give the pattern the circular aspect of a rim. The sharpness with which the outer margins of the pattern are defined varies in different parts of the world. In the Western world, where the physical evidences of settlement decrease gradually with distance from a center, the marginal lines or rims are rendered indistinct by the multiplicity of roads and highways. Each center is set as a bit of mosaic in the all-inclusive network of routes. But in other parts of the world the peripheries of settlement units stand out sharply. Human settlement, then, may be compared to a great system of wheels of varying sizes, some of which are almost completely detached from one another while others overlap or impinge upon one another.

The geometrical impression gained from so general an overview of settlement is confirmed when individual agglomerations are examined in detail. Human populations everywhere organize their respective territories in a pattern similar to that described. There are, however, important variations which must be noted. If the land surface were perfectly uniform in its physical and productive features, we might expect local settlement patterns to assume a regular or symmetrical form. The rims enclosing areas would probably not be circular, for an area cannot be entirely encompassed in a series of circles without numerous overlappings. Instead of a circle, therefore, we might expect the individual patterns to appear as hexagons or octagons.[1] But the actual patterns of settlement seldom, if ever, acquire such a neat geometric aspect. Land is neither uniform in surface features nor in productive capacity. Topographic features—mountains, streams, swamps—interrupt and indent the outer rim in many places. Routes of travel must be bent and shaped to the lines of least resistance. And centers are rarely true geometrical centers; they are pulled to one side or another by various influences. Asymmetry seems to be a much more normal characteristic of spatial arrangement than does symmetry. Nevertheless, granting this qualification, the tendency for human settlement to approximate the pattern described is well marked in all instances.

We are less concerned, however, with the distribution of settlement as such than with the spatial pattern of the activities that make up a community. At best the settlement distribution offers a very rough approximation of the organization and land uses. While occupancy of an area is indicative of use or of activity carried on there, and the existence of a road is evidence of communication between two connected points, observations of this character do not reveal the kind of activity nor the type of interdependence that may be present. Many uses of land do not require continuous occupancy. The farm family, for example, resides on a small portion of its land, though the family's activities are distributed over the whole area under its control. Likewise a hunting or pastoral people may occupy any given portion of its

---

[1] Cf. August Lösch, "The Nature of Economic Regions," *The Southern Economic Journal,* V (July, 1938), 71-78.

territory for but a few months of each year. Variations in the density of population in a large city are suggestive but fail to describe adequately the diversity and interdependence of the activities in which the population is engaged. A knowledge of the spatial pattern of collective life requires a much more intensive study than merely tracing the outlines of settlement.

Factors in the Spatial Distribution of Functions.—Why do human activities assume an orderly arrangement in space, and why, in particular, do they tend to arrange themselves about given points? The answer is to be found in the operation of certain fundamental life conditions. These are three in number and may be described as (1) the interdependence among men, (2) the dependence of activities or functions upon various characteristics of land, and (3) the friction of space. The first two account for the tendency for a pattern to develop, while the third affects the size and specific shape the pattern assumes. No one of these factors is independent of the other two. They may be treated separately only for purposes of exposition and analysis.

The interdependence among men and the dependence of human activities upon land are mutually opposed and also mutually determining influences. The one exercises an attractive force and leads to concentration of settlement, while the other exerts a dispersive influence and is in part responsible for the distribution of men and their activities. Interdependence requires that individuals and community units have access to one another and hence that they be in relatively close proximity. When exchanges carried on among related units are frequent and vital in character proximity is more essential. Persons who depend on one another for certain daily services must be closer together than those who exchange services less frequently. On the other hand, each activity has certain requirements with regard to the kind and amount of space it occupies. Administrative functions must have a central location but require a comparatively small amount of space. Manufacturing is often restricted in its selection of sites by the availability of raw materials, power resources, opportunities for transport, and other conditions inherent in the land. Agriculture, though it benefits by a central location, uses large quantities of land and consequently is usually found in a peripheral location. Its dependence upon certain types of soil further restricts its choice of site. Thus, while interdependence necessitates proximity, that proximity is qualified and limited by the diverse use values of land.

It hardly needs to be argued that interdependence among men cannot spread uniformly over an indefinite area. We observed previously that settlement is invariably nucleated, i.e., gathered closely about certain points in space. This typical formation is only partially explained by the elementary attractive and dispersive factors. They do not help us to account for variations in the size of agglomerations nor for the particular pattern of distribution of activities found in a given locality. We must look to the third factor, the friction of space, for an understanding of the spatial organization of the human community.

Human relationships, occurring as they do in a physical universe, involve the overcoming of a number of resistances which are generalized in the phrase *friction of space*.[2] Space itself is something to be passed over and thus it calls for an expenditure of time and energy. Mountains, streams, air currents, and even man-made structures may either increase or decrease the expenditure required, i.e., the friction, depending upon how these happen to be disposed with respect to a line of travel. In other words, the friction of space is small or great as distance is short or long and in the degree to which physical obstacles are present.

Since friction is always encountered in connection with a given mode of transportation or communication, it is subject to reduction —though it can never be completely eliminated—by improvements in the facilities for movement. Hence the efficiency of transportation and communication devices is a measure of the friction existing at any one time. That is to say, the resistances to contact are directly experienced, not in terms of linear distance or physical obstruction, but in units of time and energy or cost involved in moving from place to place. By this measure the distance from A to B may be greater than from B to A, provided B is upgrade from A. The distance between the two points is farther by one mode of movement than by another, say walking as compared to horseback, or the use of a horse and wagon instead of an automobile. Distance, so far as it enters into human relationships, is thus entirely relative to the available techniques for overcoming the friction of space.

The territorial pattern of collective life is largely a result of the friction of space as manifested in time-cost distance. The proximity which interdependence requires varies under different conditions of movement. Improvements in transportation and communication reflected in reductions of the time and cost components permit a wider scatter of an interrelated population without loss of contact. Similarly, the diversity of function within an area is affected by resistance

2 Robert M. Haig, *Regional Survey of New York and Its Environs* (New York, 1927), Vol. I, 21.

to movement. When the ratio of time and cost expenditure per mile of travel is great the area accessible from any one point is small and hence limited both in its variety of use potentialities and in the number of individuals it will support. Differentiation of function and increase of population are, therefore, necessarily restricted. But when the friction of space is overcome by improved systems of transportation and communication then and then only can an area develop fully its various use potentialities as well as the larger population needed to man the more complex economy.

In a very real sense, as Professor Park has said, the world within which man lives is defined less by the horizon of his geographical knowledge than by the limits imposed by his means of transportation and communication.[3] The community area is carved out of the regional territory by man's facilities for movement.

The Community Center.—The focal point in the territorial organization of the community is its center, for it is there that interdependences are integrated and administered. The center is thus a most valuable key to an understanding of the spatial patterning of collective life. If the origin of centers could be fully known, a long step would be made toward understanding the nature and development of communities. Unfortunately their origins antedate most human records and, as Sumner declared, are "lost in mystery." It may be as Baden-Powell[4] and others have suggested that a nuclear point or center first appeared as a family seat which extended its influence through the centrifugal movement and settlement of successive generations. In other instances, segmentation of a local group and the relocation of one of the parts in another area seem to have marked the beginning of a new center of activities. Or the periodic convergence of two or more groups at a site favorable to exchange may, after repeated occurences, have given rise to an enlarged fabric of relationships permanently oriented toward that point. But whatever the historic background, whether the origins of particular centers was by expansion, fission, or convergence, the basic factor which explains the nucleation of human activities is in all cases the same—the dependence of man upon his fellows.

The question of the origin of permanent centers persists, however, though in a different form. It has become a problem of site selection.

---

[3] R. E. Park, "Social Aggregation," in *Readings in Human Ecology,* ed. R. D. McKenzie (Ann Arbor, 1934), 81.
[4] H. Baden-Powell, *The Origin and Growth of Village Communities in India* (London, 1899), 292 ff.; D. W. Ross, *Early History of Land Holding among the Germans* (Boston, 1883), 27.

Why does the nucleus in the territorial pattern of settlement select a certain point rather than another? Are the sites of centers of different kinds of communities determined by a common set of factors? In seeking answers to these questions it will be helpful to begin with the independent type of community.

As long as men were nomadic they traveled in compact bands, carrying their communities with them. The center of the nomadic community was in evidence only on overnight or seasonal stopovers and then was marked by the tent of the chieftain in whose activities were integrated the affairs of the group. Under such conditions the center of the independent community was a functionary more than it was a place. Even so nomadic groups show a definite place orientation. Such groups are usually found in possession of clearly delimited territories over which they circulate in routine orbitlike fashion. Some peoples, for example the contemporary Andaman Islanders and the Negrittos of the Congo, have two or more villages of rather permanent construction which they occupy in different seasons of the year. In general, the use of a nomadic people's territory tends to be organized with reference to a number of established camping sites which are determined primarily by the distribution of natural resources. A collecting people seeks places where fruits, tuberous roots, and small rodents are abundant, hunters gravitate toward breeding grounds of game animals, while pastoral peoples are to be found in grasslands where food for their herds is available. In all instances the water supply is a factor of prime significance and fixes more precisely the site of settlement within the general area of available foods.

With the settling down of man to a sedentary mode of life centers began to come more into evidence. The village settlement was a fixed point, yet it was more than an assemblage of people and dwelling units. It became the nucleus of an organization of territory. The lands of the local area were gradually differentiated into various use zones, such as croplands, pasturelands, and perhaps woodlands, with the village itself representing a specialized residential use of the land. The settled independent community, in other words, comprised an area of diversified uses which were organized and administered from a centrally located village. It is noteworthy that this pattern of permanent settlement prevailed until late in the nineteenth century. Only in a few places, of which Norway[5] and North America under European occupancy are outstanding examples, was the land settled by scattered family units.

---

[5] Jean Brunhes, *La Geographie Humaine*, 3d. ed. (Paris, 1925), Vol. I, 164-68.

The pull of natural resources is manifested in the location of permanent as well as of temporary centers. In times past, as well as in most of the older parts of the world today, soil fertility was the decisive factor in the determination of the village site. The development of agriculture seems to have been largely responsible for the transition to a sedentary existence. Within an area of fruitful soil, of course, other factors operate to influence the selection of sites, such as adequacy of water supply, availability of minerals used in the manufacture of tools, and opportunities for defense from hostile neighbors and predatory animals. On occasion, one or more of these secondary influences took precedence over soil fertility. In arid regions, as in southwestern Asia, choice of a village site was controlled by the location of a spring or well. Likewise the need for protection from enemies has driven peoples to establish their residences upon rocks accessible only by ladders, in caves carved high on the faces of cliffs, and in other places far removed from their cultivated fields. But these should be regarded as expedient deviations from the general tendency. Another deviating factor, which should not be overlooked, is the element of chance, or rather miscalculation arising from deficiencies of knowledge.

Local self-sufficiency is the circumstance responsible for the controlling influence of geographic conditions. Early or preliterate man is not alone in his subordination to the physical environment. In China, India, medieval Europe, and other areas of civilized habitation the greater parts of the respective populations are found distributed in numerous small settlements which in turn are arranged in patterns dictated by the distribution of natural resources, especially arable land. Sometimes, as in Colonial America, the location of a salt deposit or of a waterfall, which could be used as a source of power for a grist mill, became the site of a community center. Only as self-sufficiency breaks down before the development of interdependence is the direct influence of local geographic factors significantly minimized. But even then, as we shall later have cause to show, the attractive power of physical features of the landscape remains strong.

The rise of a dependent community significantly alters the character of the center. Whereas under conditions of compact village settlement the center is simply the nuclear point in an organization of land uses, it becomes, in addition, the point of integration of the diverse functions of a more or less widely distributed population. Instead of individuals moving out each day from a centralized residence area to exploit the varied uses of lands round about, they converge upon the center from scattered outlying settlements to exchange the fruits of their many specialized activities. Residential centralization and a dispersion of functions are replaced by dispersed settlement and functional specialization. There is, of course, an accumulation of population and of settlement structures at the center; in fact, centers based upon territorial interdependence may and do grow to such giant size as to dwarf the self-sufficient community's village. But the center in this instance is a dependent unit. Its residents are a service population occupied with mediating interrelationships and with providing numerous supplemental services for the population passing through the center. The growth of the center is a measure, though a crude one, of the complexity and scope of the division of labor.

Until interdependence among spatially separated populations is well developed, however, the center as described is conspicuous neither for its function nor its size. A rudimentary division of labor usually operates with a measured periodicity, scattered population groups coming together at intervals to trade and carry on other transactions. In the interim periods interrelations are often mediated solely through itinerant merchants and craftsmen. Hence, the center exists intermittently as such, and the permanent population and physical structure concentrated there are seldom great. This was true of most of the numerous fairs of medieval Europe, many of which convened weekly, though others fortnightly, seasonally, and even annually. A village, a castle, or a church, but little more, marked the site. Similarly in Spanish Morocco many of the tribal markets are centrally located places without permanent structures of any kind. On market days they are teeming with life; on other days they are barren. Towns are known to have arisen at such places, though that has been a rare occurrence.[6]

A full expression of centralization appears only as points of periodic congregation come into continuous use as places of mediating and integrating specialized activities. Thus, as J. W. Thompson holds in his "mercatorial theory," the settling down of traders to fixed residences and shops signalized the beginnings of towns [7] or, in our terms,

---

[6] Walter Fogg, "Villages, Tribal Markets, and Towns: Some Considerations Concerning Urban Development in the Spanish and International Zones of Morocco," *Sociological Review*, XXXII (1940), 85-107.

[7] *Economic and Social History of the Middle Ages (300-1300)* (New York, 1928), 775-77. See also H. Pirenne, *Medieval Cities* (Princeton, 1925), 139 ff., and F. L. Nussbaum, *A History of the Economic Institutions of Modern Europe* (New York, 1933), 40.

Thompson thinks of the accumulation of merchants at a given point as significant not only because it gave such a place a nuclear role in the affairs of the region but also, and, in fact, primarily, because it was responsible for the growth of civil institutions and civil authority. The increasing power of the merchant class enabled them to challenge successfully the established feudal and ecclesiastical authorities. When political power eventually passed to the merchants, according to Thompson, a true municipal life emerged.

of centers which were more than mere settlement clusters or cyclical market places. The interdependences obtaining within a region and between regions were thereby brought to focus upon a specific site or sites. Such a development presupposed a population within access of the strategic location which was both sufficiently large and implicated in the division of labor to maintain a corps of service functionaries in the continuous practice of their specialties at a given location. In the absence of mechanical means of communication and transportation this also required a region well endowed with natural facilities for movement. The excellent drainage systems of Europe favored comparatively easy access to widely separated points in the continental interior.

Just as the growth of the dependent community involves an increasing concentration of population in nonagricultural pursuits, the development of permanent centralization entails a detachment and withdrawal from the land. The functions of exchange and mediation of interrelations make no demands on the land other than for space at convenient locations. Manufacturing tends likewise to be pulled to strategic transportation locations where the greatest access to the supplies of different raw materials and to markets may be had.[8] Hence natural resource sites lose much of their former value and centers are pulled toward locations of maximum accessibility. A situation on a well-traveled roadway proves to be superior to one removed from avenues of freest movement. Better still is a point of convergence of two or more thoroughfares, particularly when both land and water routes are included, for then a wider area of settlement is open to the influence of the center. Both the integration of local activities and the inclusion of the local population in an interregional division of labor are favored by a site at a route intersection.

The growth of centers at the intersections of routes is further stimulated, as Charles H. Cooley indicated in his "Theory of Transportation,"[9] by the tendency for population and wealth to collect at breaks or interruptions in routes of transportation. The interruption may be mechanical in that it is effected by a junction of routes, particularly different kinds of routes, or it may be a commercial break resulting from a change of ownership of materials in transit. In either

---

[8] There are important differences among manufacturing establishments in this respect. Plants engaged in preliminary processing of materials are usually close to the sources of material supply, while those involved in later stages of the manufacturing sequence are located closer to market centers. (See E. M. Hoover, *The Location of Economic Activity* [New York, 1948], chap. iii.)

[9] In *Sociological Theory and Social Research*, ed. R. C. Angell (New York, 1930), 75-83.

case, freight must be unloaded from one carrier and placed aboard another, and often it must be stored until a second carrier is ready or until an exchange is completed. Terminal facilities therefore must be made available in the form of wharves and docks, storage buildings, sheds for sheltering and repairing vehicles, and office space for administrative staffs. There must also be an accumulation of workers to handle cargoes, to protect and service buildings and carriers, and to carry on supervisory functions. The presence of this group calls for a large complement of craftsmen, merchants, and professional people to attend to the variety of human needs represented. The accretion of personnel and physical structure at the point of interruption is cumulative; each new addition or elaboration entails others and ultimately a large and complexly organized settlement unit takes form. Although the tendency on the part of Cooley and many of his followers to view an interruption of transportation as the essential cause of the origin and growth of centers in the modern period is an unfortunate oversimplification, there are many instances in which its influence undoubtedly has been important. The numerous port cities of the world, situated at the junctures of land and water routes, are cases in point. Likewise, Chicago sprang up on Lake Michigan at the mouth of a river link with the Mississippi Valley and on a major East-West axis of overland travel; the centrifugal swirl of waters in a great bend of the Ohio River afforded an easy landing place for down-river traffic, giving rise to what is now Cincinnati; and Des Moines, Columbus, and other centers have flourished at the intersections of railroad routes.[10] In all such examples, however, the point of convergence of routes has the additional significance of being the most accessible point for the conduct of the collective activities of the regional population.

Such is the advantage offered by a convergence of routes that a center may be established there despite formidable geographic obstacles. Not a few of the world's major centers occupy swamp lands, of which Leningrad, New Orleans, and Washington, D. C., are noteworthy examples. Venice and New York sprawl over clusters of islands which are linked together by costly bridges and tunnels. Still other centers are situated tortuously on narrow peninsulas, on plains exposed to periodic inundation by flood waters, where topography is too rugged for intramural traffic without extensive grading and leveling, or in the paths of recurring hurricanes. The most outstanding

---

[10] Cf. R. H. Whitbeck, *Urban Land Economics,* Institute for Research in Land Economics (Chicago, 1927), 90-98.

examples of man's willingness to cope with major physical inconveniences are found at the water's edge. From time immemorial watercourses have provided the lines of easiest movement and therefore have exercised a powerful attraction on human settlement. It is only in the modern period that landlocked centers of any importance have appeared, and these are relatively few in number.

The strategic advantages of a situation at the intersection of routes is shown in the persistence through the centuries of numerous towns and cities so located. Many have histories of continuous habitation reaching back thousands of years. Some antedate historic record, their origins being explained in mythology as in the case of Rome. The physical structures on these sites may have been rebuilt countless times after destruction by war, fire, or flood. The human occupants have also changed from time to time, one group being displaced by another. The great cities of the ancient world are with few exceptions important cities today.

This is not to say, of course, that once a center is established it is a permanent and immutable fixture thereafter. The rise and fall of centers is a familiar phenomenon to students of history. Changes in route patterns, whatever may be their cause, alter the advantages offered by existing locations, leaving some centers to recede into insignificance and sometimes extinction, and enabling others to rise to new heights of dominance. Many an ancient center, the victim of a river's change of course or of a new alignment of trade routes, is known now only through the researches of archeologists. The once important cities of the Euphrates-Tigris valley—Nineveh, Babylon, Baghdad—are today but subordinate towns. The same applies to Tyre and Sidon, leading commercial points on the Mediterranean seaboard in ancient times. Cairo, located close to the site of ancient Memphis, has superseded it as the principal center of the Nile valley; while Rome, after a recession, has regained its prominence as a center of political, ecclesiastical, and commercial functions. Athens and Constantinople have declined; Naples and Genoa have gained at the expense of Florence and Pisa; Milan has displaced Venice; and the list of such changes could be extended indefinitely.

The coming of the railway and of motor transportation greatly increased the variability of route patterns and hastened shifts in the positions of centers. With the close of the Civil War, in the United States, came a decline in river transportation as railways were rapidly extended westward. Pittsburgh, Cincinnati, St. Louis, New Orleans, and other river ports fell into subordination to Cleveland and Chicago, while many railway centers rose to positions of importance.

No less significant is the rise and fall of small centers. Between 1905 and 1929, 320 local trade centers in Minnesota disappeared and were replaced by 356 new centers of comparable size,[11] as a consequence of changes in transportation routes.

The requirement of accessibility, so important to the life of a center, varies with the functions served. Different types of centers seek different kinds of locations. As already indicated, the center which is a nexus of interregional relations as well as a hub of local life is found usually on the margins of regions. There routes linking together diverse producing areas converge in greatest number. But centers oriented primarily to the needs of local populations tend toward geometrically central locations in their regions. This difference is readily observable, for example, as between entrepôt cities and political capitals.

The Community Area.—As an organization of interdependences the community embraces a much wider area than the center. The latter, though of great significance, is but the nucleus of an extended pattern of interrelations. In its simplest spatial aspect the community is comprised of two generalized unit parts, the center and the adjoining outlying area. In the one are performed the processing and service functions, and in the other are carried on the raw-material-producing functions. The two develop together, each presupposing the other. But while the center is compact and readily visible, the second component, the outlying area, is diffuse and difficult of precise observation. It is just for this reason that the boundaries of the community are often erroneously regarded as coterminous with those of the village, town, or city. And it is for the same reason that the delimitation of community area poses a problem for the student of collective life.

The boundaries of communities, in fact, appear in varying degrees of distinctness. In regions of simple agricultural occupancy the concentration of settlement at village centers combined with local self-sufficiency makes for clearly defined community areas. Long-established and unvarying routines of movement to and from centers have prescribed, in most instances, incontrovertible boundaries. But in advanced agricultural and industrial regions, where settlement is scattered over the space intervening between centers and where the division of labor is highly ramified, the community area lacks definiteness.

---

[11] C. C. Zimmerman, *Farm Trade Centers in Minnesota, 1905-1929,* University of Minnesota Agricultural Experiment Station Bulletin 269 (St. Paul, September, 1930), 30-33.

In principle, however, the boundary of every community is determined in the same manner. It is fixed by the maximum radius of routine daily movement to and from a center. Thus the community includes the area the population of which, however widely distributed, regularly turns to a common center for the satisfaction of all or a major part of its needs. That distance may differ considerably, depending on the kind of transportation facility in use. Where human locomotion or animal carriage is the prevailing mode of transportation and communication the distance from center to periphery seldom exceeds five miles, but the use of mechanically powered agencies of movement enlarges the radial distance to twenty or more miles.

To speak of radial distance is not to imply symmetry or circularity in the community boundary. On flat lands the shape of the area may tend toward circularity, especially where walking is the principal mode of travel. But topography is usually irregular and the communal area reflects the limiting influence of geographic features; it is hedged in at certain places by mountains and water barriers and extended in other places as along coastal plains and river valleys. Transportation combines with topography in the distortion of boundaries. If movement in all directions from a center were uniformly free, symmetry of boundary might be expected. But this is seldom the case. Movement invariably becomes channelized into routes or highways which take natural lines of least resistance, or in any event smooth the way and facilitate travel. A point lying on an established route therefore is effectively closer to the center than is another point not on a thoroughfare though equally distant from the center. This is observable even where pedestrian transportation prevails, though that form of carriage is less bound to fixed routes than is any other type. As overland transportation becomes more mechanized, the time-cost differential from the center to equidistant points situated on the thoroughfare and not on the thoroughfare increases. Mechanized carriers are restricted to certain types of surfaces: the locomotive travels rapidly on rails but not at all where rails are absent; the automobile has much greater flexibility in this respect but performs best on hard-surfaced roads. Thus the effect of transportation facilities is to extend the bounds of the community farther on the lines of travel than elsewhere.

The community area, consequently, tends to be star-shaped rather than circular in appearance, the number of points varying with the number of radiating thoroughfares. Nevertheless, the kinds of movement are so numerous as to permit a large exercise of choice in the selection of indexes of the scope and limits of the community. In his study of Wisconsin rural service centers in 1911, C. J. Galpin [12] devised a procedure for the determination of community boundaries which, in its essentials, has since become standard practice. His method was that of plotting, on the basis of data returned on questionnaires by the farm population, the distances to which services were extended in all directions from a center. A line drawn through the points thus located inclosed a community, as shown in Figure 16.

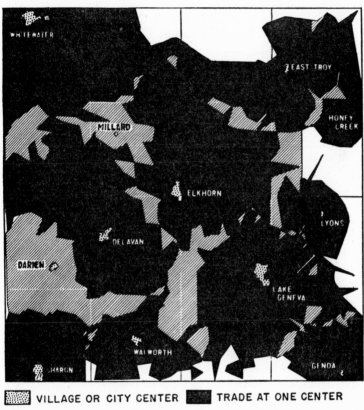

VILLAGE OR CITY CENTER   TRADE AT ONE CENTER

TRADE AT TWO OR MORE CENTERS   TRADE OUTSIDE THE COUNTY

Fig. 16.—Community areas in Walworth County, Wisconsin, 1911. (From C. J. Galpin, *The Social Anatomy of An Agricultural Village*. Agri. Exp. Stat. Univ. of Wisconsin, Research Bull. 34 [Madison, Wis., 1915]. Used by permission.)

In addition to retail grocery service, Galpin also used banking service, local newspaper distribution, milk collection, church and high school

---

[12] *The Social Anatomy of an Agricultural Village*, Agricultural Experiment Station of the University of Wisconsin, Research Bulletin 34 (Madison, Wis., May, 1915).

attendance, and public library use.[13] With such criteria it was demonstrated that subcommunities centered in villages of one to four square miles in area actually extended over areas of from less than ten to nearly one hundred and twenty square miles. Table 24 shows the areas of small village-centered communities observed in a larger sample than that studied by Galpin.

TABLE 24

Average Size of Areas of 140 Village Communities by Geographic Areas and by Size of Village, United States, 1924–30

| Geographic area | Square miles per community area | | | | | | | |
| | All villages | | Small villages | | Medium villages | | Large villages | |
	1924	1930	1924	1930	1924	1930	1924	1930
Middle Atlantic........	47	50	38	43	46	46	80	87
South...............	99	108	63	77	106	111	127	146
Middle West..........	101	114	82	96	96	113	145	148
Far West.............	240	251	119	121	346	365	213	223

Source: Edmund de S. Brunner and J. H. Kolb, *Rural Social Trends* (New York, 1933), 95.

The organizations studied by Galpin and which he called communities were actually territorial units in a larger organization commonly referred to as the metropolitan community. The much greater complexity of structure of the metropolitan community as reflected in a larger number and variety of movements to and from its center has necessitated some adaptation of Galpin's technique, mainly through the use of more appropriate evidences of territorial integration. A wide assortment of indexes of boundaries is employed such as traffic flow gradients, community services, telephone service, electric power service, wholesale and retail distribution, radio listening audience, newspaper circulation, etc.[14]

The application of indexes thus far brought into use, however, reveals that the boundaries of the modern community, instead of being

---

[13] A unique direct evidence of a community's outer limits in the form of road-turnings has been employed by Stanley D. Dodge. At the points of entry of private drives and of secondary roads into main thoroughfares the number of wheel tracks and the length of the turning arc indicate the habits of movement and the destinations of the hinterland population. This index, of course, has application only to small communities. ("Bureau and the Princeton Community," *Annals of the Association of American Geographers*, XXII (September, 1932), 175-80.)

[14] See R. D. McKenzie, *The Metropolitan Community* (New York, 1933), chap. vii.

precise lines, are blurred, if not indeterminate. Each index yields a different description of a community's margins. Figure 17 illustrates the lack of agreement among four selected criteria. In view of this peculiarity, and since each of the available indexes represents a more or less specialized relationship, nothing less than a combination of indexes is adequate for the fullest approximation to an appropriate boundary. But the use of a number of criteria produces a confusion of intertwined lines of demarcation, as shown in Figures 18 and 19. Dissatisfied with such irregularity, a few students have suspected that some one index might be sufficiently inclusive to be used alone, thus producing a sharper boundary line. Park and Newcomb suggested that the circulation radius of newspapers published in a given center provided such an index, their major assumption being that the content of the newspaper pertains to all the diverse interests that make up community life.[15] A close correlation of newspaper circulation with store delivery service, found in a Texas study,[16] lent support to this thesis. Proceeding on their supposition, Park and Newcomb delineated the metropolitan communities of the United States with the result shown in Figure 20. Further attempts to confirm the single-index hypothesis have yet to be made.

Even though a single index should prove usable, it will remain that community boundaries are zones rather than lines. They are formed where the territories of neighboring communities converge and overlap, where the integrating influences emanating from different centers meet in competition, and where, in consequence, the communal attachments of the local residents are not only divided but in a state of flux. The dynamics of the modern community is, in fact, largely responsible for the diffuseness of its boundaries. Every relative change in the time and cost of transportation and every relative shift in market conditions has immediate repercussions in the expansion or contraction of the scope of the community.[17]

A second factor involved in the indistinctness of boundaries is the interpenetration of dependent communities. Here again the terri-

---

[15] "Newspaper Circulation and Metropolitan Regions," in R. D. McKenzie, *ibid.,* chap. viii.
[16] Wm. J. Reilly, *Methods for the Study of Retail Relationships,* University of Texas Bulletin No. 2944 (November, 1929), 17.
Reilly has suggested another method for the delimitation of community boundaries which he calls the "law of retail gravitation." He states the "law" as follows: "Under normal conditions two cities draw retail trade from a smaller intermediate city in direct proportion to some power of the population of these two larger cities and in an inverse proportion to some power of the distance of each of the cities from the smaller intermediate city." Although supported by its author's findings, the principle has not been verified in other researches. (*Ibid.,* 16 ff.)
[17] See Chapter 19.

Area Served by the Clothing Store and the Drug Stores

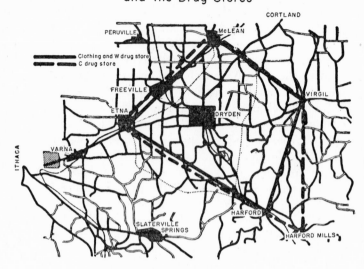

Areas from which the Presbyterian and Methodist Churches Draw Their Members

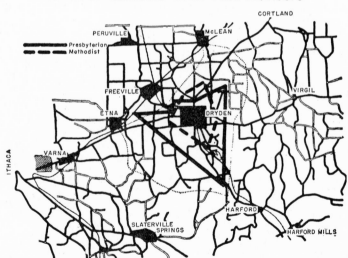

FIG. 17.—Boundaries of service areas of Dryden, New York, 1929. (From *New York*. Cornell Univ. Agri. Exp. Stat. Bull. 504 [Ithaca, N. Y., 1930]. Used

Area from Which the High-
School Pupils Come

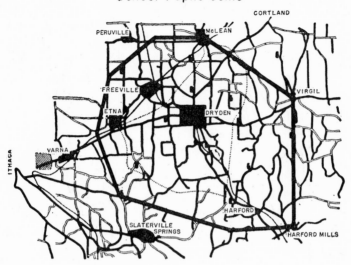

Area Served by the Bank

G. M. Kensler and Bruce L. Melvin, *A Partial Sociological Study of Dryden,*
by permission.)

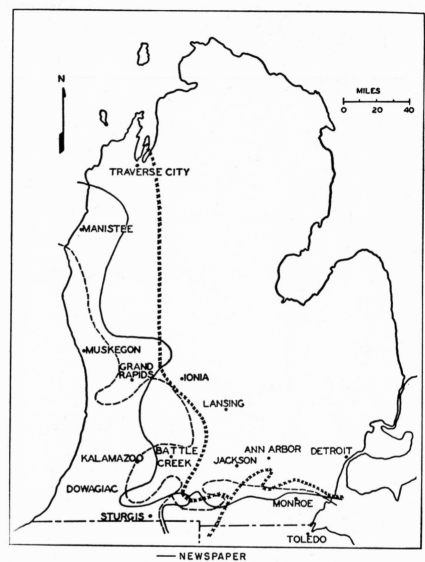

FIG. 18.—Boundaries based on three measures of Detroit's influence, 1933. (From Kenneth McGill, *Methods for Delineating the Boundary and Integration Zones of Metropolitan Regions.* Unpublished manuscript. Sociology Department, University of Michigan, 1933.)

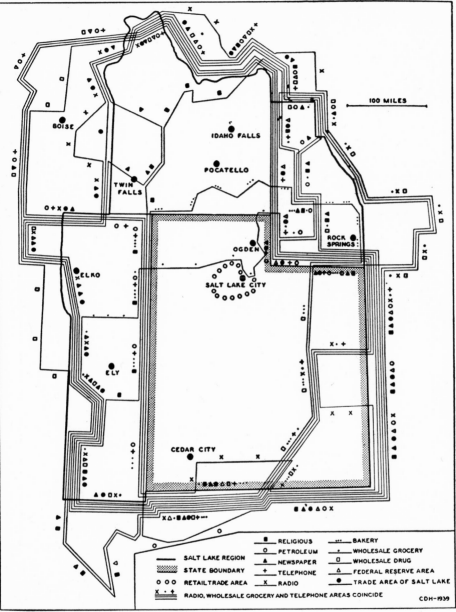

FIG. 19.—Boundaries based on selected measures of Salt Lake City's influence.
(From Chauncy D. Harris, *Salt Lake City: A Regional Capital* [Chicago: The
University of Chicago Press, 1940], Fig. 10. Used by permission of the author.)

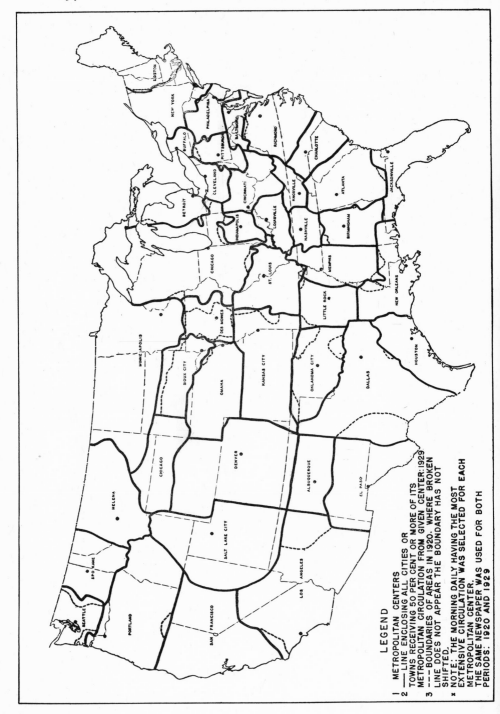

LEGEND

1   METROPOLITAN CENTERS

2 — LINE ENCLOSING ALL CITIES OR
    TOWNS RECEIVING 50 PER CENT OR MORE OF ITS
    METROPOLITAN CIRCULATION FROM GIVEN CENTER: 1929

3 --- BOUNDARIES OF AREAS IN 1920, WHERE BROKEN
      LINE DOES NOT APPEAR THE BOUNDARY HAS NOT
      SHIFTED.

x   NOTE: THE MORNING DAILY HAVING THE MOST
    EXTENSIVE CIRCULATION WAS SELECTED FOR EACH
    METROPOLITAN CENTER.
    THE SAME NEWSPAPER WAS USED FOR BOTH
    PERIODS: 1920 AND 1929

torial pattern of modern collective life is in contrast to the discrete and self-contained communities of the pre-industrial era. The introduction and rapid improvement of mechanically powered transport facilities together with their stimulation to specialization have enabled each local population to participate in the affairs of remote as well as neighboring communal groups. The organizations of spatially separate populations, in other words, have merged at many points giving rise to very extensive and inclusive communities. The term *community*, interpreted to connote a compact, easily distinguishable entity, has lost much of its meaning.

A closer examination of the spatial aspect of interdependence discloses that a community may have not one boundary, be it a line or a zone, but two or more. It is possible to observe a series of concentric zones about a center which differ in the degree of attachment of their occupants to the center, in the frequency of movement to and from the center, and in the extent to which contacts with the center are direct, involving the movement of individuals, or indirect, involving a circulation of ideas and products rather than people. The intensity of local community life appears to diminish with distance from the center, though it may not be entirely vitiated even at maximum distances.

The areas delimited by Galpin are what may be termed primary community areas; they are described by the radius of daily movement to and from a center. For those services and activities the needs for which recur after short intervals—a few hours or a day—population cannot regularly travel far. If they are to be used at all, they must be close at hand. Hence, despite the speed and efficiency of modern transportation facilities, daily face-to-face interchanges are rather highly localized. A metropolis, though it may exercise influence over a wide hinterland, is nevertheless the center of a rather restricted primary area. This may be seen in the gradient of traffic flow away from a center as in Figure 21, which shows a sharp decline at a distance of six or seven miles from the downtown section of the center. Another measure of the primary area is the commuting distance of workers employed in the center. According to Table 25, Detroit workers are reluctant to travel more than fifteen miles to work each day; 7 per cent of industrial workers and but 5 per cent of nonindustrial workers originate from beyond the fifteen-mile limit. Measured in time units, this means that seventy-five to ninety minutes is the approximate maximum that commuters are willing to spend on a one-way trip to work, though the forty-five minute or ten-mile distance is the limit recognized by 80 per cent or more of the workers. The primary area, then, comprises about three hundred square miles or, at the most,

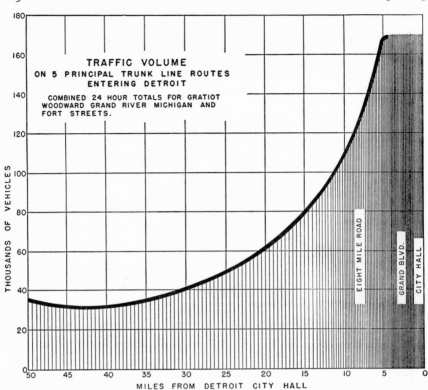

FIG. 21.—Traffic volume by distance from central business district, Detroit, Michigan. (From R. D. McKenzie, *The Metropolitan Community*, New York: McGraw-Hill Book Co., Inc., 1933, 87. Used by permission of the publisher.)

seven hundred square miles. This area coincides with what is commonly referred to as the retail shopping area.

Many routine movements which emanate from and converge upon a center, particularly a large center, extend over radii of fifty to seventy-five miles, distances too great to permit daily circulation. Such movements pertain to various special and infrequent requirements, for example, the retail purchase of durable goods, wholesale distribution, specialized medical, legal, and financial services, rare forms of entertainment, etc. The range of this kind of movement, ebbing and flowing at more or less weekly intervals, describes a secondary communal area. All the parts of this extended area are in daily contact, not by virtue of the circulation of individuals alone, but indirectly through the network of interdependences as well as through the use of the telephone, the newspaper, and the radio.

It is even possible to identify tertiary communal areas. Certain great cities perform various specialized services for vast areas, often

TABLE 25

DISTANCES TRAVELED TO WORK IN DETROIT BY INDUSTRIAL AND
NONINDUSTRIAL WORKERS, DETROIT, MICHIGAN, 1936

One way distance to work	Per cent		Cumulative per cent	
	Industrial workers	Nonindustrial workers	Industrial workers	Nonindustrial workers
Total.......	100.0	100.0	—	—
0– 4 Miles.....	42.7	46.6	100.0	100.0
5– 9 "	36.4	38.2	57.3	53.4
10–14 "	13.7	10.5	20.9	15.2
15–19 "	4.2	2.7	7.2	4.7
20–24 "	1.4	0.6	3.0	2.0
25–29 "	0.7	0.6	1.6	1.4
30–34 "	0.5	0.3	0.9	0.8
35–39 "	0.1	0.4	0.4	0.5
40 and over......	0.3	0.1	0.3	0.1

Source: Statement by Donald G. Kennedy, State Highway Commissioner of Michigan, *Hearings before the Select Committee Investigating National Defense Migration*, House of Representatives, 77th Congress, Pt. 18 (Washington, D.C., 1941), 7099.

worldwide in scope. Thus Chicago is the transportation hub and the livestock market for the whole of the United States; New York and London are the world's financial centers; and Hollywood, New York, and Paris are fashion centers for the world. Scarcely any part of the world's population today, civilized or preliterate, fails to be touched by the influences exerted from such centers. In fact, every functionally specialized center, regardless of its size, is at least a minor focus of interregional relations. But while such influences may pulsate to remote extremities with relatively high frequency, actual movements between centers and peripheries seldom average more often than once a month or once a season per inhabitant.

What, then, one may legitimately inquire, is the community: is it that which is contained in the primary, the secondary, or the tertiary area? Defined on the basis of interdependence alone, it is apparent that the community may be coextensive with the world, at least in some respects. Yet it is general practice to use the term to denote an area of local life. If we are to avoid the dilemma with which the modern situation presents us, it appears that we must incur the risk of doing violence to certain facts and adopt a working definition. Thus, from a spatial standpoint, the community may be defined as comprising that area the resident population of which is interrelated and integrated with reference to its daily requirements, whether con-

258

tacts be direct or indirect. Arbitrary as this definition may seem, it is consistent with common usage. Participation in a daily rhythm of collective life is the factor which distinguishes and gives unity to the population of a locality. In the pre-industrial period the community conformed to what we have called primary areas. Communications and people moved by the same carrier, and contacts, even though indirect, could extend no further than individuals were free to move. But in the modern period the community embraces the so-called secondary area. The separation of communication from transportation and the efficient mechanization of both have made possible daily contacts over great distances without the necessity of corresponding individual movements. Moreover, the same factors which have made for this expansion of the scope of local life have converted the earlier independent community into a dependent community. That is, while it is possible to delimit the area of daily interchange, such local organizations are linked with others in many vital relationships.

Community Area, Administrative Area, and Region.—The area factor in human life is subject to various interpretations. While the different possibilities of areal definition are too numerous to mention, consideration may be given to three typical conceptions, one or another of which is expressed in virtually every attempt to delimit areas. These are the community area, the administrative area, and the region. Unfortunately, these names are used interchangeably with the result that it is usually impossible to know what type of area is under discussion at any one time. It is partly to relieve this confusion and partly, through comparison and contrast, to clarify further the territorial limits of the community, that we turn to an examination of the three types of areas.

The administrative area is, as the name implies, represented by any area defined for the purpose of applying a policy or maintaining a public service. The most commonplace examples are political subdivisions such as school districts, townships, cities, counties, and states. There are in excess of 140,000 areas of this type in the United States. A second category of administrative area appears in extensions of municipal authority such as police jurisdictions, sanitation zones, planning regions, and so on. In metropolitan London, for instance, there are eleven distinct and overlapping administrative areas, their boundaries forming a series of concentric rings.[18] Still another type arises from subdivisions of the nation by federal bureaus

---

[18] Albert Lepawski, "The London Region: A Metropolitan Community in Crisis," *American Journal of Sociology,* XLVI (May, 1941), 826-34.

and departments to expedite policy administration. The continental area of the United States has been arranged in fourteen different combinations of administrative areas by the Treasury Department, in eleven combinations by the War Department, three by the Department of Justice, four by the Post Office Department, five by the Navy Department, fourteen by the Department of the Interior, nineteen by the Department of Agriculture, six by the Department of Commerce, one by the Department of Labor, in addition to which there are subdivisions by nearly thirty other bureaus and agencies.[19]

Among the distinctive characteristics of the administrative area are (1) its arbitrary determination, (2) its limited-purpose use, and (3) the inflexibility of its boundary. The community area in contrast is a functionally inclusive area which expands or contracts as the range of interdependences in terms of which it is described is lengthened or shortened. There is evidence that in the original layout of an administrative area some attempt is made to shape it to the functionally delineated or community area. But expedients of various sorts are allowed to enter into the plotting of the area, and not without justification. Since it is in most instances established for a specific purpose, the requirements of that purpose necessarily take precedence over other considerations. In other words, it is not always practicable to adjust the limits of the administrative area to the margins of the community. The very instability of the community's boundary makes this difficult. But what the community boundary lacks in stability the administrative area boundary possesses in excessive degree. This applies with special weight to political units. In the passage of time sentiment and vested interest, the polite and impolite names for the same thing, accumulate around political boundaries to make them well-nigh immutable. Hence the community as it grows and develops overreaches them and merges segments of and often entire political units in a single functional entity, the political boundaries remaining, however, as sources of friction to the smooth functioning of the community. A glance at Table 26 will suggest something of the administrative confusion encountered in metropolitan communities. Inflexibility in other types of administrative areas is of a somewhat different nature. It is due less to the accumulations of time than to the origin of such areas in fiat. That kind of origin does not preclude adjustments of boundaries; it simply means that needed adjustments are likely to be tardy, having to wait upon legislation

---

[19] National Resources Committee, *Regional Factors in National Planning* (Washington, D. C., 1935), 206-23.

TABLE 26

POLITICAL SUBDIVISIONS PARTLY OR WHOLLY INCLUDED IN THE TEN
LARGEST METROPOLITAN DISTRICTS, UNITED STATES, 1940

Metropolitan districts	Political subdivisions				
	Total	Incor- porated places	Town- ships	Counties	States
New York–N.E. New Jersey..	397	291	84	19	3
Chicago..................	162	118	39	5	2
Los Angeles..............	89	55	30	3	1
Philadelphia..............	174	93	71	8	2
Boston...................	90	19	64	6	1
Detroit..................	77	45	28	3	1
Pittsburgh...............	225	137	81	6	1
San Francisco–Oakland......	76	42	26	7	1
St. Louis................	106	70	29	5	2
Cleveland................	54	46	5	2	1

Source: Bureau of the Census, *Sixteenth Census of the United States, 1940*, Vol.
II (Washington, D. C., 1943).

The third type of area, the region, was discussed in some detail in
Chapter 6, which dealt with characteristics of the habitat. It will be
recalled, perhaps, that the consensus of opinion among geographers,
to whom we are indebted for the development of the concept, is that the
region is an area of homogeneity in respect to physical features or
human occupancy or both. Despite this explicit connotation, however,
the term *region* is often applied to the community area. References
to the metropolitan region and to the city region are common. But,
as we have seen, the community area is actually a different kind of
spatial unit from that described by the geographer's region. Instead
of an area of homogeneity, it is an area of heterogeneity. The diversity of the community area is evident not only in its human use
features, but also in its physical or physiographic features. Diversity
is the stuff of which interdependence is made and is thus basic to the
community.

The region and the community area are therefore different kinds
of spatial units. If we superimpose a map of metropolitan community
boundaries upon a map of regional boundaries, as in Figure 22, the
differences stand out sharply. It will be observed that in many places
community areas include portions of two or more regions. The metropolitan community of Chicago, for example, embraces segments of an
extractive industry region, a spring wheat region, a semiarid region,
and a region of mixed farming. The Houston community area con-

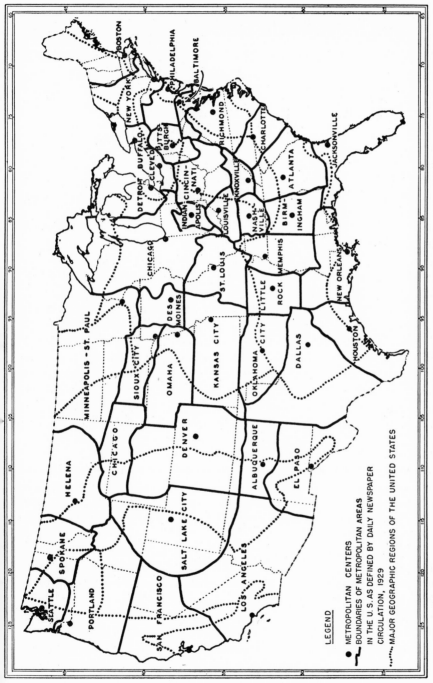

FIG. 22.—Metropolitan community areas (after R. D. McKenzie), and geographic regions (after M. C. Stark and D. S. Whittlesey) of the United States. (From National Resources Committee, *Regional Factors in National Planning* [Washington, D. C., 1935], 174 and 177.)

tains parts of the cotton region, the semiarid region, and the Southern or Gulf coastal region. In view of the manifest differences between the two kinds of area, it seems unwise to refer to both with the same term. It would make for clarity if *region* were reserved for areas of homogeneity, and *community area* were restricted to areas distinguished by interdependence.

Summary.—Viewed in its major outlines human settlement arranges itself in a pattern resembling a wheel, with a central concentration or hub, radiating thoroughfares similar to spokes along which are distributed small settlement clusters, and an outer periphery or rim. The factors that determine such a pattern are interdependence, differential location requirements, and the friction of space. The first is a cohesive influence which draws population into close spatial association. The differential location requirements, however, tend to scatter population in accordance with the various functions performed. While the third, the friction of space, or the time and cost of transportation and communication, regulates the particular shape and size of the pattern.

The center or nuclear point in the community is where interdependences are integrated and administered. In the independent community the center is the village itself and its location is fixed by the location of natural resources. With the rise of the dependent community the center becomes a settlement specialized in service and administrative functions. Its location is characteristically at strategic transport sites rather than at natural resource deposits. Such locations persist as community centers as long as the routes provide access to populous hinterlands. The community area, however, extends well beyond the limits of the center, though its boundaries are not always apparent to casual observation. In all instances the boundaries are determined by the maximum radius of routine daily movements to and from the center. That radius differs with the transportation facility in use. C. J. Galpin's method of determining boundaries by plotting the distances over which interdependences of various kinds extend has become standard practice. Many indexes of relationship are usable. The boundaries thus described prove to be broad and somewhat diffuse zones rather than precise lines. As such they reflect the interpenetration of dependent community areas. Community area is to be distinguished from administrative area and from region. The administrative area is usually an arbitrarily defined zone created for the application of some special policy or program. The region, on the other hand, is an area of homogeneous characteristics. Contrary to both these concepts of area, the community comprises that area the occupants of which are functionally interrelated.

SUPPLEMENTARY REFERENCES

FEBVRE, LUCIAN. *A Geographical Introduction to History.* New York: A. A. Knopf, 1925.

HOMANS, GEORGE C. *The English Village of the Thirteenth Century.* Cambridge: Harvard University Press, 1941.

ISARD, WALTER, and WHITNEY, VINCENT. "Metropolitan Site Selection," *Social Forces,* XXVII (March, 1949), 263-69.

JEFFERSON, MARK. "The Law of the Primate City," *Geographical Review,* XXIX (April, 1939), 226-32.

Chapter 14

SPATIAL ASPECT OF ECOLOGICAL ORGANIZATION
(CONTINUED)

The Distribution of Community Units: Concentric Zonation.—
The distribution of interrelated activities over the area comprised in
the community is controlled in the main by the friction of space and the
character of competition, the effects of the latter expressing themselves in rental charges for land.[1] Activities, or rather the units in
which they are embodied, least able to contend against the friction of
space, by virtue of their specialization and hence need for maximum
accessibility and also their adaptability to intensive land use, seek a
central location. They prove successful competitors for the more
strategic sites. The remaining units arrange themselves at distances
from the center in keeping with different abilities for bearing the time
and cost of transportation to the center. Consequently a noticeable
tendency appears for each class of land use to become segregated in a
zone situated at an appropriate distance from the center. The resulting series of more or less symmetrical concentric zones represents in
general outline a universal community pattern.

The settled preliterate community usually displays three zones. At
the core is the village frequently enclosed by a stockade; surrounding
the village is land devoted to garden use; and beyond the garden belt
are lands used for hunting and the gathering of forest products. The
medieval village community possessed essentially the same pattern.
though Max Weber detected five zones in the early German community: (1) the residential center or village; (2) garden lands; (3)
arable lands; (4) pasture lands; and (5) lands given over to forestry
and miscellaneous uses.[2] From his studies of the location of sustenance
activities von Thunen concluded that the ideal pattern of land use was
a city within a series of five concentric zones comprising in order from
the center to the periphery: (1) truck and dairy farming; (2) or-

---

[1] This factor is included by R. M. Haig as one of the frictions of space (*Robert
M. Haig, Regional Survey of New York and Its Environs*).
[2] *General Economic History*, trans. Frank H. Knight, 5. See also J. W. Thompson's description of the political organization of the medieval town (*Economic and
Social History of the Middle Ages*, 77-85).

chards; (3) grain production; (4) cattle raising; and (5) forestry.[3] Relatively little has been done to ascertain the zonal distribution of land use in communities of the United States. But there is enough evidence to indicate conformance to the general pattern.[4] Around a commercial core is a zone of intensive residential land use, the two zones comprising what is ordinarily defined as the city. A third zone is occupied largely by truck gardens, poultry farms, and nurseries, though residential and industrial uses are also conspicuous in this area. Beyond this lies a fourth zone in which dairy farming predominates. And in a fifth and ill-defined zone are found grain crops and cattle production which require large acreage.

Interest in the zonation of community activities in this country has been restricted for the most part to urban centers. In an essay on "The Growth of the City," Professor E. W. Burgess suggested that the urban pattern may be represented as a series of five concentric zones: (1) a central business district; (2) a transitional zone characterized by deterioration and obsolescence of improved property; (3) a zone of workingmen's homes; (4) a zone of middle-class residences; and (5) a zone of commuters' residences.[5] Although Professor Burgess did not reveal the empirical basis for his suggestion, the hypothesis was nevertheless widely accepted and applied and has dominated most of the discussion of the distribution of urban activities.[6]

It should be emphasized that the concentric zonal pattern is a generalized description and, for a particular community, offers merely an approximation of the actual pattern. Zonation is usually more distinct in the distribution of a given activity or index of activity than it is in respect to the distribution of all activities. As specialization develops in the dairy industry, for example, the several types of dairy activities distribute themselves about the market center in a gradient fashion which permits the delineation of fairly clear-cut producing zones. Milk, which is produced in relatively large volume per unit of land but is unable to stand high transportation costs, commands the area

---

[3] *Der isolierte Staat,* in *Beziehung auf Landwirtshaft und Nationalökonomie* (Hamburg und Rostock, 1863).

[4] See U. S. Dept. of Agriculture, Bulletin 678, *Influence of a City on Farming* (Washington, D. C., May, 1918), and Edmund de S. Brunner and J. H. Kolb, *Rural Social Trends,* chap. v.

[5] *Proceedings of the American Sociological Society,* XVIII (1923), 85-89.

[6] For supporting materials see R. V. Bowers, "Ecological Patterning of Rochester," *American Sociological Review,* IV (April, 1939), 180-89; and J. A. Quinn, "The Burgess Zonal Hypothesis and Its Critics," *ibid.,* V (April, 1940), 210-18. For criticisms see Maurice R. Davie, "The Pattern of Urban Growth," in Geo. P. Murdock (ed.), *Studies in the Science of Society* (New Haven, 1937), 133-61; and Federal Housing Administration, *The Structure and Growth of Residential Neighborhoods in American Cities* (Washington, D. C., 1939), 17 ff.

lying closest to the center. With a somewhat lower ratio of output per unit of land, cream production concentrates on lower rent lands just beyond the milk zone. Its higher value per unit of weight and lesser perishability enable cream to bear the higher costs of transportation. Butter, which derives from an even more extensive land use and having a value per unit of product higher than that of either cream or milk, predominates in remotely located lands. Yet such gradients, when rotated about the common center, do not sweep out homogeneous concentric belts of milk, cream, and butter production. This is also true of the various gradients that have been plotted for the area comprising the urban center.[7] Land values, to mention an index of general significance, if observed along a radial thoroughfare as in Figure 23, grade consistently downward from the center toward the

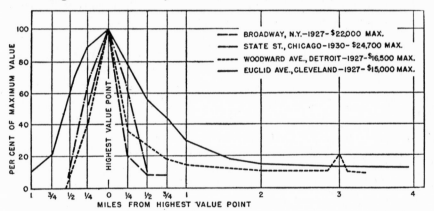

FIG. 23.—Land value gradients in four cities, equated for comparison unit: front foot value. (From R. D. McKenzie, The Metropolitan Community [New York: McGraw-Hill Book Co., Inc., 1933], 234. Used by permission of the publisher.)

periphery. But on either side of the thoroughfare land values fall off sharply. Bartholomew's tabulation of the average linear footage devoted to commercial land uses per 100 persons in half-mile concentric zones, presented in Table 27, shows the same fact. Although commercial use appears in all zones, it obviously shares the zone in each instance with other land uses.

The tendency toward homogeneity of land use in zones is offset by many factors. The limiting influence of the physical environment may intrude so that while one sector of the zone of profitable milk production has soil suitable for good pasturage, the remainder of the zone is wholly unfit for such use. Or, as is frequently the case, other

---

[7] E. W. Burgess, "The Determination of Gradients in the Growth of the City." Proceedings of the American Sociological Society, XXI (1927), 178-84.

TABLE 27

AVERAGE LINEAR FEET OF COMMERCIAL LAND IN USE PER 100
RESIDENTS IN HALF-MILE ZONES *

Mile zone	Number of cities reported †	Average linear feet per 100 residents in zone
0.5	6	69.7
1.0	6	44.3
1.5	6	30.7
2.0	6	25.0
2.5	4	20.0
3.0	4	21.3
3.5	4	26.0
4.0	2	13.0
4.5	1	10.8
5.0	1	14.0
5.5	1	7.2

* Source: H. Bartholomew, *Urban Land Uses* (Cambridge, Mass., 1932), 80.
† The six cities are: Binghamton, N. Y.; Knoxville, Tenn.; Louisville, Ky.; Sacramento, Cal.; Tulsa, Okla.; and Vancouver, B.C.

uses may prove equally, if not more, effective competitors for the available lands within the milk zone, the "zone of working men's homes," or any other concentric zone as the case may be. Thus in addition to dairying in the milk zone, there may be truck gardening, manufacturing, and residential use of the land. Heterogeneity of use may also result from changes taking place in a community: truck gardening appears in a zone before it is completely abandoned by dairying, and close on the heels of truck gardening may come residential or other types of use.[8] Still another factor of great importance in disturbing the tendency toward a neat concentric zonal arrangement is the linearity of transportation influence. Radiating routes constitute lines of superior advantage along which units cluster and compete for sites. The interstitial areas between radial routes thus acquire uses different from those attracted to the lines of travel. Commerce and manufacturing cling to the avenues of movement, whereas residence and agriculture occupy the interstitial areas. A segmented patterning in the distribution of land uses, in fact, seems more typical than the concentric zonal pattern.[9]

[8] See Edward Ackerman, "Sequent Occupance of a Boston Suburban Community," *Economic Geography*, XVII (January, 1941), 61-74.
[9] Cf. Federal Housing Administration, "The Structure and Growth of Residential Neighborhoods in American Cities" (Washington, D. C., 1939).

It is probable, however, that the lack of symmetry of the zones, which a number of critics of the concentric zone hypothesis have stressed, may be due to the use of an inappropriate measure of distance. Linear measures are crude indexes of the time and cost factors involved in traversing space. Were units of time and cost employed in the measure of distance, as James A. Quinn has suggested, smoothly circular zones would be obtained.[10] Thus all points on each of the 5-minute isochrones shown in Figure 24 are equidistant from the central business district of Detroit. Whether the distances measured by time in this illustration would be altered appreciably with the application of a cost factor is not known. Unfortunately, time and cost information is often not available in suitable form. Furthermore, their use in the delimitation of zones is complicated by the co-existence of different forms of transportation, each of which produces different time and cost radii. But despite such difficulties, time-cost distance offers the only logical approach to the determination of zone boundaries.

The Multicentered Pattern.—The concentric zonal conception, while having a limited usefulness for purposes of comparison, is apt to create the erroneous impression that the community is necessarily monocentered. In only relatively simple communities, however, does this appear to be true. Modern dependent community organization presents instead a multicentered spatial pattern. This was touched upon in the earlier discussion of the secondary area (Chapter 13) and may now be developed further.

Where the opportunity for movement is relatively free as to direction even though constrained by meager facilities, different forms of collective behavior show some tendency to focus at different points in an area.[11] In China farmers live in small village agglomerations wherein most of their routine needs find satisfaction. Periodically, however, every fifth or seventh day as determined by local custom, the farmers from the several villages in a locale meet at a centrally located village to exchange their wares, to gossip and glean the news of the area, and to carry on certain mass ceremonies.[12] The dispersed pattern of settlement characteristic of early American rural areas favored a much greater scattering of collective activities than does the compact settlement pattern of China and other old agrarian regions. Different activities as represented in schools, churches, granges, stores,

[10] *Op. cit.*
[11] Cf. Walter Christaller, *Die Zentralen Orte in Sudentschald* (Jena, 1933).
[12] Cf. Martin C. Yang, *A Chinese Village, Taitou, Shantung Province* (New York, 1945), 190-202.

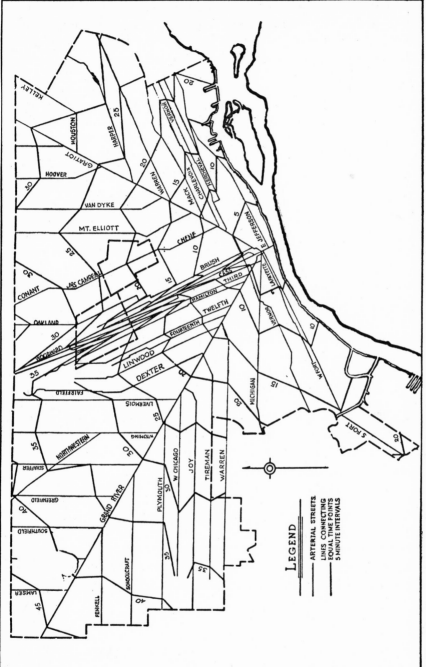

Fig. 24.—Time distances by passenger automobile, outbound peak hour traffic, Detroit, Michigan. (From Michigan State Highway Department, *Street Traffic, City of Detroit, 1936-37* [Lansing, 1937], 115.)

were not always located at a central place. Nevertheless, a market town served as a point of common orientation for the population scattered in villages, hamlets, and open country round about. But in both present-day China and early America, despite interdependences between settlements, the multicentered pattern existed in very rudimentary form. That is to say, in each instance the round of daily life revolved mainly about a single center.

Modern forms of communication and transportation have brought into being a sharply etched multicentered community pattern. Formerly semi-independent communities scattered over the hinterland about a market center were drawn into close contact with one another as well as with the major center, differentiated as to function, and transformed into units in an extensive though highly sensitive local territorial division of labor. This expanded pattern of local relations, referred to previously as the metropolitan community, has become the predominate form of the modern community. Figure 25 shows a typical distribution of various kinds of subcenters around a major center in the metropolitan community.

A conception of the number of subcenters or satellites that may be involved in the community may be gained from Table 28, which shows the number of incorporated places in the ten largest metropolitan districts in the United States. Delineated on the basis of population density rather than interrelationship, the metropolitan district is an inadequate representation of the metropolitan community.[13] In most instances community boundaries lie well beyond those drawn for the district. Table 28 also understates the number of subcenters in that it lists only places incorporated as municipalities. The number would be greatly increased were the unincorporated centers included, many of which are more important than some that are incorporated.

Of the network of interdependences in which the several centers of a communal complex are enmeshed the largest or major center forms the core. Concentrated there are communication agencies, financial and legal services, and the administrative offices of political, recreational, religious, and other services as well as of industry and commerce. Through these the manifold activities of the community are directed and integrated. Thus the special function of the principal center is that of dominance or control, a function which is further enhanced by the fact of its being a major shopping point, especially for style merchandise, a locus of the more specialized professional serv-

---

[13] In 1940 the metropolitan district contained a central city of 50,000 or more population and all contiguous land with a population density of 150 or more per square mile.

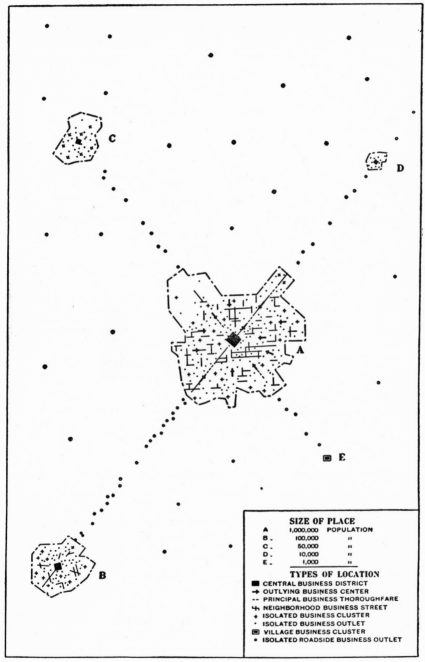

SIZE OF PLACE

A	1,000,000	POPULATION
B	100,000	"
C	50,000	"
D	10,000	"
E	1,000	"

TYPES OF LOCATION

CENTRAL BUSINESS DISTRICT
OUTLYING BUSINESS CENTER
PRINCIPAL BUSINESS THOROUGHFARE
NEIGHBORHOOD BUSINESS STREET
ISOLATED BUSINESS CLUSTER
ISOLATED BUSINESS OUTLET
VILLAGE BUSINESS CLUSTER
ISOLATED ROADSIDE BUSINESS OUTLET

FIG. 25.—The multi-centered community pattern. (From M. J. Proudfoot, "The Selection of A Business Site," *Jour. Land and Pub. Utility Econ.,* XIV [November, 1938], 371. Used by permission.)

TABLE 28

INCORPORATED PLACES BY SIZE IN THE TEN LARGEST METROPOLITAN DISTRICTS, UNITED STATES, 1940

Size of Place	New York N.E. New Jersey	Chicago	Los Angeles	Phila-delphia	Boston	Detroit	Pitts-burgh	San Francisco Oakland	St. Louis	Cleveland
Total	291	118	55	93	19	45	137	42	70	46
Under 2,500	121	54	6	45	0	12	60	13	44	24
2,500– 5,000	47	21	11	22	0	11	25	6	8	8
5,000– 10,000	56	18	14	15	0	7	24	11	6	6
10,000– 50,000	52	18	19	8	10	11	26	9	10	5
50,000–100,000	8	5	3	1	6	3	1	1	1	2
100,000 and over	6	2	2	2	3	1	1	2	1	1

Source: Bureau of the Census, *Sixteenth Census of the United States: 1940*, Vol. II (Washington, D. C., 1943).

ices, and a source of novelty and variety in every department of human interest. Its leadership in local activities is both cause and effect of its role as the agency for relating the community to the world at large. Intercommunity and interregional relations are mediated to the many territorial and other units through the institutions at the center.[14]

The subcenters clustered about are likewise specialized in greater or lesser degree. Seldom is any one complete in its service complement. In Table 29 it may be observed that small cities within twenty miles of large centers are relatively undeveloped in their service structures as compared with a random sample of cities of the same size. The extent of development in this respect varies with distance. Those beyond the thirty-mile distance appear to be somewhat specialized as retail service centers.[15] But deficiency in retail services, characteristic of places located close to large centers, is usually accompanied by a large development in one or more other activities. Some of the subcenters are devoted to manufacturing, often turning out parts or uncompleted products which are assembled or finished at plants in the metropolitan center. Other satellites specialize in the production of electric power, in collecting and redistributing farm and truck products, and in carrying on recreational services. The majority of small centers, however, are residential areas, sometimes described as "dormitory towns," from which the occupants commute to all parts of the community for employment. Of the forty-five incorporated settlements in the Detroit metropolitan district, twenty-nine are specialized residential areas and three others combine community-wide recreational services with the housing commuters. The remaining thirteen are manufacturing centers most of whose production is directly ancillary to the automobile industry of Detroit.

The multinucleated pattern is found also in the organization of land uses in centers, notably the larger ones. The focal point in the center is the "downtown" area where the various routes and agencies of movement converge and have their terminals and where, in consequence, the greatest number and variety of associational or service units are congregated. In addition to the main business district, there are in every center, depending on its size, a number of secondary business districts or subnuclei. The more important of these are found one to three miles distant from the main business district at the intersections of radial thoroughfares and heavily trafficked cross-town

---

[14] The dominant influence of metropolitan centers is intensively examined by Don J. Bogue in *The Structure of the Metropolitan Community: A Study of Dominance and Subdominance* (Ann Arbor, 1949).

[15] See also Don J. Bogue, *op. cit.*, chap iii,

TABLE 29

RATIOS OF MEAN PER CAPITA SALES IN CITIES OF 5,000-10,000 POPULATION, CLASSIFIED BY DISTANCE FROM CITIES OF 30,000 POPULATION AND OVER, TO MEAN PER CAPITA SALES IN ALL CITIES OF 5,000-10,000 POPULATION IN SAMPLE, BY TYPE OF SERVICE UNIT, UNITED STATES, 1935 *

Service units	Total (All cities)	Distance from larger city (miles)					
		0–10	10–20	20–30	30–40	40–75	75 and over
Total..........	100	61	89	110	117	123	180
Food stores........	100	90	100	101	100	103	124
Eating places........	100	110	90	100	110	105	241
General stores.......	100	83	—†	33	17	5	540
General merchandise stores...........	100	30	62	120	120	120	245
Apparel stores.......	100	70	78	117	143	143	136
Automotive stores...	100	40	72	123	130	136	192
Filling stations......	100	72	100	108	132	136	196
Household, furniture, radio stores.......	100	57	100	107	114	121	181
Lumber, building, hardware stores....	100	47	87	133	130	173	188
Drug stores.........	100	113	100	100	107	113	144
Personal service establishments.....	100	69	81	100	125	138	141
Other stores........	100	69	141	131	119	125	151
Number of cities.....	405	108	65	55	38	41	18

* Source: United States Census of Business, 1935.
† Data lacking.

streets. Lesser subdistricts appear in neighborhood locations and are dotted widely about the builtup area. This constellation of nuclei, illustrated more clearly in Figure 26 than in Figure 25, forms the essential territorial aspect of the city's service organization.

In the interstices between centers and subcenters, and, in fact, within the centers themselves, are areas of segregation, that is, areas which are internally homogeneous as to type of occupying unit. Like units, because they subsist upon the same conditions, seek the same locations. This simple principle appears to operate in all sections of the community. Producers of a given food crop are drawn by appropriate soil and favorable marketing facilities to congregate in a limited area, while growers of a different product will occupy another area for the same reasons. Industries of the same type huddle in close proximity both because they are subject to the same locational factors and because they may thus share what benefits in marketing and other

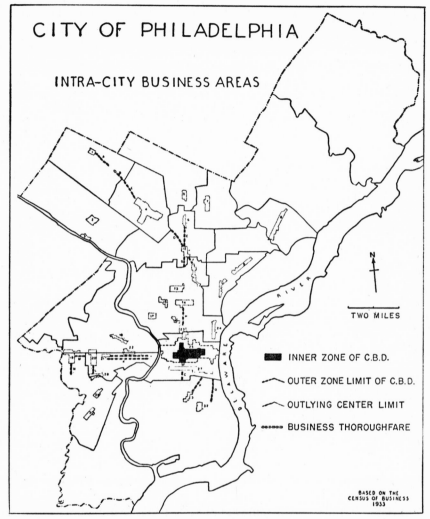

CITY OF PHILADELPHIA

INTRA-CITY BUSINESS AREAS

N

TWO MILES

▆▆ INNER ZONE OF C.B.D.

⌒ OUTER ZONE LIMIT OF C.B.D.

⌒ OUTLYING CENTER LIMIT

•••• BUSINESS THOROUGHFARE

BASED ON THE
CENSUS OF BUSINESS
1933

FIG. 26.—Central business district, secondary business districts, and business thoroughfares, Philadelphia, 1933. (From Bureau of the Census, *Intra-City Business Census Statistics for Philadelphia, Pennsylvania,* Census of Business, 1935 [Washington, D. C., 1937], 15.)

services their collective presence may yield. Even familial units are attracted to different areas in accordance with their intrinsic characteristics, such as ability to pay rent and transportation costs, ethnic affiliation, and so on. Areas of immigrant settlement, Negro and Jewish "ghettoes," areas of low, median, and high rental values, and other familiar types may be readily distinguished within the city. We shall examine this tendency more fully in the following section.

The Distribution of Community Units: Segregation.—The combination of territorial units forming the over-all spatial pattern of the community is a composite of a great number of diverse smaller units, each with its own peculiar spatial features which are expressive of its particular function. Clusters of these nonterritorial units (i.e., corporate and categoric units which are variable as to location), as was pointed out earlier, constitute territorial units and give each territorial unit its special position in the community. An examination of the community from the standpoint of the distribution of the components of territorial units reveals its spatial pattern in full detail.

It is possible to distinguish generalized patterns of distributions of units on the basis of their connection with different phases of the transportation system. One is comprised of the units involved in intercommunity relations, those, namely, that are engaged in raw-material production, manufacturing, and accessory services. Such units are located with reference to those routes and facilities—water, land, and air—which connect the community with other communities and regions. It should be noted that this phase of the transportation system, found wherever dependent communities are the prevalent type, is responsible for the main outlines of the territorial pattern. A second general distribution pattern is formed by those units occupied primarily with the intracommunity activities—retailing, wholesaling, and personal and public services of all kinds. Units carrying on functions of this kind are located along or with easy access to local transportation lanes which connect the many parts of the community. These include the highways, the streets, and rapid transit lines.

Dominated as it is by the interregional transport system, manufacturing is held close to terminal facilities. Hence the distribution pattern of manufacturing units shows a concentration in the metropolitan center and in adjacent satellites. This applies particularly to heavy industry. Units of that sort are very sparsely scattered in open country or in the more distant satellites.[16] Light manufacturing units, however, are usually much more widely scattered. Some concentration of light manufacturing establishments occurs within larger centers in zones bordering the main business districts. But such units are also found in all sizes of subcenters and at all distances from the main center.[17]

[16] Cf. Wm. N. Mitchell, *Trends in Industrial Location in the Chicago Region since 1920* (Chicago, 1933).
[17] The selection of a regional site for the location of a manufacturing unit occasions problems different from the selection of a site within the community area. The former together with the detailed cost analysis of site selection in general falls within the province of the economist and is therefore not attempted here. For economic

Nonmanufacturing units are, on the whole, distributed in a closer relationship to the population pattern than are manufacturing units. To reduce an involved set of relationships to simplest terms, manufacturing is an independent variable in relation to population while nonmanufacturing activities constitute a dependent variable. Fortunately, this simplification is more appropriate for local than for broad regional or continental areas. With few exceptions, nonmanufacturing units are directly concerned with serving the routine needs of local population. They include retailing and personal service enterprises; recreational, charitable, and religious organizations; and governmental units of various kinds such as schools, hospitals, libraries, fire stations, and so on. It is to be expected that their locations should be governed by the arrangement of population.

Differences in the distribution patterns of various types of service units are quite conspicuous, however. It may be stated as a general rule that the more specialized the function of a unit the greater is the tendency to occupy a central location. By their very nature specialized units must make themselves accessible to the largest possible number of persons. Accordingly, special financial, legal, and professional services of all sorts concentrate in the so-called "downtown" area of the community center. So also do the more specialized commercial, entertainment, and governmental units. All such units draw their support from the entire community. The converse of the rule is that the more unspecialized and standardized is a function the more pronounced is the tendency of the units so engaged to assume a distributional pattern comparable to that of the population. Grocery stores, drug stores, confectionaries, and filling stations are widely scattered and for this reason are commonly referred to as "neighborhood units." Virtually everyone uses these services, whereas the clientele of specialized units is highly selected. But there is also another factor influencing this location pattern. As was stated in an earlier connection, needs which recur with high frequency must have their sources of supply within easy reach, while those which arise infrequently may be served by units lying farther afield. Consumers cannot afford to travel far to secure food, the many emergency services of the drug store, schooling, religious services, and other routine personal requirements. Relatively few persons, on the other hand, have a daily

treatments of these matters see: Edgar M. Hoover, *Location Theory and the Shoe and Leather Industries* (Cambridge, Mass., 1937), and *The Location of Economic Activity;* Alfred Weber, *Theory of the Location of Industries* (Chicago, 1929); R. M. Kier, *Manufacturing Industries in America* (New York, 1920); and National Resources Planning Board, *Industrial Location and National Resources* (Washington, D. C., 1942).

need for specialized professional services, or for the purchase of styled clothing, furniture, and other such shopping goods. Hence a longer journey does not prove excessively burdensome. Individuals and units having daily requirements for such specialized services are usually located close to them.

Table 30 describes the location pattern of retail service units in a more or less representative metropolitan center, Philadelphia. It may be observed that the central business district contains but 9 per cent of all units, while the neighborhood districts contain 69 per cent, the remainder being located in large secondary districts and on radial thoroughfares. The scatter of units, however, is much greater than the scatter of sales. Units in the central business district, though they comprise less than a tenth of the total number, account for more than a third—37 per cent—of all sales. The neighborhood districts, despite the fact that they have two thirds of all store units, account for only 40 per cent of sales. This peculiarity is due not only to differences in size of units but also to differences in the combinations of units in the different locations. In the central business district unspecialized units, such as food, automotive, and drug stores and filling stations, are relatively few, while in the neighborhood districts these units are proportionately more numerous. Specialized units, conversely, predominate in the central district and are very infrequent in the neighborhood areas. Large secondary districts resemble the central business district more closely than neighborhood districts both in kinds of units and in the ratio of sales to units. Except for automotive retailing, radial thoroughfares are comparatively unimportant as service locations.

A second major locational characteristic of service units, exhibited principally in the central business district but evident in slighter degree in the more important secondary districts, is the existence of distinct groupings. There is a well-defined tendency for units of the same general type to cluster together. The commercial core of a large center usually contains a financial district, a wholesaling district, a theater district, a hotel district, and a retail shopping district.[18] Within the latter may be distinguished smaller groupings: shoe stores in one or two adjacent blocks; men's and women's clothing shops in another

---

[18] That this tendency is not a novel one is evident in the following: "In medieval London the names of streets indicate the special business of its occupants; examples are Ironmongers Lane, Hosiers Lane, and Bowyers Row. The fishmongers were located near Billingsgate, on the water front, and the money lenders on Lombard Street, where Italians or Lombards dominated the loaning and changing of money after the expulsion of the Jews." (N. S. B. Gras, *An Introduction to Economic History* [New York, Harper & Bros.], 136).

TABLE 30

Per Cent of Total Service Units and Per Cent of Total Sales Located in Four Types of Service Districts, Philadelphia, 1935

Type of service unit	Central business district		Business thoroughfares		Neighborhood districts		Large secondary centers	
	Per cent of stores	Per cent of sales	Per cent of stores	Per cent of sales	Per cent of stores	Per cent of sales	Per cent of stores	Per cent of sales
All units................	9.2	37.4	2.8	3.3	69.4	40.1	18.6	19.2
Food....................	2.5	5.7	2.3	3.0	81.9	69.3	13.3	22.0
Automotive..............	5.0	9.5	7.0	20.3	70.5	35.4	17.5	34.8
Filling stations.........	1.8	2.2	4.7	8.5	85.4	78.5	8.1	10.8
General merchandise.....	4.9	71.5	3.1	0.1	63.5	21.7	28.5	6.7
Apparel.................	22.1	63.2	1.9	0.5	36.8	9.4	39.2	26.9
Furniture—household.....	18.0	34.9	3.7	4.4	42.6	22.1	35.7	38.6
Lumber—building—hardware.	7.3	15.3	4.2	4.0	66.9	59.8	21.6	20.9
Restaurant..............	14.6	37.4	2.8	2.2	67.1	41.0	15.5	19.4
Drug...................	5.7	25.2	3.0	3.0	77.2	51.0	14.1	20.8
Other retail.............	17.6	37.0	2.3	2.2	60.5	41.5	19.6	19.3

Source: U. S. Census of Business, *Intra-Business Statistics for Philadelphia, Pennsylvania*, 1935, 26-27.

sector; and florists and other units combined in still other locations.[19] This attraction of competitors for one another results partly from the greater customer drawing power their concentration makes possible. A cluster of shoe stores, for example, does a greater volume of sales than the same number of units scattered widely over the area.[20] There is also the fact that a common location permits joint support for necessary services to business, thus spreading their costs. Units which compete with each other are also capable of combining their resources to increase their chances of survival.

On the other hand, there are definite symbiotic combinations in the distribution of units in the central business district. The financial district, though occupied by units which are alike in that all are concerned with money matters, is actually quite differentiated in its composition. Not only does it include banking houses which themselves are often specialized in various banking functions, but also stock exchanges and brokerages. Supplementing these units and rounding out the complement of financial services are legal, engineering, accounting, and other related agencies.[21] Likewise in the retail shopping district, supplemental units cluster together. Theaters, restaurants, and florists' shops locate in close proximity to one another, as do variety, department, shoe, and women's clothing stores.[22]

Familial units are distributed with references to land values, the locations of other types of units, and the time and cost of transportation to centers of activity. Since familial functions constitute a relatively unintensive use of land, they cannot compete successfully in most instances with business and industrial functions for the most accessible locations. Families are thus relegated to less accessible sites, i.e., to low-value lands. They take up positions in the area lying around the districts occupied by associational units. Such districts exercise a repellent influence on residences in another way. The traffic conditions and the noise and dirt they create are unfavorable to the performance of the family's functions. On the other hand, schools, churches, recreational facilities, and various other services attract residences, for they are directly involved in the day to day functions of the family.

---

[19] In New York City, Park Avenue from Forty-second Street to Forty-sixth Street is occupied almost exclusively by men's high quality clothing shops. It is an American counterpart of London's Bond Street. Further north on Park Avenue women's furnishing shops predominate. From Forty-second to Sixtieth Streets there are no grocery stores, butcher shops, delicatessens, cigar stores, barbers, or chain stores.

[20] R. U. Ratcliff, *The Problem of Retail Site Selections.* Michigan Business Studies, Vol. IX, No. 1 (Ann Arbor, 1939), 66.

[21] See *Regional Survey of New York and Its Environs,* Vol. I, 48-104, for an excellent description of the financial district of New York City.

[22] R. U. Ratcliff, *op. cit.,* 25 ff.

But the familial unit must maintain a degree of accessibility to the principal centers of activity in the community. Its members must be able to participate freely in the division of labor of the community and the various services should be able to reach the residence location without excessive cost. Hence the time and cost of transportation, by which accessibility is measured, limit the scatter of familial units around the locus of specialized functions toward which they are oriented. For example, where the time and cost of transportation to a possible residence location approximate or exceed the savings in rental payments that location would permit, the selection of a site tends to shift to a higher rent but less distant location.

The influences of the three factors are combined in a single measure, namely, rental value for residential use. The residential property on high-priced land is usually in a deteriorated condition, for since it is close to business or industrial areas it is being held speculatively in anticipation of its acquisition by a more intensive and therefore more remunerative use. In view of that probability owners of such property are not disposed to spend heavily for maintenance or to engage in new residential construction. Hence the property can command a relatively low rent for family use. Moreover, its proximity to various objectionable uses and its distance from family amenities also contribute to low residential rental values. Its accessibility, however, tends to counter the depressing effects on rent of deterioration and nearness to undesirable conditions. Conversely, new residential structures appear on low value lands, lands that have few if any alternative uses. Since the buildings are newer and presumably better equipped for family use than those found on high-priced land, they can command a higher rent. Their protection by distance from objectionable land uses and their access to the services and utilities family life requires also favor a high rental charge. But again, the tendency to high rental valuation is minimized somewhat by the lowered general accessibility to places of employment and specialized services that greater distance involves. Thus while land values, in the main, grade downward with distance from concentrations of associational units, rental values for residential buildings grade upward.[23] That is, rental values for residential property tend to vary inversely with land values.

<hr/>

[23] In the centers of communities based primarily on an agricultural economy, as in many parts of contemporary Latin America, the rent gradient runs in the opposite direction: residential rents decrease with distance from the central service or business district. Such a pattern is doubtless a result of the effort to minimize the time-cost distance involved in pedestrian travel. Thus agricultural laborers who occupy peripheral low-rent areas are near their places of work, while the landowners, having more time for travel at their disposal, occupy the interior or central

Rent, operating through income, is a most important factor in the distribution and segregation of familial units. Those with comparable incomes seek similar locations and consequently cluster together in one or two selected areas within the community. This tendency is shown on a block basis for different cities in Figure 27. Although there is considerable homogeneity in most blocks, there is also a fair amount of heterogeneity in many, e.g., the $40.00-$49.00 monthly rental blocks. This lack of uniformity results partly from the fact that one side of a block may be exposed to influences different from other sides. A block, in other words, may lie on the boundary between distinctive larger areas. Figure 28 presents a better view of the segregation pattern in a single city. Different rental areas are clearly distinguishable in the Richmond map. The importance of income is not only in that it measures the ability to pay rent but also in that it is an index of other family characteristics which express themselves as location requirements. Families of the same income class tend to have like needs for public transportation service, for access to schools, for size of residence and yard space, etc. The attraction of similar family units for one another in residential site selection has its basis, to a large extent, in the uniformity of their location requirements.

There is also the fact, however, that the presence on a site of a given type of familial unit is a localizing factor for others of that type. A number of similar units can create by their congregation various amenities that are not inherent in the location. If together in sufficient number, they can attract special services to their area, can engage in their own peculiar forms of collective behavior, and can when necessary offer relatively effective opposition to undesirable encroachments from without. The attraction of similar units for one another on this basis is apparent in the foreign immigrant settlements found in many communities, particularly in the inner sectors of the central cities. The same principle doubtless applies in some degree in most areas of homogeneous settlement. But such an attraction can operate only in a zone where the rents do not exceed the purchasing power of the familial units involved.

The generalization concerning the selective effects of rental charges is sometimes subjected to severe criticism. Walter Firey [24] argues

residential areas. The relationship between land values and residential rents in communities of this type has not been investigated so far as the author is aware. (See N. S. Hayner, "Mexico City: Its Growth and Configuration," *American Journal of Sociology*, L (January, 1945), 295; and John Gillin, "Parallel Cultures and Inhibitions to Acculturation in a Guatemalan Community," *Social Forces*, XXIV (October, 1945), 2-3.)

[24] *Land Use in Central Boston* (Cambridge, 1947).

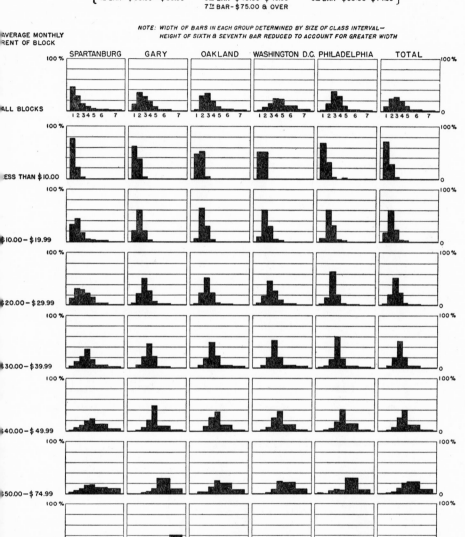

FIG. 27.—Distribution of residential rents in blocks, by average rent of block, for selected cities, 1934-36. (From Federal Housing Administration, *The Structure and Growth of Residential Neighborhoods in American Cities* [Washington, D. C., 1939], 33.)

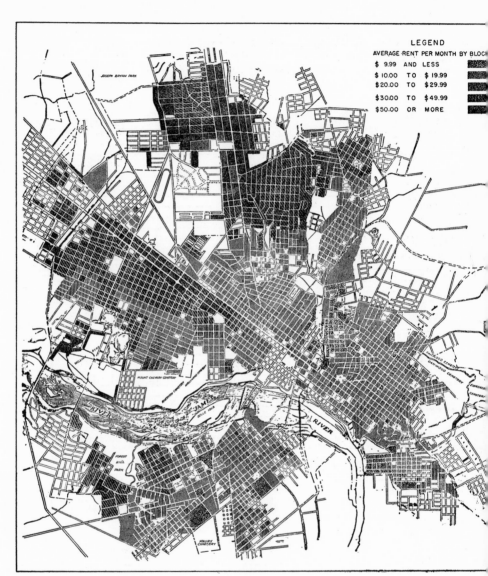

Fig. 28.—The distribution of residential rents in Richmond, Virginia, 1934. (From Federal Housing Administration, *The Structure and Growth of Residential Neighborhoods in American Cities* [Washington, D. C., 1939], 35.)

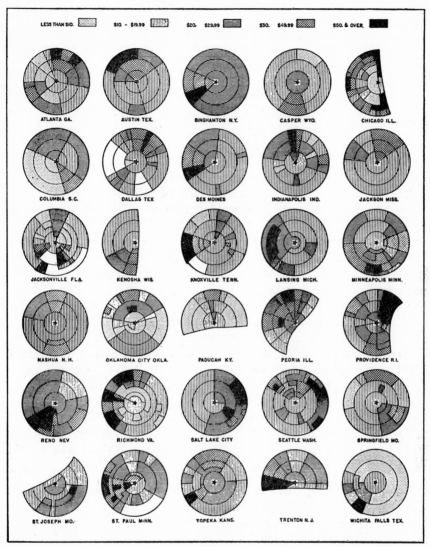

FIG. 29.—Theoretical pattern of distribution of rent areas in 30 American cities. (From Federal Housing Administration, *The Structure and Growth of Residential Neighborhoods in American Cities* [Washington, D. C., 1939], 77.)

that such a position attributes too great a rationality to human behavior. He suggests that sentimentalism and other "nonrational" considerations may intrude and offset an otherwise rational process. Firey cites Boston's Beacon Hill as an instance in which residences are held in an area by sentimental attachments and at great expense to the occupants. Another example, the Commons, though it lies on a valuable business site in the downtown area of Boston, is preserved as a park because of its historical associations. Assuming the accuracy of his conclusions regarding the reasons for the persistence of apparently uneconomic uses—which accuracy is itself in doubt— Firey's reasoning confuses motive with an external limiting factor. Regardless of the motive for the occupancy of a site, that occupancy involves certain costs which must be paid. If the family can pay the costs, then it may exercise any conceivable motive. It is worth noting, furthermore, that the limiting influence of rent declines with increase in income. The very wealthy may locate their residences anywhere: they may even dislodge business uses and take possession of their locations. Hence the existence of expensive residential properties near the downtown areas of many large cities.

The community pattern is thus a constellation of centers superimposed, as it were, upon a patchwork of areas of segregated land uses. It is a combination of territorial units of both corporate and categoric types each of which is closely dependent on all others. This pattern, it should be noted, is in a developmental stage. Collective life has not yet become fully adapted to the new scale of distance introduced by the automobile and telephone. The inertia existing in an established physical structure of buildings and roadways has made change slow and faltering. In all probability, however, the differentiation and interdependence of territorial units will become more sharply defined as populations succeed in freeing themselves from the spatial patterns built about mass carrier and pedestrian travel.[25] But before the one cycle is done a new one has begun. The airplane, radio, television, and so on will inevitably introduce extensive modifications in the territorial pattern of the community. What these will be still remains a matter for speculation.

Summary.—Units of the community distribute themselves about a central point in relation to their ability to bear the time and cost of transportation to and from the central point. The result of this tendency is a series of concentric zones, a pattern which is universally observable in all types of communities. Analysis reveals that that pattern is a very generalized description, for the zones are neither entirely symmetrical nor entirely homogeneous. Topography, transportation routes, and change affect both the shape and the content of the zones. Moreover, instead of a single center, as the concentric

---

[25] According to *Automobile Facts* (March, 1941), published by the Automobile Manufacturers' Association, there are 2,130 incorporated places in the United States, ranging in population from 2,500 to 50,000, that depend exclusively on private automobiles for transportation. No street cars or buses of any type operate in these cities.

zone description implies, the dependent community possesses a multi-centered pattern. Every center and subcenter in the metropolitan community tends to be a specialized territorial unit with the largest or major center serving as the integrating point for all functions in the community. The multinucleated pattern is also to be observed within centers : the central business district shares the service function with numerous smaller business districts scattered over the city.

Different kinds of units are distributed with reference to different phases of the transportation system. Manufacturing units are arranged along the interregional transport network, while retail and service units are located in close relation to the intramural transport system. The former are relatively independent of population location, but the latter are highly dependent on the distribution of population. The more specialized is the function of a service unit the greater is the tendency toward a central location. Associational units carrying on similar functions seek similar locations, for thus they are able to compete more effectively and also to share the costs of commonly needed facilities. Familial units are distributed by their abilities to pay rent, giving rise to areas of segregated family types. As with associational units, families of the same type make like demands on the environment which serve as an additional segregating factor. The community pattern, then, may be described as a constellation of centers set upon a patchwork of small internally homogenous areas.

SUPPLEMENTARY REFERENCES

BOWERS, R. V. "Ecological Patterning of Rochester, New York," *American Sociological Review,* IV (April, 1930), 180-89.

DAVIE, M. R. "The Pattern of Urban Growth," in G. P. Murdock (ed.), *Studies in the Science of Society.* New Haven: Yale University Press, 1937.

DEBOER, S. R. *Shopping Districts.* Studies in City Planning. Washington, D. C.: American Planning and Civic Association, 1937.

FRAZIER, FRANKLIN E. "Negro Harlem: An Ecological Study," *American Journal of Sociology,* XLIII (July, 1937), 72-89.

GILMORE, W. "The Old New Orleans and the New: A Case for Ecology," *American Sociological Review,* IX (August, 1944), 388-94.

HAIG, ROBERT M. "Toward an Understanding of the Metropolis," *Quarterly Journal of Economics,* (February-May, 1926), 179-208 and 402-34.

HANSEN, ASAEL T. "The Ecology of a Latin American City," in E. B. Reuter (ed.), *Race and Culture Contacts.* New York: McGraw-Hill Book Co., 1934.

MCKENZIE, R. D. "Spatial Distance and Community Organization Pattern," *Social Forces,* V (June, 1927), 623-27.

MOSCHELES, JULIE. "The Demographic, Social, and Economic Regions of Greater Prague," *Geographical Review,* XXVII (1937), 414-29.

OGBURN, WM. F. *Social Characteristics of Cities: A Basis for New Interpretations of the Role of the City in American Life.* Chicago: The International City Managers' Association, 1937.

OLSSON, W. WM. "Stockholm: Its Structure and Development," *Geographical Review,* XXX (1940), 420-28.

Chapter 15

TEMPORAL ASPECT OF ECOLOGICAL ORGANIZATION

Time, like space, is a limiting factor of great significance. It is at least in part the limitation of time, manifested in the urgency of vital needs, that leads individuals to relate themselves to one another. All forms of collective behavior are in one way or another adaptive to time and hence may be measured on the temporal dimension.

Space and time are separable from one another only in abstraction. It has been observed repeatedly in preceding chapters that space is experienced within the framework of a time system. Space has been described as a time-cost variable. The distance that may be traveled for any purpose, assuming a given amount of time at the disposal of the traveler, is contingent on the speed and efficiency of existing transport facilities. Hence the territorial scope of the community and, to a large extent, the number of individuals who may live in close mutual dependence, are fixed by the time required for the overcoming of distance. Similarly, the distribution of units within the community varies with the time used in movement. A temporal pattern is implicit in each and every spatial pattern.[1]

But the time available for travel is no less important than the speed of movement in affecting the spatial distribution of interrelated units. The various functions comprising a given mode of life must be so arranged in the time space that each will be adequately performed. If those functions are slow in operation as a result of crude tools, insufficient working population, or other frictional conditions, they cannot be far removed from one another in space. The time remaining for movement is apt to be brief. Or if the time span is crowded with numerous functions, the opportunities for movement may be restricted. It is for such reasons that frequently recurring needs must have their sources of supply close at hand and, too, that closely related functions tend to locate in proximity to one another. One of the chief advantages of a large population and specialization is that they permit certain units or functionaries to concentrate on movement, i.e., trans-

---

[1] See Gladys Engle-Frisch, "Some Neglected Temporal Aspects of Human Ecology," *Social Forces,* XXII (October, 1943), 43-47.

portation and communication, thus enabling others to approach maximum efficiency through continuous operation at fixed locations.

What we are saying, in effect, is that there is a temporal as well as a spatial distribution of community units. And while each is necessarily involved in the other, nevertheless the two kinds of distributions may be examined separately. Since the two preceding chapters were devoted to an analysis of space with only unavoidable reference to time, the present chapter is concerned almost exclusively with temporal patterns.

Rhythm, Tempo, and Timing.—Time is experienced as duration and recurrence. Duration is the means whereby events are quantitatively distinguished from one another. Recurrence provides the measure of duration. The repetition of small events measures the difference between before and after in reference to larger events. It is probable that were it not for recurrence there would be no conception of time. Moreover, it is unlikely, as Whitehead has suggested, that there would be any appreciation of order and measurement without the phenomenon of rhythmic recurrence.

The great recurrences of things are very obvious in our ordinary experience. Days recur, lunar phases recur, the seasons of the year recur, rotating bodies recur to their old positions, beats of the heart recur, breathing recurs. On every side we are met by recurrence. Apart from recurrence knowledge would be impossible; for nothing could be referred to our past experience. Also, apart from regularity of recurrence, measurement would be impossible. In our experience, as we gain the idea of exactness, recurrence is fundamental.[2]

Recurrences exhibit various characteristics, three of which may be noted. There is the aspect of rhythm, the regular periodicity with which events occur. Tempo, a second characteristic, pertains to the number of events per unit of time or the rate of recurrence. Thus rhythms differ with respect to their tempos. Moreover, since in any defined situation there are manifold rhythms, many of which have different tempos, coordination or timing of their unlike pulsations is essential to the avoidance of confusion. Rhythm, tempo, and timing, therefore, represent three different aspects in which the temporal factor may be analyzed, especially as it bears upon the collective life of organisms.

Several different types of rhythm may be distinguished: physical, physiological, and functional. Although these forms of fluctuations are interrelated, each has its own peculiar manifestation. The rhythms

---

[2] A. N. Whitehead, *Science and the Modern World* (New York, 1931), 47. Copyright 1925 by The Macmillan Company and used with their permission.

of the physical world are much varied, ranging from the regular and periodic movements of heavenly bodies to the violent changes in the weather. They differ on different parts of the earth's surface. Pulsations are more pronounced with distance from the equator, and there is a great variety in weather and in other physical fluctuations within every belt of latitude.

Physiological rhythms are fundamentally internal; they derive from the heredity nature of the organism. Every species of organism has a physiological rhythm, a reproduction and life cycle, peculiar to itself. Pulse and metabolism likewise differ from species to species. Most physiological rhythms, however, are affected by conditions in the habitat. Periodic hunger contractions, the alternating periods of rest and activity, and changes in the thickness of outer coverings, for example, vary with the food supply, the day and night cycle, and the seasons.

Functional rhythms are observable in the concerted activity of the organism engaged in securing and maintaining its livelihood. The search for food, shelter, and mates recurs with a more or less regular periodicity, varying with the species. To a large extent such routine activities are external manifestations of internal physiological rhythms. But so far as there is flexibility in organic behavior the opportunities for habit formation cause functional rhythms to be susceptible to indefinite elaboration. The acquisition of a habit, by definition a repetitive act, involves a time spacing which becomes an integral part of behavior. As the variety of activities is increased the different habits are redistributed in the restricted time span with the result that the functional rhythm is accentuated. The food-getting, eating, and sleeping habits of an individual are forced into a sharper pattern with the addition of the time-consuming responsibility for progeny. But the necessity that numbers of individuals act in concert for the achievement of most objectives gives rise to habit systems in which the functional rhythms of individuals are blended in a rhythm of the whole. Here too the rhythm varies in amplitude with the accumulation of demands on available time. Accordingly every type of community possesses a functional routine peculiar to itself.

Rhythms differ quantitatively as well as qualitatively. Every kind of recurrence seems to have a unique rate or tempo. In physical phenomena the range of variation in tempo extends from the relatively rapid day and night alternation, at one extreme, to age-long geological cycles, at the other. Physiological rhythms likewise differ widely. The life cycles of species vary roughly with size; generations recur at intervals of a few seconds in the smallest organisms and at intervals of twenty to thirty years in the largest species. The rates of other organic rhythms also differ in different species. Functional rhythms, no less than physical and physiological rhythms, are differentiated as to tempo. Each type of individual and collective activity possesses a distinctive periodicity.[3] The variability of behavior, moreover, allows for change of tempo.

The most important factor in connection with rhythms is the necessity of adjustment of one to another. Of the three types the physical rhythm is dominant; all other kinds of fluctuation are constrained to conform to the pulsations in the physical environment. The organism, if it is to survive, must adapt its life cycle and routine to the rhythms in the physical world—to the diurnal cycle, to the changing seasons, to the oscillations in temperature and humidity. The geographic distribution of plants and animals in existence at any one time reflects the timing of physiological with physical rhythms that has been achieved.

The timing of physiological rhythms is fundamental to the establishment of symbiosis among species. In order that diverse organisms may live together, their respective routines must fit into a pattern which is congenial to the needs of all. Thus the pulse of life in a given species is often a determining factor in its attaining a niche in a particular community. In this connection considerable significance attaches to differences in tempo. Recalling our earlier discussion [4] of the pyramid of numbers, organisms at each level differ not only in size but also in length of life cycle. The quick succession of generations of small organisms at the base of the communal hierarchy enables them to maintain a food supply for larger organisms and at the same time assures survival of their own species. Apart from the meshing of rhythms involved in food-chains, co-occupancy of the habitat also entails an adjustment of routines differing in tempo. Since a species, by virtue of the periodicity of its activity, does not continuously use the part of the habitat it occupies, it leaves a time-space for occupancy by other species. Many of the small flowers that carpet the floors of deciduous forests in the early spring succeed in living there because they bloom before the leaves of the trees come out and shut off their light. Other flowers survive because of inactivity until the leafing of trees furnishes the shade which they require.

Timing has the same vital importance when, as with man, the rhythmic character of functioning arises more from behavioral adapta-

---

[3] Since periodicity provides one basis for the identification of types of activity, this statement is somewhat redundant.

[4] Chapter 3.

tions than from genetic constitution. But the task of dovetailing interdependent activities is necessarily more difficult in human society as a consequence of the exceptional variability of man's behavior. Controls must be devised and implemented in order to assure a coherently functioning system. Every increase in the number and variety of activities carried on simultaneously in an aggregate further emphasizes the need for control. The control function introduces an additional rhythm and that, too, must be adjusted to the rhythms of the functions over which it exercises dominance.

But timing involves an adjustment of the similar rhythms of like organisms or units as well as of the dissimilar rhythms of differentiated units. In order for like units to supplement one another in a commensalistic relationship they must achieve a synchronization of their individual activities. Synchronous activity, of course, follows more or less automatically from similarity of functions; that is, individuals that carry on the same kind of activities tend to do so at the same periods. Plants of a given species germinate from seeds, grow, pollinate, and die in concert. Likewise the members of an animal species feed, mate, rest, and breed in a common rhythm. The tendency is much the same in every functional category of men. Yet the opportunities for divergence from a central tendency in human behavior are such that considerable temporal disorder may occur among the activities of similar units. If, however, the individuals or units of any one type are to realize the greatest mutual support, they must synchronize their functions.

Man's Adjustment to Physical and Biotic Rhythms.—Man as an animal has a distinctive physiological rhythm. The human life span and reproduction cycle are features of man's phylogenetic nature, and have marked uniformity throughout the species. As in the case of other organisms, man's physiological rhythm and duration are responsive within limits to external factors. Growth may be accelerated or retarded and the life cycle may be modified by environmental conditions. Modern science has advanced the average length of life, but it has not extended the reproduction period or the ultimate span of human duration.

Man's early and widespread distribution over the surface of the earth has resulted largely from his behavioral achievements rather than from his physiological adaptation to the varying physical and biotic rhythms of the different parts of the world. By nature he is a tropical or subtropical animal. Yet man's most generalized form of physiological adaptations to the variations of his environment re lates to the day and night alternations with the corresponding intervals of activity and rest rather than to the seasonal cycle. He is primarily a diurnal animal, a fact which should be borne in mind when considering the rhythms of his communal life. Adjustments to the seasons and to other fluctuations in external nature depend upon his plasticity and ability to accumulate contrivances. The discovery of fire and its use in combating the severity of the elements were decisive factors in man's early adaptation to environmental rhythms. Other technological developments too numerous to mention have enhanced his ability to thrive in regions of radical environmental fluctuations.[5]

The chief problem of adaptation pertains to the rhythm of the food base. By fire, shelter, and clothing man everywhere has attained a considerable degree of mastery over the inorganic environment. Greater difficulty is encountered in maintaining an adjustment to fluctuations in the biotic environment. In this respect man's catholic food tolerance stands him in good stead. A survey of human adjustments to the food supply in different regions of the world, however, reveals that they are oriented primarily to the adverse periods in the cycle of fluctuation. It is possible to classify peoples with regard to their modes of meeting periodic adversities. Three general though not mutually exclusive types of adjustment appear, namely, movement, storage, and circulation.

All nomadic peoples, including the simple hunting and collecting groups as well as those nomads who depend upon domesticated animals as their main source of sustenance, accommodate to the environmental rhythms through movement. Such peoples move with the seasons and with the fluctuations of the food base. That is, they respond to the exhaustion of the food supply by moving to a new location. The seasonal round leads them through an orbit which is repeated year after year.

As peoples adopted settled habitation and began to cultivate plants and animals, they narrowed the range of their movements and were compelled to rely more exclusively upon their ability to stabilize their local food supplies. Thus storage became one of the principal means of guarding against adversities of seasonal change. Storage of course constitutes an important method of food stabilization even among collecting and hunting peoples. The flocks and herds of pastoral nomads are animated repositories of food surpluses. But the use and necessity of storage attain paramount significance in sedentary communities.

---

[5] Cf. S. F. Gilfillan, "The Coldward Course of Progress," *Political Science Quarterly*, XXXV (September, 1920), 393-410.

The unit which assumes responsibility for storage is sometimes the family, sometimes the residence group comprising several families, and on occasion a centralized governing agency. In most simple agricultural economies the family or the kinship group constitutes the basic unit of mutual obligation in production and consumption. Neighboring families, however, frequently combine to form a larger unit for the supplementation of family storage. In the most advanced agricultural civilizations of the past, in which centralized governments obtained, the maintenance of public granaries was quite common. This practice prevailed in China until the overthrow of the Manchu regime. Every year the farmers were required to turn over a portion of their grain crops for storage in the public granaries. A surplus for distribution in time of want was thereby maintained.[6] Unfortunately, with the establishment of the Republic, this age-long policy was discontinued, with calamitous consequences in recent decades.

Obviously the problem of adjustment to adverse conditions is not the same in every locality. This is clearly evident from a survey of the incidence of famine. While famines may occur anywhere, their frequency is correlated with the variableness of the environment. In other words, the famine areas of the world are the regions of marked climatic and physical fluctuation, such as the valleys of erratic rivers and the plains of irregular rainfall. On the other hand, areas of relative constancy, the monsoon regions of southern Asia and the valley of the lower Nile, for example, are seldom affected by famine. In such areas the communal structure is characteristically stable. A constant food supply is usually associated with a more highly developed community organization than is found in areas of uncertainty. Peoples who depend principally on sea foods are particularly fortunate in this respect.

The third major form of adjustment to the adversities of the habitat has been described as circulation. By this is meant the intercommunity exchange of food and other commodities. Through exchange a local population may compensate for a restricted growing season or for deficiencies of supplies resulting from whatever cause, without either leaving its place of residence or engaging in large-scale storage. While trade was more or less common among preliterate peoples and characterizes all the more advanced peoples, trade in foods and other such necessities remained local in nature until the advent of steam transportation. Luxury goods for the upper classes were exchanged

---

[6] W. H. Mallory, *China: Land of Famine* (New York, 1926), 68.

over wide areas quite early in human history. Even cereals and other nonperishable foods were traded and moved over considerable territory by ancient peoples, notably the Romans. But it was not until the nineteenth century that circulation of the necessities of life reached worldwide dimensions; and there are still many parts of the world untouched by such exchange. With the extension of trade in basic necessities man has become less restricted to the foods and other staples of his local habitat. He is therefore able to specialize in exploiting the resources at hand and to exchange the products for those the local area does not provide. This process has led to a high degree of regional specialization in production and also has made possible an increasing diversity of consumers' goods. Accordingly, circulation has become progressively more important in meeting the hazards of local environmental rhythms. Storage has come to play a decreasing role, at least so far as the family and the local community are concerned.

Time Systems.—The rhythm of man's collective life, which we have been viewing in a very general way, is actually a synthesis of numerous functional rhythms. Some of the latter are no doubt outward manifestations of physiological processes, but a large and increasing proportion are acquired habits, that is, temporal adaptations of behavior to pre-existing or for other reasons unyielding recurrences. Even man's physiological rhythms are, to a considerable extent, modified and shaped in the process of habit formation. In fact, since man is not provided with any well-marked physiological fluctuations by which he might accommodate to physical oscillations or, for that matter, to the behavior of his fellows, he must rely upon a constructed time system for the ordering of interrelated behavior.

All peoples have some form of time reckoning, however crude. One of the most primitive groups in this respect was the California Indians, no one of whom, it is reported, was aware of his own age. Nor was anyone able to indicate how remote was an event that had occurred six, eight, or more years previously.[7] Yet they employed for daily needs a system of time units based on familiar recurrences. The Andaman Islanders identify the seasons by the predominating odors of the flowers in bloom,[8] the Bushmen shed their winter garments with the first thunderstorm,[9] and agriculturalists are guided in their succession of plowing, planting, and harvesting by the movements of birds and animals. Each local group possesses a time system

---

[7] A. L. Kroeber, "Elements of Culture in Native California," *University of California Publications in Archaeology and Ethnology* (1917-23), Vol. XIII, 260-328.
[8] A. Radcliffe-Brown, *The Andaman Islanders* (London, 1922), 311 ff.
[9] Martin P. Nilsson, *Primitive Time-Reckoning* (London, 1920), 48.

expressive of its own peculiar routine of activities. The units are marked off by periodic events and by the duration of essential tasks.

Important events become the primary reference points for the measurement of extended durations. The death of Alexander, the founding of Rome, the birth of Christ, the founding of the Japanese Empire and other similar incidents have served as bases for time systems.[10] It is noteworthy that even formal calendrical and astronomical systems, which in the last analysis are but social fictions, are based on such reference points. More proximate occurrences mark the beginning of shorter periods, as represented in such colloquialisms as "since the year of the Plague," "since the landing of the Pilgrims," and "since Pearl Harbor." Designations of this character are vastly more meaningful than since 1665, December 21, 1620, or December 7, 1941. Shorter intervals are likewise measured by familiar happenings. The natives of Madagascar speak of things being done in a "rice-cooking"—about half an hour; and in the "frying of a locust" —approximately a minute; while the Cross River natives describe the equivalent of fifteen minutes as "less than the time in which maize is not yet completely roasted." [11] Similarly, "before you can say Jack Robinson" and "in the twinkling of an eye" are commonplace American expressions.

Two natural recurrences—the diurnal cycle and the lunar phase —serve as universal time units. Although of irregular duration from place to place, the day seems everywhere to have the same social import. The daylight period provides a more or less standard interval for the flow of activity while nightfall and darkness bring a lacuna nicely suited for rest and recuperation. It is the variation of light and darkness and the concomitant alternation of waking and sleeping that supply the fundamental rhythm of community life. The lunar phase lends itself to the reckoning of longer durations. As with the day, one lunar cycle follows another in a continuous series, and after each cycle there is a hiatus of one or two days which is sufficient to mark the end of one time unit and to announce the start of the next.

Subdivisions of the lunar cycle arise from functional rhythms and are delimited by the recurrence of market days. Thence derives the concept of the week, the length of which varies in different groups from three to ten days. In general the spacing of market days is closer among the simpler than among the more advanced peoples. According to Hutton Webster, "The shorter intervals of three, four, and five

[10] P. A. Sorokin and R. K. Merton, "Social Time: A Methodological and Functional Analysis," *American Journal of Sociology,* XVII (March, 1937), 623.
[11] Martin P. Nilsson, *op cit.,* 42.

days reflect the simple economy of primitive life, since the market must recur with sufficient frequency to permit neighboring communities, who keep on hand no large stocks of food and other necessities, to obtain them from one another. The longer cycles of six, eight, and ten days, much less common, apparently arise by doubling the earlier period, whenever it is desired to hold a great market for the produce of a wide area." [12] Both the week and the lunar cycle have entered into the determination of our conventional month.

Time units of less than a day occur in great variety. We have already referred to the use of familiar durations, such as the time involved in cooking a certain food, in walking to a habitual destination, or in carrying to completion any one of the many routine tasks of daily life. Where eating is regularized, the intervals between meals may constitute recognized time units. The changing positions of the sun and the lengthening of shadows are widely employed to measure the passage of time. Fire, too, is often used to gauge duration, as, for example, the passing of night.[13]

For the most part, however, independent communities do not require an intensive subdivision of time. There are relatively few activities to be coordinated and synchronized and the tempo of life is governed by the slow progress of the seasonal succession. Hence the collective life is ordered with reference to large units of time. A traveler from the Occidental world discovers this as he waits to keep an appointment with an old world peasant or with a member of a preliterate group. Either may arrive for such a meeting anywhere within several hours of the appointed time without any awareness of being early or late. It is only where the diversity of interrelated activities is great and the tempo is rapid that the need for precise time units arises.[14]

The extension of the web of human symbiosis, with its multiplication of forms and complexities of collective activity, requires the development of an abstract time system, one that is mutually comprehensible to persons from widely divergent backgrounds. Thus the earliest astronomical or mathematical time systems appeared in cities.[15] At the outset the more rigorous systems of time calculation repre-

---

[12] *Rest Days* (New York, 1916), 117-18.
[13] Walter Hough, "Time Keeping by Light and Fire," *The American Anthropologist*, VI (1893), 207-10.
[14] A. Irving Hallowell, "Temporal Orientations in Western Civilization and in a Preliterate Society," *The American Anthropologist*, XXXIX (October-November, 1937), 656.
[15] W. Ward Fowler, "Calendar," in *Encyclopedia of Religion and Ethics*, III, 133.

sented in the calendar served primarily for the periodic mobilization
of the population for religious and certain administrative activities.
Progressive involution in the broadened pattern of interdependences
called for further refinement and standardization of time units. The
timing of manifold interlocking sustenance activities, each with a
rhythm peculiar to itself, depends on a system composed of minute
and exact units. Under such conditions time came to be conceived
as an uninterrupted continuum made up of uniform interchangeable
parts. The clock, declares Lewis Mumford, rather than the steam
engine, is the key to the industrial age.[16]

The standardization of time has greatly facilitated travel and communication over wide distances.[17] It is important to note, however,
that while time is standardized, communities on different meridians
are at different periods in the solar or clock day. When it is twelve
o'clock noon at Greenwich, it is seven A.M. in New York and four A.M.
in San Francisco; or, to put it another way, when the day's work ends
at six in the evening, in London, it is ten A.M. in San Francisco—the
time for the opening of banks. Such differences in time have considerable significance in world communications and business under-
takings. Only half the world is light at one time, and since modern
civilization is primarily an east-west girdle of the globe, it is difficult
for all points to communicate with one another simultaneously or
even on the same day. For instance, the stock exchange in London
closes for the day at about the time the New York stock exchange
opens. One important outcome of this situation is the tendency for
world communications to be relayed westward rather than eastward.
Thus a bank in New York which has branches in all the largest cities
of the world wires instructions to its branches in San Francisco,
Tokyo, Hong Kong, Calcutta, Cairo, and London. The instructions
arrive at each point in time for the opening of the business day.

Once developed a time system becomes as set in the "cake of custom" as are the activities themselves. The Irish farmer, Arensburg
informs us, is "less free to choose the date of sowing than his wife

16 *Technics and Civilization* (New York, 1934), 14.
17 The concept of standard time did not arise officially until after the introduction
of the railway. The railways in the United States developed a system of standard
time in 1875, some ten years before the convening of the international conference to
consider the adoption of a standardized system of time that would apply to the world
as a whole. It was then agreed by most of the nations attending the conference that
Greenwich, England, should be adopted as the prime meridian for reckoning longitude, and that a series of time belts, each comprising 15 degrees of longitude, should
be used in reckoning time east and west of Greenwich. In the United States, zones
were established at intervals of approximately 15 degrees from east to west across
the continent. Various other nations have followed the American example and established similar zones. (See Lewis Mumford, *op. cit.,* 198.)

the hour of dinner." [18] Ancestral experience has determined the best times to begin different tasks and the annual round is defined in traditional prescriptions from which few dare to depart. Urban populations are only somewhat less bound by habit in this respect. Whenever a community attempts to shift from standard to daylight saving time there is immediate protest from the public, as evidenced by the riots in Chicago when that city sought to adopt Eastern Standard Time; and by the more recent opposition to War Time. The resistance to changing Thanksgiving Day from the fourth to the third Thursday in November, and to calendar changes in general are expressive of the inertia of habit.

Time and the Independent Community.—The temporal order of the community is based on the synchronization and coordination of numerous periodic activities. Functions which are alike in character display similar periodicities as a consequence of their common requirements. They thus tend to operate synchronously, especially where they are mutually sustaining. The temporal relationship among the components of a categoric unit is of this order. Diverse activities, however, differ in periodicity. A temporal coordination is therefore essential to their interdependence as is evidenced by all corporate groupings.

In the independent community the rhythm and tempo of human affairs is set by the fluctuations of the physical and organic spheres. Even so, there is considerable variation among communities. Differences in food supply, in climatic conditions, and in other habitat factors limit and qualify the temporal organization in various ways.

The least systematic of peoples, so far as temporal routine is concerned, are those who gain their subsistence through collecting seeds, roots, and other readily available materials. For such groups success in securing food is irregular and often fortuitous, making impossible any strict scheduling of activities. The precariousness of life, furthermore, enforces a relentless quest for food which all but excludes activities not immediately related to sustenance. Although the Shoshonian Indians, a collectional economy people, observe a nominal seasonal schedule, their movements are in fact highly erratic.[19] Food supplies are uncertain and village groups and even individual families are drawn far afield by the promise of greater abundance elsewhere. The division of labor is minimal in groups of this character; all individuals

---

[18] *The Irish Countryman*, 48.
[19] Julian H. Steward, *Basin-Plateau Aboriginal Sociopolitical Groups* (Washington, D. C., 1938), 19-20.

do approximately the same thing. Timing of activities is therefore principally a matter of synchronization rather than of coordination.

Virtually all groups that subsist on surface resources are necessarily nomadic, shifting the sites of their operations with the seasons. As they pass through their annual orbits they adapt their systems of communal timing to the requirements of life in the different habitats. The yearly rounds of hunting groups in many areas involve their aggregation and disaggregation. "The horde is an unstable economic group whose membership and size are regulated by the seasonal cycle." [20] The Plains Indians, who lived on the bison, customarily organized in large hunting groups in the spring and autumn; and scattered along the small wooded creeks in the midsummer and again in the winter. The Eskimo pursue a somewhat similar cycle. An interesting feature of such groupings and dispersions is their accompaniments in other aspects of collective life. Marcel Mauss has observed that during the periods of banding the Eskimo become imbued with pronounced religious interests, which they express in elaborate ceremonial forms, but when they break up into small aggregates in periods of scatter these activities completely disappear. [21]

A stable food base, such as fishing and hunting groups enjoy, permits a marked routinization of community life. The rather precise calendar of activities of the natives of Labrador is described by Junek as follows:

Latter part of June to the end of July: cod-fishing and "making" of cod, with occasional sealing by trap-nets. August: advent of dog-fish, end of cod-fishing, washing and drying of cod, repairing of herring nets, berry picking. September: herring-fishing, salting of cod, beginning of wood-gathering. October: wood-gathering with dog-teams. December to March: fox and weasel trapping. March: sealing on ice floes. April to May: sealing by trap nets, seal-skin curing and sealhide "barking." [22]

Settled agriculturalists develop an even more rigid and routinized system of timing. They are committed to a protracted series of processes involved in cultivation and the raising of animals which bind them to a local area. Lacking the nomad's opportunity to escape local hardships, they must maximize the productivity of their habitat. The limited growing season and the multiplicity of tasks connected with growing, preparing, and storing of food, the care of animals, and

---

20 W. Lloyd Warner, *A Black Civilization* (New York, 1937), 138.
21 "Essai sur les variations saisonnières des societés Eskimaux," *L'Annee Sociologique*, IX (1904-5), 39.
22 O. W. Junek, *Isolated Communities* (New York, American Book Co., 1937), 43. See also C. Daryll Forde, *Habitat, Economy and Society* (New York, 1934), 109-15.

the maintenance of equipment and of permanent shelters require a careful timing of activities. Functions must be adjusted to the seasonal shifts and changes within seasons and also to one another in a relatively complex division of labor.

The temporal patterning of interdependent activities, if it may be generalized, reveals the same outline in all but the simplest of communities. Each type of activity tends to occupy a particular place in the time span which is determined by its importance in the livelihood of the community and its relation to other functions. Sustenance activities usually take precedence over all other activities and thus occupy the primary position. The remaining functions are fitted into the temporal interstices occurring in and about the sustenance function. Eating is spaced in the rest intervals between work periods, and leisure pursuits come at the close of the work day. In areas of marked seasonality lengthy periods of intense sustenance activity are usually followed by seasons of relative inactivity. The latter are commonly devoted to numerous affairs which are crowded from the work seasons, such as religious ceremonials, visits abroad, trading, repairing equipment, etc.

The succession of activities comprising the daily and seasonal round of the independent community is accentuated at each period through the synchronization of the efforts of many individuals. This is perhaps the most striking temporal feature of the independent community and is the source of its distinctive rhythm. Mass participation characterizes all major activities. Hunting, canoe-building, preparing for ceremonies, agricultural processes, and so on, are done in concert often with a definite and precise cadence. There is, of course, a division of labor in which a number of functions are carried on concurrently and are timed to come to fruition at moments which make for greatest efficiency. Thus while the males are afield seeking food or caring for crops the other members of their households are gathering fuel, preparing food for consumption, and attending to various customary chores. Such coordination is of vital importance, though it is often obscured by the preponderating rhythm of synchronous behavior.

Time and the Dependent Community.—The growth of interdependence among scattered groups initiates a new temporal regime in community organization. Through the extension of communications and trade relationships man is freed from the dominance of seasonal cycles. He is released from sole reliance upon the resources of the local habitat and is enabled to draw his sustenance from widely scattered supplies. It is therefore possible to bridge the gaps between

periods of local abundance and to reduce materially the threat of
famine. Where this occurs the round of life assumes greater regularity and, in fact, is increasingly subject to human control. Timing
becomes more and more a matter of adjusting the functions of communal units in a progressively more complex division of labor. Even
the extractive functions, which remain exposed to the influence of
physical fluctuations, yield at many points to the timing of the division
of labor as expressed through the market phenomena of pricing and
credit. In other words, the dependent community develops a rhythm
within itself which is more responsive to what takes place in other
communities with which it is related than to the cycles of physical
variation in its immediate area.

The diurnal cycle, in the modern dependent community as in all
independent communities, constitutes the primary unit in the rhythm
of activity. The hours of sunlight are devoted to work and those of
darkness to recreation and rest. Collective activities are typically
day-spaced and within that phase of the cycle that routinization of
activity is precise; the night phase marks a temporary suspension of
most functions and a relaxation of routine and timing in those that
are carried on. This is observable in the movements of the community population. Each morning a significant portion of the population converges at a number of locations for the conduct of various
functions and each late afternoon it redistributes itself once more,
flowing back into its residential pattern. The pulsations of traffic
flow with reference to the central business district are shown in Figure 30. The curve for all movement attains an abrupt peak at
8 : 00 A.M. as a result of the movement of workers to places of employment. An influx of shoppers begins after 10 : 00 A.M. and reaches
a maximum between 12 : 00 noon and 1 : 00 P.M. A very heavy out-
flow of workers and shoppers sets in about 4 : 00 P.M. and continues
until 7 : 00 P.M. After the dinner hour there is a return to the central
district for various recreational services. The gradual decline of the
curve after 8 : 30 P.M. is in contrast to the precipitous decline after
5 : 30 P.M.

The daily cycle is interrupted periodically by the termination of
the longer weekly cycle. From Monday through Friday the rhythm
of community life as revealed in the ebb and flow of movement retains
the same pattern. On Saturday and on Sunday, however, different
patterns appear, as may be seen in Figure 31. Saturday, which begins
like any other weekday, shows a somewhat different rhythm. The
volume of movement continues high throughout the afternoon and
the evening, with peaks at 8 : 30 A.M., noon, 5 : 30 P.M., and 8 : 30 P.M.,

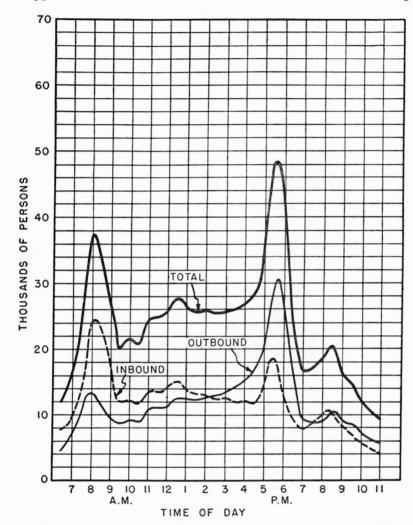

FIG. 30.—The volume of traffic flow into and out of the central business district, by hours of the day. (From John Paver and Miller McClintock, *Traffic and Trade* [New York: McGraw-Hill Book Co., Inc., 1935], 16. Used by permission.)

evincing the combination of shopping and recreational activities to which the day is devoted. That Sunday is primarily a recreational day is shown by its unique pattern of hourly movements. The large volumes of Sunday movement occur at hours different from other days of the week and also in different parts of the community. Movement gravitates not so much to the business center as to the highways and outlying residential areas.

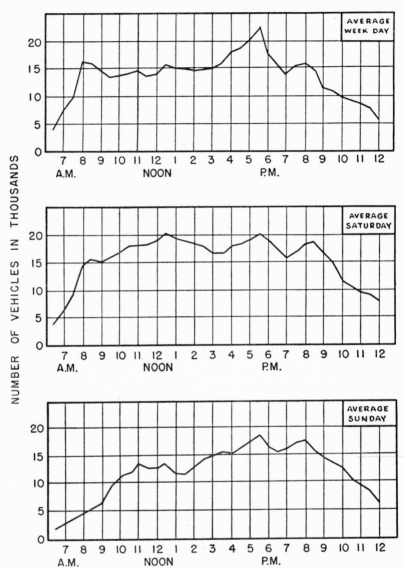

Fig. 31.—The volume of vehicular traffic into and out of the central business district, by hour and day of the week. (From John Paver and Miller McClintock, *Traffic and Trade* [New York: McGraw-Hill Book Co., Inc., 1935], 20. Used by permission.)

The rhythms of collective life, however, vary considerably in different-sized communities. In small communities there is a well-defined staggering in the operating times of work and recreational units. Work is restricted to the daylight hours and recreation to the evening hours. Corporate units offering specialized leisure time services function with a less than daily periodicity: motion picture theaters operate two or three times a week, while churches are active biweekly, weekly, and sometimes monthly. But as the size of the community increases marked temporal divisions tend to disappear.[23] Every increase in size increases the number of individuals requiring a service at any given time. Thus in the large city many different units function simultaneously and some continuously around the clock. Technological changes, notably the development of electric illumination, have exerted an important influence to this end. The incandescent lamp brought light conditions under control, minimizing the limiting effects of night on the spacing and duration of activities. Consequently a host of new units, serving amusement interests for the most part, came into existence to occupy the former period of darkness. The nocturnal phase of the daily round has steadily approached equivalence to the diurnal phase, especially in the larger communities. As periodicity gives way to continuity the community acquires greater temporal and functional symmetry.[24]

A noteworthy result of the more even or arhythmic flow of activity through the twenty-four-hour cycle is an increased efficiency in the use of community facilities. Where the day and night fluctuations are marked, facilities lie comparatively idle through a fourth or more of the twenty-four hour period. It has been observed that although the number of seats in motion picture theaters per capita is less in large cities than in small, per capita motion picture attendance is considerably greater in the larger cities.[25] This applies in like manner to physical equipment of all kinds—to sidewalks and streets, to sewer, water, and power lines, and to a large variety of buildings open to use by the public. But complete symmetry is never achieved. Most units require an interim for the repair and maintenance of equipment. Moreover, the custom of a daylight work routine remains strong even in the large metropolitan centers. Not only is the nocturnal phase incomplete, it tends toward specialization with reference to recreation and amusement.

---

[23] See Robert S. Lynd and Helen M. Lynd, *Middletown* (New York, 1929), 263.
[24] Cf. Orlando Park, "Concerning Community Symmetry," *Ecology,* XXII (April, 1941), 165.
[25] National Resources Committee, *Our Cities, Their Role in the National Economy* (Washington, D. C., 1937), 20.

In fact, even in large places there is a definite temporal succession in the peaks of activity, and to a certain extent of opening times, of different types of associational units from the early evening hours on through the night. Restaurants are filled between the hours of 5 :00 and 8 :00 P.M.; theaters from 8 :00 to 11 :00 P.M.; supper clubs and night clubs from 10 :00 P.M. to 2 :00 A.M.; and the remaining hours of the night are claimed by units offering services having a more tenuous community sanction. For the most part, the spacing of activities becomes less orderly as the night advances. It appears that as man's work is more definitely set to the clock and paced by the machine his leisure activities become more random and whimsical. Nighttime activities are therefore much less routinized than are those of the daytime. Evidences of this may be noted, in Figure 30, in the gradual decline in the volumes of traffic flow with the progress of the night.

The tendency toward community symmetry has its counterpart in the acceleration of the tempo of rhythms. Every advance in specialization and in the elaboration of mechanical technology has increased the rate of recurrence; and in the modern community an unprecedented pace has been reached. The power-driven machine applied to assembly line production has tremendously speeded human effort by a subdivision of tasks to extremes of minutia. In many instances, the tempo is carried well beyond the limits of man's reaction time by the incorporation of manual skills in precision machinery. Mechanical communication permits a continuous flow of instantaneous contacts between physically separated points with little or no regard for distance. Even transportation is approaching the speed of sound. Numerous ramifications of these mechanical conquests of time are felt throughout the structure of the community, affecting the tempo of all human relations.

The tempo of life is quicker in the community center than in the outlying area. Movements are faster and more frequent, relationships more transitory and doubtless more enervating than elsewhere in the community. The metropolitan center, with its concentrations of communication, its specialized units that carry on services for extended territory, and its selected personnel working intensively in an intricate pattern of relationships, manifests the extreme in the tempo of modern life. The nerve centers of the metropolis—the exchanges and news agencies that are in continuous contact with happenings near and far—are the points of most feverish activity. There man is in the midst of the most stimulating context that human ingenuity has thus far devised. By bringing into instantaneous focus the opportunities, the risks, and the tragedies of life, man's behavior is made to resemble that of an animal treated to a rapid succession of electric shocks. It is not surprising that the incidence of mental disorder is highest in metropolitan centers.[26]

The reduction of time has intensified competition in the production and sale of goods and this in turn has made time a factor of paramount importance in the success of enterprise. Interest, rent, and wages are all items of cost which are directly related to time. Since "time is money" in the operation of business, there is a constant stimulus to shorten the period between the extraction of raw materials and the sale of the finished product. "The quicker merchandise can be moved from the raw material to the ultimate consumer and the less merchandise, of whatever it may consist, is involved in the 'float,' so to speak, the more efficient and the more stable industry becomes." [27] This involves a speeding up of the production processes all along the line; and every invention of time-saving import is seized upon with avidity. The effect of accelerating tempo on railroad service is described in the passage following:

Silk trains, valued in millions, speeding from Pacific Coast ports to silk centers the width of a continent away, were heavily insured. The insurance was high, and was calculated not in days but in hours; the road which could promise accurate delivery could save in insurance sums large enough to make special schedules for silk a paying proposition. Vitamin research and the necessity for stimulating the jaded palate of America with fresh fruits and vegetables next laid their toll on the railroader. For instance, lettuce can be picked during only two or three hours of the day if it is to remain fresh and firm, and a delay of an hour or two in delivery to a commission house means that morning auctions are missed, buyers are surfeited, and huge losses must be sustained. The radio and telegraphic reports on the market give sellers and buyers instantaneous information on which they may act, but the goods put in transit on that information must reach their destination within the range of a few hours if they are to meet the market for which they were intended. Railroads bidding for the milk business must guarantee schedules as accurate as those of passenger trains if losses due to spoilage are not to eat up profits. Even though beef can be refrigerated and kept indefinitely, its delivery to meet a certain day's market, or to keep the production line of a packing house going, means that cattle trains have to be put on penalty schedule if a competing road is not to get the business.[28]

---

[26] C. Landis and J. Page, *Modern Society and Mental Diseases* (New York, 1938), 44 ff.

[27] Alfred P. Sloan, Jr., quoted by Arthur Pound, *The Turning Wheel* (New York, 1934), 334.

[28] Reprinted from *The Railroader*, 1940, by W. Fred Cottrell with the permission of the author and of the publishers, Stanford University Press, Stanford University, Calif., 64.

The standardization of grades, prices, and measurements has also contributed greatly to the increase of tempo and the tightening of the web of time relationships. The effect of standardization in accelerating the work of the factory is obvious. It has made for a smoother and more rapid flow of commodities; and has also made possible the purchase and sale of goods without personal inspection. Retail merchandising underwent a pronounced quickening of pace as fixed prices for commodities replaced the old higgling and dickering between buyers and sellers.[29] Instalment buying has likewise facilitated the movement of inventories. Prices are closely geared to the rate of turnover of stocks and the larger business units are continuously making price studies in order to establish up-to-the-minute standards for different commodities.

The incentive to save time is not limited to manufacturing and distribution. It is evident as well in the production of organic materials. Agriculturalists and students of biology are constantly at work endeavoring to accelerate the life processes of domesticated plants and animals. By the selection of seeds, the crossing of strains, grafting, the substitution of chemical solutions for soils, etc., it is possible to increase the tempo and also to effect important changes in the quality and distribution of organic resources. "By crossing Red Fife wheat with early-maturing hard Red Calcutta, Saunders produced the celebrated Marquis wheat which can be harvested in 103 days after sowing."[30] As a result the wheat belt was pushed approximately two hundred miles north into the western provinces of Canada.

The increasing speed of the machine and the greater standardization of tasks involved encourages a sharper separation of time into work and leisure periods. Compensation for monotony and relaxation from the tiring pace of machine processes assume major importance for the worker. Organized labor is continuously striving to shorten the work day and the work week and, in fact, to reduce the speed of work activity. This shortening of work time and the lengthening of leisure time has profound effects upon the structure of the community. It has greatly encouraged a multiplication of recreational

---

[29] Industrialization in an old agrarian area, such as China, is hampered by the standardization it involves, as, for example, in wage payments. Higgling with employers for wages is the worker's ancient prerogative; it is a basis of competition among workers from which prestige is derived. Only with great reluctance, therefore, does the Chinese worker submit to the impersonal standardized wage-scale of the modern system. The same difficulty is encountered in respect to the need for uniform starting and stopping times. See Kuo-Heng Shih, *China Enters the Machine Age,* trans. Hsiao-Tung Fei and Francis L. V. Hsu (Cambridge, Mass., 1944), 63-77.

[30] Enid Charles, *The Twilight of Parenthood* (New York, 1934).

services, which together have come to form a major industry and a further complication of the community's temporal pattern.

The rhythmic functioning of the dependent community, with its multiplicity of differentiated parts and its rapid tempo, requires a closely articulated timing system. Even such a minor thing as the failure of the milkman or the postman to call at his regular time creates disturbances which may disrupt the activities in a number of inter-related units. Any interruption in the schedule of a transportation facility, any change in opening or closing hours of banks, stores, the-aters, and other agencies is always productive of more or less con-fusion. The timing system is subjected therefore to various explicit and formalized controls. Timing specialists such as traffic managers, dispatchers, efficiency experts, and the like are employed to maintain and improve the routines of activities; and time units, operating sched-ules, and holidays are enacted into laws.

The timing system of the dependent community resembles that of the independent community in that it is paced and controlled, to a very large extent, by the routine of the unit, or units, which carry on the principal sustenance activity. In one instance it may be a mining enterprise, in another a number of factories, a complement of service agencies, or a university. Since the major industry is the chief source of employment, it determines the beginning and the ending of the working day and thus regulates the movements of population and the operating times of many if not of all the other communal units.

That influence is evident in the rhythm of family life. The hour of rising, the schedule of meals, the periods of recreation, and the time of retiring in the family are governed by the routine of the employing agency. And just as there is functional differentiation in the com-munity so there is diversity among familial rhythms. Families whose working members are employed in subordinate occupations operate on schedules which differ from those of families whose members hold executive and professional positions.[31] In general the latter begin their daily round later and end it earlier than do the former and also enjoy a greater freedom from fixed routines. Hence prestige tends to be correlated with starting time.

All other units likewise accommodate their routines to that set by the dominant units, though they differ in this respect in accordance with their respective functions. The adjustment of recreational serv-ices to the after-work and holiday hours has already been noted. The

---

[31] See Robert S. Lynd and Helen M. Lynd, *Middletown* (New York, 1929), 53-54, and George A. Lundberg, Mirra Komarovsky, and Mary A. McInerny, *Leisure: A Suburban Study* (New York, 1934), 92 ff.

operations of passenger transportation agencies are regulated by the starting and ending of the working day and the resulting tides of population flow. Daily newspapers time their activities so that the news reaches the people when it may be read—in the early morning and late afternoon. Banks, legal firms, freight carriers, and numerous other units serving business and industry arrange their schedules so as to maximize the accessibility of their services. Nor are churches, schools, courts, and government offices free from the controlling influence of the basic rhythm in the community.

The intricate temporal pattern formed by the interweaving of numerous different functional rhythms acts as a coercive force on the behavior of the community's members. They may ignore it only at the risk of isolation from a large part of the collective life. The resistance of workers to night shift assignments grows out of just such an experience. Night work confuses the individual's family life and excludes him from many neighborhood and community affairs.[32] The railroad worker, particularly the trainman, is more or less permanently committed to a passive role in his community of residence, for his work schedule bears no relation to the rhythm of the community. He cannot accept civil responsibility nor can he maintain an active membership in a local group. If his family accommodate themselves to the temporal pattern of the community, they see him at irregular intervals, or if they adjust to his time schedule, their participations in community activities are intermittent.[33]

The dominating influence of the rhythm of the principal sustenance unit is clearly revealed in the effects of its interruption. If severe enough, an interruption may lead to a complete breakdown in the community timing system. That result was observed by Dr. Lazarsfeld and his colleagues in their excellent study of protracted unemployment in Marienthal, Austria.[34] The closing of the rayon plant there deprived the community not only of the major source of employment but of the very basis of the rhythm of collective life as well. Lacking the sustaining routine of plant operation, the tempo of all activities was visibly slowed, schedules were disrupted and fell into confusion, and, for a large part of the population, time seemed to lose its meaning. Leisure time activities, which might have been expected to multiply and absorb the energies of the people, actually decreased. Memberships in clubs lapsed and reading matter in the library was neglected.

---

[32] Paul and Faith Pigors, *Human Aspects of Multiple Shift Operations* (Cambridge, Mass., 1944), 33. See also Robert S. and Helen M. Lynd, *op. cit.,* 55.

[33] W. F. Cottrell, *op. cit.,* 71-74.

[34] *The Unemployed of Marienthal* (Leipzig, 1933), trans. Adelaide R. Hesse, F.E.R.A. Research Library, chap v.

Holidays and week-end days became like all other days. Only the children, by virtue of the continuation of school, retained their former routine.

What was an exceptional situation in Marienthal occurs, though in more orderly fashion, with seasonal regularity in a vacation resort area. The primary industry of such a place is of course the provision of services for a population of periodic vacationers. If that is the only basis of sustenance, as is the case of Ocean City, New Jersey,[35] the fluctuations may be extreme. In Ocean City the resident population annually varies from about 5,000 in the winter months to 60,000 or more in the summer months.[36] During the busy season the place burgeons with closely timed activities, but in the off-seasons the tempo slows and the timing is relaxed. Shops close their doors and their operators depart, the personnel of public services turn leisurely to maintenance tasks, and family life assumes a different pattern. The number of workers per family declines and the volume of public relief increases, as may be observed in Tables 31 and 32.

TABLE 31

PERCENTAGE DISTRIBUTION OF FAMILIES BY NUMBER OF WORKERS PER FAMILY, SUMMER AND WINTER SEASONS, OCEAN CITY, N. J., 1940

Workers per family	Summer	Winter
Total	100.0	100.0
0	2.7	7.6
1	14.0	50.9
2	30.0	25.2
3	26.4	11.8
4	14.0	2.7
5	7.9	—
6 or more	5.2	1.8
Average number per family	2.8	1.6

Source: J. Ellis Voss, *Ocean City: An Ecological Analysis of a Satellite Community* (Philadelphia, 1941), 65.

A comparable fluctuation takes place on a larger scale as a result of what is called the business cycle, a type of rhythm peculiar to the modern dependent community. Whatever may be its cause, which it is not our purpose to investigate, the business cycle manifests itself as a periodic rise and fall in the rate and volume of economic activity.

[35] J. Ellis Voss, *Ocean City: An Ecological Analysis of a Satellite Community* (Philadelphia, 1941).
[36] *Ibid.*, 42.

TABLE 32

FREQUENCY OF WORK RELIEF AND DIRECT RELIEF ASSISTANCE,
BY MONTHS, OCEAN CITY, N. J., 1939

Month	Assignments to W.P.A.	Direct relief orders
Total	1,048	1,216
January	234	342
February	180	312
March	94	245
April	62	109
May	12	56
June	2	6
July	8	6
August	21	7
September	55	6
October	100	7
November	77	26
December	203	94

Source: J. Ellis Voss, *Ocean City: An Ecological Analysis of a Satellite Community* (Philadelphia, 1941), 128.

Since they are contingent upon and paced by the functioning of sustenance-producing units, all other activities fluctuate with the business cycle. The effects are more numerous than might appear at first glance: they penetrate every aspect of the round of community life.

The impact of business cycles is most obvious with respect to employment. Unlike the peasant farmer who, though he may be underemployed because of his small holdings, is never unemployed, the worker in any industry in the dependent community is exposed periodically to the threat of enforced inactivity. Often it is possible for disengaged workers to find employment elsewhere. But the difficulty in securing off-season work is great where workers and the units are highly specialized in their occupational and industrial activities. Moreover, as the size of the producing unit—factory or shop—increases with the growth of mass production a temporary shutdown or retrenchment leaves disproportionately large numbers of individuals unoccupied at one time and place. This is vividly demonstrated by the automobile industry, which is highly concentrated geographically and the units of which employ tens of thousands of workers. The results are aggravated by the sensitive interlinkages among units, which necessitate that the closing of one unit be followed by the closing of others. Thus a cessation of activities in the automobile industry throws such large numbers out of work that it is impossible for the community to absorb them in other types of employment.

Nor is modern agriculture immune to the effects of business fluctuations. As agriculture becomes specialized it becomes market-oriented. The farmer turns to the production of cash crops, his household industries migrate to the city, and he becomes more and more like the specialized urban worker in his subjection to the business cycle. He is employed, even overemployed, in certain producing seasons, while in others he is almost totally unemployed. One of the outstanding features of the great depression of the 1930's was the extent to which the agricultural population was affected, especially in those parts of the world where specialization was most highly developed. Government aid to destitute farmers was as extensive—and in some places even more extensive—as the aid to unemployed in towns and cities.

Much of the efficiency which might accrue from work specialization in our modern order is cancelled by losses resulting from successive intervals of inactivity. Wages and costs are high in part because of the discontinuity of employment in the different spheres of activity. The fact that the individual must consume regularly whether he works or not necessitates high wages during the periods of employment in order that he may carry through the periods of unemployment. One of the major problems of the present age is to obtain the advantages of specialization and at the same time stabilize employment.

Alternating expansion and contraction of the volume of business activity reaches beyond employment as such to influence the succession of generations in the labor force. An important problem in every society is the fitting of each new generation into the division of labor. This problem has grown more acute as a consequence of the extension of the average length of life which has made for an overlapping of generations far beyond that of former times. Usually the overlapping is adjusted by expansion of the economy: the younger generations are absorbed by the rise of new industries. But when expansion ceases, as in periods of depression, youths are forced into competition with the older workers of the community for employment. Since the depression phase of the cycle frequently lasts for from five to ten years, the upward swing takes on a new generation, leaving many of the older workers permanently unemployed.

Incident to the fluctuations of employment are numerous correlating cycles. Births and deaths, marriage and divorce,[37] migration,[38] and still other phenomena are distributed in time in close

---

[37] Maurice B. Hexter, *Social Consequences of the Business Cycle* (New York, 1925).

[38] Harry Jerome, *Migration and Business Cycles* (New York, 1926).

correspondence with the ebb and flow of business activity. Sustenance units regulate the flow and distribution of income through which a very large and increasing proportion of relationships in the dependent community are mediated.

The recurrent phases of the business cycle leave their marks on the physical structure of the community. During the upward swing of business the community expands its plant and equipment, for it is in this period that expenditures on capital goods—dwellings, factories, streets and utilities, etc.—attain their maximum momentum. Conversely, with the onset of business decline and falling prices, expenditures on capital goods recede to a minimum. Accordingly, the business cycle leaves an impress on the community somewhat analogous to the effect of rainfall cycles on the yearly rings of growth in trees. It must be noted, however, that current policies of deficit spending may reduce the effects of cyclical change and smooth the rate of capital replacement and expansion.

Summary.—Although space and time are different aspects of the same thing such that it is difficult to experience one without reference to the other, the discussion in this chapter deals primarily with temporal distribution and organization. Time is a dimension on which all activities and their interrelations are measurable. Rhythm, tempo, and timing are distinguishable characteristics of time experience. Rhythm refers to the phenomenon of regular recurrences and is evident in the physical environment, the physiological processes of organisms, and overt behavior of all kinds. Tempo pertains to the rate of recurrence: the three principal types of rhythms differ in tempo and also include many variations of tempo. Timing relates to the tendency toward mutual adjustment of rhythms. It may take the form of synchronization where rhythms with similar tempos are concerned or of coordination where rhythms of different tempos are involved.

Man's adjustment to the physical world seems to involve a timing of physiological with physical rhythms only in respect to the diurnal cycle. Adjustments to climatic or seasonal fluctuations is accomplished through the timing of behavioral or functional rhythms. His greatest problem in this connection concerns the rhythm in his food supply. Three general modes of accommodation to temporal variations in food supplies are observable; these are: movement, storage, and circulation. Movement or nomadism is characteristic of simpler peoples. The use of storage to bridge the gaps between growing seasons is found in sedentary peoples, particularly those who live in independent communities. Circulation, involving the exchange of goods, displaces storage where the dependent type of community prevails.

The collective life of every human group embodies a system of reckoning time by which its many activities are ordered. Major happenings serve as primary reference points in the calculation of lapsed time and the before and after periods are subdivided in terms of the durations of familiar recurrences. The lunar cycle and the diurnal cycle are universally recognized units of time. In independent communities there is small need for precision in the temporal order; hence such communities usually deal in large units of time. But the complexities of the dependent community call for an intensive subdivision of time and the units employed tend to approach the infinitely small.

The basic rhythm of the independent community is closely adjusted to and governed by the rhythms in the physical and biotic environment. In the temporal organization of the community the sustenance function occupies the primary or key position: other functions are distributed in the unoccupied time spaces preceding and following that claimed by sustenance activity. Since there is relatively little differentiation in the independent community, synchronization is a more conspicuous phase of temporal organization than is coordination.

The dependent community develops a rhythm of functioning that is more responsive to what is taking place in other communities than to fluctuations in the local environment. A diurnal cycle is much in evidence, however, as the ebb and flow of traffic reveals. Size of community accounts for differences in the amplitudes of rhythms: rhythm is most pronounced in small places and tends to diminish in amplitude with increase in size. In very large communities temporal symmetry, or arhythmic functioning, tends to characterize the daily round, though complete symmetry is never achieved. Tempo likewise increases with size of community. The multiplication of activities and of population involved in activities accelerates the rate of recurrence. Competition plays an important part in speeding the tempo of purchase and sale and of moving goods from place to place. The reduction of time involved in production processes even extends into agriculture. Numerous closely geared rhythms require that studied attention be given to their control and regulation, hence the emergence of various timing specialists. Dominance over the temporal pattern is exercised by the rhythm of the principal sustenance unit. That is evident in the consequences of interruptions in its routine of operations: such an event spreads chaos through the temporal order of the community. But where interruptions are themselves rhythmic, the community acquires an over-all rhythm which is accommodated to the fluctuations in its sustenance units. The business cycle is a type of rhythm peculiar to the dependent community and has wide ramifications among all the manifold rhythms comprising the temporal order.

SUPPLEMENTARY REFERENCES

BREESE, GERALD W. *The Daytime Population of the Central Business District of Chicago with Particular Reference to the Factor of Transportation.* Chicago: The University of Chicago Press, 1949.

CARREL, ALEXIS. "Physiological Time," *Science,* LXXIV (1931).

COTTRELL, W. F. "Of Time and the Railroader," *American Sociological Review.* IV (April, 1939).

FRANK, LAWRENCE K. "Time Perspective," *Journal of Social Philosophy,* IV (1939).

MALINOWSKI, B. "Lunar and Seasonal Calendar in the Trobriands," *Journal of the Royal Anthropological Institute,* LVII (1927).

McSPARRAN, J. A. "Why the Farmers Oppose Daylight Saving," *National Municipal Review,* XII (September, 1923).

PART IV

CHANGE AND DEVELOPMENT

Chapter 16

INTRODUCTION

Much of what has already been said pertains to the development and change of organization. It is very difficult even in abstract discussion to achieve a complete separation of structural and dynamic aspects. But since in the preceding section our emphasis has been upon the former, in this section it shall be upon the latter, for one is as important as the other.

We shall define change as any irreversible or nonrepetitive alteration of an existing pattern of relationships. This, it should be noted, excludes such routine sequences as the diurnal and seasonal cycles in the functioning of a community, the succession of generations in the division of labor, the daily ebb and flow of population, and so on. These are stable elements in an established order. Change occurs when one pattern of relationships is replaced by another or, what amounts to the same thing, when an existing functional rhythm gives way to a new and different rhythm.

The workings of change, however, whether it concerns social phenomena or phenomena of any other kind, has long been a philosophical problem for which as yet there is no final solution. The issue involves a number of perplexing questions; for example: What are the units of change? How much difference must there be in before and after states to constitute a change? And what is the context in which change is to be observed? Such questions are differently resolved in two views of the matter that occupy the center of attention in most debates. They may be described as the continuous and discontinuous conceptions of change.

According to the one view, change is a continuous and uninterrupted process. It proceeds constantly and inexorably by infinitely small alterations. In short intervals of time, therefore, change is often imperceptible. Still, nothing is at rest; nothing is the same in successive instants. And the changes we observe are but the cumulative effects of innumerable modifications which together form a continuum.

In the second view, the discontinuous conception, change is regarded as a cyclical process in which variation alternates with stability. It is the assumption of this conception that every phenomenon is so constituted as to be resistant to modification for limited periods of time. Each object or combination of objects represents an equilibrium of mutually sustaining forces. External pressures build up against that equilibrium until eventually it is broken and change follows rapidly. The modifications which ensue work toward the reestablishment of equilibrium on a new or different basis. Inertia sets in again and a new cycle is begun. The explosive character of change implied in the discontinuous conception is responsible for its being described as the "catastrophic theory." [1]

It must be granted that both theories have their merits. The superiority of one over the other seems to depend primarily upon how the problem at hand is stated rather than upon a judgment as to the relative truth of each.[2] For the study of problems involving a limited number of measurable variables the continuous conception of change is easily applicable. It assumes a fairly mature knowledge of the subject matter or at least considerable agreement as to what are the relevant operating factors. But for problems concerning intricately constituted events, many of the factors in which are of undetermined importance, the continuous theory raises almost insuperable obstacles to observation. Thus it is necessary to stress the more salient and accessible manifestations of change to the neglect of the many less conspicuous and minor evidences. Accordingly change appears as a discontinuous process. Major changes are usually the cumulative results of numerous minor changes and are therefore spaced at intervals through time.

Social scientists have generally found the cyclical or discontinuous theory more congenial to their subject matter and type of problem.[3] The human community is so complex as to defy simultaneous observation of all its parts or of all factors influencing its form. Moreover, those students who attempt to deal with the community as a whole are interested only in changes which concern the whole. Changes in the parts become important only so far as they alter fundamentally the general structure of the community. And, inasmuch as fundamental structural alterations are observed to be widely spaced in time,

---

[1] See R. E. Park, "Succession, An Ecological Concept," *American Sociological Review,* I (April, 1936), 175.

[2] In many instances in which the two interpretations are opposed the difference appears to be a confusion of the fact of change with the form of change. Change may be assumed to be constantly going on and is therefore continuous. But without contradicting that position the discontinuous conception holds that change proceeds unevenly, in a series of stages.

[3] F. J. Teggart, *The Theory of History* (New Haven, Conn.: Yale University Press, 1925) ; and W. I. Thomas, *Source Book for Social Origins* (Chicago, 1909), chap. ii.

community change seems to be most adequately accommodated in the discontinuous conception.

There are, moreover, characteristics of human activity which lend further support to this view of change. Man's behavior is notoriously inert as to form. As behavior is adapted to the conditions of life it crystallizes in habit and becomes unyielding to novel circumstances. The rigidity of the individual habit is reinforced, in part, by that of complementing habits which together form a stable system of behavior. And the habit system of a people, the "cake of custom," as Bagehot described it, limits the field of perception and fixes the universe of comprehension. It is thus the arbiter of what is useful and good and, in effect, is sooner or later identified with the good. To these bases of rigidity must be added the fact that man builds his habits into roadways, tools, and all the physical equipage of daily life. The existence of a building or tool preserves appropriate behavior patterns at least for the duration of the usefulness of the instrumentality and often for long after obsolescence has set in. Collective life, in short, is inflexible at many points and therefore resistant to change. A fundamental change seems to require a cataclysmic disturbance, one which threatens the very existence of life itself.

These considerations proved so convincing that the cyclical interpretation of change, or natural history as it came to be called, gained a tremendous vogue among social scientists. The huge success achieved by biologists with the concept was, of course, a factor of no small consequence in giving it both prestige and promise. Accordingly the histories of a large assortment of social phenomena, including the family, private property, the newspaper, revolution, and many more, were reconstructed as natural histories. The subject matter of virtually every discipline of the social sciences was exposed to the hypothesis. It made its appearance in ecological literature as the concept *succession*. In this more recent application the idea was used originally to describe the series of events or stages involved in the replacement in an area of one type of occupant or land use by another.[4] The meaning of succession, however, was subsequently enlarged to embrace the emergence of entire communities and, in fact, the development of everything that may be regarded as having had a history.[5]

Criticisms of the attempts to deal with change in this fashion have been numerous and, in a large measure, justified. Although the nat-

---

[4] R. D. McKenzie, "The Scope of Human Ecology," in E. W. Burgess (ed.), *The Urban Community* (Chicago, 1926), 181.

[5] See Andrew W. Lind, *An Island Community: Ecological Succession in Hawaii* (Chicago, 1938), "Introduction," by R. E. Park, *ix-xvi*.

ural history or succession concept is an intriguing theoretical construct, it turns out to be a rather impracticable research tool. No stable criteria for the identification of stages have been developed, nor is there any means for determining the number and order of stages comprising a sequence. Verification of expositions of change in terms of a series of discrete stages each of which unfolds from a preceding one is therefore made extremely difficult, if not impossible.[6] For these reasons we shall restrict our use of succession to instances of change in which it has been shown to have utility.

A more productive approach to change is with reference to the patterns it displays. Only three will be mentioned here and but one will be treated in the following chapters. The three may be termed *expansion, conversion,* and *contraction.* By expansion is meant change of a developmental character in which a community is enlarged and extended, becoming not only more inclusive but also increasingly complex in its internal structure. Conversion, the second type, refers to that change in which one form or structure of relationships is replaced by another of essentially the same degree of complexity. In other words, conversion entails no long-run progression in the direction either of growth or decline. The third pattern of change, contraction, is merely the converse of expansion; it envisions the progressive reduction and, possibly, disappearance of a community. Both conversion and contraction are, with few exceptions, incidental to expansion. Hence, instead of receiving independent treatment, they will be discussed in conjunction with expansion.

Expansion is clearly the most important of the several patterns of change. It is through expansion, or cumulative change, that new types of communities replace old and that man's relations to habitat and to other forms of life are significantly altered. The study of expansion has the further advantage of revealing the many and varied manifestations of change that together constitute a continuing process. Before turning to an intensive examination of that process, however, it will be helpful to consider human mobility in some detail, for if change is to be at all visible, it must express itself in the movements of men.

SUPPLEMENTARY REFERENCES

CHAPIN, F. STUART. *Cultural Change.* New York: Appleton-Century-Crofts, Inc., 1928.
COOLEY, C. H. *Social Process.* New York: Chas. Scribner's Sons, 1918.

---

[6] It must be admitted that part of the problem grows out of the fact that the theory has been treated not as an hypothesis but as an *ex post facto* interpretation and as a means of generalizing historical data.

HOBHOUSE, L. T., WHEELER, G. G., and GINSBURG, M. *Material Culture and Social Institutions of the Simpler Peoples.* London; Chapman & Hall, 1915.

OGBURN, W. F., *Social Change: With Respect to Culture and Original Nature.* New York: B. W. Huebsch, 1923.

PRINCE, SAMUEL H. *Catastrophe and Social Change.* New York: Columbia University Press, 1920.

SPENCER, HERBERT. *Principles of Sociology,* 3d ed. New York: Appleton-Century-Crofts, Inc., 1923. Vol. 1.

Chapter 17

MOBILITY AND CHANGE

Change without movement is impossible. In organic life change-ability is the measure of adaptive capacity, and mobility is the mechanism of change. This is to say that wherever there is life there is movement: as the one ceases, so does the other. The scope and content of life, moreover, are defined by the facilities an organism possesses for overcoming distance.[1] That may be observed in the cycle of individual existence. Starting life with a minimum of activity, the individual gradually expands his sphere of movement as he advances from infancy, reaching his maximum attainment in early adulthood. As senility sets in the range of movement contracts and arrives again at the point from which it started. The extent of participation in the events of the life context varies along a correlating cycle.

Forms of life may be scaled and rated on the basis of capacity for movement. Plants and animals differ fundamentally in this respect. The stationary plant must achieve an adaptation to an environment delineated by the reach of its roots and leaves. Within its individual life span the plant is limited to tropismatic movements. The mobile animal lives in a wider world. His power of locomotion enables him to exploit a larger food area and also to adjust more quickly and selectively to environmental change. Accordingly the animal is regarded as a higher form of life than the plant. Perhaps it is because of superior mobility that we are more disposed to attribute consciousness to animals than to plants.

In man the ability to move is developed to an extraordinary degree. While many other organisms can move more swiftly, few are able to move so selectively and none is able to extend his power of mobility as can man. In addition to his native capacity for locomotion, man can call to his aid secondary agencies for conquering distance. Thus he has greatly enlarged his environment and has spread his settlement pattern more widely than has any other animal species.

---

[1] "The quality of life most useful in nature, from the point of view of the domination of a wider environment," wrote George W. Crile, "is the quality of changeableness, plasticity, mobility, or versatility." (*Man: An Adapting Mechanism* [New York, 1916], 18.)

It is largely, if not entirely, through the development of his capacity for movement that man has arrived at a position of world domination.

There are of course great inequalities among men with respect to mastery of the physical environment. And these are intimately associated with the comparative efficiency of the facilities used in transportation and communication. The so-called preliterate peoples are uniformly the least mobile. They are bound to a local habitat from which they can escape only with great difficulty and usually with outside aid. If one studies a map showing the distribution of ethnic groups about the world, he will observe that contemporary preliterate peoples are either isolated from or bypassed by interregional thoroughfares. Civilized peoples, on the other hand, are those peoples who have attained a high degree of mobility. This is reflected in the diversity of techniques and materials that have been assembled to make up the content of civilization as well as in the frequency and distance of movement by such peoples. So far as it is feasible to rank human groups on a qualitative scale, the capacity for movement provides a useful criterion.

Types of Mobility.—The manifestations of movement are numerous and varied. They differ in form, frequency, function, and in many other ways. Obviously, an adequate treatment of a phenomenon so diverse must proceed from a classification of some kind. In this respect there is also opportunity for considerable variation, since every classification reflects a special interest or problem. It may be helpful to examine a few different classifications before setting forth one suited to the problem of ecology.

Walter Heape, the zoologist, in his study of the breeding habits of animals, utilized a threefold classification of movement, namely, migration, emigration, and nomadism.[2] The first of these he defined as movement out of an area followed by a return to the point of origin. Emigration refers to movement involving a change of habitat but without a return to the home area. And nomadism is characterized by a continuous change of habitat, usually assuming a cyclical pattern.

A somewhat different scheme reflecting a preoccupation with the history of civilization is suggested by James Bryce.[3] Transference, according to Bryce, occurs when a large population forsakes its homeland and settles in a new area. In contrast to transference is dispersion which involves the expansion of a people over progressively wider

2 *Emigration, Migration and Nomadism* (Cambridge, 1931), chap. i.
3 "The Migration of the Races of Men Considered Historically," *Annual Report of the Smithsonian Institution, 1893* (Washington, D. C., 1894), 567-88.

areas while at the same time maintaining its hold on the original habitat. A third form of movement, described as permeation, is actually what is commonly referred to as cultural diffusion. Permeation denotes the movement of ideas, forms of behavior, and institutions rather than of individuals. This may be more appropriately regarded as an effect of the intergroup contacts occasioned by movements of people through space.

A third classification is that of Karl Bucher, an economic historian.[4] Bucher's types are much like those of Heape. He lists (1) migration with continuous change of locality, or nomadism; (2) migration with temporary change of settlement, i.e., followed by a return movement; and (3) migration with permanent resettlement at the destination.

Although these three classifications of movement emerged from different contexts, they bear a certain resemblance to one another. Both Heape and Bucher recognize a class of movements that are routine and implicit in an established mode of life, i.e., nomadism. And all three authors observe a kind of movement that is unique in the sense that it is expressive of change. Bryce's classification is concerned entirely with this type of movement. Thus it appears that the several schemes may be merged in a simpler dichotomous grouping. Two general types, which may be called recurrent and nonrecurrent movements,[5] appear to be sufficient to contain virtually all instances of mobility and also to identify the distinction of principal importance among them.

Recurrent movements, as the name indicates, comprise all those movements that are routine and repetitive. They might also be called functional, for it is by this type of movement that the functioning of a community is carried on. All the comings and goings, transportations and circulations, that make up the daily, weekly, and seasonal rounds of collective life fall into this category. The recurrent movements are expressive of the rhythm and timing of community activities.

In addition to the routine movements occurring within a circumscribed communal area, there are a number of special forms of recurrent movement. Nomadism, for example, is of this order. The nomadic group moves over a well-defined orbit with calendrical regularity. Likewise, the shuttlings or transhumance of sedentary pastoral peoples are implicit in an established mode of life. The seasonal moves of casual workers, the circulations of itinerant merchants, preachers, and other professionals, and the more recent vacation travel are similar in character. From the standpoint of the functioning of the commu-

---

[4] *Industrial Evolution,* trans. S. M. Wickett (New York, 1907), 352.
[5] Cf. Clements and Shelford, *Bio-Ecology,* 61.

nity these differ in no significant respect from the daily trip to the office or grocery store, or the weekly trip to the theater. Each is an integral part in an established organization and is therefore essential to the maintenance of that organization. Recurrent movements involve no break with the past, no disruption of an established order. They are the means by which an existing equilibrium is maintained. They are the basic and the visible manifestation of stability. As such they differ markedly from the movements which comprise the second category.

Nonrecurrent movements are movements out of and without return to a given context of life conditions. They follow from an alteration of fundamental conditions which requires a readjustment of population in a modified or entirely new structure of relationships. In the sifting and sorting of population which ensues nonrecurrent movements may take the form of a complete displacement of some portion of the total population for resettlement elsewhere, of a local redistribution of some individuals in a different alignment of relationships, or of an influx of individuals from other localities. Such movements are therefore symptomatic of change; they involve a transition from one pattern of organization to another. Nonrecurrent movement is both the means by which change is effected and the most accessible and measurable evidence of change. It is to this type that the term *migration* is usually applied,[6] and it is, of course, in this type of movement that we are primarily interested in the present chapter.

Migration is unquestionably one of the most impressive of the phenomena of human behavior. It has dominated the thoughts of chroniclers of man's activities since time immemorial. To some observers migration is an occurrence so common as to suggest in all men a migratory "instinct" or wanderlust which is forever propelling them onward.[7] Others, however, have been impressed by the novel and revolutionary character of migration. These students look upon man as inherently stable or sedentary, to be dislodged from his accustomed habitat only by events of cataclysmic dimensions.[8] Such differences of interpretation recall the old tale of the seven blind men and the elephant. To the historian who seeks to grasp the broad sweep of human events in its entirety it may well appear that migration is the

---

[6] P. K. Whelpton, *Needed Population Research* (Lancaster, Pa., 1938), 123-25; W. F. Willcox (ed.), *International Migrations*, Vol. II (New York, 1931), 85-86; and Julius Isaac, *Economics of Migration* (New York, 1947), 4-5.

[7] Cf. Ragnar Numelin, *The Wandering Spirit, A Study of Human Migration* (London, 1937).

[8] Cf. Arnold J. Toynbee, *A Study of History* (London, 1934), Vol. III, Annex II to IIIA.

rule rather than the exception. Indeed it is probable that migration has provided most of the stuff of which history is composed. The spectacular breaks with the past, the downfalls of sovereigns, the conquests of peoples, the collapse of civilizations, the rise of new regimes mark the beginnings or the endings of migrations. Such events quicken the minds of men and cause them to create legends and documentary records. The large historic perspective, however, obscures much that is important. It is as definitely a human tendency to maintain habit systems as to change them. But to regard man as essentially sedentary, though this may lie closer to the truth, is likewise reflective of incomplete perception. It stems from a preoccupation with a given local situation which is seen only in its general outline. Rather than categorize man's behavior as of one pattern or the other, it is more profitable to enquire into the factors that influence migration.

Causes of Migration.—A proper understanding of migration requires a knowledge of its causes. Too often, however, the search for causes becomes a matter of ascertaining the motives of migrants, though the announced motives may or may not have any connection with the factors of change attending the migration. It is said that the Puritan Pilgrims moved to secure religious freedom, the Palatinate Germans to find opportunity for free political expression, and the peasants of Southern Italy for the more vulgar end of economic gain. Some have suggested that migration is psychological in origin, beginning with an idea which spreads and gathers impetus through contagion.[9] Interpretations such as these locate the cause of migration in the individual migrants and only secondarily, if at all, in the environmental and communal context. No doubt migration involves psychological elements, but it is also a manifestation of external changes. For an understanding of the general phenomenon it is important to know not why the migrant thinks he has moved but the conditions or characteristics common to all instances of migration and lacking in situations from which there is no migration.

A circumstance which seems to attend all occasions of migration is what may be called overpopulation. The term overpopulation is used advisedly, for it describes a relative condition; it is a matter of the ratio of number to the opportunities for life. A surplus number of people may come about through excessive natural increase such as occurs in each generation in many old agrarian areas. Excess population, however, is often produced by an abrupt reduction in the food supply. Famines are usually a consequence of crop failures or other

---

[9] A. H. Carr-Saunders, *The Population Problem* (New York, 1922), 301.

cataclysms rather than of slowly accumulated deficiencies of food supplies. A similar effect resulted from the destruction of cotton crops by the boll weevil in southern United States during the first quarter of the present century. It was pointed out in an earlier chapter that overpopulation also may be a function of the ratio of numbers to jobs available as well as to the supply of food or raw materials. Thus an area with more wage workers than opportunities for employment is overpopulated in the same sense as an agricultural area in which famine conditions prevail. This kind of situation, since it is a product of market conditions, is far more dynamic than one harnessed to seasonal changes. It may give way very quickly to a condition of underpopulation with a revival of production or a realignment of market relations.

Migration involves, however, a destination as well as a starting point. Overpopulation is the stimulus; it describes the conditions in the home area which make migration advisable. For the stimulus to become effective there must be a destination, a place or area in which circumstances are favorable to the absorption of additional settlers. The cause of migration, in other words, appears to be twofold: it consists in an excess of numbers in the area of origin, and underpopulation in the area of destination. These correspond to the "push" and the "pull" factors set forth by A. C. Haddon [10] and others.

In other words migration seems invariably to be a matter of the comparative desirability of areas. Contrary to the older view of historians and anthropologists, it is likely that there have been few if any instances of blind wandering or spontaneous desertion of areas. The abrupt and violent invasions of Europe by Asiatic hordes so often cited as evidence of sheer expulsion appear to have been inadequately described. Penetrating study such as that of Gilbert Murray [11] reveals that the early Barbarian invasion of Hellas was preceded by a long period of small scale movements to and from the area by families singly and in small groups. In this way the peninsula was explored and knowledge of the superior opportunities it afforded became available to the band which subsequently overran and occupied the land. Virtually all extended movements are similarly prefaced by periods of discovery. Incidental contacts, bold pioneering, sallies by venturesome individuals, trading relationships, or even chance departures from a beaten track may be the initial source of information about a neighboring area. Not infrequently the appraisal of opportunities to be found in a possible place of destination may be inadequate or

---

[10] *The Wandering of Peoples* (Cambridge, 1919), chap. i.
[11] *The Rise of the Greek Epic* (Oxford, 1911), 67.

misleading. But whether correct or incorrect, based on facts or hearsay, information or misinformation, as the case may be, these reports are a decisive element in releasing and directing the flow of migration.

The outpouring of Europeans to colonial frontiers, though at first organized and supervised by business enterprises in the form of the plantation, was initiated and continuously stimulated by the knowledge of unused resources at the various destinations. That the "free land" slogan was at odds with the land requirements of the modes of life of native peoples did not modify the force of the "pull" felt in Europe. To the European farmer and raw-material producer lands serving as breeding grounds for game animals or for periodic pasturage were unused lands and therefore available for their occupancy.[12] The superior opportunities in overseas areas provided a release to the pent-up pressures in the homeland and surplus population drained into a stream of migration.

The operation of "push" and "pull" influences is very nicely illustrated by the ebb and flow of European migration to the United States. Harry Jerome observed a close correlation between immigration and the business cycle as measured by pig iron production.[13] He found that changes in the flow of overseas migration lagged approximately six months behind business cycle alternations. Jerome's findings were confirmed in a later study of Swedish migrations to this country by Dorothy S. Thomas.[14] The movement of the Swedish population to the overseas destination, she pointed out, occurred chiefly when economic conditions in Sweden were depressed and opportunities in the United States were abundant. No other combination of circumstances in the two areas produced an appreciable volume of migration from the one to the other.

Stated differently, it appears that migration flows from areas of low rates of capital investment to areas of high rates of capital investment. Thus may be understood the failures of attempts of modern nations to induce emigration of their citizens to agricultural dominions.[15] The unwillingness to move, despite the promise of subsidies, reflects a lack of suitable opportunity as defined in the industrial economy of the present era. Agriculture is a depressed industry, subordinated economically and politically to mechanical industry.[16] It attracts rela-

---

[12] See the discussion of "open" and "closed" resources in H. J. Nieboer, *Slavery as an Industrial System* (The Hague, 1910), 418.

[13] *Migration and Business Cycles.*

[14] *Social and Economic Aspects of Swedish Population Movements, 1750-1933* (New York, 1941), 166-69.

[15] See Chapter 9.

[16] Cf. Owen Lattimore, "The Mainsprings of Asiatic Migration," in Isaiah Bowman (ed.), *The Limits of Land Settlement* (New York, 1937), chap. v.

tively little capital and yields a low level of living. Hence the trend of settlement is away from rather than toward agricultural settlement.

The effect of knowledge is displayed indirectly in the distance covered by migration. Ravenstein, in his studies of rural migration to European cities, observed a predominance of short-distance moves.[17] Evidently the knowledge of alternative opportunities varies with distance. The northward movement of Negroes in the United States, prior to 1916 especially, also followed the short-distance pattern, proceeding as a state-to-state displacement.[18] In the more recent migrations to war-industry centers workers who moved the shortest distances found better jobs and found them more quickly than workers who moved long distances.[19] In general, long-distance migrants are solicited or recruited. Agents of employers and others interested in adding to the population of a locality are sent out to propagandize, offer inducements, and provide assistance to potential immigrants. Without such carriers of information the flow from distant places would be slow. A large part of European migration to North America was solicited as is also much of the interregional movement of labor in the United States.

That the information which guides migrants is frequently inadequate or erroneous is evident in the large back-flow that has attended modern migrations. In earlier periods the price of error was a heavy mortality rather than a return movement. Of the 60 million Europeans estimated to have moved overseas in the 19th century, approximately 20 million returned to Europe. In other words, a minimum of 80 million moves was needed to produce a net migration of about 40 million.[20] Likewise, to establish a net migration from farms to cities in the United States of 6.3 million, in 1920-30, and of 2.2 million in 1930-40, required 31 and 22 million moves, respectively. The lost motion and wastage of resources resulting from misguided migrations are tremendous.[21] It is for this reason that modern governments

---

[17] E. G. Ravenstein, "The Laws of Migration," *Journal of the Royal Statistical Association*, XLVIII (1885), 167-235; LII (1889), 241-305; see also S. Stouffer, "Intervening Opportunities: A Theory Relating Mobility and Distance," *American Sociological Review*, V (December, 1940), 845-68.

[18] National Resources Committee, *The Problems of a Changing Population* (Washington, D. C., 1938), 99.

[19] *National Defense Migration,* Hearings before the Select Committee Investigating National Defense Migration, House of Representatives, Part 27, Washington Hearings, Feb. 1942 (Washington, 1942), 10322.

[20] A. M. Carr-Saunders, *World Population,* 49-50.

[21] In a study of intrastate migration to Flint and Grand Rapids, Michigan, during the depression years 1930 to 1935, it was found that while the unemployment rate prior to migration was significantly higher for migrants than for nonmigrants, the differential was much greater in the post-migration period. That may have been

have sought to regularize and facilitate migration through systems of employment exchanges.

As a simplified statement of causation, therefore, it may be concluded that migration presupposes a condition of disequilibrium in the form of an excess number of people in one locality, and either incompletely used resources or disequilibrium in the form of too few people in an alternative place of settlement. The effect of migration is to permit a restoration of equilibrium at both the point of origin and the point of destination. Like every other simple theoretical formulation this one assumes all related conditions to be constant. That related conditions are not constant in practice is evident in the vast differences in the responsiveness of peoples to migratory stimuli. Apparently there is a more complex causation than that contained in complementing conditions of overpopulation and underpopulation. If so, we should expect to find the complicating factors as elements of different types of community structure. As already observed, the existence of destinations for movement is contingent upon available knowledge which is in itself incidental to the structure and functioning of the community. But the organization of the community conditions the migratory tendency in other ways as well.

Migration and the Independent Community.—The independent community, by virtue of its self-sufficiency and insularity, imposes numerous restraints on migration. Self-sufficiency necessitates a steadfast adherence to proved techniques and arrangements, and stability, in turn, preserves the independent existence. This is both cause and effect of the nature of the community's relation to the land. The population, in producing its own sustenance directly from local resources, is bound to the land by a routine of long-run processes, such as the maturation of plants and the breeding cycles of food animals. It is thus immobilized. Nomadic peoples are only somewhat less restricted than sedentary. Although the former are mobile in the sense that they circulate over relatively large areas in the course of the seasonal round, nomadic life is stabilized on the basis of movement. The pastoral economy involves a commitment to seasonally governed processes from which the population is seldom able to extricate itself.

The attachment to place which arises in the isolation of self-sufficient existence is in itself a powerful deterrent to movement and re-

due to unequal access to sources of information concerning available jobs. Whether the high unemployment rates of migrants at destinations resulted in a return movement is not known. (Ronald Freedman and Amos H. Hawley, "Unemployment and Migration in the Depression, 1930 to 1935," *Journal of the American Statistical Association,* XLIV [June, 1949], 260-72.)

settlement elsewhere. Behavior becomes intimately and almost inextricably bound up with the objects and characteristics of the universe of daily life. This association is reinforced by the interlocking of habit systems in which each behavior pattern is contingent upon every other, the whole constituting an effective mode of life. Habit and habitat are in fact inseparable abstractions; the habitat is simply that segment of the physical world to which the habits of the group apply. Thus where the objects of the habitat are stable over long periods of time there is a strong disinclination to move, not only because of the profound implication in a familiar context but also because habits are probably not applicable elsewhere. It is not surprising, therefore, to find in the members of the independent community a pronounced identification with the place of abode. Rather than the lands belonging to them, many preliterate peoples regard themselves as belonging to the land.[22] Similarly among peasant peoples the family is often identified with the land it occupies. A family bereft of its land holdings is without status and by the same token is excluded from active group membership.

Not only is there a fixity as to place, but the very cohesiveness of the community enables it to withstand many migration stimuli. The interdependences among its individuals are overlaid by sentiments of right and duty and cemented by common loyalties. Thus the shock of adverse climatic fluctuations or of depredations by enemies, which produce temporary shortages, are absorbed by the systems of mutual aid and sharing. Adjustments are made in the rate of consumption of the entire population which, though they may not prevent increased mortality, nevertheless make it possible for the community to survive the crisis. The resiliency of the independent community is the principal source of its strength, without which it probably could not retain its foothold in a hostile environment. So vital an element is group cohesion, in fact, that migration must be a mass movement, if it is to occur at all. An individual or even three or four individuals together cannot subsist apart from the larger whole. There are no facilities for life outside the community of which one is a member.

The lack of preparation for movement becomes acutely apparent when migration offers the only hope for survival. In the absence of very efficient transportation facilities, movement requires large amounts of per capita wealth in the form of food reserves to sustain the migrants through the time of transit, and transport for the car-

---

[22] M. Mead, *Cooperation and Competition among Primitive Peoples* (New York, 1937), 21; and W. I. Thomas, *Primitive Behavior, 32.*

riage of necessary tools and possessions. Even after a destination is reached the need for food stores continues, since the migrants must be tided over the long period of waiting for crops to mature. But these requirements may seldom be fulfilled, especially in view of the expediency of migration of people adapted to a self-sufficient mode of life. Hence an extraordinary mortality usually attends their attempts to move and take up residence in a new area. Mortality risks are aggravated further by an indefinite prolongation of the period of adaptation at the destination resulting from the inappropriateness of the migrants' techniques for working the land and the trial and error search for new techniques which ensues.

Migration from the independent community, therefore, tends to be a last resort to which recourse is had only after all other solutions to overpopulation have failed. In most instances a major catastrophe seems required to set a migration in motion. Minor and recurrent occasions of disequilibrium find their remedies not in movement but in higher than normal mortality rates.

Migration and the Dependent Community.—Population living under conditions of dependent community organization is unhampered by the resistances which beset the independent community, though it is confronted by a different set of restraints peculiar to its more complex mode of life. The primary orientation of the dependent community is not to the land but to a network of intercommunity relations. And that network of relations or market situation, since it constitutes a highly flexible and changeable sustenance base, presupposes maximum mobility. In consequence, population in general, if not individuals in particular, is prepared for and habituated to readjustment through migration. Nor are migrants deterred, assuming employment opportunities to be available at the selected destination, by the prospect of a long period of waiting for the income flow to begin. The wage job with its weekly or monthly payment simplifies the problem of establishment in a new context of relationships. It should be noted, however, that a great part of the mobility required by market fluctuations does not issue in migration. It occurs as a movement of capital, materials, and products to people, as a flow of communications, and as extensive daily journeys to and from places of work and service. Nevertheless, migration is a commonplace response to changes in opportunity and is relatively uninhibited by deep involvement in the seasonal round.

Nor do the community units possess the resiliency and thus the restraining power observed in the independent community. It was

noted in an earlier chapter [23] that associational units, through which
are carried on most of the activities of the dependent community, are
based on a market and when the market is reduced below a minimum
the units cease to operate. The associational unit cannot retain its
personnel through periods of severe adversity. There is thus an element of insecurity of position in the organization of such a unit which
supplies, if not an incentive, at least a low resistance to migration.
And when curtailment or loss of function occurs, migration may become a necessity. It is of more than passing interest in this connection to note that the progressive transfer of manual skills to machinery,
which has given rise to large numbers of semiskilled workers, has
further enhanced the readiness to move in that portion of the labor
force. On the one hand, the loss of skill means for the worker less
security of job tenure, and, on the other hand, it gives him a much
greater industrial versatility. He can acquire proficiency in any of a
wide assortment of machine-tending jobs in a few hours or a few days.

Migration is facilitated also by the existence of a highly developed
transportation and communication system. Instead of having to provide their own vehicles and sources of power, migrants to and from
the dependent community, even though they possess but little wealth,
may secure passage to distant points. The risks as well as the costs
of movement are small. Furthermore, the relatively free flow of communications gives wide dissemination to news and information about
opportunities available elsewhere.

All aspects of the relation of the individual to the large and intricately organized community seem to make for a readiness to move.
The standardization of techniques and forms of communications provides a broad universe of familiarity within which individuals may
circulate relatively unrestricted by traditional resistances. Local
loyalties and the rule of sentiment are irrelevant in such a context.
Dependences involve strangers for the most part rather than kinsmen,
and strangers may be replaced by other strangers without seriously
disturbing the rhythm of functions. Rights to possessions and land,
which are an important basis of the attachment to place in the independent community, are rendered convertible by the aid of money.
With money the individual may carry his rights abstractly in his
pocket and convert them to specific rights of one kind or another as
the occasion may warrant. Through this means he may delegate his
rights and their complementary responsibilities, as he has in regard
to political, charitable, and even religious participation. These activi-

[23] Chapter 12.

ties are carried on by professional representatives while the individual is left free to move.

The very circumstances in the dependent community that encourage migration operate also as controls upon movement. Although, for example, the dynamic market nexus is more or less continuously provoking movement and redistribution, it at the same time sets limits on the range of migration. Settlement is held within the scope of the market, to use Adam Smith's phrase; that is, interdependent individuals and community units cannot scatter so widely as to lose access to one another.[24] It is for this reason that large expanses of relatively unused though productive lands are to be found on the peripheries of highly developed areas, as in the western sections of Canada and the United States and in the interior of Australia.[25] Transportation costs from such zones to market centers are too great to permit an economic use of the lands.

Transportation time and cost measure, in general, the practicable distance from a market center that migration may carry a population. Settlement is held to areas served by the railway and the all-weather road. It has been estimated that thirty miles is the maximum distance from a railway that wheat growing may be profitable.[26] That, of course, will differ with the type of carriage to the railway shipping point. But other elements of cost qualify the scope of the market measured in time-cost distance. The price of a product, for example, varies from time to time and with it varies the area of market relations. A spectacular instance of this occurred in connection with wheat during and after World War I. High prices for wheat occasioned by wartime demands prompted a heavy migration to the Great Plains for wheat farming, an area formerly used for grazing purposes. A sudden recession of wheat prices following the war reversed that movement and led to an abandonment of farm lands which accelerated in ensuing years. While bulky commodities such as wheat and food products generally are limited to low-cost transportation, exotic materials which are used in small quantities may be produced at great time-cost distances from a market center. Opium, tung oil, quinine, teakwood, and many other such items are produced in the remotest

---

24 According to F. J. Turner, at one time in the colonial period of North America settlers were held within the coastal area wherein was located the only known deposits of salt. The inland spread of settlement was limited to the distance that could be traveled periodically to obtain salt. (*The Frontier in American History* (New York, 1921), 17-18.)

25 See, for example, T. C. Feldman, *The Federal Colonization Project in the Matanuska Valley, Alaska* (Seattle, Wash., 1942-43).

26 Isaiah Bowman, *The Pioneer Fringe* (New York, 1931), 66.

parts of the world. It is doubtful, however, that opportunities in the production of materials of this character would attract and support many settlers, even were they not produced as now in areas of dense population. The greater the distance between units, at any given stage of development of transportation, the more specialized it seems the dependency between them must be.

Interestingly enough, motor vehicle transportation seems to have introduced a new resistance to migration. The lengthening commuting radius afforded by the automobile has reduced the amount of migration necessary, at least within local areas. Instead of having to live within walking distance of the job or of a public transportation facility, the worker may locate his residence 10 or more miles away. Thus he has acquired a wider area in which he may seek employment without having to move his residence. Investigation would probably show a declining ratio of residence changes to job changes since 1900.[27] It has been observed that new mining operations may be started without the necessity of providing housing facilities at the mine site. Workers show an increasing disposition to live in permanent towns and cities and to travel 20 to 40 miles daily to the mine shaft.[28] One result of this has been to bring into use many small raw material deposits that were neglected formerly because of the transportation and overhead costs of working them. The full effect of the increasing commuting radius on the amount of migration, however, has yet to be felt.

The limitation of market scope is an index of a more diffuse resistance to migration which has developed with the rise of the dependent community. The progressive subdivision and subsequent rationalization of tasks has produced an intensive organization of virtually all elements of life. There remain few interstices into which movement may occur unhampered by institutional restraints. All lands and resources are blocked out and owned. Enterprises are secured and protected by franchises and other monopoly controls. They offer a job structure into which a migrant may be fitted only if there is a vacancy and if he meets stated specifications. Additional controls are imposed by labor unions and professional groups which strive to maintain a scarcity of their skills by limiting the numbers admitted to membership. So compact is the organization of the dependent com-

---

[27] A Detroit traffic survey brought to light the fact that of all industrial workers who changed jobs in 1936, only 10 per cent changed residences. Unfortunately, similar data for earlier years are not available. (Reported in *National Defense Migration,* Part 18, Detroit Hearings [Sept., 1941], 7102.)

[28] Carter Goodrich, *et al., Migration and Economic Opportunity* (Philadelphia, 1936), 311-15.

munity that the potential migrant must wait for a relaxation of controls before he may move. And even then he must be guided by a fund of detailed information.

An increasing number of controls on migration tend to gain formal expression in law and to be articulated and exercised by the political agency of the community. Since it is the function of that agency to maintain conditions favorable to an uninterrupted and productive operation of community organization, its concern logically includes the regulation of population. In some instances this may involve discouraging the migration of native peoples. The custom of villenage in the feudal system, by which the peasant was permanently bound to the land, was a highly effective method of retaining a necessary population. Later, under mercantilism, central governments systematically prohibited the emigration of workers. Similar though abortive attempts were made in the United States by the early governments of Atlantic coastal States with reference to westward migration, and again, in 1916-19, by municipalities and States in the South in regard to the northbound migration of Negroes.[29]

In other instances, as for example in period of economic expansion, governmental units may induce immigration to overcome a condition of underpopulation. With the rise of proprietary towns in the latter part of the feudal era the need for population to occupy the towns was so great the proprietors actively proselyted among the manorial serfs. Sanctuary was offered in the town and it became the custom to make a freedman of any who succeeded in staying there for a year and a day. The policy of aggressive recruitment of migrants is common in colonial ventures. Many States in this country, during the 19th century, maintained agents in various European cities, advertised, and resorted to other means to attract additional settlers. The Homestead Act of 1861, which opened public lands to foreigners as well as to the native born, was the first positive effort of the federal government to encourage immigration.

Sooner or later, however, an area acquires a population sufficient to man its organization. Inducements to immigrants are then withdrawn and in their place are substituted controls which qualify and restrict the opportunities for entrance until eventually the area is closed to all but a few outsiders. This was occurring in the United States through the latter part of the 19th and the early part of the 20th centuries, and was brought to completion in the Immigration Acts of

---

[29] United States Department of Labor, *Negro Migration in 1916-17* (Washington, D. C., 1919).

1917 and 1924.[30] Within the space of a few years similar controls were imposed throughout the new world.[31]

The same tendency is manifested by local governmental units. Immigration meets a stiffening resistance as population threatens to exceed the number of opportunities. The economic depression of the 1930's, which created general overpopulation, crystallized numerous local controls that had been developing for some time and brought many new ones into being. Laws specifying a minimum period of residence in a state to establish eligibility for public assistance are examples. In 1931, there were fourteen states which had no residence laws and five states which required periods of six months or less. By 1940 no state was without residence laws; seventeen states specified three years or more residence, and one required no less than ten years. The consequences of such legislation are indicated by experience in an Iowa county in which the principal industry, coal mining, had been in decline for some years. The evacuation of the area by the unemployed miners was brought to a halt, after 1930, through the enactment of residence laws, and the county thereafter developed the highest incidence of relief in the State.[32] In the most explicit attempt to restrict internal migration yet to appear twenty-eight states, following the leadership of California, prohibited the entrance of persons who were or might become public charges.[33] Similar, if less striking, controls were imposed by cities and minor civil divisions throughout the country. The necessary redistribution of population was thus impeded and inequalities in the distribution of opportunities were preserved.

Finally, there is the phenomenon of attachment to place which often operates as an effective restraint. Nostalgia, the acute form of homesickness which seems to render the afflicted temporarily incapable of sustained activity, is generally recognized as a disease requiring treatment.[34] No doubt much of the backflow from migration is due to that ailment. Carefully conceived resettlement projects have attempted to anticipate disruptions arising from nostalgia by moving

---

[30] See R. D. McKenzie, *Oriental Exclusion* (New York, 1927) ; Donald R. Taft, *Human Migration* (New York, 1936), chaps. xiii and xiv; and Maurice R. Davis, *World Immigration* (New York, 1939), chap. viii.

[31] Harold Fields, "Closing Immigration throughout the World," *American Journal of International Law,* XXVI (October, 1932), 671-99.

[32] Howard Bowen, *Report on Oppamoose County,* Iowa State Planning Board (Iowa City, 1935).

[33] Laws of this character were declared unconstitutional by the United States Supreme Court in Edwards vs. California, 1941. For a full account of the Edwards case and related laws, literature, etc., see *National Defense Migration,* Part 26, Washington Hearings, January, 1942 (Washington, D. C., 1942).

[34] "Nostalgia," *Encyclopaedia Britannica* (11th ed., 1924), XX, 457.

entire communities rather than selected individuals or families.[35] The reluctance of many of the skilled workers to accompany the movement of industries from Hartford and New Haven, Connecticut, in 1929, despite the inducements that were offered them, was based on a preference to remain in a familiar environment. In many instances the decision to stay behind meant employment in jobs requiring less skill and paying lower wages.[36] The fluidity of contemporary life notwithstanding, there seems to be a pronounced tendency to become involved in a local complex of relationships from which it is difficult to extricate one's self.

Selectivity of Migration.—Thus far we have dealt solely with resistance factors which apply generally to whole populations. In the independent community only such factors tend to influence migration, for the group must necessarily move as a unit. But in the dependent community there are facilities and other supporting conditions for movement by detached individuals. It might be expected, therefore, that migration between dependent communities would have a differential incidence corresponding in some way to the differentials existing in the population.

This is clearly true in respect to age composition. Young adults, who comprise the more vigorous, self-reliant, and adaptable segment of population, are more migratory than are other age groups. Tables 33 and 34 show the marked preponderance of this age group in foreign immigration and in internal migration.

The sex distribution of migrants also reveals a selectivity. The sex selection, however, is not so simple as that observed for age. Table 35 indicates that while males were predominant in the migration to the United States in 1907, their number had declined to or below the expected proportions by 1930. Evidently in long-distance migrations, especially those involving a radical readjustment at the destinations, males are the first to move. The females follow after the males have succeeded in establishing themselves in the new community. This seems to be what is indicated in the last two columns of Table 35. That is, the relatively high ratios of married women to married men, in 1930, suggest that immigration in that year was bringing family members who had been left behind until the principal hazards of resettlement were overcome.

---

[35] See Carter Goodrich, *et. al., op. cit.,* 548-50.
[36] Ewan Clague and Walter J. Couper, *After the Shutdown* (New Haven, 1934), 50-51.

TABLE 33

AGE COMPOSITION OF IMMIGRANTS AT TEN-YEAR INTERVALS,
UNITED STATES, 1820-1930

Year of Immigration	Total	Under 15	15-40	Over 40
1820	100.0	14.8	68.1	17.1
1830	100.0	27.5	62.2	10.3
1840	100.0	23.7	68.0	8.3
1850	100.0	21.9	67.3	10.8
1860	100.0	16.0	74.6	9.4
1870	100.0	23.0	64.8	12.2
1880	100.0	19.1	71.6	9.3
1890	100.0	19.0	69.2	11.8
1900	100.0	15.5	73.8	10.7
1910	100.0	14.9	74.7	10.4
1920	100.0	18.4	66.8	14.8
1930	100.0	16.3	68.2	15.5

Source: W. F. Willcox (ed.), *International Migrations* (New York, 1931), Vol. II, 114.

TABLE 34

PER CENT AGE DISTRIBUTION OF TOTAL POPULATION, NONMIGRANTS
AND MIGRANTS, UNITED STATES, 1935-40 *

Age †	Total Population	Nonmigrants	Migrants
Total	100.0	100.0	100.0
Under 5	8.0	9.2	.....
5-13	15.2	15.2	15.8
14-17	7.3	7.5	6.4
18-19	3.9	3.7	4.3
20-24	8.8	8.1	13.4
25-29	8.4	7.6	14.0
30-34	7.8	7.2	11.6
35-44	13.9	13.7	15.7
45-54	11.8	12.2	9.6
55-64	8.0	8.4	5.3
65 and over	6.9	7.2	3.9

* Source: U. S. Bureau of the Census, *Population, Internal Migration 1935 to 1940. Age of Migrants* (Washington, D. C., 1946).
† Age is reported as of 1940, though the migrations occurred during the 5-year period 1935 to 1940.

TABLE 35

PER CENT MALE OF ALL IMMIGRANTS, 1907 AND 1930, AND MARRIED FEMALES
PER 100 MARRIED MALES, 1910 AND 1930, BY SELECTED NATIONALITY GROUPS,
UNITED STATES.

Nationality of immigrant	Per cent male		Married females per 100 married males	
	1907	1930	1910	1930
Bulgarian...............	97.3	31.7	5	1,063
Dutch and Flemish.......	67.1	59.5	69	98
English.................	64.8	49.6	77	104
French..................	57.8	55.3	86	107
German.................	60.5	50.5	65	146
Greek..................	96.5	41.3	8	656
Irish...................	56.5	48.8	70	97
Lithuanian..............	72.3	29.8	38	643
Mexican................	81.3	53.0	62	121
Polish..................	73.0	46.7	23	171
Romanian...............	92.6	28.7	10	611

Source: W. F. Willcox, *op. cit.,* 112-113.

But in short-distance migrations, rural to urban movements in particular, females tend to be numerically dominant. In Table 36 it may be observed that 52 per cent of the migrants to cities within states are females, and that this proportion drops to 51 per cent in urban-ward movements which cross state lines and to less than 50 per cent in movements between noncontiguous states. Females begin their migration from rural areas at an earlier age than do males, concentrating much of their movement between the ages of eighteen and thirty years. After age thirty and until age fifty-five males move in larger proportions than females. The latter return to predominance in the years following age fifty-five. This age-sex pattern is undoubtedly a result of the scarcity of economic opportunities for unattached females in rural areas.

In fact, the differential movements of age and sex groups are almost entirely expressive of an occupational selection at work in migration. Disequilibrium, of course, is felt first and most forcefully as unemployment or labor shortage. Furthermore, it may concern any number from one of to all the occupations represented in the communities in question. Migration is a means of redistributing that part of a population most directly affected by conditions of disequilibrium in closer conformity with the distribution of opportunities. Unfortunately we lack systematic studies of the operation of occupational selection. But its workings are abundantly illustrated in labor re-

TABLE 36

PER CENT AGE AND SEX DISTRIBUTION OF ALL MIGRANTS TO URBAN PLACES BY DISTANCE OF MIGRATION, UNITED STATES, 1935-40.

Age	Within states			Between contiguous states			Between noncontiguous states		
	Total	Male	Female	Total	Male	Female	Total	Male	Female
Total............	100.0	47.7	52.3	100.0	48.6	51.4	100.0	50.4	49.6
Under 5............	—	—	—	—	—	—	—	—	—
5–13............	13.6	6.9	6.7	12.9	6.5	6.4	11.2	5.6	5.6
14–17............	5.7	2.7	3.0	5.3	2.5	2.8	4.6	2.2	2.4
18–19............	4.3	1.6	2.7	4.3	1.7	2.6	3.7	1.8	1.9
20–24............	14.3	5.6	8.7	15.0	6.2	8.8	14.7	7.2	7.5
25–29............	14.7	6.9	7.8	15.9	7.5	8.4	16.6	8.4	8.2
30–34............	12.4	6.2	6.2	12.9	6.6	6.3	13.0	6.7	6.3
35–44............	16.1	8.5	7.6	16.9	9.1	7.8	17.0	9.1	7.9
45–54............	9.5	5.0	4.5	9.3	5.1	4.2	9.8	5.2	4.6
55–64............	5.2	2.5	2.7	4.5	2.2	2.3	5.4	2.5	2.9
64 and over......	4.2	1.8	2.4	3.0	1.2	1.8	4.0	1.7	2.3

Source: U. S. Bureau of the Census, *Population, Internal Migration 1935 to 1940; Age of Migrants* (Washington, D. C., 1946).

cruiting practices, such as indenture, slavery, contracting, and direct solicitation. The entire rural to urban migration, moreover, has been, and still is a movement of occupationally dispossessed agriculturists to unskilled and semiskilled jobs in mechanical and service industries.

Differentials in migration, however, may also indicate variations in ability. It would appear that the task of moving and beginning life anew in a strange situation entails risks which many individuals are biologically and perhaps psychologically unable to assume. This may, for example, partially account for the age variations just noted. If true, such differences should be observable within as well as between age groups. Here again the existing knowledge is inconclusive. There is some evidence to support the conclusion that the biologically fit or the healthy move more readily than the unhealthy.[37] A recent study by Ronald Freedman, however, indicates that in the United States rural migrants to cities experience more days of disabling illness than do nonmigrants in the cities of destination. Furthermore, this differential is consistent in all income classes.[38] Information on selectivity with reference to mental health is no more satisfactory. Data on commitments to mental institutions in New York State show higher frequencies of mental disorder among migrants than among other native residents of the State.[39] It is not possible to determine from these data, however, whether the higher rates are due to selectivity or to difficulties of adjustment to the circumstances of life in the State of New York.

There is even greater confusion over the selectivity of migration in respect to intelligence, possibly because of the larger amount of research that has been done. Since migration may be assumed to require initiative and aggressiveness, it is reasonable to expect that the more intelligent individuals are most likely to move. The immediate difficulty encountered in testing this hypothesis lies in securing an

[37] A. B. Hill, *Internal Migration and the Effects on the Death Rate, with Special Reference to the County of Essex* (London: Medical Research Council Report Series, No. 95, 1925), cited in *Research Memorandum on Migration Differentials* (New York: Social Science Research Council, Bull. 43, 1938), 92-97, and E. P. Hutchinson, "Internal Migration and Tuberculosis Mortality in Sweden," *American Sociological Review*, I (April, 1936), 273-85.

[38] "Health Differentials for Rural-Urban Migration," *American Sociological Review*, XII (October, 1947), 536-41.

[39] Benjamin Malzberg, "Rates of Mental Disease among Certain Population Groups in New York State," *Journal of the American Statistical Association*, XXXI (September, 1936), 545-48. A more recent study dealing with a section of Baltimore indicates that mental and personality disorders are more closely associated with intracity mobility than with urban-rural and intercity movements. (See Christopher Tietze, Paul Liemkau, and Marcia Cooper, "Personality Disorder and Spatial Mobility," *American Journal of Sociology*, XLVIII (July, 1942), 29-39.

adequate measure of intelligence. A few studies using school achievement as a gauge of intelligence have indicated a better than chance migration of the more advanced individuals.[40] But uncertainty is injected into these findings by another study using grade performance data which revealed that children of migrants are no better than average,[41] though whether the children of migrants are the proper subjects for study is open to question.

A more recent study reveals that the level of educational achievement of migrants does not differ significantly from that of nonmigrants at either the source or the destination when age, sex, marital status, occupation, previous occupational mobility, and employment status are held constant.[42] Still another research based upon intelligence test scores of rural youth in Kansas found that the more intelligent by that measure not only moved in larger numbers but also moved farther and to the larger cities.[43] It is probable, of course, that selectivity in Kansas may differ from that operating in other places.

Thus while the weight of evidence seems to support the hypothesis of intelligence selection, considerably more research is necessary. The control of two factors should produce more stable results than have been attained heretofore. First, a distinction should be observed between primary and secondary migrants, or those who are responsible for the migration and those who merely accompany the primary migrant.[44] Albert H. Hobbs noted rather important differences between these two groups both in respect to educational achievement and grade-point scores in school.[45] Secondly, the characteristics of the community from which migration proceeds should be controlled. It is entirely likely that a community in which opportunities are permanently depleted may produce a type of migrant different from one in which opportunities are but temporarily restricted.[46] Obviously more detailed information than has yet been available is required to ascertain the effects on migration of differentially distributed intrinsic factors.

----

[40] Wilson Gee and Dewees Runk, "Qualitative Selection in Cityward Migration," *American Journal of Sociology*, XXXVII (September, 1931), 254-65; and T. C. McCormick, "Urban Migration and Educational Selection—Arkansas Data." *Ibid.*, XXXIX (November, 1933), 355-59.

[41] Otto Klineberg, "The Intelligence of Migrants," *American Sociological Review*, III (April, 1938), 218-24.

[42] Ronald Freedman and Amos H. Hawley, "Educational and Occupational Selectivity of Migration in the Depression, 1930-35." (Unpublished manuscript.)

[43] Noel P. Gist and Carroll D. Clark, "Intelligence as a Selective Factor in Rural-Urban Migrations," *American Journal of Sociology*, XLIV (July, 1938), 36-58.

[44] Suggested by Otto Klineberg, *op. cit.*

[45] *Differentials in Internal Migration* (Philadelphia, 1942), 66-78.

[46] Jane Moore, *Cityward Migration: Swedish Data* (Chicago, 1937), 28-42.

Summary.—It has been the purpose of this chapter to indicate the relationship between mobility and change. Mobility is a generic concept and embraces a large variety of movements. For the purposes of ecology the many kinds of mobility may be reduced to two, recurrent and nonrecurrent movements. Recurrent movements are those by which a community functions: they include all routine movements regardless of how widely spaced in time is their occurrence. Nonrecurrent movements are unique and are involved in change. They are transitional in that they entail a shift from one organization to another. The terms migration and nonrecurrent movement are used synonymously. Migration is both the means by which change is effected and the most accessible evidence of change.

Whatever may be the factors making for change, the phenomenon is manifested in the community as disequilibrium. Overpopulation in one community combined with underpopulation in another, each an instance of disequilibrium, together constitute the generalized cause of migration. Causation as thus stated, however, is immediately complicated by the presence of numerous special conditions found in communities of different types. The degree of dependence of a community and, in consequence, the nature of its relation to the land and the character of its internal organization influence the responsiveness of the members to disequilibrium.

The organization of the independent community contains numerous resistances to migration. A self-sufficient existence necessitates a close adjustment of behavior to the seasonal cycle the effect of which is to immobilize the population for at least a season's duration. This seems to have its counterpart in a strong attachment to place. Furthermore, the cohesiveness of such a community enables it to withstand many influences which might otherwise result in migration. Since there are no facilities for living outside the community, migration must occur as a mass movement. The absence of efficient transportation and the lack of sufficient surpluses to provide the population during the period of adjustment at a destination constitute further resistances to migration. In view of all such circumstances, migration from the independent community is usually a final expedient.

In many of its aspects the dependent community favors a high degree of migration. The frequent readjustments in a flexible market situation, the rather tenuous membership in functional units, the rapid flow of income permitting relatively easy establishment at destinations, the existence of an efficient transportation system, and the emancipation of population from many restraining loyalties all facilitate the flow of migration. Nevertheless, there are many resistances.

Population cannot move beyond the bounds of the market as measured by time and cost. Moreover, the automobile and mechanical forms of communication have increased commuting distances and thereby have lessened the need for migration. The intensive organization of all activities leaves few unoccupied niches into which the migrant may settle. Political agencies impose further restrictions by limiting the number who may enter an area at any one time.

The selectivity of migration is clear with reference to age and sex. Young adults are disproportionately numerous in all migration streams. Females are numerically dominant in short distance migrations. The evidence of selectivity with reference to health and intelligence is contradictory. In the latter case it is probable that the control of type of migrant and type of area involved might yield consistent evidence of selectivity.

SUPPLEMENTARY REFERENCES

ANDERSON, NELS. *Men on the Move.* Chicago: The University of Chicago Press, 1940.

McKENZIE, R. D. "Movement and the Ability to Live,"*Proceedings of the Institute of International Relations* (1926), 175-80.

MOORE, JANE. *Cityward Migration: Swedish Data.* Chicago: The University of Chicago Press, 1938.

SAUNDERS, HAROLD W. "Human Migration and Social Equilibrium," Journal of Business (University of Iowa), XXIII (March, 1943), 11-15.

Chapter 18

EXPANSION—INTERREGIONAL ORGANIZATION

Expansion is a progressive absorption of more or less unrelated populations and land areas into a single organization. The term connotes movement away from but without loss of contact with a place of settlement. It involves an inner locus or center of activity and an outwardly advancing periphery of influence. Two patterns of movement are implied in the concept, namely centrifugal and centripetal. Centrifugal movements constitute the process by which outlying resources and settlers are drawn into relations with the center. Centripetal movements make possible a sufficient development of the center to insure reciprocal relations within an ever widening range of territory.

The Locus of Expansion.—Expansion proceeds from an important conflux of movement. The principal advantage of such a location is, of course, its accessibility. This attribute favors expansion in two respects. In the first place, ease of access from surrounding regions to the point of intersection of routes and the flow of population through that site enables the group occupying the area to become familiar with the knowledge and skills of widely scattered peoples. Culture accumulates rapidly where the frequency and the diversity of intergroup meetings are great. A people so situated, therefore, is likely to acquire a technical superiority over the occupants of neighboring and more insular areas. Secondly, a highly accessible location stimulates the development of a mediating function. Buying and selling gravitate to accessible sites and create demands for numerous services to the persons engaged in exchange. Such activities, moreover, multiply and diversify as the individuals carrying them on become increasingly sophisticated in the cultures of other groups. In other words, culture accumulation and the development of a mediating or service function prosper at the crossroads through the action of one upon the other.

Thus a group whose habitat lies athwart an intersection of well-traveled thoroughfares is diverted from self-sufficiency to specialization in serving the needs of residents in adjoining areas. Once begun specialization seems to provide its own stimulus to further specialization. Every opportunity to enhance the mediating role is seized upon.

Transportation improvements in particular find ready encouragement in the strategically located settlement, for they make possible a widening of the area of influence. Historically it was from such points that overland thoroughfares were first extended and water routes were explored and charted. Needless to say, all this describes an urban location, for sooner or later a city appears at the heavily trafficked route intersection. Some form of city is invariably the center of expansion.

Transportation Improvements.—Every improvement in transportation and communication extends the potential, if not the actual, territorial scope of interdependence. Improvements may take any one or more of three generalized forms : they may reduce the time and cost of travel between points ; they may minimize the effects of weather on goods or persons in transit ; and they may increase the bulk or capacity of carriage. Whatever their nature, increases in the efficiency of movement bring spatially separated groups within access of one another, making possible the development of supplementary relations.

Under the simplest conditions of movement and carriage population is found in independent village communities scattered more or less uniformly over the area of settlement. Such communities differ in size and complexity according to whether transportation is by means of human locomotion or by animal-powered vehicles. Human carriage is practicable only over very short distances and the interdependences it may sustain are limited to personal services and light materials. Village isolation and self-sufficiency are therefore virtually complete. An exception appears in regions where agricultural resources are capable of maintaining dense populations, as in parts of China. There intercourse among neighboring villages is relatively easy despite rudimentary transport facilities. The community comprises a cluster of villages which are interrelated through a major village or market town.[1]

The introduction of the animal-drawn vehicle does not so much lengthen the radius of movement to and from a center as increase the volume of materials or the number of persons that can be transported. The degree of dependence among settlements situated within short distances of one another is thus increased manyfold.[2] Whereas for-

---

[1] Martin C. Yang, *A Chinese Village* (New York, 1945), 190-202.

[2] See Edward C. Kirkland, *Men, Cities, and Transportation* (Cambridge, Mass., 1948), Vol. I, 48-59.

Wagons, according to J. W. Thompson, first came into general use in twelfth century Europe. *Economic and Social History of the Middle Ages* (300-1300) (New York, 1928), 565.

merly interdependences were confined principally to the exchange of luxuries, they subsequently involve essentials such as food and bulky raw materials. A more complex local community life tends to develop, therefore.

Until the hard-surfaced road appeared, however, the occupants of an area were rather loosely knit together and relations were often suspended during seasons of inclement weather. Because of impassable roads in the eighteenth century, according to Mantoux, "districts in England, with no artificial barriers dividing them as in France and Germany, were nevertheless for a long time almost completely cut off from one another. . . ."[3] The improvement and extension of roads into surrounding territory follows closely upon specialization in service activities in a settlement.[4] A greater regularity of movement and the use of heavier vehicles becomes possible, and the reliability and diversity of relations increase accordingly.

Nevertheless, until quite recent times, roadways afforded a very meager basis for expansion. Road improvements greatly stimulated short haul and occasional travel. But long-distance use of roadways was restricted to the conveyance of information and items of high value per unit of weight.[5] With only animal power overland movement remained laborious and slow. The very casualness of the interlinkages that could be maintained among widely scattered populations accounts for the loose integration of empire in ancient times.[6] Such circumstances prevailed until late in human history. In early America, for example, the cost per ton-mile of freight moved by wagon ranged from thirty cents to three dollars and passenger travel by stagecoach varied from six to twenty-five cents per mile, depending on the condition of the roads.

In the absence of low-cost overland transportation the enlargement of a center's area of influence is conditioned mainly by the existence and character of water routes. Water offers much less resistance to movement, especially of bulk goods, than does land.[7] Thus, as Adam

---

[3] Paul Mantoux, *The Industrial Revolution in the Eighteenth Century.* Trans. Marjorie Vernor (New York, 1927), 117.

[4] See Joseph A. Durrenberger, *Turnpikes, A Study of the Toll Road Movement in the Middle Atlantic States and Maryland* (Valdosta, Ga., 1931), 26-45 ff.

[5] According to Mantoux, despite the extensive building of roads in England during the eighteenth century, potatoes, sugar, and cotton were still unknown in many villages at the end of that period. (*Op. cit.,* 123.)

[6] Apparently it is for this reason that a military domination was required to preserve an empire, for no fundamental interdependences could be supported by the transport facilities then in existence.

[7] It has been estimated that, while a ton of goods could be carried across the ocean from Europe to America, in 1817, for $9.00, the same weight could not be transported overland more than thirty miles at that price. (Chester W. Wright, *Economic His-*

Smith noted, the growth of a territorial division of labor usually begins at a maritime location and progresses along the water courses.[8] History records few important exceptions to this generalization. Most of the major empires from antiquity to the present have developed on the basis of water transportation.[9] And until rather late in the modern period expansion was primarily a function of improvements in water-borne transportation. Developments in navigational techniques, increases in the size and speed of vessels, the construction of canals, and the dredging of rivers and harbors contributed to the reduction of distances and the heightening of accessibility of marketing centers.

The introduction of the railroad marked the first major conquest of overland distance. The early lines, however, like the roadways before them, were built as feeders to the water transportation systems. Short lines were constructed from established centers into otherwise relatively inaccessible producing areas. But the great speed and adaptability of the railroad soon became apparent and traffic began to be diverted from the water routes. This encouraged the extension of railway systems farther inland to provide direct links between remote areas and market centers. Consequently there developed a new network of relationships independent of water transportation.

Both water and rail transportation tend to foster interregional to a greater extent than intraregional relationships. The fact that they are adapted to the carriage of heavy cargoes results in high terminal charges for the maintenance of loading equipment, docks, warehouses, and repair shops. Costs of this nature are constant regardless of the length of haul. But since the longer the haul the more widely may fixed charges be distributed, total transfer costs increase less than proportionately with distance. The effect is to minimize the significance of distance.[10] Resources located close to markets have a slight and often negligible advantage over more remote resources. Moderate differences in productivity may be sufficient to more than cover the added costs of transportation. With distant resources occupying

tory of the United States (New York, 1911), 267.) In 1929 the cost of moving a bushel of wheat by water from Sydney to Liverpool, a distance of 14,050 statute miles, was about 18 or 20 cents. For that price a bushel of wheat could be moved only about 100 miles by cart in China.

[8] The Wealth of Nations, 18.

[9] Exceptions such as the inland empires of the Incas and Aztecs, though they attained a remarkable development, were limited both in extent and duration.

[10] Before the coming of the railroad, turnpikes carried long distance overland traffic. After the establishment of railroads most of the main line turnpikes were abandoned with the exception of a few miles near cities and villages. (Joseph A. Durrenberger, op. cit., 118 and 140.)

a favorable competitive position, a relatively free rein is given to the formation of interregional dependences.

In Table 37 various types of transportation are compared in respect to per day speed, average load, per ton-mile cost, and maximum range of movement assuming that the carrier hauls nothing but its own food or fuel. Thus it is apparent that the maximum radial distance a porter can travel and return to his point of departure is 150 miles. If the porter carries a 50 per cent pay load, his maximum radial distance drops to something like 75 miles. By contrast, the horse and wagon can cover a radial distance of 675 miles at about a fourth the ton-mile cost, though the average speed is no greater than the porter's. A

TABLE 37

SPEED, AVERAGE LOAD, COST PER TON MILE, AND MAXIMUM DISTANCE OF
HAUL FOR DIFFERENT TYPES OF TRANSPORTATION *

Type of transportation	Speed: miles per day	Average load: tons	Cost per ton mile†	Maximum distance with full load of food or fuel: miles
Human porter.......	15– 20	.03	$0.10 –$1.00	300
Horse team..........	15– 20	1.40	0.07 – 0.25	675
Pack animal.........	15– 25	.14	0.10 – 1.00	500
Liberty ship (10,000 tons)......	250	12,000.00	0.001– 0.005	110,000
Motor truck (12 tons).	250– 600	—	0.02 – 0.08	40,000
Railroad (Steam and diesel)..	400–1,000	2,500.00	0.007– 0.05	13,000–85,000
Airplane (July, 1943).	4,000–6,000	9.00	0.14 – 0.33	3,000– 6,000

* Source: *Atlas of World Maps*, Army Service Forces Manual, M-101 (Washington, D. C., 1943), 23.
† Costs in all parts of the world approximated in U. S. currency.

substitution of pay load for food for horses and driver again shortens the radius, but less than proportionally since lightening the wagon should increase the speed of travel. Note the great speeds, low costs, and enormous ranges of modern mechanized transport facilities. The possibility of refueling en route, excluded from consideration in this comparison, extends the range of movement for all types of carriers.

Intercommunity Relations.—The extension of routes and the improvement of transportation facilities establish contacts between isolated communities and make possible the development of relations of mutual dependence. Such relationships begin in an exchange of goods, carried on sometimes by means of silent trade, occasionally through a ceremonial exchange of gifts, but usually in direct barter. At the outset the trading relationship may deal only in trifles of one sort or another, and until transportation facilities are well developed it seldom involves other than luxury goods.   Nevertheless, the trading relationship, however simple, carries tremendous implications for the organization of all communities concerned.   Trade is unquestionably one of the most revolutionary of human relations.   This is not only because it establishes a contact where none may have existed before, but also because it necessitates cultural diffusion and ultimately the reorganization of entire communities.

Trade immediately broadens the sustenance base.   For example, where community A provides yams grown in its territory to community B for axe heads made from stone found in B's habitat, the resources of A and B are to that extent pooled and each becomes dependent on a larger area.   The area added in this way to the original domain of the one community is utilized by that community through the agency of the other community.   In other words, trade has also the effect of enlarging the cooperating population.   By entering into a division of labor with scattered community groups each community gains the benefits of a much larger producing population than it can contain within its own organization.   Although it is not often recognized as such, the development of intergroup dependences represents a most important form of population increase.

The effects of exchange reach much further, however.   A continuing exchange leads to specialization on the basis of whatever local advantages a community may possess.   Specialization, in turn, disturbs the traditional equilibrium of functions in the community.   A realignment of relations becomes necessary in order that more energy may be devoted to the specialty while at the same time the remaining requirements, not supplied through trade, may continue to be satisfied. Obviously, the extent to which specialization develops varies with the frequency of trade and the importance of the items acquired thereby to the life of the local group.   Although the trade between the Malays from Timor and Macassar and the Murngin of Australia was intermittent and of no vital importance to either group, it brought about a noticeable reorganization of the latter's collective life.   Before the coming of the Malays the Murngin discarded the shells of sea turtles as worthless objects.   But when iron axes were offered for the shells they took on a new value for the Murngin, who subsequently spent larger amounts of time in turtle hunting.   This led some of the hunters to discard the flimsy, easily constructed bark canoe, which was not suited to the heavy work of harpooning turtles, for the sturdy, more costly dugout canoe.[11]　The appearance of the European trader in Blackfoot territory is reported to have had a somewhat more pronounced effect. Firearms and ammunition received in exchange for furs soon converted the Indians to the business of fur production on a comparatively large scale.　That, incidentally, divided them into a number of warring camps each attempting to enlarge its territory at the expense of the others in order to produce still more furs.[12]　A similar situation developed in New Zealand with reference to the European demand for hemp and in Hawaii with respect to sandalwood.　Prior to the arrival of Europeans some of the Melanesian communities in New Guinea had forsaken their agricultural economy and were devoting themselves exclusively to trade.[13]

While specialization develops and absorbs a larger proportion of the total working force, the influx of new products through trade eliminates many pristine industries and occupations.　Numerous other changes take place, for what was appropriate to a self-sufficient mode of life proves to be more or less irrelevant to one of specialization and interdependence.　The authority of the chieftain or elder wanes, mores are modified, and a different class structure displaces the old.[14]　Peculiarities of language, religion, art, and virtually all aspects of behavior tend to be leveled by the standardizing influences of the give and take of exchange.[15]　How radical may be the revolution in the local community organization depends on the number and character of meetings with members of the alien group.

The Maori of New Zealand illustrate an almost complete dissolution of tribal organization.　The process began with trade.　Restraint, which at first marked the native's acceptance of muskets, blankets, iron hoops, articles of clothing, etc., soon gave way to an avid demand for more and more of the curious and useful items of Western civilization offered by the invader.　The accelerating interchange of products, ideas, and techniques meant a degree of prosperity for both parties; more than that, it implicated the native in the white man's economy, and afforded the white man an increasing knowledge of the resources

[11] W. Lloyd Warner, *A Black Civilization* (New York, 1937), 459-62.
[12] Clark Wissler, "European and American Indian Cultures in Contact," in E. B. Reuter (ed.), *Race and Culture Contacts* (New York, 1934), 115-16.
[13] C. G. Seligman, *The Melanesians of British New Guinea* (London, 1910), 526 ff.
[14] An excellent illustration of the effect of change to a different type of land use on the class structure is had in Ralph Linton's description of the response of the Tanala tribe, in Madagascar, to the substitution of irrigated for dry rice cultivation. *The Study of Man* (New York, 1936), 348-54.
[15] See Robert Redfield, "Culture Changes in Yucatan," *American Anthropologist*, XXXVI (January-March, 1934), 57-69.

of the island which finally led to the attraction of a growing number of European settlers. With the importation of European organization, the old cohesive community of the Maori disintegrated. The time-worn system of communal work and sharing yielded to the individualization of land ownership and employment. The authority of the chieftain and the priest lost most of its former significance and the once influential kinship group was relegated to a position of inferiority. Each family head began to work his own land holding, to sell his produce, and to spend the money on himself and his immediate family. At present the Maori population is rapidly being absorbed in the inclusive organization dominated by Europeans.[16]

This, however, is an extreme instance of community disintegration such as occurs only where the frontier area is appropriated by large numbers of settlers from the center of expansion. But even where that happens the new community structure assumes a semi-independent character. Interregional relations created on the basis of water and rail transportation are limited for the most part to exchanges of materials and manufactured products. The economics of the long haul and of the full load cargo operate against the extension of more intimate relationships, such as direct services to individuals and interpersonal associations of whatever kind. The latter are relatively untransportable. Hence although the projection of water and rail routes permits the expansion of an economy and occasions significant changes in the organizations of the communities brought into that economy, each remains a distinct territorial unit with a local life of its own.

Reorganization of Land Uses.—The phenomenon of expansion involves widespread changes in the uses to which the lands encompassed by the transportation and communication system are put. The changes begin with the first appearance of the trader on the frontier and they end only when the reorganization of the territorial division of labor is completed.

As we have seen, the beginnings of specialization in independent communities on the periphery of an expanding organization results in more intensive uses of the lands by the native populations. The trader may even stimulate the development of resources that have been neglected by the occupants of the invaded area. So long as the market for such materials remains small, however, no radical changes in use of the land may occur. But if a growing market for the output of frontier resources is found, supplying the demand may necessitate

---

[16] Raymond Firth, *Primitive Economics of the New Zealand Maori* (London, 1929), chap. xiv, especially 470-471.

numerous changes. Since the populations of independent communities are usually too small and too poorly equipped for production in great volume, the exploitation of the resources in keeping with market requirements requires the importation of a large labor force and quantities of tools. The appearance of large scale business enterprise, taking the form of the plantation in many cases,[17] brings with it various related activities mainly of a service character and these introduce further alteration of the land use pattern. The end result is often a complete displacement of the native population with its traditional practices of land use and the substitution of an alien population with an entirely different orientation to resources.

Labor force and transportation considerations may recommend a shift of large scale production, particularly of agricultural staples, to more convenient areas. Newbigin writes:

As regards products which can be obtained from wild plants or animals, it is possible to say generally that when the demand becomes large and constant, the area of production tends to shift from the region to which the form concerned is native to another non-adjacent area where cultivation or domestication is possible. The shifting is in this case the important point; for it is less remarkable that natural resources should be easily exhausted than that attempts to replace them should so rarely be made in the producing area. Rubber production, which has moved from inter-tropical South America to Asia; cinchona for quinine from Colombia to India; wattle bark for tanning from Australia to Natal; fur production from the Canadian sub-arctic forest to the fox farms of Prince Edward Island, may be given as examples. Among the factors explaining the movement one is that areas yielding wild produce on a considerable scale are necessarily thinly populated and undeveloped, with little surplus capital and often poor lines of communication.[18]

The opening of frontier resources reacts back upon the center to stimulate its growth thereby producing a redistribution of activities. Established industries are enlarged and new ones appear to utilize the more abundant or the new raw materials and to serve the expanded market. As the central city grows adjacent agricultural lands are taken over by industrial, residential, and commercial activities. Urban growth, in turn, sends out ripples of change over wide areas round about; additional acres are brought under agricultural production to supply the increased needs of the city, lumber and other building material resources must be developed to house the increased

---

[17] Edgar T. Thompson, "The Plantation System," *American Journal of Sociology,* XXXV, (November, 1935), 314-26.
[18] Marion I. Newbigin, *A New Regional Geography of the World* (London, Christophers, 1929), 405.

population, etc.[19] But urban growth is not confined to the center. Villages and towns spring up along route extensions to provide services to settlers and to function as collecting points for produce to be trans-shipped to manufacturing locations. Large entrepôt cities take form at the gateways of regions to serve as administrative centers and as major staging points for population and goods flowing into and out of their regions.

Actually land use changes tend to occur over the whole area touched by the lines of movement. Owing to the fact that interregional expansion proceeds on the basis of long-haul or large bulk types of transportation—water and rail—the settlement pattern is pushed out in narrow ribbons along the routes of travel, its inland depth held at all points to a distance of 20 to 30 miles from the route. This pattern is very marked where water transportation is predominant. The ribbon type pattern, however, is extended into interiors of regions with their penetration by overland routes. Canals were frequently constructed in the prerailway era to open land interiors and with few exceptions the lands thus made accessible were quickly settled and brought within the territorial division of labor.[20] Describing the effects of the Illinois and Michigan Canal as observed in Chicago, its eastern terminal, an early writer states:

When the canal was opened all of a sudden, these farm wagons disappeared and our merchants were greatly astonished and nearly panic-stricken at the wonderful change. The farmers could get for their farm products at the towns on the canal from 30 to 80 miles from Chicago within a cent or two as much per bushel (for their wheat) as in Chicago.[21]

The railroad, of course, was of much greater consequence in the development of interior areas. Although the main outlines of the railway route system were originally determined by the pre-existing settlement pattern, once the rail routes were established they shaped the subsequent distribution of land uses. Terminal points and their adjacent areas acquired a distinct advantage over neighboring localities by virtue of their more direct contact with market centers. Similarly lands adjoining the railroad right of way, formerly devoted to marginal uses, if indeed they were used at all, were converted to more

---

[19] See Homer Hoyt, *One Hundred Years of Land Values* (Chicago, 1933), 48 ff.
[20] The completion of the Erie Canal, for example, lowered freight rates between Buffalo and New York from $100.00 to $5.00 per ton and reduced the time to a third of what had previously been required. (Joseph Durrenberger, *op. cit.*, 132.)
[21] J. W. Waughop in *Chicago Tribune*, September 28, 1884, cited by Homer Hoyt, in *One Hundred Years of Land Values in Chicago* (Chicago, University of Chicago Press, 1933), 60.

or less intensive production of market commodities.[22] Thus settlement accumulated along the railroad route, clustering thickly here and there at station and terminal points. Because of its greater speed and flexibility the railroad drew many industries away from the water's edge, particularly industries producing perishable and high-value goods.[23] Writing on the development of the northwestern section of the United States, Robert R. Martin says:

> As rail lines began to be pushed out over the country, after 1880, villages hitherto scattered along the rivers and streams, at the crossing of old trails, or in the gold fields, were drawn to the railroad and distributed at convenient distances along the lines. The growing of agricultural products was accelerated and rapidly took first place in the industry of the new territory. The horse and wagon being the only means of transportation, farming was limited to the lands contiguous to the railroads.[24]

It is of interest to note that an efficient form of interregional transportation such as the railroad provides may permit distant producers to compete effectively for a market with local producers. That competition has often been felt by agriculturalists in the vicinities of large cities. If the latter had been sustained only by a transportation cost advantage prior to the construction of the railroad, they usually succumbed to the competition and their lands either fell into disuse or passed to a different activity. Much of the abandoned New England farm land which is now classed as marginal appears not to have suffered any loss of productivity in the past one hundred years or more.[25] As in so many other instances, its productivity has simply proved inadequate to the competition offered by western lands. An alternative to abandonment, however, is a shift to a different crop. Areas of specialized production, for example, are sometimes forced into diversified farming. The more balanced economy that results provides a stabler basis for local service centers. This has occurred in many of

---

[22] Prior to the advent of the railroad in northwestern United States cattle growers could find markets only for the hides of animals which were therefore slaughtered in the fields, their carcasses being left where they fell. After the completion of the railroad the raising of cattle as food for distant markets became profitable. (Robert R. Martin, "Integration in the Inland Empire Region of the Pacific Northwest," *Social Forces*, 17 (October, 1938), 34.)

[23] Arthur Redford describes such changes in mid-nineteenth-century England. Settlements located on the new railway routes grew rapidly, while those on the old post roads and canals passed into decline. (*Labour Migration in England, 1800-1850* [Manchester, 1926], 162 ff.)

[24] "Village Changes in the Pacific Northwest," *Social Forces*, 15 (May, 1937), 539. See Robert R. Martin, *op. cit.*, 33-35.

[25] Kenneth MacLeish and Kimball Young, *Culture of a Contemporary Rural Community: Landaff, New Hampshire*, Bureau of Agricultural Economics Rural Life Studies: 3 (Washington, D. C., 1942), 15.

the older agricultural areas of the country, e.g., in the hop-growing section of New York,[26] and the cotton-producing areas of the Southeast.[27]

Population Redistribution.—As already indicated, the interrelating of a progressively larger territory through the extension of routes and the perfection of transportation and communication facilities produces both centripetal and centrifugal population movements. These were implied in our discussion of the reorganization of land uses. Population flows inward to the center to staff the developing marketing, servicing, and industrial units through which the growing number and variety of dependences are integrated. The rise of the center as a focus of dominance proceeds hand in hand with the development of its organization. Its size and diversity of activities are together a measure of the extent to which expansion has been carried. Concurrent with the centripetal movement is a centrifugal movement which carries population outward toward the periphery to develop the new resources and to provide the many supplementary functions required. Each type of movement presupposes the other.

Population flows into the two streams of movement from several sources, which are themselves incident to the growth of organization. One of the most important of these is natural increase. The greater security of the supply of sustenance materials made possible by technological advancement, particularly in respect to transportation and communication, permits declines in mortality and hence an increasing excess of births over deaths.[28] But where there is no corresponding increase in job opportunities or where technological change is not cumulative growth is short-lived. The added numbers soon absorb the increased supply of sustenance and a resurgence of the death rate occurs. Population size stabilizes at a higher figure. Expansion, however, creates opportunities elsewhere; therefore the surplus population tends to drain out of its home area and to distribute itself in accordance with the requirements of the enlarged division of labor.

The displacement from agricultural sections sooner or later applies to the parent population as well as to surplus progeny. As the center grows it offers a larger market to producers of food and other agri-

---

[26] W. G. Mathes, Jr., T. H. Townsend, and Dwight Sanderson, *A Study of Rural Community Development in Waterville, New York.* Cornell Agricultural Experiment Station Bulletin 608 (Ithaca, New York, 1934).

[27] Walter Wynne, *Culture of a Contemporary Rural Community: Harmony, Georgia.* Bureau of Agricultural Economics Rural Life Studies: 6 (Washington, D. C., 1943), 17-20.

[28] For a more extended discussion of the mechanics of population growth see Chapter 7.

cultural products. Subsistence farming gives way to specialized production for the market. And once it is drawn into the market nexus agriculture becomes involved in fiscal considerations and therefore seeks a maximum level of efficiency. Efforts to achieve greater efficiency take the form of increased application of mechanical techniques to production processes and increase in the size of farms. The result is a reduced ratio of man-hours per unit of product and a relative decline in the number of people needed in agriculture.[29] Still more individuals therefore are released into the centrifugal and centripetal currents.

A third source of population available for redistribution develops in the competition between old and new producing areas. We noted that new resources of superior quality, even though they lie more remotely from the market, are often effective competitors with resources long in use. For this to occur the differential productivity favoring the new resources should exceed the differences in transfer costs to the market. In view of the fact that water and rail rates increase less than proportionally with distance, comparatively slight production cost advantages in outlying areas enable them to capture the market for their products. The old producing areas often drop out of use and their populations eventually drift toward areas of increasing opportunity.

The displacement of population from old producing areas near the center resulting from excessive growth, technological progress, and interregional competition is followed by a functional as well as a territorial redistribution. The resorting of the population in functional positions has been described by J. A. Hobson as "the normal law of evolution of employment," [30] and by Colin Clark as the "morphology of economic growth." [31] Both phrases pertain to the same sequence of events. In brief, that involves, first, a rapid increase of agricultural and mining employment as new territories are added and industrial centers are enlarged. Subsequently, however, the amount of employment in the extractive or primary industries enters upon a progressive decline, inasmuch as the market for their products is relatively inelastic. In the meantime, employment in fabricating functions— industries of a secondary type—increases rapidly. This is a period of accelerating centripetal migration and burgeoning urban growth. But eventually, owing to continuous technological development, a rela-

---

[29] The relative decline of agriculturalists turns into an absolute decline when the rate of population growth begins to subside, because of the inelastic market for agricultural purposes.

[30] *The Evolution of Modern Capitalism* (London, 1908), 397-99.

[31] *The Conditions of Economic Progress* (London, 1940), 337-73.

tive decline of employment begins in the secondary industries. As that happens the tertiary or service industries absorb an increasing proportion of the labor force. Perhaps it is in this stage that the decline of opportunities in primary industries turns from a relative to an absolute decrease. Investigation might also show that expansion from a given center has run its course. Further research on the relation between functional and territorial redistribution is needed before the full significance of either can be known.

The Limits of Expansion.—The territorial extent to which an organization may expand is restricted by one of two factors. In any given state of transportation facilities expansion is limited by the time and cost involved in reaching the center or market. There tends to be a point on any given route beyond which the cost of transfer to the market equals or exceeds the difference between the cost of production and the market price.[32] That point marks the maximum scope of the area of interdependence. Without improvements in transportation the radial scope of organization may be increased only by a fall in production costs of the materials produced at the periphery or by a rise in their market price.

Expansion from a particular center is also checked by the development of rival centers of expansion which tend to appear in all the outlying regions. In the early phases of expansion the relation between periphery and center is that of the specific to the general: the one or two special products, i.e., raw materials, of the region are exchanged for a large assortment of services provided by the center, including manufacturing of all types, retailing, financing, policing, administration, etc. But this relationship tends to be reversed as population accumulates in the raw material producing area. Local services develop, many of them administratively independent and hence in competition with those provided by the older center. With the appearance of manufacturing establishments the outlying region becomes a market for its own raw materials as well as those of other regions. Thus the region, through the agency of its principal city, becomes self-sufficient in respect to an increasing number of requisite services. Conversely, its dependence on the center of origin narrows to one or a few special requirements such as financial service, or perhaps only for an exchange of manufactured products.

The two centers, in fact, become active competitors, especially as the activities carried on in one are duplicated in the other. The new

---

32 This varies for different products, that is, with the ratio of production costs to market price. For a few products, such as diamonds, opium, and exotic metals, there may be no distance limitation.

metropolis in what was once a frontier needs raw material supplies and outlets for its manufactured products and other exportable services just as does the parent city. It is, in short, a competing center of expansion. To the degree to which the new center succeeds in extending its dominion that of the older center is hemmed in and checked. There may even be contraction of the area tributary to the older center, for competition arises over the traffic with intervening settlements. Many of these may find advantages in the new center that are not to be had in the old.

The Expansion of Europe.—An illustration of the principles discussed will aid in their clarification. The expansion of Europe offers an excellent example for this purpose. It must be noted, however, that illustration is not an adequate substitute for inductive procedure. Yet inferences from comparative historical materials of the type treated in this connection do not lend themselves to quantitative demonstration. The inferences that have been set forth, even though neatly illustrated in the following, remain, therefore, as hypotheses to be tested.

The [33] history of modern civilization is largely the story of European expansion which, slowly at first, then with increasing momentum, brought different regions and peoples within a common economic order and a common cultural milieu. While this development, extending over four centuries, is a single process, it is by no means a simple one. The rate of change has not been uniform; there have been periods of rapid expansion followed by periods of relative stagnation. Different European peoples have taken the lead at different times. Frequent changes have occurred in political and economic alignments of centers and frontiers. The general trend, however, has been toward an ever thickening of the web of relationships, toward the development of a more clearly outlined settlement structure, a contraction of space as measured in time and cost, an extension of territorial limits, the inclusion of an ever increasing number and variety of peoples, and a general leveling of cultural differences. Mantoux has likened the expansion of industrial society to a river ". . . which does not always flow at the same pace, but sometimes slackens its course, sometimes rushes on, now running through narrow gorges, and now spreading back over the plain, now breaking up

---

[33] The content of this section is reproduced with minor changes from R. D. McKenzie, "Industrial Expansion and the Interrelations of Peoples," in E. B. Reuter (ed.), *Race and Culture Contacts* (New York: McGraw-Hill Book Co., 1933) with the kind permission of the publisher.

into many divergent branches, and now winding about, so that it seems to curve back on itself." [34]

In tracing the development of western civilization scholars have found it convenient to recognize distinguishable historic periods, the number of divisions depending upon the special interest of the investigator. For our purpose here, which is to indicate in broad outline the development of the ecological organization of world society, the history of European expansion may be viewed as having three phases.

The first, beginning with the age of discovery in the fifteenth century and extending into the nineteenth century, represents an era of transoceanic rim-settlement. During this period various European peoples—Spanish, Portuguese, English, French, and Dutch—established outposts at different points along the seacoasts of the New World, Africa, and Southern Asia. These marginal settlements were of three different types: (1) farm-family colonies of European migrants in the temperate belts; (2) sugar and spice plantations in the tropics, owned and operated by European capitalists but worked by colored slaves; and (3) the trading stations along the coasts of India and southern China.

Trade consisted primarily of articles of luxury—precious metals, spices, sugar, tea, and manufactured commodities of handicraft production. The attitude and practice of the different European powers throughout this period were predatory and exploitative. As Knowles relates, "Overseas possessions were regarded at this time by all the colonizing powers as estates to be worked for the benefit of the mother country, and the colonial system was designed so to shape the development of colonies that they should become producers of raw materials or tropical products such as sugar and spices, and should provide good markets for the manufacturers of the mother country." [35] Almost to the close of this era the plantations and Eastern trading posts were considered by the home countries of greater importance than the agricultural colonies in the temperate belts. The great distance, as measured in sailing time, which separated the European centers from the overseas frontiers, prevented the development of effective territorial division of labor and created conditions favorable to piracy and exploitation. On the other hand the lucrative trade in plantation and Eastern products furnished certain of the European powers, notably England, with the capital reserves for the subsequent development of manufacturing.

---

[34] *Op. cit.*, 488.
[35] L. C. A. Knowles, *Economic Development of the British Overseas Empire* (London, 1928), Vol. I, 10.

A second phase of European expansion began early in the nineteenth century and continued with increasing momentum almost to the outbreak of the first World War. This era was initiated by the succession of mechanical inventions which brought about a transformation in methods of production and means of transportation. It is characterized by the rise of industrial cities, by increasing movements of European peoples to overseas settlements, by an inland expansion of those settlements,[36] by a more extensive and varied interchange of products between centers and frontiers, and by the growth of European dominance.

England assumed the lead in the industrialization process. As the power-driven factory displaced handicraft production and the steamship and railway became the leading agencies of transportation a new basis for territorial division of labor was introduced. The process was cumulative, advancing with accelerated speed throughout the nineteenth century. Industrial cities sprang into existence, first in England, later in surrounding European countries and in the United States. Population moved inward to the growing centers of industry and commerce and outward to the expanding frontiers. The complementary exchange of products which ensued, consisting mainly of the trade of manufactured goods for food and raw materials, furnished the most effective territorial division of labor the world has ever known. It made possible the doubling of the white population in the course of half a century, coupled with a substantial increase in the level of living.

Meanwhile the rising dominance of Western European centers and the increasing concentration of industry and wealth stimulated a demand for larger quantities and greater varieties of plantation and mineral products, also for the luxuries of the Orient. This led to an extension of European capital and business enterprise into a wide range of territory occupied by peoples of different race and culture. It likewise led to large scale movements of colored peoples, first African slaves, later East Indians and Chinese contract coolies, to meet labor requirements in the new plantations and mining areas. Thus the number of interracial settlements increased, each organized on the pattern of white direction and control of colored labor.[37]

---

[36] "During the whole of the past century it has been a question of the development of interiors—the moving inland from a port or coastline to control the land behind, and then the continuous pushing back of the frontier, a process enormously quickened by railways. . . ." (L. C. A. Knowles, *ibid.*, 79.)

[37] The expansion of Europe involved an overseas movement of approximately 90 million people, including 60 million Europeans, 20 million Africans, and 10 million Asiatics. The volume of internal migration must have been almost as great.

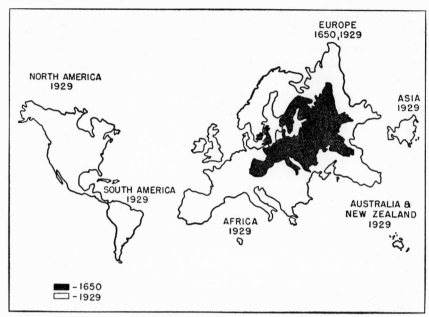

FIG. 32.—The redistribution of European population, 1650 to 1929. (Land areas proportional to unmixed European stocks.) (From National Resources Committee, *The Problems of A Changing Population* [Washington, D. C., 1938], 19.)

The midcentury gold discoveries on the Pacific coast of North America, in Australia and New Zealand gave rise to a somewhat different type of multiracial settlement.   These new mining ventures became foci of rapid convergence of both white and colored—mostly Chinese—peoples, and provided the initial stimulus for settlement in previously undeveloped regions.   They expedited railroad construction and hastened the recession of the frontiers of Western civilization.   Their chief significance, however, derives from the fact that they renewed interracial conflict in areas only subdued by Europeans. That eventuated in the erection of legislative barriers against all Asiatic immigrants to those countries and a quickening of national racial consciousness among peoples bordering on the Pacific.

Concurrent with the formation of interracial plantation and mining settlements another type of European outpost suddenly acquired new economic and cultural significance, namely, the commercial center in Oriental countries.   For several centuries different European powers had "traded with" the peoples of India and southern China.   But after the middle of the nineteenth century—with the advent of the steamship, cable, telegraph, and railway—power-driven factories began to appear at shipping points along the coast of Asia; and Japan was opened to Western commerce. The completion of the Suez Canal in 1869 and of a trans-American railway line in the same year opened a new route around the world. By cutting in half the time required to encircle the globe the completion of that thoroughfare reduced correspondingly the distance between the East and the West.

The effect of these various developments was revolutionary in character. Whereas the earlier contacts of Western traders and missionaries with the peoples of the Orient made but slight imprint on these older civilizations, the coming of power-driven factories, railways, banks, and other elements of the furniture of modern capitalism started a series of economic and cultural changes the repercussions of which have been worldwide in scope. Japan, perhaps because of its more developed internal organization, responded more quickly than her Oriental neighbors to the impact of Western culture. Within a single generation that country rose from a feudal state to the rank of a world power.

By the turn of the twentieth century the basic structure of modern civilization had been laid. The steamship had brought the land masses of the earth into easy economic access and the railways had penetrated the inland regions. Consolidated national states had been formed by the coalescing and federation of formerly isolated settlement units. Great cities had arisen along the coastlines and at strategic inland points of the New World and Asia, integrating vast hinterlands and coming into competition with European centers. Tariff barriers—symbols of the growing consciousness of nationality and interregional competition—had been introduced in the United States and the British Dominions. England alone of the European states still maintained a policy of free trade.

The third and present phase of industrial expansion began early in the twentieth century and was accelerated by the dislocation occasioned by World War I. This may be styled an era of cultural maturation of frontier settlements and general emergence of economic nationalism. It is characterized, on the one hand, by the decline of European dominance in Western civilization and a decrease in the transmaritime movements of European peoples, capital, and goods, and, on the other hand, by the rise of the United States, of Japan momentarily, and of Russia as centers of world expansion, by the growth of manufacture in hitherto backward countries, and by an all but universal proliferation of political barriers to interregional movement.

While some of these tendencies were in evidence during the latter part of the nineteenth century, they have all increased in tempo since the turn of the present century and particularly in the inter-World

War period. They are, of course, related to the utilization of petroleum and electric energy in industry, transportation, and communication. Thus new forms of energy supply furnished the basis for the extraordinary economic and social changes that have come to be regarded
as the "second industrial revolution."

Inasmuch as the United States led the world in the mechanization
of movement and production she rapidly acquired a dominant position
in the territorial organization of modern civilization. By the early
twenties this country had shifted her role from a debtor to a creditor
nation and during that decade became the world's center in the export
of capital. With the surplus of wealth accruing from mass production
and the optimism engendered by a rapidly rising level of living, capital
flowed out of the United States in unprecedented quantities.[38]

The extensive foreign loans, especially the capital investments in
the more backward and sparsely populated areas, stimulated a new
centrifugal movement of settlement. In response to the increasing
demand for raw materials, new plantation and mining settlements suddenly burst forth and older ones grew larger. Each such development
invoked fresh movements and mixtures of peoples entailing manifold
adjustments to large scale capitalistic organization. To the extent
that these growing frontier settlements came to depend on the United
States as a source of capital and as a market for their export products
they fell under the economic dominance and, in some cases, the political hegemony of this country.

A significant aspect of the rapid expansion of the American
economy is that it produced extreme specialization of the outlying
countries affected and on that basis implicated them in a highly sensitive market situation. This has worked to deny the younger areas of
industrial development full incorporation in the total economy. Lacking well-rounded industrial and service structures, the peoples of such
areas are at the mercy of favorable market conditions and are forced
from time to time to make radical readjustment to shifting markets.
While most of the large cities of the modern world can accommodate
to changing markets without involving substantial redistribution of
population, the settlements located outside the political boundaries of
their leading market and which specialized in raw material production

---

[38] "At the beginning of 1931 the foreign investments of the United States were
distributed as follows : $5,600,000,000 was in Europe, Germany alone being indebted
to the extent of nearly $1,500,000,000; $4,000,000.000 in Canada ; $3,000,000,000 in
Central America ; and an equal amount in South America. Over half of the capital
placed in various American countries was represented by direct investments, while
at least three fourths of the capital exported to Europe was represented by American
investments in bonds." (M. Palyi, "Foreign Investment," *Encyclopaedia of the Social
Sciences,* Vol. 6, 373.)

find it difficult and often impossible to do so. This difficulty is aggravated by the fact that the older countries are tending to rely more intensively on their own resources and are erecting tariff walls against foreign products. It is not surprising, therefore, that interracial conflict and political revolt have become endemic in recent years throughout the so-called backward regions of the world. Nor is it possible any longer to impute blame or responsibility to parent countries for the adverse conditions prevailing in their colonies. The interrelations of contemporary peoples have become depersonalized: they are now determined more by the vicissitudes of world markets than by the policies of imperial powers.

While the economic expansion of the United States gave impetus to the development of regions throughout the New World and induced various realignments of peoples, the industrial and commercial maturation of Japan produced effects in world relations of almost equal importance. Unlike the expansion of the United States, which has been confined to the export of machine-made products, capital and technical specialists, that of Japan has involved an emigration of people for resettlement as well. During the first two decades of the twentieth century Japan's contact with the Western world consisted largely of the migration of its citizens to white dominated countries bordering the Pacific. This migration became a disturbing factor to Western peoples not only in itself but because it presaged a new era of competition with a rapidly expanding Oriental nation.

After 1920 the expansion of Japan assumed a different aspect. The emigration of its citizens—restricted since 1924 almost exclusively to Brazil—became relatively less important but the expansion of Japanese economy advanced apace. Japan's location at the outer margin of European and American influence afforded a strategic position from which to wage commercial warfare against the Western world. Thus Japan succeeded in capturing much of England's trade with India and South Pacific regions and pushed westward into Africa and eastward into New World territory. This together with the fact that other Asiatic peoples have been "coming of age" in the new industrial regime started a general withdrawal of European dominance from all Eastern territory. That withdrawal continues for most European peoples despite the downfall of Japanese economy as a result of the second World War. The disposition of the United States in this respect is still in doubt, as is also the future of Japan. It is evident, however, that for some time to come the Orient will constitute a zone of competition between the United States and a new and vigorous expanding power, Russia.

Surveying the world as it is today, its land surface is divided into about a hundred major political areas or countries. These countries range in size from a few thousand to over four million square miles and in population from less than a million to over four hundred millions. Although each country may be considered as the home of a people possessing sufficient cultural homogeneity and belief in a common destiny to be thought of as a unit, they are nevertheless economically and to an increasing degree culturally bound together in a web of vital relationships.

These different human groups vary greatly in the influence they exert in the modern world. Some are aggressive forces pushing out beyond their recognized political domains; others are playing a defensive role, either seeking to free themselves from foreign political entanglements or to guard the territory they occupy against the intrusion of foreign commerce. Some are entering upon a new cycle of expansion; others seem to have reached their expansion crest and are beginning to recede; still others are in a condition of relative stagnation. All, however, are being drawn closer together with the advance of communications and each is becoming more conscious of the presence of the rest.

Summary.—Expansion is the spread and elaboration of organization. It begins at an intersection of heavily traveled routes, e.g., a city, and proceeds with the extension and improvement of transportation and communication facilities. The phenomenon involves centrifugal and centripetal movements. Centrifugal movements are the process by which new lands and populations are incorporated into a single organization. The centripetal movements make possible a sufficient development of the center to maintain integration and coordination over the expanding complex of relationships. The analysis of expansion is in terms of intercommunity relations, reorganization of land uses, population redistribution, and limits of expansion.

Projections of routes bring previously isolated communities into contact with one another and involve them in a more inclusive organization. The process begins with trade, which incites specialization of producing activity, especially in the more self-sufficient of the communities. Specialization disturbs the prior organization, requiring a realignment of relations within the community. If the dependence established by trade grows in significance, it is apt to result in a complete absorption of one group by another. Normally, however, where water and rail communications are the linkages the creation of interdependences reorients the economy of the communities concerned but leaves each a more or less discrete unit. Accompanying the establishment of intercommunity relations is a reorganization of land uses. Specialization of resource exploitation at the frontier is one of the first manifestations of that reorganization, and specialization often leads to large scale production and the appropriation of the lands by population from the center of expansion. The development of frontier resources has its counterpart in the multiplication of urban land uses at the center and, in fact, at intervals along all interregional routes. Competition as between new and old producing areas often causes the latter to drop out of use or to shift to other uses. Both intercommunity contacts and changing land uses presuppose population movement. The population that supplies the additional manpower needs of an expanded organization comes from natural increase, technological progress which displaces workers from handicraft industries, and the substitution of more productive for less productive resources. The limits of expansion are set in some instances by the time and cost of transportation from the center—a point being reached beyond which it is not practicable to go, and in other instances by the competition between rival organizations based on different centers. The various aspects of interregional expansion are illustrated by the expansion of Europe. Although most data on expansion are derived from modern experience, it may be assumed that the phenomenon has occurred much more widely and differs from that of Europe only in details.

SUPPLEMENTARY REFERENCES

BRIDENBAUGH, CARL. Cities in the Wilderness (1625-1742). New York: The Ronald Press Co., 1938.

GABRIEL, RALPH HENRY. The Evolution of Long Island. New Haven: Yale University Press, 1921.

HOOVER, EDGAR M. The Location of Economic Activity. New York: McGraw-Hill Book Co., 1948.

KOHN, HANS. Western Civilization in the Near East, trans. E. W. Dickes. New York: Columbia University Press, 1936.

KUCZYNSKI, R. R. Colonial Population. New York: Oxford University Press, 1937.

MANDELBAUM, K. The Industrialization of Backward Areas. Oxford: B. Blackwell & Mott, Ltd., 1945.

McKENZIE, R. D. "The Concept of Dominance and World Organization," American Journal of Sociology, XXXIII (July, 1927), 28-42.

———. "Ecological Succession in the Puget Sound Region," Publications of the American Sociological Society, XXIII (1929), 60-80.

OGBURN, W. F. The Social Effects of Aviation. Boston: Houghton Mifflin Co., 1946.

TOUTAINE, JULES. The Economic History of the Ancient World. New York: Alfred A. Knopf, Inc., 1930.

Chapter 19

EXPANSION: THE GROWTH OF THE CITY

It will be recalled that the growth of the city or center of expansion is a necessary concomitant of the enlargement of the scope of interdependence. Otherwise the integration and coordination of an ever more complex fabric of interdependences would be impossible. The city is both creature and creator of expansion. An analysis of the growth of the city therefore will enable us to illuminate further the expansion process.

Multiplication of Cities.—The city is of ancient origin and has been represented in varying degrees of development in every civilization for which we have written records. Throughout most of human history, however, the number of inhabitants of cities comprised a very small fraction of the total population. Very few early cities achieved populations of 100,000 or more and this order of magnitude was probably of temporary duration in most instances. At the birth of Christ there were approximately twelve cities of 100,000 population in the Mediterranean area. It is said that Carthage at one point in its history attained a population of 700,000, and Rome may have surpassed the 500,000 mark. One or two such agglomerations also may have appeared in Asia in ancient times, notably at Peiping. Nevertheless, the populations of the areas containing these great cities were preponderantly rural.

The reasons for the relatively small amount of urban settlement in early times are to be found in the simple techniques of production and the clumsy transportation facilities then in existence. Since the yield from the soil over and above the day to day requirements of the producers was very slight, the proportion of nonagricultural workers that could be maintained in cities was correspondingly small. The number of city dwellers was further held in check by a lack of quick and inexpensive transportation. Without such facilities the distribution of food, a product which is both bulky and perishable, is closely restricted. This partly explains the much greater growth of early cities located on water routes as compared with inland cities.

Large scale urban growth is actually of very recent occurrence. Although the Middle Ages brought a marked increase of town popula-

tion in Europe, the numbers involved were not great. This is indicated by the fact that in 1800 there were only twenty-one cities of
100,000 or more population in the world.[1] But in the following century and a quarter the growth and multiplication of cities were extraordinary. By 1900 the number of cities with at least 100,000 inhabitants
had increased to 146; in 1920 the number was 202, in 1927 the number
stood at 537, and in 1940 there were about 720. London, in 1802,
was the first city to reach the size of the 1,000,000 population. Thirty-
six more cities entered that size class in the ensuing years.

Striking as these facts are, they very inadequately portray the total
amount of city growth in the modern period. The great city is symptomatic of a general development of cities, especially in the western
part of the world. Yet a measurement of the total growth of urban
settlement is virtually impossible, owing to the extreme diversity of
definitions of the city in different nations. A partial indication of the
proportion of population residing in cities and the change in that respect is given in Table 38.

TABLE 38

Percentage of the Total Population Residing in Places of 10,000 or
More, Selected Areas, 1850 and 1890

Area	1850	1890
England and Wales	22	62
Scotland	17	49
Belgium	13	34
Netherlands	29	33
Prussia	7	30
United States	3	27
France	4	26
Denmark	11	24
Ireland	8	17
Austria	4	16
Sweden	3	13
Norway	3	12
Russia	3	9

Source: A. F. Weber, *The Growth of Cities in the
Nineteenth Century* (New York, 1899), 151.

The trend in the United States may serve to indicate more fully the
rapidity and extent of urban growth. In 1790, the date of the first
official census, 97 per cent of the population lived in rural areas and
places of less than 8,000 inhabitants. By 1930 this proportion had

---

[1] A. F. Weber, *The Growth of Cities in the Nineteenth Century* (New York,
1899).

declined to 49 per cent. The 54 places with 2,500 or more people, in 1820, contained 7 per cent of the total population, whereas the 3,464 incorporated places above that size in 1940 contained 56.5 per cent of the national population. Table 39 describes the trend, from 1890 to 1940, in the proportions of the population occupying different sizes of urban places.

TABLE 39

PERCENTAGE OF POPULATION IN URBAN PLACES, BY SIZE OF PLACE,
UNITED STATES, 1890-1940

Size of place	1890	1900	1910	1920	1930	1940
2,500 or more........	35.4	40.0	45.8	51.4	56.2	56.5
10,000 or more........	27.6	31.8	37.0	42.4	47.6	47.7
25,000 or more........	22.2	26.1	31.0	35.8	40.2	40.0
50,000 or more........	18.6	22.4	26.6	31.0	35.0	34.4
100,000 or more........	15.4	18.8	22.1	26.0	29.7	28.8
500,000 or more.......	7.1	10.7	12.5	15.5	17.1	17.0
1,000,000 or more.......	5.8	8.5	9.2	9.6	12.3	12.1

Source: U. S. Bureau of the Census, *Fifteenth Census of the United States: 1930,* "Population," Vol. I (Washington, D. C., 1931), 14; and *Sixteenth Census of the United States: 1940,* "Population: United States Summary" (Washington, D. C., 1943), 12.

This entire phenomenon of urban growth in the United States, as elsewhere, is a function of expansion. The centers of expansion, however, are found primarily, though not exclusively, in the largest cities. Most of the small cities are clustered about great metropolitan centers and serve as appendages to the central urban organs. They transmit the influences of the metropolis to the area round about and carry on many of the processes which enable the metropolis to maintain relations over a broad area.

Sources of Growth.—As we noted in the preceding chapter the reorganization of interrelationships involved in expansion produces overpopulation in the producing or rural areas. This results from excessive natural increase and, sooner or later, from an absolute displacement of people by increasingly efficient technology. It is that surplus population which constitutes the principal source of numbers for cities. The pressure of overpopulation in the producing areas and the multiplication of opportunities in centers of exchange and administration cause centripetal migrations and the growth of urban populations.

The surplus population created in the established producing areas, however, does not find, in the early phase of expansion, an adequate outlet in cityward migration. Rural displacement seems at first to proceed much more rapidly than the development of urban opportunities. This leaves a segment of the local population for which there is no immediate need either in extracting or in manufacturing and service activities. It is that population which supplies the manpower requirements for the development of frontier lands. Thus while many individuals converge upon cities, centrifugal movements carry many others toward the outer periphery of influence. As industrial expansion got under way in first one area and then another in nineteenth-century Europe each area in turn was a source of large scale migration to overseas settlements. But eventually each area, and in approximately the same order as industrialism originally spread from one to the other, ceased exporting population. The accelerating growth of cities absorbed the local rural excess, and cities even entered into competition with frontier zones for population.

Migration, we have said, accounts for the major part of urban growth. Although natural increase occurs in city populations, it is usually contingent upon migration.[2] That is, the annual excess of births over deaths results from a favorable age composition produced by sustained in-migration, for age specific fertility rates are commonly as low as and often lower than age specific death rates. If migration were suspended, therefore, the preponderance of young adults would soon pass out of the population and natural increase would either come to an end or give way to natural decrease.[3] There are exceptions to this rule, of course, especially among small cities. Whether such a ratio of births to deaths constitutes a permanent characteristic of cities is not known.

The measurement of the relative importance of migration to the growth of cities is hampered by inadequate data. According to the National Resources Committee, "seventy-five of the 93 cities with more than 100,000 population in 1930 had received at least one third of their total population from foreign countries or from States other than that in which the city is located. An appreciable number even of those born in the same States came from outside these cities. It is safe to say that, with the exception of a few southern cities, a large

---

[2] This applies principally to modern cities. In the pre-industrial cities natural decrease seems to have prevailed despite their favorable age compositions. Lack of sanitation, ignorance of contagion, and other hazards arising from congested settlement produced exorbitant death rates. Migration was necessary, therefore, not only for growth but for the maintenance of numbers at any given size. (See Mabel Craven Buer, *Health, Wealth, and Population in the Early Days of the Industrial Revolution* [London, 1926], 33.)

[3] The intrinsic rate of natural increase in cities in the United States was −2.3 per thousand in 1905-10 and reached −11.4 per thousand in 1935-40 (*Sixteenth Census of the United States, 1940,* "Population, Differential Fertility, 1940 and 1910," Table 7.)

share of the 1930 population of all large cities (ranging from 30 to 80 per cent for the individual cities) was born elsewhere."[4] Another indication of the significance of migration may be gained by forecasting the urban population of an area, first, on the assumption of a continuation of the past migration trend, and, secondly, on the assumption of no migration to cities. This is done in Table 40 for the urban population in the United States for the period 1930 to 1960. The further assumption is made in this calculation that birth and death rates will follow their respective trends as they had developed to 1930. It is evident that, with rural to urban migration continuing to draw the same proportion of rural natural increase, urban population would grow during the three decades following 1930 at a decreasing rate. But without migration urban population growth would fall off more sharply and give way to an absolute decline by 1950.

TABLE 40

Expected Urban Population in the United States,
With and Without Migration, 1930-1960.

Year	With migration			Without migration		
	Population (000's)	Amount of increase (000's)	Per cent increase	Population (000's)	Amount of increase (000's)	Per cent increase
1930.......	60,180.1	14,663.8	27.0	69,180.1	14,663.8	27.0
1940.......	76,038.8	6,858.7	9.9	70,785.0	1,604.9	2.3
1950.......	80,861.7	4,822.9	6.3	70,657.6	−127.4	−1.8
1960.......	82,436.3	1,574.6	1.9	68,548.7	−2,108.9	−3.0

Source: National Resources Committee, *Population Statistics: 3. Urban Data* (Washington, D. C., 1937), 27.

Functional Organization.—The reorganization of the scope and character of collective life which gives rise to cities involves a multiplication and diversification of nonagricultural activities. The development of this tendency in the United States is shown in Table 41 for the period 1820 to 1940. In 1820, agriculture provided employment for 72 per cent of the working force, while the nonagricultural industries employed but 28 per cent of the total. By 1940 these proportions were reversed. Agriculture declined steadily to less than a fifth of all employed workers. The nonagricultural, and for the most part urban, activities increased to the point where they comprised four fifths of the working population. In this transition employment in manufac-

---

[4] *The Problems of a Changing Population,* 99.

turing and mechanical industries increased at a moderate rate, reached a peak in 1920, and declined thereafter. But the more distinctively urban functions—transportation and communication, trade, public service, and professional service—have increased rapidly and without interruption.

TABLE 41

PERCENTAGE DISTRIBUTION OF EMPLOYED WORKERS BY INDUSTRY GROUPS, UNITED STATES, 1820-1940.

Industry	1940*	1930†	1920†	1910†	1900‡	1880‡	1860‡	1840‡	1820‡
All Industries..	100.0	100.0	100.0	100.0	100.0	100.0	100.0	100.0	100.0
Agriculture........	18.8	21.4	25.6	32.5	36.8	48.9	59.7	68.6	71.9
Mining...........	2.0	2.0	2.6	2.5	2.0	1.5	1.6	0.3	0.3
Manufacturing and Mechanical......	28.0	28.9	30.8	27.9	27.0	24.1	18.4	14.6	12.2
Transportation and Communication..	8.4	7.9	7.4	7.0	} 18.7	12.2	7.4	3.8	2.5
Trade............	16.7	12.5	10.2	9.5					
Public Service.....	3.9	1.8	1.8	1.1	—	—	—	—	—
Professional Service........	10.5	6.7	5.2	4.5	4.2	3.5	2.9	2.7	2.8
Domestic and Personal Service.	11.7	10.1	8.1	9.8	10.6	9.3	9.5	9.6	10.0
Clerical..........	—	8.2	7.5	4.5	—	—	—	—	—
Other......	—	0.5	0.8	0.7	0.7	0.5	0.5	0.4	0.3

* From U. S. Bureau of the Census, *Sixteenth Census of the United States: 1940*, "Population: United States Summary" (Washington, D. C., 1943), 10.

† From U. S. Bureau of the Census, *Fifteenth Census of the United States: 1930*, "Population," Vol. 5, 39.

‡ From P. K. Whelpton, "Occupational Groups in the United States, 1820-1920." *Journal of the American Statistical Association*, XXI (September, 1926), S. No. 155, 340.

The development of manufacturing is an important factor in the rise of cities. The extensive centripetal movements of the nineteenth century were initiated in part at least by the growth of mechanical industry. Factory workers and their dependents clustered in dense concentrations in and around established urban sites. The effect was cumulative. Large scale specialization such as is represented in masses of factory workers requires numerous persons in supplemental functions to provide the necessary complement of services. Actually the indirect effects of manufacturing on the growth of cities are at least as important as the direct effects, if not more so. Manufacturing supplies the mechanical devices for releasing manpower from onerous tasks, it produces the transportation and communication equipment essential for extensive territorial specialization and interdependence; and it calls into being numerous administrative and service functions.

That these effects are relatively slow to mature is evident in the delayed expansion of the service sector of the economy. Thus while in the early part of the nineteenth century the urban population was paced by the increase in manufacturing employment, since 1890, as may be seen in Table 42, the former has outstripped the latter. The dominating importance of nonmanufacturing or service functions is apparent in the fact that they employ 60 per cent or more of all gainfully employed workers in cities, in contrast to the approximately 30 per cent employed in manufacturing (Table 7).

TABLE 42

Total Urban Population, Total Employed Workers in Manufacturing, and Ratio of Employed Workers in Manufacturing to Urban Population by Census Year, United States, 1890 to 1940.

Year	Urban population (in thousands)	Wage earners in manufacturing (Average for the year)		Ratio of workers in manufacturing to 100 of urban population
		Year	Number (in thousands)	
1940.........	74,424	1939	7,887	10.6
1930.........	68,955	1929	8,808	12.8
1920.........	54,305	1919	9,000	16.6
1910.........	42,166	1909	6,615	15.7
1900.........	30,380	1899	4,713	15.5
1890.........	22,298	1889	4,252	19.1

Source: U. S. Bureau of the Census, *Sixteenth Census of the United States: 1940*, "Population" (Washington, D. C., 1942), Vol. I; and "Manufacturing" (Washington, D. C., 1942), Vol. I.

Manufacturing is not indispensable, however, to the growth of every city, though every city must produce some commodity or service for "export" to populations in adjacent or more distant areas. That may be governmental service, higher education, health and recreational opportunity, or marketing service. Hence the number and sizes of manufacturing establishments are highly variable from city to city. Some fairly large cities have no manufacturing establishments within their boundaries, while others, particularly those situated close to larger cities, may have more wage jobs in manufacturing than they have resident population. If these individual differences are ignored and the averages of size-classes of cities are compared, as in Table 43, it is found that the number of establishments increases with size of city. But the size of establishments tends to decline as city size increases. The net effect of these countervailing tendencies seems to be for the

number of wage jobs in manufacturing per city to approximate a ratio
to population which, over the range of size classes, has limited variability. Stated in other terms, for every wage job in manufacturing,
in 1940, there are between nine and fourteen residents in the city.
This, as said before, represents a smaller ratio than prevailed in earlier
periods.

Corporate units which serve the day-to-day needs of the local population comprise in the aggregate what is here termed the service structure. Such units bear a relation to the local population different from

TABLE 43

Manufacturing Establishments per City, Wage-Earners per Establishment, and Wage Jobs per 100 of the Resident Population,
by Size of City, United States, 1940.

Size of city	Number of cities	Establishments per city	Wage-earners per establishment	Wage-jobs per 100 resident population
All cities......	1,009	125.3	42.4	8.7
500,000 and over...	14	4,371.8	30.2	8.3
200,000–499,999....	29	632.7	38.3	7.5
100,000–199,999....	49	229.7	57.5	10.0
90,000– 99,999....	7	168.1	57.2	9.9
80,000– 89,999....	13	125.9	54.2	8.1
70,000– 79,999....	18	113.5	70.3	10.8
60,000– 69,999....	33	93.7	57.4	8.3
50,000– 59,999....	28	90.9	66.0	10.9
40,000– 49,999....	50	73.4	71.6	11.7
30,000– 39,999....	82	58.4	60.2	9.2
20,000– 29,999....	147	39.7	57.8	9.1
10,000– 19,999....	539	20.1	57.9	8.5

Source: U. S. Bureau of the Census, *Sixteenth Census of the United States: 1940*,
"Manufacturing" (Washington, D. C., 1942), Vol. III.

manufacturing establishments and other similar units which produce
for interregional exchange. The latter make up the economic base of
the city and to a considerable extent determine the number of people
who may live there. Service units, on the other hand, since they are
adapted to the consumption habits of the local population, are dependent in respect to both their number and their characteristics on the
size of that population. This, of course, is a much simplified statement of the relationships involved. Producing units are somewhat
dependent on population size for their labor supply and for adequate
services to their workers. Service units, conversely, may influence
population size by making a given city an attractive place in which

to live. Producing units are relatively more independent and service units are relatively more dependent on the size of the local population at any given time.

Population increase influences both the diversification and the amount of service activity in the city. Each increase in size affords greater opportunity for specialization. In a small place many types of services can be provided only if they are dovetailed in one or a very few establishments. With increases in size of urban place the probability that there will be a continuous demand for any one service also increases. Jointly offered services separate and appear in individual units. In addition, growth in size permits the emergence of altogether new types of services. Hence the service structure is elaborated and made more complete with advances in city size. In Table 44 this process is described for one part of the country.

TABLE 44

APPROXIMATE MINIMUM POPULATION OF TOWN IN WHICH GIVEN TYPES OF
SPECIALIZED RETAILING FIRST APPEARS, TEXAS, 1929 *

Type of specialized store	Approximate population of town in which specialized stores first appear
Men's and women's apparel and dry goods (together)...	500
Hardware, furniture, and undertaking (together)......	500
Meats and groceries (together).....................	500
Hardware...	500
House furnishings (incomplete lines)................	1,000
Women's apparel (without shoes)...................	1,000
Jewelry and musical instruments or optometrist service..	1,000
Hats and dressmaking..............................	1,000
Music and musical instruments......................	2,500
Men's apparel.....................................	3,000
Furniture	4,000
Men's and women's shoes and hosiery...............	6,000
Men's and women's shoes...........................	10,000
Women's shoes and hosiery.........................	30,000
Women's hats.....................................	40,000
Women's shoes....................................	60,000
Men's shoes......................................	60,000
Men's hats.......................................	60,000

* Wm. J. Reilly, *Methods for the Study of Retail Relationships,* Univ. of Texas Bull. 2944 (Austin, 1929), 26.

Likewise the volume of service activity, as represented in retailing and the sale of personal services, increases with size of city. This is partly because the denser the population the fewer things are individuals able to do for themselves. But also specialization develops and

intensifies dependence. The relationship of volume of service activity
to population, however, is not so clearly indicated by number of establishments as by a measure such as per capita sales, for the reason that
the size of establishment also varies with size of city.[5] This applies
to many forms of nonpecuniary services, e.g., religious, eductional,
and the like; however, the relation between the number of such units
and city growth has not been investigated.

The influence of population size on the variety and amount of
service is subject to modification resulting from the characteristics
of the population. Service structure, in other words, tends toward a
close adaptation to population composition. Thus in cities with high
income the amount of service activity is significantly greater than in
low income cities, when size and distance from a larger city are controlled.[6] Although the effect of income is observable over a wide
range of types of services, it is most marked in respect to the more
specialized services. Cities with large concentrations of people over
45 years of age have a larger volume of service activity than do cities
in which persons under 20 years of age are exceptionally numerous.
Moreover, old population cities have a much greater development of
restaurants, drug stores, and personal services than is found in young
population cities. No doubt part of the effect of age, though not all,
is a function of income. Differences in sex ratio appear to have no
important bearing on the amount of service activity except in suburban
cities, and there it is probable that sex ratio differences are closely related to income differences. Nativity differences, while not associated with differences in amount of service, are related to differences
in types of services. Food store and restaurant services are much
greater where the foreign-born are numerous than where they are
few. Perhaps this is because food habits are more persistent than
any other kind of habit.

It is worth noting that single-industry cities possess essentially
the same kind of service structure as multiple-industry cities. Specialization of production and generalization of consumption go hand
in hand in the dependent community. This observation, parenthetically, is in keeping with the point made earlier that service activity is

---

[5] Amos H. Hawley, "An Ecological Study of Urban Service Institutions," *American Sociological Review,* VI (October, 1941), 631-32. Number of establishments
has been suggested as an index of population where data on numbers are lacking (T.
Lynn Smith, *Farm Trade Centers in Louisiana,* 1901-31, Louisiana Bull. 284, Louisiana State University, 1933), but contrary evidence has been supplied by V. H.
Whitney, ("The Estimation of Population for Unincorporated Places," *American
Sociological Review,* XI [February, 1946], 98-103.)
[6] Amos H. Hawley, *ibid.,* 636 ff.

relatively more dependent on population than is production. But cities in which manufacturing employment is disproportionately large have less developed service structures than cities in which manufacturing employment is of comparatively minor importance. Type of employment is doubtless an index, however, of other population characteristics.

The variations in manufacturing and service activity with size of city are also apparent, as might be expected, in the employment structure of the urban labor force. Table 45 indicates that the proportions engaged in transportation and communications, wholesale and retail trade, finance, recreation, and government increase with city size. On the other hand, manufacturing, extractive, and professional activities decline as size increases. These data describe not where the jobs are but where the workers reside. Many workers may reside in one size of city and work in another, and this applies to certain classes of workers more than to others. Professional workers are particularly inclined to seek residences in small suburban cities adjacent to large cities in which their employment is located.

TABLE 45

Percentage Distribution of Employed Persons 14 Years of Age and Over, in a Sample of 101 Cities, by Industry and Size of City, United States, 1940

Industry	Total United States	Cities			
		10,000–24,999	25,000–49,999	50,000–99,999	100,000–999,999
Total....................	100.0	100.0	100.0	100.0	100.0
Construction................	4.6	4.7	4.5	4.3	5.0
Manufacturing..............	23.4	29.8	34.5	30.3	28.0
Transportation..............	4.8	5.7	4.3	4.6	6.4
Communication.............	0.9	1.2	1.1	1.3	1.3
Utilities.....................	1.2	1.7	2.0	1.9	1.4
Wholesale trade.............	2.7	3.3	3.0	3.8	4.0
Retail trade.................	14.0	16.8	17.0	18.0	18.7
Finance....................	3.2	3.9	3.5	5.2	5.0
Personal and Business Services..	10.8	12.5	12.9	12.0	12.3
Recreation..................	0.9	0.9	1.0	0.8	1.1
Professional................	7.3	10.0	9.2	9.9	8.3
Government.................	3.9	4.0	3.7	4.4	4.9
Extractive and Other..........	22.3	5.5	3.3	3.5	3.6
Number of Cities..........	101	60	20	11	10

Source: U. S. Bureau of the Census, *Sixteenth Census of the United States: 1940*, "Population" (Washington, D. C., 1943), Vol. II, Pts. 1-7.

Physical Structure and the Spatial Pattern.—The growth of population and the development of its organization obviously must be accompanied by the construction of dwellings, streets, and other equipment essential to the daily functioning of the collective life.[7] All such equipment we refer to as the physical structure of the city. The distribution of the elements of that structure form a pattern of land uses which presumably is expressive of the interdependences among the various activities comprised by the city.[8] In this section we are concerned with the effects of growth on both the physical structure and the spatial pattern of the city.

The significance of transportation in the development of the physical structure of the city needs only brief mention. Urban population owes its increase largely to improvements in transportation which enhance the city's opportunities for participating in the interregional economy. And from increases in both population and activities arise needs for additions to the physical structure.[9] On the other hand, reductions of the time and cost of intramural movements increase the number of individuals who may live together in the city and also the size of the area over which they may be scattered. The extension of the builtup area of the city has followed closely upon changes in transport, beginning with pedestrian travel, succeeded by the horse-car, then the street railway, rapid transit lines, and finally the motor vehicle. These changes have not only permitted projections of the city into the countryside, they have altered its shape and affected its composition.

As a city adds to its territory to accommodate the increased need for space it overruns and engulfs many small villages and cities. For example, Figure 33 indicates that Detroit has absorbed twenty-eight such places in its growth. Some of these have a vestigial survival as secondary business districts, others are remembered only as place names for ill-defined locations within the city.

Various conceptions of the pattern of the city's territorial spread have been put forth. In an early work Richard M. Hurd observed that growth is both central and axial. "A continual contest exists

---

[7] From a study of seventeen cities, between the years 1875 and 1933, W. H. Newman concluded that changes in the rate of building activity lagged one to two years behind changes in the rate of population growth. ("The Building Industry and Business Cycles," *The Journal of Business of the University of Chicago* [July, 1935], 32-39.

[8] See Chapters 13 and 14.

[9] According to Walter Isard, every important innovation in transportation is followed by an upsurge of industrial and residential building activity. ("Transport Development and Building Cycles," *Quarterly Journal of Economics*, LVII [November, 1942], 90-112.)

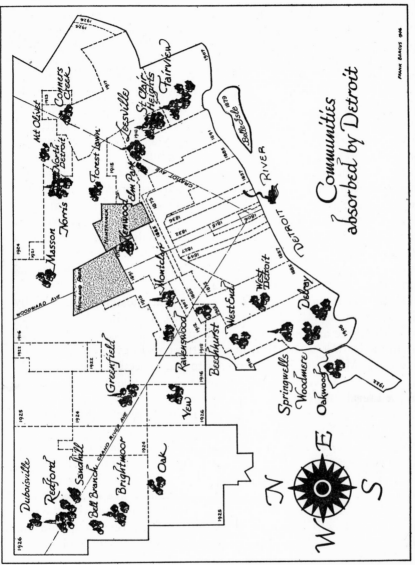

FIG. 33.—Communities absorbed by the growth of Detroit. (From Detroit City Plan Commission. *Proposed Generalized Land Use Plan* [Detroit, 1947]. Used by permission.)

between axial growth, pushing out from the center along transportation lines, and central growth, constantly following and obliterating it, while new projections are being made further out on the various axes." [10]   In consequence the city acquires a star-shaped pattern, there being relatively little development of lands in the triangular spaces between radiating thoroughfares. A second conception is that of E. W. Burgess which holds that the pattern of a city is a series of concentric zones differentiated as to type of land use and of structure. [11] Growth proceeds more or less symmetrically as the result of pressure from the center, with each zone expanding into the next outer zone. Yet another suggestion, which is actually a refinement of Hurd's and Burgess' statements, is that growth occurs in sectors. [12] That is, sizeable areas are subdivided and developed as units, acquiring characteristics at the time which remain to distinguish them for long thereafter. The tendency is for such sectors to extend radially from the center to the periphery of the city. Thus, "if one sector of a city develops as a low rent area, it will tend to retain that character for long distances as it extends itself in the process of growth." [13]

Of these patterns of growth it seems that the one suggested by Hurd is most useful for general purposes, though the differences among the three are more apparent than real. The tendency to axial growth projecting outward from a builtup core is evident in virtually every city. Moreover it corresponds to the expected effect of established routes of travel upon the extension of settlement. On the other hand, a literal interpretation of the concentric theory would involve an assumption of equal ease of movement in all directions from a center. But such an assumption has no support in fact. The concentric pattern appears to have its clearest expression in what Hurd referred to as central growth, and even then the expansion of one zone into another is irregular, occurring more rapidly along radial routes than elsewhere. The sector theory concerns certain details of growth and does not contradict the axial pattern. In any case, however, the pattern of city growth is subject to many modifications in specific instances. Factors such as local topography, the amount and rate of growth, the character of transportation, and the availability of utilities may introduce deviations from the generalized pattern.

---

[10] Richard M. Hurd, *Principles of City Land Values* (1924), 39 ff.

[11] E. W. Burgess, "The Growth of the City: An Introduction to a Research Project," *op. cit.,* and *Supra,* Chapter 13.

[12] Arthur M. Weimer and Homer Hoyt, *Principles of Urban Real Estate* (New York, 1939), 60-70; and Federal Housing Administration, *The Structure and Growth of Residential Neighborhoods in American Cities* (New York, 1939), 17 ff.

[13] Arthur M. Weimer and Homer Hoyt, *ibid.,* 61.

The character of transportation is by all counts the most significant factor influencing the distribution of additions to the physical structure of the city. Most other influencing factors exert their effects indirectly through affecting transportation. The network of streets establishes the major and subsidiary axes along which construction may occur. A street pattern based on a number of radial avenues favors a spreading out of building and gives rise to the star-shaped appearance to which Hurd alluded. A grid pattern, however, encourages a compact physical structure, though even in that instance the main traffic arteries intersecting at right angles in the business center become radii along which extended development takes place. Topographic features may necessitate departures from a symmetrical street pattern in which case building construction will be likewise affected. A steep hill close by the city's center may result in streets skirting its base with construction developing in a semicircle about the hill. The first settlement at what is now Rio de Janeiro selected a small coastal shelf approachable from the interior only through two or three narrow defiles.[14] In consequence most of the residential area has grown up on the far sides of the hills that hem in the old section of the city. A stream or even a railroad, both of which present problems of crossing, tend to channelize growth along their opposite sides. Large segments of land long held out of use may be analogous to topographic features in their effects. Thus Boston Common and the old Hudson's Bay Company property in Edmonton, Canada, forced the central business districts of the two cities into U-shaped patterns.

The type of carrier in use is also of importance to the shape assumed by the city. Mass carriers such as street railways and rapid transit lines accentuate the star-shaped pattern. The lands intervening between radial routes are difficult to serve by facilities of that type and therefore tend to be developed only a convenient walking distance from the main thoroughfare. But an individual carrier, notably the automobile, is not confined to major avenues, but may go wherever a road surface sufficient to bear its weight has been laid down. Accordingly, the automobile has permitted much of the interstitial area in the star-shaped pattern to be filled in and cities have taken on a more circular appearance. Detroit, more than any other large city, has developed on the basis of automobile transportation. Nevertheless, the radial pattern with sparsely occupied interstices is clearly evident in Figures 34 and 35, which show Detroit's builtup area in 1890 and

---

14 Norman D. Wilson, "Some Problems of Urban Transportation," in H. A. Innes (ed.), *Essays in Transportation* (Toronto, 1941), 99-100; see also Margaret T. Parker, *Lowell: A Study of Industrial Development* (New York, 1940), 95-97.

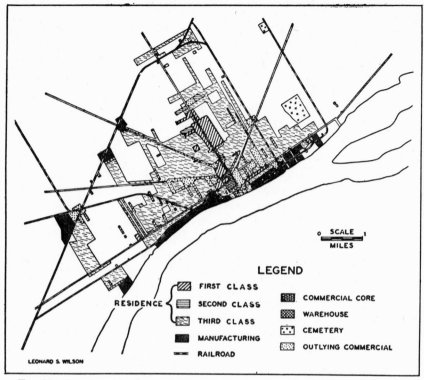

LEGEND

RESIDENCE
  FIRST CLASS
  SECOND CLASS
  THIRD CLASS

MANUFACTURING
RAILROAD

COMMERCIAL CORE
WAREHOUSE
CEMETERY
OUTLYING COMMERCIAL

SCALE
MILES

LEONARD S. WILSON

FIG. 34.—Developed land uses in Detroit, 1890. (From L. S. Wilson, "Functional Areas in Detroit, 1890-1933," *Papers Michigan Academy of Science, Arts, and Letters,* Vol. XXII [1947], 399. Used by permission.)

1900. After 1900 the lands lying between radiating thoroughfares became more densely occupied, as may be observed in Figures 36, 37, and 38. But even in 1933 traces of the radial pattern were still noticeable.

Turning to the process of growth and its effects on the pattern of land uses, it is well to note at the outset that in the very small city there is seldom a very distinct pattern. Industrial, business, residential, and other activities seem to be distributed more or less at random over the entire city area. A service or business district is discernible as a section in which there are relatively more business and service activities and relatively fewer residential uses of the land than elsewhere in the city. The rather amorphous pattern of the small city is doubtless due in part to the fact that distances between points are usually short and there is, in consequence, very little competition for accessible sites. Moreover, the limited variety of land use and population types and the small number of representatives of each type offer but a negligible encouragement to the segregation of each type. Such circumstances as these disappear, however, with increase in size and a more sharply etched pattern takes form.

Growth proceeds through accumulation and pressure at the center and accretion at the periphery of the city. The center, formed by the intersection of the principal interregional and local routes, is the point

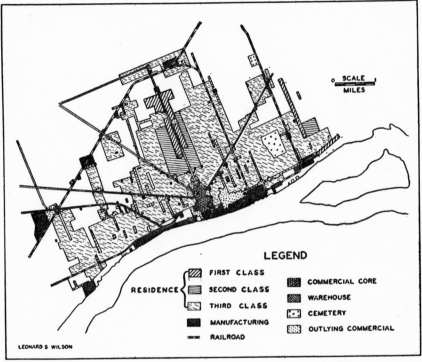

FIG. 35.—Developed land uses in Detroit, 1900. (From L. S. Wilson, *loc. cit.*, 402. Used by permission.)

of maximum accessibility from both within and without. Accordingly, it is there that building density increases first and most rapidly. As available space in and immediately adjacent to the strategic transportation point is filled in competition for sites becomes progressively more severe. That is indicated by rising values of land at the center. Functions for which maximum accessibility is of vital concern tend more and more to dominate the central area—typically retail and specialized service functions, able to withstand high land values only through ability to use land intensively. Others using land less intensively are excluded from or forced out of the focal area. They take up positions around the highest land-value zone at distances from it which vary inversely with their capacity for intensive land use and need for accessibility. Financial and central office functions tend to locate on lands adjacent to the highest value area, while recreational activities and the retailing of many types of staple goods are apt to be found even further removed. Such extensive uses as are represented in automotive sales establishments and secondhand goods stores gather at the margin of the central business district, often pressing out along the radial thoroughfares.

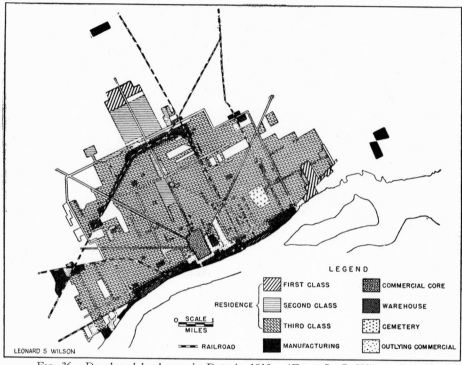

Fig. 36.—Developed land uses in Detroit, 1910. (From L. S. Wilson, *loc. cit.,* 404. Used by permission.)

The lateral projection of the business area tends to be arrested somewhat by a vertical extension of the city at the point of highest land values. This seems to occur when city growth races ahead of improvements in local transportation. Competition for site, under such conditions, raises land values well above what most functions can sustain alone. Only through a pooling of their rent-paying capacities in the construction of a skyscraper—"a street stood on end" —are they able to maintain the choice location. Homer Hoyt describes the vertical growth of Chicago in the following manner:

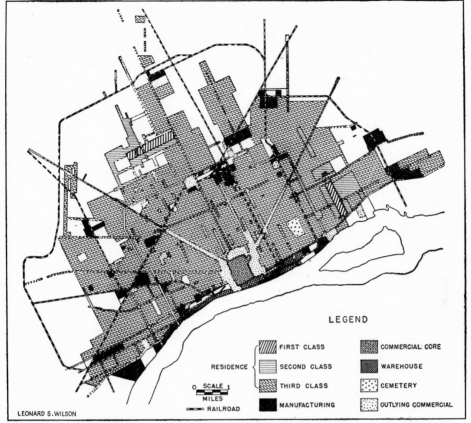

Fig. 37.—Developed land uses in Detroit, 1920. (From L. S. Wilson, *loc. cit.,* 407. Used by permission.)

. . . the Chicago Loop buildings under the pressure of expanding business confined to a limited area have tapped successively higher layers of air. By 1893 over 10 per cent of the air layer from 7 to 12 stories had been filled with buildings, and the highest towers extended to 16 stories. By 1923, when the new zoning laws permitted tower buildings that contained as many as 44 stories, 37 per cent of the area from 7 to 12 stories had been occupied, 17 per cent of that between 12 and 16 stories, and over 6 per cent of that between 16 and 22 stories.[15]

The growth of the inner zone of the city as a business district produces numerous changes in its character. Its space is given over more and more to specialized retailing, recreational, administrative, and other services. Furthermore, these functions tend to regroup form-

---

[15] Homer Hoyt, *One Hundred Years of Land Values in Chicago* (Chicago, University of Chicago Press, 1933), 329-330.

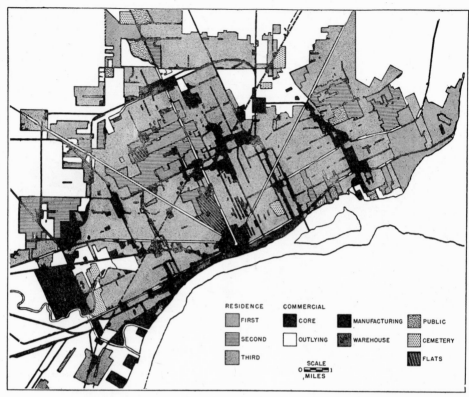

RESIDENCE   COMMERCIAL
FIRST   CORE   MANUFACTURING   PUBLIC
SECOND   OUTLYING   WAREHOUSE   CEMETERY
THIRD   FLATS
                 SCALE
                 0 ▬▬▬ 1
                 ,MILES

Fig. 38.—Developed land uses in Detroit, 1933. (From L. S. Wilson, *loc. cit.,* 408. Used by permission.)

ing relatively homogeneous clusters such as were described in Chapter 13.[16] The changes in composition and distribution of uses in the central business district are reflected in rapid obsolescence of structures and frequent rebuilding. For example:

In the 60 years since the Chicago fire, practically the entire loop district has been rebuilt twice, more than half of it three times, and much of it four times. A survey of lower Broadway, New York City, below Cortlandt Street, shows only three buildings more than 40 years of age, all of which were marked for demolition, except one, which had been substantially rebuilt within the last ten years, and showed only seventeen buildings more than 25 years of age.[17]

---

[16] "In 1880 the banks and stockbrokers' offices (in Stockholm)—most sensitive of all business activities to situation—were not concentrated; by 1930 they were clustered in the south-east of Norrmalm and formed the true 'core' of the city." (Robert E. Dickinson, *City, Region and Regionalism* [London, 1947], 139.)

[17] *The Bulletin,* The National Association of Building Owners and Managers (December, 1930), 107.

Manufacturing industry effects a rather complete withdrawal from the central district to lower value areas. Oriented more toward interregional than toward intramural transportation routes, manufacturing may remove itself from the highest value zone and, at the same time, actually improve its accessibility to interregional markets. Transportation changes have accelerated the movement from the business district. The development of the railroad opened an abundance of cheap lands for manufacturing use in the outer sections of the city yet within reach of the working population. The abandonment of business district and waterfront sites results in areas of industrial concentration along railroad belt lines and switching yards. If the buildings vacated by manufacturing are not immediately replaced by structures adapted to other uses, they tend to be occupied by miscellaneous light industries, often of a marginal economic status, and by warehouse uses. The latter, however, are also strongly attracted to cheap land and railroad siding facilities.[18] These changes in industrial location are evident in the series of illustrations of Detroit's growth, Figures 34 through 38. The redistribution of industry and the growth of the central business district in Chicago are portrayed in Figure 39.

Evacuation of the central business district is no less marked in the case of residential uses. Figures 34-38 show the process in Detroit. Expansion of its commercial core was accompanied by a steady outward movement of residential areas along the radial traffic arteries—highest priced first, moderately priced residences next, lowest priced areas last.[19] Relocation of high rental residential areas in six American cities is shown in Figure 40. The movement represents not only a withdrawal before rising land values, but also an escape from the inconveniences generated by congestion. The extent of the removal appears to be associated with the ability of population to pay the costs of transportation to and from the center.

Although the changing locations of industrial and residential areas have been referred to as movement much of it occurs in the form of

---

[18] Warehousing has steadily declined as an urban function and in the amount of land it uses. The increasing efficiency of transportation has made for direct and quick deliveries from manufacturer to retailer, and has thus reduced the need for the stocking of large inventories.

[19] That this is not a novel tendency is indicated in the following quotation: "The wealthier people settled in their new town houses in the seventeenth and eighteenth centuries (often moving in from the countryside) in the quieter quarters of the town, usually on its outskirts inside the walls or on pleasant sites—high land or a high river bank. In London the wealthy began to shift outwards to Chelsea and Islington so as to avoid the noise and smells of the city." (Robert E. Dickinson, *City, Region and Regionalism: A Geographical Contribution to Human Ecology* [London, Routledge & Kegan Paul, Ltd., 1947], 99.)

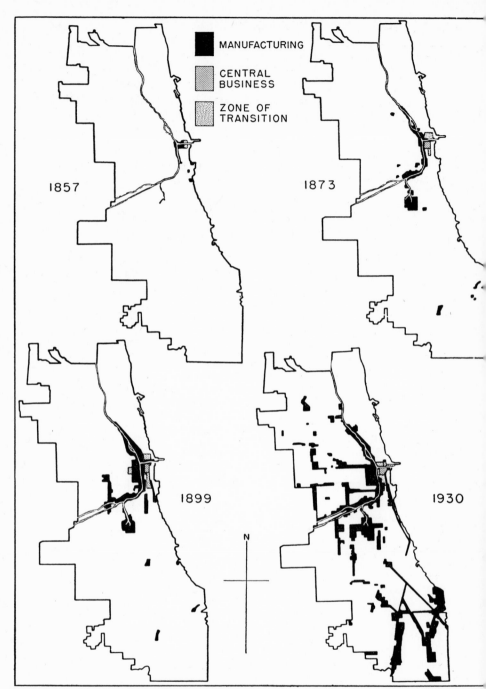

Fig. 39.—The redistribution of manufacturing and the growth of the central business district, Chicago, 1857-1930. (From Federal Housing Administration, *The Structure and Growth of Residential Neighborhoods in American Cities* [Washington, D. C., 1939], 110.)

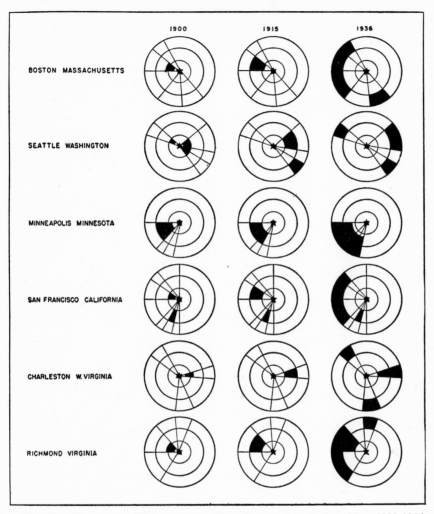

1900   1915   1936

BOSTON MASSACHUSETTS

SEATTLE WASHINGTON

MINNEAPOLIS MINNESOTA

SAN FRANCISCO CALIFORNIA

CHARLESTON W. VIRGINIA

RICHMOND VIRGINIA

Fig. 40.—Movements of high rent residential areas in selected cities, 1900-1936. (From Federal Housing Administration, *The Structure and Growth of Residential Neighborhoods in American Cities* [Washington, D. C., 1939], 115.)

peripheral growth. The encroachment of business uses upon adjoining areas devoted to different uses hastens the obsolescence of the structures adapted to those uses. Replacements are made not in the established areas, whether they be residential or industrial, but in new areas that are protected from the invasion of high land values. Also in the new areas considerable accretion from without takes place. But the repelling influence of the business district, and of industrial areas when residences alone are considered, is never completely lacking in the growth at the periphery.

Accompanying the relocation of residential areas is a movement of
the central business district, which is visible in Figures 34 through
38. The movement may be regarded as having two phases. We have
already referred to the lateral extension of the business core. That
impinges upon adjacent residential areas and presses them outward
as residential lands pass into commercial uses. A second phase appears in the tendency of the business district to shift its "center of
gravity" in pursuit of the residential areas and particularly the better
or higher priced areas.[20] This is partly a result of the inclination on
the part of services to retain as close proximity to their clienteles as
conditions permit. But it is also due to increasing pressure from
traffic congestion at the center which accelerated rapidly as the use of
the automobile spread. Cities situated on a waterfront are especially
subject to such pressure. Since their populations cannot be distributed in full circles around their centers, traffic must enter the centers
from a limited number of directions in each instance. Some relief
from the resulting congestion is obtained in an uptown movement of
the business district.[21] The business and traffic center appears to seek
the center of population distribution.

Traffic congestion at the center is also influential in the development of outlying business districts. These appear at the intersections
of important radial and cross-city thoroughfares and at transfer points
of public carriers. The accessibility of such locations to a heavy traffic
flow, their relative abundance of automobile parking space, and their
low land values rapidly attract an accumulation of service functions
of the less specialized sort. Outlying business districts, though they
vary greatly as to size, may emerge as significant competitors of the

---

[20] Federal Housing Administration, *op. cit.*, 108; and Calvin F. Smith, *Social
Saga of Two Cities* (1937), 44-45.
"The central business district of Chicago, which in previous years had been pulled
southward by the influence of fashionable homes on Prairie, Calumet, and Michigan
Avenues, received a powerful tug from the North Side when the center of fashion
shifted to the Lake Shore Drive. The effect was slow to manifest itself, however.
The growth of the Gold Coast on the North Side had proceeded far by 1900, but
the northward thrust of the Loop did not come until the Michigan Avenue bridge
was opened on May 14, 1920." (Homer Hoyt, *One Hundred Years of Land Values
in Chicago* [Chicago, University of Chicago Press, 1933], 242.)
[21] Norman D. Wilson, *op. cit.*, 99.
The average daily money loss from traffic density in Detroit in 1936, based only
on low operating speeds, was estimated at $28,081 (*Street Traffic, City of Detroit,
1936-1937*, 57-58). An estimate for Boston placed the figure at $18,000 per mile per
year (*The Role of the Federal Government in Highway Development* [Washington,
D. C., 1944], 23.) Speeds as low as 4.5 miles per hour are not uncommon. J. L.
Sert, describing traffic conditions on Broadway, in Los Angeles, observed that a
distance which required 10 minutes and 20 seconds to traverse by horse and buggy,
in 1910, now consumes 14 minutes and 12 seconds by automobile (*Can Our Cities
Survive* [London, 1942]).

principal business center. New services generally make their initial appearance in the central business district, for their very novelty gives them a specialized character. But as their functions become established in the habits of the population the units multiply or subdivide as by fission, sending out counterparts to neighborhood shopping districts and to satellite locations.[22] This has been the experience of motion-picture theaters, dry-cleaning establishments, beauty shops, and to a considerable extent of banking units. A dispersed locational pattern is likewise steadily developing in all kinds of retail activities.[23]

Population Redistribution.—As has been noted, the prevailing direction of residence changes in the growing city is centrifugal. In the early city and in the small city of today maximum densities of population are found at or near the focal points of activity. But as residences are displaced from that zone by more intensive uses of the land population retires to lower value lands. The zone of maximum density shifts outward leaving an unpopulated core. This is illustrated with Chicago data in Figure 41 in which a hollow place at Madison Ave. can be seen to develop after 1880.[24] Paul F. Cressey observed: "In 1898 Chicago was relatively compact, half of its population living within a radius of 3.2 miles from the center of the city. In subsequent years the median point has moved steadily outward, being located at 4.1 miles in 1910, 5.0 miles in 1920, and 5.8 miles in 1930."[25] Table 46 shows the same tendency at work in Frankfurt, Germany. In general, the area within a 2- to 4-mile radius, differing with the size of the city, from the central business district has lost population almost continuously since early in the twentieth century, while the area beyond that distance has gained just as continuously.[26] This may be seen for the 1930 to 1940 period in Table 47 which describes population changes by distance zones in selected cities.

As in intercommunity migration, the centrifugal movement within the city proceeds by short-distance moves. Families tend to move within or to adjacent census tracts, i.e., but a few blocks at a time.[27]

---

[22] Cf. *Regional Survey of New York and Its Environs,* Vol. I.

[23] United States Bureau of the Census, "Intra-City Business Census Statistics for Philadelphia, Pennsylvania," *op. cit.,* 8 ff.

[24] This refers, of course, to the resident or sleeping population. The daylight population of the central business district is normally denser than that of most other sections of the city.

[25] "Population Succession in Chicago, 1898-1930," *American Journal of Sociology,* XLIV (July, 1938), 59.

[26] See R. D. McKenzie, *The Metropolitan Community* (New York, 1933), 176.

[27] Howard W. Green, *Movements of Families Within the Cleveland Metropolitan District, 1935;* Real Property Inventory of Metropolitan Cleveland, Report No. 7 (Cleveland, 1936), 23; and Richard Dewey, "Peripheral Expansion in Milwaukee County," *American Journal of Sociology,* LIV (September, 1948), 120.

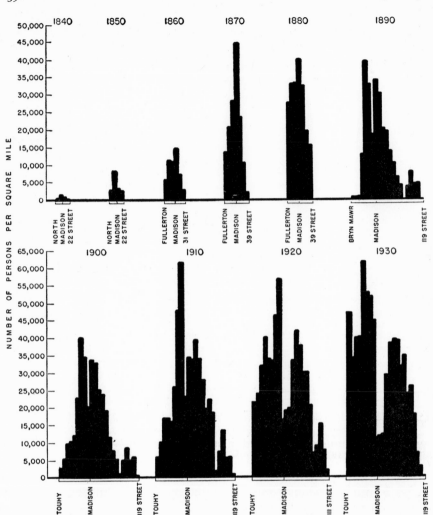

Fig. 41.—Population per square mile in a zone of land extending along the lake from the northern to the southern limits of Chicago, 1840-1930. (From Homer Hoyt, *One Hundred Years of Land Values in Chicago* [Chicago: The University of Chicago Press, 1933], 360. Used by permission.)

That may result from both an inverse correlation of information on alternative places of residence with distance and the difficulty of making a complete withdrawal from a set of relationships based on neighborhood. If the experience in Cleveland in the years between 1933 and 1935 is reliable, however, the latter factor making for short-distance moves would seem to be rather unimportant; the median length of residence of all families in the houses they occupied in that

year was 3.6 years.[28] Furthermore the intracity movement is primarily from low-value residential areas to higher-value residential areas
and from old to newer houses. This is to be expected in view of the
general centrifugal drift. The newer and higher rental homes are the
greater distances from the city center.

TABLE 46

POPULATION PER ACRE BY DISTANCE FROM CENTER,
FRANKFURT, GERMANY, 1890 AND 1933

Distance Zone (Kilometers)	Density per acre	
	1890	1933
0.0- 0.5.........	200	121
0.5- 1.0.........	76	69
1.0- 2.0.........	33	68
2.0- 3.0.........	7	25
3.0- 4.0.........	4	12
4.0- 5.0.........	2	7
5.0- 6.0.........	6	10
6.0- 7.0.........	1	5
7.0- 8.0........	1	2
8.0-12.0........	1	2

Source: Cited by Robert E. Dickinson,
City, Region, and Regionalism (London,
1947), 129.

The selective effects of population movement within the city are
portrayed in Figure 42. The pyramids in this illustration describe the
age and composition of population in census tracts located at approximately 1.5-mile intervals on Madison Avenue, Chicago, from the Loop
to Oak Park. In Tract 298, situated less than a mile from the business district, the predominance of males increased from 1919 to 1930.
Evidently most of the families remaining in that Tract in 1910 had
departed by 1930. A similar, though more pronounced, change took
place in Tract 226. The tendency in the more distant tracts has been
toward a more uniform sex distribution and a declining family size.
The latter trend may reflect the concentrations of apartment houses
and other types of multiple residences along the traffic artery. Families lead the outward movement, while unattached individuals are last
to evacuate areas passing from residential to other uses.

---

[28] Howard W. Green, *ibid.*, 49. For house owners the median was 9.6 years and
for renters it was 1.3 years. The medians by type of residence were as follows:
apartment houses, 10.6 months; four-family houses, 1.6 years; row houses, 1.7 years;
two-family houses, 2.6 years; and single-family houses, 7.0 years.

TABLE 47

PERCENT OF INCREASE OF POPULATION IN GROUPS OF CENSUS TRACTS LYING WITHIN GIVEN DISTANCES FROM CENTER OF CITY, SELECTED CITIES, 1930–1940

Distance from center of city	Los Angeles	New York	Chicago	Philadelphia	Cleveland	Cincinnati	Boston	Pittsburgh
Total	21.5	7.6	0.6	−1.0	−2.5	1.0	−1.3	0.3
0– 1 mile	3.9	−10.6	−7.2	−10.5	−11.5	−6.6	−11.8	−5.1
1– 2 miles	7.4		−10.7	−8.9	−7.9	−7.5	−8.3	−1.1
2– 3 "	10.8	0.7	−8.4	−1.8	0.2	2.0	0.9	−0.3
3– 4 "	9.6		−1.5	−2.3	−3.4	1.3	4.6	2.5
4– 5 "	9.0	7.4	0.6	−2.4	−4.6	3.0	4.2	5.5
5– 6 "	16.6			2.5	0.5	13.9	6.7	
6– 7 "	34.8			19.7	0.7	16.9		
7– 8 "	65.2	8.3	3.9	35.1				
8–10 "	82.4	12.8	4.9	20.3	5.0	13.2	8.1	−1.2
10–12 "	109.8							
12 and over	52.6	21.1	4.7					

Distance from center of city	Buffalo	St. Louis	Indianapolis	Columbus, Ohio	Washington, D. C.	Nashville	Dayton	New Haven
Total	0.5	−0.7	6.3	5.3	36.2	8.8	4.8	−1.3
0–1 mile	0.6	−18.3	0.4	6.7	20.9	2.3	8.3	−3.1
1–2 miles	0.6	−4.6	5.6	1.7	31.2	8.3	1.1	−0.3
2–3 "	−3.6	−2.7	4.5	3.7	45.3	10.1		
3–4 "	−2.3	−0.7	5.8					
4–5 "	3.1	2.7						
5 and over	16.8	14.3	21.7	12.2	83.3	16.7	8.3	−0.2

Source: U. S. Bureau of the Census, *The Growth of Metropolitan Districts in the United States: 1900–1940* (Washington, D. C. 1948), 9.

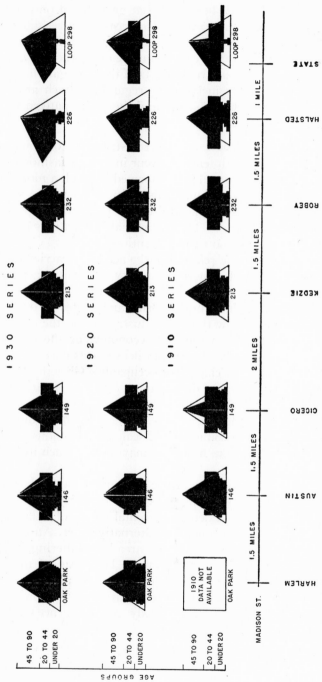

FIG. 42.—Age and sex composition of populations in selected census tracts located on Madison Avenue, Chicago, 1910, 1920, and 1930. (From R. D. McKenzie, *The Metropolitan Community* [New York: McGraw-Hill Book Co., Inc., 1933], 181. Used by permission.)

It is clear from what has been said that growth not only enlarges and extends the physical structure, it also occasions a reshuffling and redistribution of land uses and population. There thus arises a mosaic pattern made up of numerous areas each more or less homogeneous in its building type. Such areas are products of the segregation tendency which operates most freely in large aggregations. Each area, however, is constantly subject to change, and the entire pattern remains in flux so long as growth continues.

The Redistribution Process.—The redistribution of components of the city incident to growth tends to occur in orderly fashion. Areas of homogeneous use are formed and reformed through a more or less routine process called succession. This term refers to the sequence of changes by which units of one land use or population type replace those of another in an area.[29] The theoretical implications have been discussed already and need no further mention here.[30]

Any event that alters the relation of the activities carried on in an area to those carried on elsewhere in the city may initiate succession in that area. Occurrences such as the obsolescence and physical deterioration of property, shifts in the forms and routes of transportation, the introduction of new types of industry into or the elimination of established industry from the local economy, or the erection of buildings having either attractive or repellent effects may singly or in combination bring about a change of occupants. Growth of the city constitutes the most general of disturbances. The competition for location and space resulting from growth may release waves of succession that ripple across the entire city. The growth of the central business district is apt to produce broad-scale repercussions. Growth in a given residential section, however, may have a much more localized effect.

The displacement of one type of use by another has its beginnings in the obsolescence of the buildings and other property improvements in the area. This leads to a decline of rental values of buildings and opens the way for the invasion of an alternative use. An occupying group may thus eliminate itself from its area by so altering the buildings, through prolonged use, that they are better suited to another type of use. Actually, however, obsolescence seldom results entirely from physical deterioration. The latter is usually a symptom of the former. Rather is obsolescence generally a consequence of the ap-

---

[29] Population types are comparable with land use types so far as they represent different demands for land and buildings and yield different rentals for use of the land.
[30] See Chapter 16.

pearance of an external threat to the established occupants. The encroachment of industry or business upon a residential area, for example, hastens, if it does not start, the obsolescence of the residential structures. This may work in two ways. The noise, dirt, and congestion that accompany industrial and business activities render the area unsuitable for residential purposes. At the same time, the prospect of deriving higher returns from more intensive uses of the land causes land values to rise above the maximum warranted by residential uses. Accordingly residential properties begin to lose their usefulness as such and the process continues as the competing land use, i.e., industrial or business, draws nearer and enters the area.

The result is essentially the same when a "low order" residential use, as represented by a low income or minority group, threatens to invade an area of "higher order" residential use. This may stem from the development of extreme congestion in the rental space available to the invaders or from a rise of income level among certain of their members. In either case, the properties in the threatened area tend to lose their use-value for the established occupants. Market values, however, may increase, should the invading group promise a more intensive use of the land. If there is a rise of market values, the invasion may proceed rapidly. If not, it may be delayed by opposition from the established residents. Colored groups have met opposition on this score many times in northern cities.[31] Having experienced failures in various of their attempts at opposition, white groups have sought protection against invasions of their neighborhoods by colored groups through writing restrictive covenants into property deeds.[32]

A residential area adjacent to an expanding business district may experience a series of successions, passing from one population type to another before finally being occupied by business uses. A typical sequence is native American to German, to Italian, to Russian, to Negro.[33] Each successor may represent a lower economic level and a more intensive occupation of the area.

The succession approaches its culmination with the achievement of numerical preponderance by the invading population or land use type. It reaches completion with the importation of the customary institu-

---

[31] The succession of Negro groups has been carefully studied by Harold A. Gibbard, *Residential Succession: A Study in Human Ecology* (University of Michigan, Ph.D. Thesis 1938).

[32] See Herman H. Long and Charles S. Johnson, *People vs. Property: Race Restrictive Covenants in Housing* (Nashville, Tenn., 1947).

[33] Louis Wirth, *The Ghetto* (Chicago, 1928), 226-28; C. W. MacFarlane, "Three Primary Laws of Social Evolution," *Annals American Academy of Political and Social Science*, XX (1902), 390; and Paul F. Cressey, "Population Succession in Chicago: 1898-1930," *American Journal of Sociology*, XLIV (July, 1938), 59-69.

tions and services of the new occupant. Control of the area has thus
passed to the invader and a condition of relative equilibrium is established. This may last, however, only until the next growth phase of
the city, or until the beginning in the vicinity of a redevelopment
project of some sort. Often a second succession is under way before
the preceding one is done. The extent to which city growth follows
a cyclical pattern has considerable bearing on the spacing of successions and the manifestations of equilibrium after each succession.

A further qualification on the application of the succession concept
arises in connection with city size. Since the observability of such a
well-marked sequence as implied by the term presupposes the existence
of highly homogeneous use areas, it has its principal utility in the large
city. In small cities where segregation of land uses is not far advanced redistributions of land uses do not involve large scale replacements of one type of occupant by another. Locational changes concern individual families or service establishments and may occur
without disrupting activities in the area to which the move is directed.
The extent to which a redistribution is amenable to the formalized description connoted by succession, in other words, may vary with city
size.

Summary.—Although cities developed in ancient civilizations, few
exceeded in size populations of 100,000 or more. The producing
techniques and the means of transport in the pre-industrial period
were too inefficient to supply the needs of large aggregations of nonagricultural population. Large scale urban growth is of recent occurrence and is confined, for the most part, to the Western world.
The phenomenal rise of cities in this area is a function of expansion.
Cities grow primarily through migration, the migrants originating as
surplus population in areas of extractive industry. Natural increase
in cities is generally inadequate to maintain a given size of population,
not to mention increase of size.

The development of manufacturing has both direct and indirect
significance for city growth. Manufacturing operates directly by assembling a labor force and a core of service workers to supply the
requirements of the industrial workers and their families. Indirectly,
manufacturing produces labor-saving devices which displace more
people from extractive functions, the transportation and communication equipment by which scattered populations are interrelated, and
numerous marketing and administrative functions. Basic as it is,
however, manufacturing is not essential to each and every city; many
cities carry on specialized functions exclusive of manufacturing. In

general, the number of manufacturing establishments increases and the size of establishment decreases with size of city. Wage jobs in mechanical industry vary between 7 and 12 per 100 of the total population in cities of different size. Retail and service functions also increase in number and variety by size of city, though that association is affected by income level, age and nativity composition, and type of employment. Industrial specialization seems to have no influence on service structure.

The growth of the city is accompanied by extensions of its area and elaborations of its physical structure. This is closely geared to changes in both interregional and intramural transportation. The city pushes out along radiating routes in a star-shaped pattern, the interstitial areas filling in more slowly. Factors that affect transportation, such as the street layout, topography, and lands held out of use, introduce modifications in the pattern of physical growth. Increase in size involves a redistribution of land uses because of pressure at the center and accretion at the periphery. Specialized functions accumulate at the center of the city and drive out unspecialized and low intensity land uses. The development of the central business district brings a change in its character which is indicated by the rapid obsolescence and frequent rebuilding of improvements on the land. Manufacturing withdraws from the inner zone and clusters on cheaper land adjacent to rail and highway routes. Residences also abandon the central area for cheaper lands, their distance of removal varying directly with their rental value. The central business district shifts its location from time to time partly to maintain a central location relative to population distribution and partly in response to traffic congestion. Secondary business districts appear in outlying sections as the total area of the city increases and traffic density at the center mounts. New services appear first in the central district and subsequently scatter to secondary districts. The prevailing population movement is centrifugal, proceeding by a series of short-distance moves. The outward movement is led by families, unattached individuals being the last to evacuate declining residential areas.

The redistribution process has been conceptualized as a sequence of stages or succession in which one land use or population type replaces another in an area. Any event that alters the established interrelations may initiate a succession. Growth is the most general source of disturbance. The process begins with obsolescence of buildings in the area affected, which results from the encroachment of other uses and changes in land values. Thus the prior use abandons the land and the succession is completed when the new use attains numerical dominance in the area. The utility of the succession concept, however, seems to depend on the extent to which urban growth proceeds by starts and stops. Furthermore, it seems to have greater applicability in large than in small cities, for in the latter segregation is not sufficiently marked to permit observations of succession.

SUPPLEMENTARY REFERENCES

Building the Future City. The Annals of the American Academy of Political and Social Science, CCXLII (November, 1945).

DAVIDSON, DEWEY, and ANDERSON, PERCY E. *Occupational Trade in the United States.* Stanford University: Stanford University Press, California, 1940.

OLIVER, HENRY M. "Income, Region, Community Size, and Color," *Quarterly Journal of Economics,* LX (August, 1946), 588-99.

SCHLESINGER, ARTHUR M. "The City in American History," *Mississippi Valley Historical Review,* XXVII (June, 1940), 43-66.

SPENGLER, EDWIN H. *Land Values in New York in Relation to Transit Facilities.* New York: Columbia University Press, 1930.

WU, PEK SI. *Social Characteristics of Increasing, Stable, and Decreasing Cities.* Unpublished Ph.D. Thesis. Department of Sociology, The University of Chicago, 1945.

Chapter 20

EXPANSION: THE LOCAL COMMUNITY

Although vast centrifugal movements were released in the course of the development of an interregional division of labor producing numerous cities, many of unprecedented size, the communities so affected emerged as highly compact settlement agglomerations. Increases in the size of the nucleus, or city, were not matched by corresponding increases in the scope of the community.

This was due primarily to the character of water and rail transportation which, as previously noted, favored the long haul and unavoidably discriminated against the short haul. Under such conditions proximity to markets offers but a negligible advantage over more distant locations. Moreover, the scheduling of trips of such carriers was seldom conducive to the "spontaneous" movement involved in the daily round of community life. Hence there was no great incentive or opportunity for nearby settlements to ally themselves closely with one another. Apart from industrial specialization each settlement unit remained a more or less discrete entity. Each had its own independent services, clubs, and schools, and each had its own water supply and communications facilities. Only in a more pronounced orientation toward a major market center was local independence perceptibly modified. And communities located more than a day's horse and wagon journey from the nearest railway station or water route were almost as completely isolated as before the establishment of the rail or water route.

Transportation Improvements.—The expansion of the area of local community life requires a reduction of the time and cost involved in short distance movements and small lot shipments. Various adaptations of the railway, in the form of commuter trains, interurban electric trains, and street railways, contributed to this end. That is, they extended the radial distance that could be traveled in an hour's time —the unit which generally measures the zone of daily interchanges. The horse-car lengthened the distance of an hour's journey from two and a half or three miles to four or five miles, and electric traction

405

further extended the sixty-minute radius to seven or eight miles.[1]
Rapid transit electric lines added ten to twenty miles to the distance
that could be traversed in an hour. The zone of easy daily contact
would then have been enlarged from about twenty-eight square miles
to nearly three thousand square miles were it not for the fact that rail
transportation systems developed in star-shaped patterns, leaving large
pie-shaped interstitial areas as inaccessible as before. Nevertheless,
the adaptations of rail transportation to intracommunity movement
enlarged the builtup areas of cities and created radial strings of
suburban settlements. The lack of flexibility in such carriers, however, imposed rather close restrictions on the territorial extension of
the community as a whole.

TABLE 48

RAILWAY AND HIGHWAY TRAVEL TIME BY LENGTH OF HAUL,
UNITED STATES, 1936 *

| Mileage range | Average haul (miles) | Elapsed hours | | |
		Railway	Highway	Per cent highway is of railway
Under 50........	33	28	4	14.3
50–100.........	88	33	9	27.3
100–200.........	156	38	13	34.2
200–300.........	259	45	18	40.0
300–500.........	396	57	27	47.4
500 and over.....	781	85	51	60.0

* Adapted from National Resources Planning Board, *Technological Trends and
National Policy* (Washington, D. C., 1937), 185.

It was the motor vehicle, more than any other single factor, which
revolutionized the pattern of local relations.[2] Unlike rail and water
transportation, the motor vehicle is well suited to short-distance use,
inasmuch as its terminal costs are low and its operating costs therefore
tend to increase directly with distance. Cost-distance gradients for
the three types of carriers are shown in Figure 43. Within a radius

---

[1] Norman D. Wilson, *Some Problems of Urban Transportation, op. cit.,* 86.
[2] Introduced just prior to 1900, the number of motor vehicles in use increased to
365,000 by 1910, to 7,500,000 by 1920, and to 30,600,000 by 1940. Passenger automobiles expressed as ratios per 1000 population for these dates numbered 5.0, 77.2,
and 207.3 respectively. The telephone, and later the radio, also played an important
part in the change of the scope of the local community. The number of telephone
installations, which was 2,500 in 1876, increased to 339,000 in 1895, to 13,329,000 in
1920, and to 17,424,000 in 1935, an increase from less than 1 to about 14 per 1000
population.

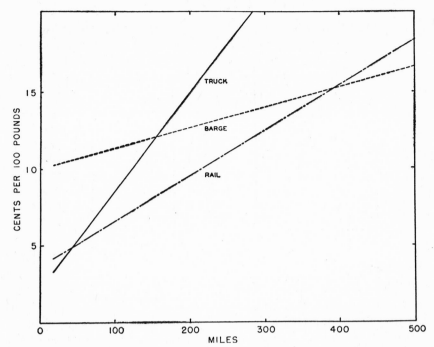

Fig. 43.—Mileage cost scale for commodity movements in carload lots or equivalent in the lower Mississippi Valley area, 1939-40. (From Board of Investigation and Research, *Comparisons of Rail, Motor, and Water Carrier Costs*, 79th Congress, 1st Session, Senate Document No. 84 [Washington, D. C., 1945], 9.)

of approximately thirty miles of a shipping point the motor vehicle, in this instance the truck, offers the cheapest mode of transportation. But in view of the rather important saving of time afforded by the motor truck, as is indicated in Table 48, it is probable that the zone of motor truck advantage extends well beyond the sixty-mile radius.

As may be inferred from these materials, the motor vehicle is preponderantly a short-distance carrier. This fact is shown in Table 49. More than four fifths of all trips are less than twenty miles one way. Within this range fall 85 per cent of all passenger car trips and 80 per cent of all truck trips.[3]

This intensive local use of the automobile derives not only from its short-distance cost advantage but also from its greater use flexibility. To be sure, the flexibility of the motor vehicle is partly represented in its low cost of operation. The meager terminal facilities

---

[3] Likewise over 90 per cent of all telephone traffic is comprised of exchange or local calls. (See National Resources Planning Board, *Transportation and National Policy* [Washington, D.C., 1942], 218.)

TABLE 49

MOTOR VEHICLE TRIP LENGTHS AND VEHICLE-MILES TRAVELED,
UNITED STATES, 1939 *

Trip lengths (miles)	Per cent of total trips	Cumulative per cent of trips	Per cent of total miles travel	Cumulative per cent of miles travel
Less than 5......	37.5	37.5	6.2	6.2
5– 9.9........	26.3	63.8	13.1	19.3
10– 19.9........	20.3	84.1	20.1	39.4
20– 29.9........	6.8	90.9	11.2	50.6
30– 39.9........	3.0	93.9	6.9	57.5
40– 49.9........	1.4	95.3	4.1	61.6
50– 99.9........	3.1	98.4	15.5	77.1
100–249.9........	1.3	99.7	15.1	92.2
250–499.9........	.2	99.9	4.2	96.4
500 and over.....	.1	100.0	3.6	100.0

* National Resources Planning Board, *Transportation and National Policy* (Washington, D. C., 1942), 385.

required and its accommodation to small lot cargoes, both of which are elements of flexibility, make for low costs. But there is also the fact that the motor vehicle is free of fixed routes and hence of fixed operating schedules.[4] It may be moved immediately and in any direction. Thus the automobile tremendously increased the possible number and variety of relationships within a local area.

The short-distance superiority and flexibility of the motor truck are illustrated in the following example:

If a Sioux Falls jobber could sell a bill of goods to a merchant in Brookings, S.D., to be shipped by rail, it would be best to go via the North Western, and the route taken would be west from Sioux Falls to Salem, S.D., a distance of 40 miles, then north to Huron, a distance of 68.3 miles, and then east to Brookings, a distance of 72 miles, making a total haul of 180.3 miles, and the time consumed would require second morning delivery in Brookings. The total distance from Sioux Falls due north to Brookings by truck is 58 miles and the schedule now in effect (1930) by truck is a departure from Sioux Falls at 11:00 a.m. and a delivery at Brookings at 3:00 p.m. the same day.[5]

And the use of the motor truck in combination with the telephone is indicated in a second illustration:

---

[4] It should be noted that this flexibility presupposes an elaborate system of roadways. Roads, moreover, are sufficiently wide in most instances to accommodate a large number of vehicles simultaneously. However, where traffic congestion develops a great part of the flexibility is lost.

[5] Armour's Livestock Bureau, "The Motor Truck in the Food Industry," *Monthly Letter to Animal Husbandmen*, XI (November 1931), 9, quoted in R. D. McKenzie, *The Metropolitan Community* (New York, 1933), 142.

A department store in New York may ascertain from the Weather Bureau Friday afternoon that Saturday will probably be a rainy day. In the Saturday morning papers the store will advertise a special sale of overshoes and rubber coats, telephoning a manufacturer, probably 150 miles away, Friday afternoon to furnish the sizes and styles desired. The shipment is loaded out that night in trucks and delivered at the store's door early enough the next morning to permit display before the advertised hour of the sale.[6]

The development of highways, therefore, produced an entirely different pattern from that of the railways. Whereas the railroad gave rise to a system of through line routes primarily,[7] which left local transportation unchanged, highway construction wove a tight web of

TABLE 50

PERCENTAGE DISTRIBUTION OF MAIN HIGHWAY TRAFFIC (PRIVATE, AUTOMOBILE, BUS, AND TRUCK) IN SELECTED STATES, BY ORIGIN AND DESTINATION, 1940 *

Region and state	Origin *and* destination urban	Origin *or* destination urban	Origin and destination rural
New England: New Hampshire..........	35.3	49.1	15.6
East North Central: Ohio..............	67.5	29.7	2.8
West North Central: Nebraska..........	49.1	37.9	13.0
South Atlantic: West Virginia..........	60.3	25.9	13.8
East South Central: Tennessee..........	57.8	34.7	7.5
Mountain: Utah........................	8.7	59.1	32.2
Pacific: Oregon.......................	23.4	46.6	30.0
All Regions, Average..................	49.6	36.6	13.8

* *Interregional Highways,* A Report of the National Interregional Highway Committee (Washington, D. C., 1944), 41.

local routes in the territory about cities and towns. The network of motor roads thins out with distance from the service center, and beyond the range of daily automobile commuting it gives way to a number of radial main line highways. Of the 1,556 thousands of miles of surfaced roads in 1940, however, only 24 per cent was in primary rural or intercity highways.[8] And much of that, of course, must be regarded as included in local road systems about service centers. Table 50 indicates that 37 per cent of main highway traffic has a city as its origin or destination and that 50 per cent is intercity

---

[6] National Resources Committee, *Technological Trends and National Policy* (Washington, D. C., 1933), 185.

[7] Of the 268,600 miles of steam railroad track (excluding 115,920 miles of yard and siding track) in use in 1939, short-haul or feeder lines comprised approximately 10,000 miles of track. (National Resources Planning Board, *op. cit.,* 33.)

[8] National Resources Planning Board, *Transportation and National Policy,* 44.

traffic, though it does not indicate how much of the latter is comprised of short-distance journeys. Less than 14 per cent of such traffic was rural in both origin and destination.

The convenience and speed of the automobile together with the hard-surfaced road created a new scale of local distance. The sixty-minute radius was extended to as much as fifty miles, depending on the density of traffic. Daily movements thus could reach well beyond the builtup areas of cities to encompass large expanses of rural territory and its scattered villages and cities. The old compact community was eliminated and replaced by a diffuse type of community composed of numerous territorial units whose functions are integrated and administered through the agency of a central city.

The effect of this revolution in transportation is strikingly, if somewhat inadequately, indicated in Figure 44. In the prerailroad period, prior to the 1850's, Baltimore, Washington, D. C., and Chicago were small and compact settlements. Through the latter half of the nineteenth century the three settlements increased in size but retained their compact form. Some scattering of settlement appears in the 1900 silhouettes. Most of the outlying or suburban units which existed at that time were products of steam railway transportation and were not, therefore, closely related to nearby centers. By 1936 the motor vehicle had come into full use and the three settlements seem to have exploded into their surrounding areas. But since these illustrations represent merely the builtup areas within and about the cities, they fail to reveal the full effect of the motor vehicle on the respective communities.

The events which follow from the extension of the motor road and the telephone line from a center into its surrounding area are, in a general way, similar to those produced by the interlinking of producing regions. There occurs a redistribution of population and land uses, a specialization of activity in each segment of the total area, and an absorption of all segments and their inhabitants in a single, comprehensive organization. But the effects of these changes penetrate much more deeply into the daily affairs of the local groups contained within the ambit of accessibility.

Redistribution of Community Units.—A highly important feature of local community expansion is the redistribution and reorganization of producing activities involved. In regard to manufacturing the prevailing tendency is centripetal with reference to administrative functions and centrifugal with reference to processing functions. The separation of communication from transportation which occurred with

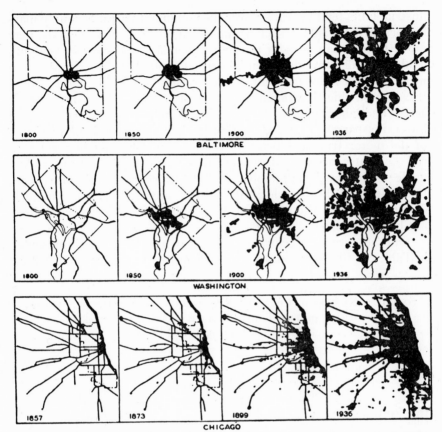

Fig. 44.—Local community expansion, 1800-1936. (From *Interregional Highways*, Message from the President of the United States, 78th Congress, 2nd Sesion, House Document No. 379 [Washington, D. C., 1944], 55.)

the advent of the telegraph and telephone makes possible a removal of administrative from processing functions without loss of contact between them. Hence, the former congregate in the central city where they may have immediate access to marketing and various ancillary services. The insularity of extractive enterprises and of manufacturing establishments that are necessarily situated at raw material deposits is thus dissipated and they are integrated with the activities of the market center.

On the other hand, the railroad, motor truck, and electric power, together with the facilities for instantaneous point to point communication, have enormously enlarged the element of freedom of site selection for producing plants. No longer bound to water routes, to large population concentrations, and to the points of power production, in-

dustrial units tend to scatter over the community area. Strongly market-oriented industries, such as those manufacturing style goods, may
move from urban sites to the more abundant and cheaper outlying
lands and still retain the essential market contact.[9] Centrifugal movement is much more frequent, however, among durable goods industries whose chief locational requirements are usually transportation
access and labor supply. The costs of railroad terminal facilities are
lower in sparsely occupied sections, while the short-haul efficiency
of the motor truck compensates for many deficiencies in respect to
rail or water access. Moreover, the extended commuting radius
made possible by the automobile brings an adequate supply of workers
to the doors of the plant located at almost any site in the community.
The restraints on site selection, though they have been relaxed, have
not been eliminated.

One measure of the centrifugal scatter of manufacturing is presented
in Table 51. Throughout the 20-year period shown, 11 counties have

TABLE 51

SMALLEST NUMBER OF COUNTIES REQUIRED TO OBTAIN EACH SPECIFIED
FRACTION OF THE TOTAL NUMBER OF WAGE EARNERS IN
MANUFACTURING, 1919-1939 *

Fraction of total number of wage earners	Number of Counties		
	1919	1929	1939
One fourth	11	11	11
One half	46	51	54
Three fourths	198	209	214

* Source: R. D. McKenzie, *The Metropolitan Community* (New York, 1933), 55;
and U. S. Bureau of the Census, *Sixteenth Census of the United States: 1940,* "Manufacturing" (Washington, D. C., 1942), Vol. III.

contained one fourth of all wage workers in manufacturing. But the
smallest number of counties required to include one half of all workers
increased from 46, in 1919, to 54, in 1939, and the smallest number
required to contain three fourths increased from 198 to 214 during
the two decades. This suggests that the movement was restricted to
local areas, for the most part. Table 52 indicates that to be the case.
The principal industrial cities have lost wage jobs in manufacturing
consistently since 1899, most of which seems to have moved to their
adjacent areas. The peripheries of lesser industrial centers have also

---

[9] So far as such units are marginal producers and do not require specialized buildings, they tend to remain in obsolescent structures within the congested areas of cities.

gained in manufacturing employment, though not at the expense of their centers.   This, plus the increase shown for important industrial counties without large cities, represents the amount of interregional movement that has taken place.

Although manufacturing plants are becoming more scattered, their interrelations are becoming more numerous and sensitive.[10]   To an increasing extent the relations of plant to plant are being arranged on an assembly line basis in which the operation of one plant is contingent

TABLE 52

PER CENT DISTRIBUTION OF WAGE JOBS IN MANUFACTURING BY TYPE
OF LOCALITY, UNITED STATES, 1899-1933 *

Type of locality	1933	1931	1929	1919	1899
Total..........................	100.0	100.0	100.0	100.0	100.0
Principal cities†.....................	33.1	35.2	35.1	36.1	39.5
Satellite cities‡.....................	2.6	2.9	2.9	3.6	3.7
Industrial peripheries§...............	18.7	18.2	18.2	18.6	14.6
Other cities of 100,000 population ‖	6.7	6.9	6.9	6.3	5.9
Peripheries of other cities of 100,000 population#......................	1.6	1.7	1.6	1.6	1.1
Important industrial counties**.........	10.3	9.7	9.3	8.3	8.4
All other.............................	27.0	25.4	26.0	25.5	26.8

* Daniel B. Creamer, *Is Industry Decentralizing?* (Philadelphia, 1935), 10.
† Largest cities in each of the 33 industrial areas identified by the U. S. Bureau of the Census.
‡ Cities of 100,000 or more population located in 33 industrial areas, but excluding principal cities.
§ All other areas in 33 industrial areas.
‖ Not located in 33 industrial areas.
Remainders of counties in which are located "other cities of 100,000 population or more."
** Counties with no city of 100,000, but with at least 10,000 wage jobs in manufacturing.

upon that in another.   In many forms of production, the finished article represents the assemblage of a large assortment of parts manufactured in separately located plants.   The increasing speed and reliability of transportation facilities within the local area makes possible the assembling and using of the various parts as needed instead of, as formerly, stocking them in advance.   The economic incentive to the reduction of stock inventories, in turn, encourages greater interdependence among manufacturing establishments.

The organization of the automobile industry in the Detroit area affords an excellent example of this type of hand-to-mouth practice.

10 This and the following paragraph are adapted from R. D. McKenzie, *The Metropolitan Community*, 79, with the permission of the publisher.

The completed vehicle is assembled in Detroit from parts manufactured in a multitude of plants scattered throughout southern Michigan and in other districts. The transportation channels along which the different parts are conveyed to the assembling factory might almost be considered as extensions of the factory's assembly lines, as the intake from the trucks and railways is about as sensitively adjusted to the time factor in production as is the speed of the belt lines within the plant itself. Moreover, the entire process is directed and controlled from central offices, most of which are located in the city of Detroit. In fact, without the centralization of administrative control the integration of widely spread industrial activities would be impossible.

While the railroad brought distant and local agriculturalists into competition for urban markets, the motor vehicle confronts agriculture in the areas about cities with a competition for rural lands.[11] The enlargement of the builtup areas of cities and the diffusion of urban functions, such as manufacturing, recreation, residence, etc., over the countryside raises the values of land well above what many forms of agriculture can sustain. The withdrawal of agriculture in the face of such competition leaves only the most intensive forms of cultivation in the immediate vicinities of cities.[12] No satisfactory measure of the effects of the competition between agriculture and urban activities for rural land has been prepared for this country. But in England, between 1928 and 1937, the spread of manufacturing and residence absorbed an estimated 460,000 acres of agricultural land, while recreational uses took another 108,000 acres. From 1937 to 1939 about 80,000 acres per year were taken for nonagricultural purposes.[13]

Even more revealing of the reorganization of the community on an expanded scale is the redistribution of retail and personal services that takes place. This follows as a consequence of the competition among service agencies located in different territorial units occasioned by the automobile, the telephone, and also the newspaper. The large city with its great population and its strategic location on transport routes is better able to provide specialized retail services, the so-called shopping goods lines—i.e., those of a durable character and those subject in considerable degree to style considerations. Purchasers

[11] As late as 1920 farming was carried on in Queens County, New York, a now solidly builtup area. (Edwin H. Spengler, *Land Values in New York in Relation to Transit Facilities* [New York, 1930], 121.)

[12] See Edmund de S. Brunner and J. H. Kolb, *Rural Social Trends* (New York, 1933), 125-43.

[13] A. W. Ashby, "The Effects of Urban Growth on the Countryside," *The Sociological Review*, XXXI (October, 1939), 367-68. See also E. N. Torbert, "Evolution of Land Utilization in Lebanon, New Hampshire," *Geographical Review*, XXV (April, 1935), 209-30.

of such goods seek the opportunity for selection that variety presents. Hence establishments that retail furniture, clothing, millinery, jewelry, and other specialty goods tend to decline both in number and volume of sales in the small city and village and to concentrate in the large city.[14] The same tendency is observable in regard to professional services.[15] On the other hand, services which originated in the large city and which have become progressively more standardized have diffused outward. Thus hardware, automobile, plumbing, cleaning and dyeing, and beauty establishments have appeared and multiplied in outlying settlement clusters.[16] The incidence of these changes appears to have been greatest beyond the ten-mile radius about a large center—in the area not formerly accessible to the center.[17]

The increased range of routine movement creates competition among small cities and villages as well as between the large city and its satellites. Subcenters that are favorably located tend to enlarge their service areas at the expense of others that are not so well situated. This is evident in Table 53, in which the service areas measured by Galpin in 1913 [18] are compared with the areas of the same villages in 1929. Not a few village centers wane and ultimately disappear.[19] Benton MacKaye writes:

The typical colonial village which we have described has become, in the up country of New England, for the most part a deserted village. The church and steeple remain, and the bell also, but it rings, if it rings at all, for a season only, and then for a waning congregation. The town hall is there, but the town meeting has been moved to a more populous precinct. The school house stands, but the pupils who are left in town are 'merged' by motor bus in some other center. The thirty dwelling houses have become thirteen—or three. The outlying fields and pastures have largely become brushland, and the woodlots are cut off a little faster than they grow. Below in the valley the grist mill has

[14] Walter B. Mitchell, *Furniture Distribution in the West Midcontinent,* U. S. Bureau of Foreign and Domestic Commerce, Domestic Commerce Series No. 68, 1932, 16; *The Automobile and the Village Merchant,* Bureau of Business Research Bull. 19, Univ. of Illinois, 1928; P. D. Converse and R. V. Mitchell, "The Movement of Retail Trade within a Metropolitan Area," *Marketing Journal,* II (July, 1937), 61-67; and *The Influence of Automobiles and Good Roads on Retail Trade Centers,* University of Nebraska Studies in Business No. 18 (Lincoln, 1927).
[15] C. R. Hoffer, *Changes in the Retail and Service Facilities of Rural Trade Centers in Michigan, 1900 and 1930,* Michigan State College Agricultural Experiment Station Special Bulletin No. 261 (East Lansing, 1935), 30.
[16] *Ibid.,* 20-23.
[17] Joan Halloran, "Effects of Changes in Communication upon Business Services in Iowa Agricultural Villages, 1920-35," *Journal of Business,* University of Iowa (November, 1937), 14.
[18] Chapter 13.
[19] See C. C. Zimmerman, *Farm Trade Centers in Minnesota,* 1905-1929, University of Minnesota Agricultural Experiment Station Bulletin 269 (St. Paul, September, 1930), 30-33.

TABLE 53

PER CENT NET CHANGE OF SQUARE MILES IN SEVEN TYPES OF SERVICE AREAS OF VILLAGE CENTERS, WALWORTH COUNTY, WISCONSIN, 1913-29 *

Service center	Total	Library	Milk marketing	High school	Groceries	Churches	Dry goods	Banking
Total	25.8	143.3	63.7	48.7	22.4	10.0	6.5	3.1
Whitewater	48.2	143.3	121.2	190.2	8.5	25.9	-2.1	39.1
Delavan	4.7	128.9	23.1	29.4	-18.2	10.0	-24.1	-9.8
Lake Geneva	13.9	19.2	48.1	65.7	-2.0	36.3	7.7	-13.0
Elkhorn	38.5	70.9	151.7	40.0	84.9	-13.7	13.7	13.2
East Troy	49.2	100.0	111.8	5.1	110.3	-40.6	115.7	5.6
Sharon	27.8	100.0	37.2	33.3	5.3	100.0	-14.9	-14.2
Genoa City	14.5	100.0	44.8	-51.5	6.4	72.5	-8.6	-11.2
Darien	30.7	100.0	-5.0	24.0	20.9	25.4	7.2	26.3
Lyons	6.1	—	73.5	—	14.3	12.0	-10.8	-19.5
Honey Creek	7.5	—	21.1	—	-6.9	114.5	15.4	-4.8
Millard	61.4	—	-100.0	—	200.0	54.5	—	—
Walworth	17.0	—	74.7	79.2	-5.5	39.1	-7.2	11.7

* Source: J. H. Kolb and R. A. Polson, *Trends in Town-Country Relations*, Research Bulletin 117, Agricultural Experiment Station of the University of Wisconsin (Madison, Wisconsin, Sept. 1933), 33.

gone; the shoddy mill went long ago; the sawmill run by water power has been replaced by the steam portable.[20]

Irwin, Iowa, (1940 population: 345) has had a similar, if less radical, experience:

There is no longer an attorney in the community, and the number of doctors, grain dealers, blacksmiths, and general merchandise dealers has declined. A millinery shop, a livery stable, a furniture store, and a hotel that previously operated are no longer there. Only one bank remains of the three banks that operated between 1910 and 1930. The number of automobile sales agencies had not changed between 1914 and 1940, but the number of garages had increased and five service stations were operating. The movies, a pool hall, and "beer joints," confectioneries, and a hamburger shop were fairly recent enterprises.[21]

A favorable location is conditioned to an increasing extent by highway access. An intersection of highways becomes more important than a junction of road with railway line. This is evident in the relocations of the business sections within subcenters; they have tended to pull away from railroad stations to redevelop at the intersections of major motor thoroughfares. Type of roadway is often of decisive importance to the survival of the subcenter. Those situated on unsurfaced roads decline and often become extinct, while those located on paved roads are more apt to survive and grow.[22]

The subcenters that survive the competition and the new ones that emerge at strategic locations created by the elaboration of the local transport system assume more or less specialized roles as territorial units in an enlarged community. In the redistribution of service and other functions that takes place some subcenters are reduced to positions of minor importance, such as providing only the least specialized of services, while others acquire quite distinctive functions.[23] This is because population is released from close attachment to neighboring service agencies and may, with the aid of the automobile, the telephone, and other forms of rapid communication, range freely and selectively over a wide area, turning to one place for employment, to another for

---

[20] *The New Exploration: A Philosophy of Regional Planning* (New York, Harcourt, Brace & Co., 1928), 69-70.

[21] Edward O. Moe and Carl C. Taylor, *Culture of a Contemporary Rural Community: Irwin, Iowa,* Bureau of Agricultural Economics, Rural Life Studies: 5 (Washington, D. C., 1942), 64.

[22] C. R. Hoffer, *op. cit.*, 9.

[23] See, for example, Earl H. Bell, *Culture of a Contemporary Rural Community: Sublette, Kansas,* Bureau of Agricultural Economics, Rural Life Studies: 2 (Washington, D. C., 1942), 71-72; Kenneth MacLeish and Kimball Young, *Culture of a Contemporary Rural Community: Landaff, New Hampshire,* Bureau of Agricultural Economics, Rural Life Studies: 3 (Washington, D. C., 1942), 16; and Edward O. Moe and Carl C. Taylor, *op. cit.*, 64.

a given service, and to still more distant subcenters for various other services: The movements of the residents of Irwin's (Iowa) trade area, which is situated in the hinterland of Omaha, are typical:

Irwin as a village is a retailing, local produce, service, and residence center. The goods and services available in the village are generally those for which there is frequent call and which are of relatively low cost. Shopping excursions are often made by Irwin people to Harlan, the county seat, a town of 3,500, and to Manila, Dennison, and Manning, where a greater variety of goods and services are available. Less frequent trips are made to Omaha and Council Bluffs. Sales of farm produce, particularly livestock, are made in the metropolitan center, as are purchases of livestock for feeding, men's and women's clothing, furniture, household utensils, and other goods and services of a somewhat special character. Council Bluffs and Omaha newspapers and radio stations supply the town with news and entertainment and exert great influence through the control devices of propaganda and advertising. Styles, fashions, and fads flow out into the locality from these cities.[24]

The service structure of the expanded community is thus based on a hierarchy of territorial units—hamlets, villages, and cities, in which the most specialized services are concentrated in the largest unit or community center, lesser degrees of specialized services are carried on in subcenters depending on their sizes, and all units providing the least specialized, lowest cost, and most frequently demanded services.[25] Over this pattern the community center exerts a controlling influence, in part because it is the locus of the greatest number and variety of services, and in part because among its services are many which in one way or another govern and integrate the service functions of subcenters.

The wide-ranging circulation of population for its employment and consumer service has repercussions in every other aspect of daily life. To be sure, what affects fundamental patterns of activity is bound to affect all other kinds of behavior. Increased selectivity in the one respect necessarily applies to interest satisfactions of whatever type. The expanded community, furthermore, offers to the mobile population a stimulating variety of opportunities in comparison with which the offerings in the residence locale appear meager and mundane.

---

[24] Edward O. Moe and Carl C. Taylor, *ibid.*, 48. See also Eaton Van Wert Read, *An Analysis of the Retail Trading Relationships of Elgin, Illinios: A Satellite City* (Chicago, 1938).

[25] C. C. Zimmerman reports an experience in the settlement of a section of western Canada that suggests an element of necessity in this pattern. The plan of the settlement called for a number of large service centers which were established before any other villages or cities appeared. Nevertheless scattered subcenters grew up in the same proportion as in the older sections of Canada. ("Centralism versus Localism in the Community," *American Sociological Review*, III [April, 1938], 158.)

Hence the traditional support of local government, the church, the family, and neighborhood groups, based as it was on a restricted radius of movement, is greatly weakened and often vitiated entirely. The personal services formerly derived from such units, if they are sought at all, are found in larger, better equipped, and more widely scattered units.

These take the form, for the most part, of highly specialized categoric associations. The great ease and individuation of movement expose persons to a large variety of contacts and novel situations. Whim or reason, as the case may be, operates therefore with comparatively few restraints in the determination of one's associates. Hence the common interests around which individuals gather in groups submit to progressive subdivision. Kinship loses much of its former importance and the neighborhood's function is alienated to other agencies.[26] This produces an enormous increase in the number of categoric associations, each with a very narrow focus and with a membership drawn widely from the community area.[27]

The development of a new type of service, organized recreation provided by specialized units, has absorbed a large part of the energies that used to be spent in traditional communal units. Prospering from the habit of formal association that has come with a heightened mobility and from the increased leisure time made possible by a more efficient community organization, recreational service has grown to the status of a major industry. This has involved a fundamental change in orientation similar to that taking place in all other aspects of collective life: in contrast to the older local focus of attention, the orientation of recreational interests and movements has swung outward to the wider community. The automobile has been instrumental in scattering recreational activities far afield. Strung along the highways and distributed over the open spaces are night clubs, open air theaters, golf courses, resorts, and numerous other agencies of a similar character. Moreover, the facilities within each center and subcenter have become accessible to the residents of every other territorial unit in the community. Thus further inroads are made on the recreational function of the family which it has been in process of yielding up to the school, the library, the motion-picture theater, and the mu-

---

26 See E. R. Roper-Power, "The Social Structure of an English Country Town," *Sociological Review*, XXIX (October, 1937), 391-413.

27 Studies indicate that memberships in categoric groups vary with possession of an automobile, telephone, and residence location on a hard-surfaced road. (N. L. Whetten and E. C. Devereux, Jr., *Studies of Suburbanization in Connecticut, 1. Windsor: A Highly Developed Agricultural Area*, Storrs Agricultural Experiment Station Bull. 212 [Storrs, Conn., 1936], 123-24.)

nicipal playing field. Likewise, the church, itself primarily a leisure time institution, has experienced an intensified competition for the time of its nominal adherents. The same applies to neighborhood associations which have been reduced, for the most part, to functioning intermittently as pressure groups for the protection of vested interests.

But while leisure time movements have acquired a centrifugal character, there is still a prominent centripetal phase in this aspect of community activity. A large volume of movement converges upon the metropolitan city or community center, for there is found a highly varied and exotic assortment of recreational opportunities. Of much greater importance, however, is a less obvious centripetal movement —the centralization of administrative control over recreational service units scattered throughout the community. The chain organization of such service, notable in respect to motion picture theaters, locates its central offices in the center. Likewise as special interest associations develop federations of one sort or another their headquarters concentrate there. And of course in the center are located the supply companies and the financial, legal, advertising, and other services to business without which units providing recreation would be as helpless as any other type of corporate association.

A general leveling of culture differences occurs over the entire area absorbed by the process of expansion.[28] The habits of consumption, the fashions and fads, and the idiom of the metropolis diffuse over the community displacing the many local peculiarities of behavior. Culture generalization, of course, is nothing more nor less than a symptom of the development of a common organization in a previously segmented population. The realignment of relations tends to remove all vestiges of local autonomy over recreational, religious, and many other interests as well as over functions of a more distinctly pecuniary nature.

Expansion of the scope of daily exchanges and contacts through the development of rapid transit and instantaneous communication, therefore, produces not only a larger but an altogether new type of community. The expanded community with its multi-nucleated pattern gains its unity, unlike its predecessor, through territorial differentiation of specialized functions rather than through mass participation in centrally located institutions.

Population Redistribution.—The reorganization of the community on a new scale of distance sets in motion numerous population relocations. Many of these have been referred to already, at least by

---

[28] Cf. Walter O. Cralle, "Social Change and Isolation in the Ozark Mountain Region of Missouri," *American Journal of Sociology*, XLI (January, 1936), 435-46.

implication. The rises and falls of villages, the dislodgement through competition of one land use type by another, and the shifting fortunes of satellite cities are all indicative of change in the pattern of population distribution. But the most important of all redistribution trends is the centrifugal movement from the metropolis and, in fact, from virtually all sizeable cities in the metropolitan area.

The scatter of population about urban centers is a direct response to the increased ease of movement. The huge compact urban agglomerations formed under the dominating influence of water and rail transportation prove unnecessary and in many respects inefficient in the new context of mobility. The automobile, the telephone, and the radio enable population to escape the disutilities of the large city and yet retain participation in the community center. While the deconcentration trend has not been adequately measured, it is made apparent, on the one hand, by the failure of large cities to continue growth and by substantial net out-migrations in many instances, and, on the other hand, by the very rapid growth of population in areas adjacent to large cities. The results of these tendencies may be observed in Table 54. Population in the outlying areas of metropolitan districts has

TABLE 54

PERCENTAGE INCREASE IN POPULATION IN METROPOLITAN DISTRICTS, BY SIZE OF DISTRICT, UNITED STATES, 1930-40 *

Size of district	District total	Central cities	Area outside central cities
Total	8.2	5.0	15.8
50,000-75,000	17.6	13.3	38.1
75,000-100,000	11.6	8.2	26.7
100,000-250,000	10.9	5.8	26.1
250,000-500,000	8.5	4.9	19.7
500,000-1,000,000	9.0	6.2	15.8
1,000,000-2,000,000	4.8	-0.3	11.6
2,000,000 and over	7.2	4.8	12.4

* Source: Amos H. Hawley and Don J. Bogue, "Recent Shifts in Population: The Drift Toward the Metropolitan District, 1930-40," *Review of Economic Statistics,* XXIV (August, 1942), 145.

grown three times as fast as the population of central cities in the 1930-40 decade. In fact, the most rapidly growing populations in the United States, at least since 1920, have been those in rural areas and small cities within metropolitan districts. This is indicated in Table 55, when it is remembered that the growth of the total population of the country, in 1930-40, was but 7.2 per cent, while that

TABLE 55

Percentage Increases of Population in Satellite Cities and in
Unincorporated Area Within Metropolitan Districts,
United States, 1920–40 *

Type and size of place	1920–30	1930–40		
		96 districts existing in 1930	37 districts first reported in 1940	133 districts reported in 1940
100,000 and over.........	12.5	3.9	—	3.9
50,000–100,000..........	20.5	2.0	—	2.0
25,000– 50,000..........	32.8	3.2	—	3.2
15,000– 25,000..........	26.6	8.5	—	8.5
10,000– 15,000..........	39.6	7.6	9.0	7.6
5,000– 10,000..........	47.7	11.3	17.2	11.4
2,500– 5,000..........	69.8	12.1	8.8	12.0
Unincorporated area......	54.8	28.2	37.3	28.8

* Source: Amos H. Hawley and Don J. Bogue, *op. cit.*, 146. Satellite cities and unincorporated area are classified according to their size and type in 1930.

for all urban areas was 7.9 per cent. The metropolitan district, however, is not sufficiently inclusive to contain the full force of deconcentration. High growth rates prevail as far as forty-five miles from central cities of 500,000 or more inhabitants and as far as twenty-five miles from small central cities.[29]

Population deconcentration occurs in both an absolute and a relative sense. That large cities suffer a net loss in the exchange of population with their hinterlands has been shown in a number of studies.[30] But there is also the fact that much of the intercommunity migration stops short of the city and settles in the adjacent zone. This seems to be true not only of the large city but to some extent of all cities of 10,000 or more population. Thus the scattering of urban population seems to be partly due to accretion at the periphery. It is unfortunate that census data do not permit a measurement of the relative growth in urban hinterlands resulting from actual centrifugal migration and of that produced by the accumulation of inter-community migrants.

While improvements in transportation and communication are a necessary condition to the outward movement of urban population, a

[29] Don J. Bogue, "Metropolitan Decentralization: A Study of Differential Growth," a paper read at the Annual Meeting of the Population Association of America, Philadelphia, May 22, 1948.
[30] Howard W. Green, *Movements of Families within the Cleveland Metropolitan District* (Cleveland, 1936), 18-19.

full explanation of that trend must include the influences of other factors. Some of those factors are represented in the distinctive characteristics of residents in the outlying zone. Table 56 shows that, for the very large metropolitan communities, the population living outside central cities is younger, is more highly educated, and includes more people in upper social-economic groups than does the population of central cities. The relatively large proportions under 21 years of age and not in the labor force reflect the concentration in the outer area of young family units, with husband, wife, and children present, which, incidentally, reside primarily in single family, owner occupied dwelling

TABLE 56

PERCENTAGE OF POPULATION IN METROPOLITAN DISTRICTS WITH CENTRAL CITIES OF 500,000 OR MORE HAVING SELECTED CHARACTERISTICS, UNITED STATES, 1940 *

Characteristic	Districts total	Central cities	Remainder of districts
Under 21 years of age.....................	30.8	29.8	32.4
One or more years college education †.....	10.7	9.8	12.4
Not in labor force ‡......................	44.6	44.0	46.4
Self-employed §	9.8	9.6	10.3
Professional and proprietor manager and official §	14.0	13.2	15.5

* Source : U. S. Bureau of the Census, *Sixteenth Census of the United States: 1940,* "Population," Vol. III (Washington, D. C., 1942).
† Based on population 25 years of age and over.
‡ Based on population 14 years of age and over.
§ Based on population 14 years of age and over and in the labor force.

units. It appears, then, that the centrifugal movement is an effort on the part of those who are willing and able to pay higher costs for travel and perhaps for residential services to secure more suitable conditions for family life.

An examination of the reasons given by centrifugal migrants for the direction of their moves adds support to the inference drawn from a comparison of population characteristics. The results of two separate inquiries are presented in Table 57. Although the desire to improve conditions for children was mentioned only in the Milwaukee investigation, the search for more space which was a prominent reason in the migration from both Milwaukee and Flint doubtless has the same connotation.[31] Table 57 also suggests a belief that the more

---

[31] See also M. C. Branch, Jr., *Urban Planning and Public Opinion* (Princeton, 1942), and R. B. Andrews, "Urban Fringe Studies of Two Wisconsin Cities," *Journal of Land and Public Utility Economics,* XXI (November, 1945), 375-82.

TABLE 57

Per Cent Frequency of Reasons Given for Centrifugal Migration from
Milwaukee and from Flint

Reason for move	Centrifugal migrants	
	From Milwaukee *	From Flint †
Better for children	32.0	—
Less congested area	18.0	34.8
Cleaner	17.0	15.9
Larger lot	15.0	13.0
Lower taxes	10.5	23.0
Forced to move	5.0	15.9
Cheaper land, cheaper to build	4.0	5.8

* Richard Dewey, "Peripheral Expansion in Milwaukee County," *American Journal of Sociology*, LIV (September, 1948), 121.
† Betty Tableman, *Intra-Community Migration in the Flint Metropolitan District*, University of Michigan Social Science Research Project, mimeographed (Ann Arbor, 1948), 40.

abundant space in the outlying area is to be had at less cost.[32] That the costs of living are actually less in the outer areas, however, is not established; in fact, there is evidence to indicate the contrary.[33] Nevertheless, the presumption that living costs are cheaper outside of large cities and particularly in open country area seems to be widespread.

Table 58 compares some of the more frequently recurring reasons for residence changes given by centrifugal migrants with those given by centripetal migrants in the same metropolitan community, Flint, Michigan. It appears in these data that the outward movement is directed largely toward home ownership; almost a third of the centrifugal migrants expressed such a motivation, while fewer than 10 per cent of the families moving into the city moved with that objective in mind. Moreover, 14 per cent of the former group indicated that they sought escape from apartment type residences. On the other hand, the inward movement seems to be governed by convenience considerations. Almost two fifths of all centripetal migrants expressed a desire to live nearer their places of work and another 13 per cent stated that they moved as a result of job changes. Neither of these reasons was mentioned by centrifugal migrants. Another noteworthy reason for cen-

[32] A study of centrifugal migration from Cleveland shows that movement is to higher rental value residences; conversely, the centripetal migration to Cleveland is to lower rental value housing. (Howard W. Green, *op. cit.*, 69 ff.)
[33] *Annexation*, Dayton City Plan Board (Dayton, Ohio, 1946).

tripetal movement is to secure better schools for children. This factor might not be so important in another metropolitan district in which there was less unincorporated area than exists in the Flint district.

How large a proportion of the total metropolitan community population may ultimately be absorbed by the outlying area or to what extent large cities will lose residents in the centrifugal movement cannot be foretold at present. That the process of scatter will continue for some time into the future seems unquestionable. But there are resistances to the spreading distribution which accumulate and which may eventually check the movement.

TABLE 58

PER CENT FREQUENCY OF SELECTED REASONS GIVEN FOR CENTRIFUGAL MIGRATION FROM AND FOR CENTRIPETAL MIGRATION TO FLINT, MICHIGAN *

Reason for move	Centrifugal migrant	Centripetal migrant
Wanted to own home	30.4	9.7
To secure more housing space	11.6	12.9
Involuntary	15.9	12.9
Job change	—	12.9
To live closer to work place	—	38.7
To secure more yard space	13.0	—
To secure more satisfactory neighborhood	10.1	—
To escape apartment residence	14.4	—
To secure better schools	—	9.7

* Betty Tableman, *op. cit.,* 36.

Frictions in Expansion.—The expansion of the local community introduces numerous strains and frictions in the organization and functioning of the community. Many of these may be attributed to the unevenness of change, to the differences of time lag in the readjustment of various elements of the community. Others represent problems that may find no solution in the maturation of the new community structure and which, therefore, may remain as permanent stresses in the expanded community.

An expanding organization engulfs and spreads over many political subdivisions, such as smaller cities, villages, townships, school districts, and parts of states.[34] But there is no redistribution and reorganization of administrative or governmental functions comparable to that we observed in connection with manufacturing and service func-

[34] See Chapter 13.

tions. Each political entity tends to persist as a semi-autonomous unit, retaining the powers granted in its charter or constitution. Expansion seems even to foster a multiplication of political units, for the population that occupies unincorporated area sooner or later seeks some form of local rule in order to provide itself with urban utilities. The net result is a confusion of jurisdictional boundaries, of unequal governmental powers, and of conflicting administrative policies in what in other respects is a single functionally integrated unit. Concerted action in dealing with communitywide problems is virtually impossible.[35] The protection of public health, the efficient exercise of police power, the control of land use, the development of flood control measures, the equitable distribution of tax burdens, and many other such matters are severely hampered, therefore, if indeed they are accomplished at all.

Perhaps in time this anomalous situation, which incidentally is more or less peculiar to the United States,[36] will be corrected by the merging of the many minor civil divisions into a single governmental unit with boundaries approximating those of the community. At present, however, there is no strong disposition to undertake so "radical" a political reorganization. Annexation, the legal device by which cities may enlarge their areas, is becoming increasingly difficult to employ.[37] Smaller cities whose territories are contiguous to larger cities are unwilling to join the latter. And many large cities are so hemmed in by municipalities that there is very little unincorporated area available for annexation. Even that which is available is often occupied by individuals who prefer to provide their own services.

There is also a general rise of living costs to be considered. This probably has part of its basis in the multiplicity of governmental units. Many political subdivisions are doubtless too small to operate efficiently; their governmental services must either be of low quality or very expensive to their residents. If it were possible to control differences in quality, it could probably be shown that per capita costs of government decrease with increase of size of population. But the rise of costs applies to all kinds of utilities. A thinning distribution of population means fewer subscribers per mile of telephone line, of water main, of sewer trunk line; fewer residents per mile of road surface,

---

[35] Cf. Arthur W. Bromage and John A. Perkins, "Willow Run Produces Bombers and Intergovernmental Problems," *American Political Science Review*, XXXVI (August, 1942), 689-97.

[36] See National Resources Committee, *Urban Planning and Land Policies* (Washington, D. C., 1939), 312 ff., for material on the control of surrounding lands exercised by European cities.

[37] S. E. Sanders and A. J. Rabuck, *New City Patterns* (New York, 1946), 22 ff.

etc. It means also that delivery services of all kinds are apt to be more costly.[38] The time, effort, and money spent in daily journeys to places of work, school, and shopping are likewise increased. Dewey has conservatively estimated that every added mile of distance to place of work raises the individual's annual outlay for transportation by about $25.00.[39] Whether the gains in real income derived from living outside large cities compensate for the added money expense involved in satisfying routine requirements cannot be determined until appropriate measures of each variable are available. But many such costs may be reduced by continued growth of peripheral population.

Rising costs of living also threaten the occupants of cities. Undeveloped lands in cities tend to remain undeveloped, while hollow places in the form of parking lots and one- and two-story buildings appear on high value lands in the central business districts. New building construction occurs in growing volume outside rather than within the city and that, coupled with the progressive obsolescence and depreciation of old buildings, results in a reduction of the total assessed valuation of property. One estimate places the decline in assessed valuations in the five cities of 1,000,000 or more population, between 1930 and 1940, at 40 to 60 per cent.[40] Shrinkages in the tax base create serious problems of financing ordinary municipal services. There are numerous instances in most large cities of high-pressure water mains, expensive fire fighting equipment, and other costly utilities "serving" vacant lots.[41] The investment in Flint, Michigan, in sewer, water, sidewalks, and street grading on which 19,791 vacant lots fronted in 1939 was estimated to be $3,000,000.[42] Such capital outlays are unused investments, the costs of which either are charged against the properties adjacent to vacant lots or spread on the tax roll of the city. The consequent rise of per capita costs of government may be expected to be cumulative, for every increase of costs is an additional discouragement to construction within the city and that, in turn, induces further increases in costs.

---

[38] Kate K. Liepmann quotes an author who states: "As building density (in England) rose from 250 to 350 houses per mile, there was a fall in weekly delivery costs (of milk) per household of 9.3 per cent in congested areas and of 7.7 per cent on housing estates." (*The Journey to Work* [New York, 1944], 103.)

[39] *Op. cit.,* 121.

[40] Lent D. Upson, "The Future Service Structure of Cities," *Municipal Finance,* XIV (May, 1942), 22-27. No doubt some of that loss was due to the general depression of values in the 1930's.

[41] Leverett S. Lyon, "Economic Problems of American Cities," *American Economic Review,* XXXII (March, 1942), Supplement, 307-23.

[42] Edward N. Bacon, "A Diagnosis and Suggested Treatment of an Urban Community's Land Problems (Flint, Michigan)," *Journal of Land and Public Utility Economics,* XVI (February, 1940), 81.

Despite the actual or expected decline of taxable values in large cities, they continue to provide and in effect subsidize a number of services for the community at large. The financial burden of these services increases even where the city is growing, if at the same time settlement in the outlying area is growing at a faster rate. The maintenance of an elaborate equipment of streets and other utilities which make the city attractive to business and industry and thus to the entire community as a shopping and employment center is a service of no small importance. Industries that locate outside the city pay no taxes to the city yet rely upon it to supply large portions of their labor forces with urban amenities. Metropolitan centers underwrite the costs of many direct services such as airports, museums, zoos, stadiums, and auditoriums that are used regularly by nonresidents.[43] It is understandable, therefore, why some cities, notably Philadelphia and Toledo, have introduced a system of taxation that applies to residents and nonresidents alike—i.e., a one per cent tax on wages and salaries chargeable on all who live in the city and work elsewhere and all who live elsewhere and work in the city. But while such a tax may meet the immediate need for more revenue, it may in the long run accelerate the centrifugal movement.

Limits of Expansion.—The limits of expansion of the local community are fixed in much the same fashion as are those of interregional organization. Transportation time and cost involved in the maintenance of daily contacts impose an effective limit to the scope of the community. The influence of transportation, however, is subject to some modification by changes in the costs of services at the center. A decline in prices at a center will make possible the expenditure of more time or cost in travel and thus will permit a further enlargement of the community area. Yet, unless they are of considerable magnitude, it is unlikely that such changes can exert an appreciable effect on the dimensions of the local community, for the element of convenience appears to be fully as important as the element of cost in deciding the frequency of contacts between spatially separated units.

In sparsely populated regions, such as the western parts of the United States, transportation tends to operate as the decisive limiting factor on the scope of the community. Its influence is more or less absolutė. Only those improvements which lower the time and cost of movement afford a significant enlargement of the area of daily functioning interdependences. But in regions of dense settlement the

---

[43] See Edward Blythin, "The Dangers of Metropolitan Decentralization," *National Municipal Review*, XXXI (September, 1942), 442-44.

comparative time and cost involved in moving to alternative centers becomes the limiting factor. A close juxtaposition of centers, as in northeastern United States, makes impossible the development around each of community area of maximum size. Each area infringes upon others. Hence the scope of any one community depends upon the relative accessibility of its center. Where all communities are served by the same kinds of transport facilities, as is true of regions such as the one mentioned, differences in accessibility of centers are contingent upon variations of transport service—e.g., the attractiveness of service, the scheduling of trips, rate computations, and monopolistic practices. Differential changes in transportation features of this ·type permit the expansion of one community at the expense of others.

Of greater importance in regions of closely spaced cities, however, are differences in the character and efficiency of services available in each neighboring city. Superior marketing facilities and related services may compensate for transportation disadvantages or the time and cost of a longer haul to a given center. Thus the community area may be extended beyond what transportation costs alone would warrant. It is partly for such a reason, of course, that large cities usually have more extensive community areas than smaller cities.

In other words, where one community impinges upon others intercity competition operates as the most effective limiting factor on expansion. The relative competitive strength of each center in securing the patronage of residents in the intervening spaces and in attracting to itself administrative and marketing functions determines the extent to which the community area may be enlarged. Competition is observable not only in the struggle for transportation and communication advantages and superior services of all kinds; it also appears in efforts to accelerate rates of population growth. Elaborate publicity campaigns are frequently launched to implement the competition.[44]

But even after the principal outlines of community areas are marked out and established,[45] the expansion process may continue for some time as their internal organizations are developed and adjusted to the new scale of distance. This is due to the differential responsiveness to change that exists among the various phases of community structure. For example, the speed of automobiles may be increased within a season, but the widening, straightening, and surfacing of roads may

---

[44] See R. D. McKenzie, *The Metropolitan Community*, 160-62.
[45] Some indication that this has taken place is had in the tendency in recent years for metropolitan newspapers to contract their circulation areas. Having discovered that their trade areas have become more or less stationary, merchants are unwilling to pay for advertising which is extended into unproductive territory.

require years; a village may lose its function long before its population is redistributed; and local government units may be reduced to ineffectiveness a generation or more in advance of their consolidation in larger units.

Summary.—Interregional expansion gave rise to large compact cities but did not enlarge the scope of the local community. Not until efficient, highly flexible means of movement and communication over short distances appeared did the expansion of the local community begin. The motor vehicle, the telephone, and the radio supplied the required facility, introducing revolutionary changes in the scale of local distance. The sixty-minute radius was extended to forty or fifty miles and tight networks of roads developed about major cities. Paralleling this change is a redistribution of functions and population in the entire area made easily accessible from the central city which gives rise to a more complex and more dispersed community organization.

Redistribution affects all functions of the community. Administrative offices of industrial enterprises congregate in the metropolis but without loss of contact with their scattered producing activities. Manufacturing, originally concentrated at the center to benefit from close access to labor supplies, markets, sources of power, and shipping facilities, finds its range of choice of site location greatly enlarged and therefore tends to move centrifugally. Despite the local scatter of manufacturing functions, their interrelations become more numerous and more sensitive. Agriculture is faced with a new competition arising from the invasion of rural lands by urban functions, including not only manufacturing but recreational, commercial, and residential activities as well. Service centers likewise are brought into competition with one another. The more specialized services gravitate to the large cities, leaving only the most routine services in the small places. On the other hand, new services initiated first in the metropolis, when they become generally accepted, diffuse outward to smaller subcenters. In the shifting and realignment of relations many old villages and towns disappear, while new ones take form at more strategic locations. Each service center or subcenter tends to assume a more or less specialized role in the service structure of the expanded community. Traditional categoric units also yield to the change. Kinship and neighborhood units lose many of their functions and are replaced by specialized units the members of which are often widely scattered.

These changes are accompanied by population redistribution. That movement is essentially centrifugal in character and is expressed in both absolute and relative respects. That is, there is movement outward from the center and there is accretion in the peripheral areas from intercommunity movement. Population scatter is explainable largely in terms of the increased speed of commutation travel and of communication afforded by the new forms of overcoming distance. It involves disproportionate numbers of young people in the upper social-economic group. The reasons given by migrants from central cities of metropolitan districts to the outlying areas indicate that the movement is an effort to secure better conditions for family life.

A number of frictions develop in the course of local community expansion. The inclusion of numerous political subdivisions within the scope of a single community interferes with an efficient operation of the organization in many respects. Effective concerted action with reference to communitywide problems is all but impossible. A general rise of living costs represents another friction. This is due partly to the maintenance of too many small and inefficient governmental units, but more importantly to the increased expense involved in distributing services to a more thinly scattered population. The annual outlay for transportation by the resident is also increased. On the other hand, the costs of maintaining services in large cities that are losing population to or are growing more slowly than their outlying areas tend to rise. The contraction of the assessed valuation of real property within their boundaries results in increased taxes or a deterioration in the number and quality of municipal services. These observations argue for a general reorganization of the governmental function in the expanded community.

The limits of expansion in the local community are fixed by the time and cost of movement to and from the center and by expansion from neighboring centers. But even after the principal outlines of the enlarged community are marked out and established the expansion process continues internally as its organization develops and is accommodated to the new scale of distance.

Supplementary References

Hartsough, Mildred L. *Development of Twin Cities as a Metropolitan Market.* Minneapolis: University of Minnesota Press, 1925.

Hauser, Phillip. "How Declining Urban Growth Affects City Activities," *Public Management* (December, 1940).

Hughes, Everett C. *French Canada in Transition.* Chicago: The University of Chicago Press, 1943.

Jenkins, David Ross. *The Growth and Decline of Agricultural Villages.* New York: Columbia University Press, 1940.

Liepmann, Kate K. *The Journey to Work: Its significance for Industrial and Community Life.* New York: Oxford University Press, 1944.

Mayer, Harold M. "Patterns and Recent Trends of Chicago's Outlying Business Centers," *The Journal of Land and Public Utility Economics,* XVIII (February, 1942), 4-17.

NELSON, LOWRY, and JACOBSON, E. "Recent Changes in Farm Trade Centers of Minnesota," *Rural Sociology,* VI (June, 1941).

SMITH, THOMAS R. *The Cotton Textile Industry of Fall River, Massachusetts.* New York: King's Crown Press, 1944.

TREWARTHA, GLENN T. "The Unincorporated Hamlet: One Element in the American Settlement Fabric," *Annals of the Association of American Geographers,* XXXIII (March, 1943), 32-81.

WILSON, WARREN H. *Quacker Hill: A Sociological Study.* New York: Columbia University Press, 1907.

NAME INDEX

Ackerman, E., 267
Adams, C. C., 8, 9, 10
Alihan, M., 74
Allee, W. C., 19, 40, 42, 48, 52, 57, 65, 67
Alverdes, F., 40
Anderson, E. L., 233
Anderson, N., 347
Anderson, P. E., 404
Andrews, R. B., 414
Angell, R. C., 201, 233, 242
Arensberg, C., 158, 299
Ashby, A. W., 414

Bacon, E. N., 427
Baden-Powell, H., 238
Bagehot, W., 321
Bailey, E. W., 51
Baker, J., 65
Baker, O. E., 146
Baldwin, J. M., 51
Barnes, H. E., 82
Barrows, H. H., 71, 74
Bartholomew, H., 266, 267
Barton, R. F., 194
Bell, E. H., 417
Bernard, L. L., 23, 70
Bews, J. W., 3, 9
Binghamton, M. T., 158
Blatz, W. E., 183
Blythin, E., 428
Boas, F., 18, 28
Bogue, D. J., 273, 421, 422
Bossard, J., 197
Boulding, K., 77
Bowen, H., 339
Bowers, R., 90, 265, 287
Bowman, I., 162, 330, 336
Branch, M. C., 423
Branford, V., 89
Braun-Blanquet, J., 39, 40
Breasted, J. H., 60
Breese, G., 316
Bridenbaugh, C., 370
Briffault, R., 213
Bromage, A. W., 426
Brunhes, J., 71, 87, 239
Brunner, E. de S., 229, 265, 414
Bryan, P. 72
Bryce, J., 325
Bucher, K., 326
Buck, J. L., 116
Buer, M. C., 374
Bunzel, R., 18
Burgess, E. W., 8, 10, 31, 90, 265, 266, 321, 384
Bushee, F. A., 229

Byron, L., 79

Cairnes, J. E., 209
Carpenter, J. R., 7, 39
Carr, W. G., 147
Carr-Saunders, A. M., 91, 105, 110, 171, 328, 331
Carrel, A., 316
Chapin, F. S., 322
Charles, E., 63, 308
Child, C. M., 51
Christaller, W., 268
Clague, E., 167, 340
Clark, Colin, 360
Clark, C. D., 139, 140, 345
Cleland, W., 107, 173
Clements, F. E., 3, 39, 42, 43, 45, 49, 50, 53, 55, 67, 326
Colby, C. C., 71
Comte, A., 207, 209
Connelly, W. E., 159
Conrad, H. S., 39
Converse, P. D., 415
Cooley, C. H., 201, 242, 243, 322
Cooper, M., 344
Cort, W. W., 65
Cottrell, W. F., 307, 310, 316
Coulter, C. W., 166
Couper, W. J., 167, 340
Cowles, H. C., 41
Cralle, W. O., 420
Creamer, D., 166, 413
Cressey, P. F., 395, 401
Crile, G. W., 324

Dalton, H., 171
Dampier, Sir W., 34
Darling, F. F., 40
Darwin, C., 4, 5, 15, 16, 17, 19, 23, 30, 33, 34, 35
Darwin, F., 4
Davidson, D., 404
Davie, M., 265, 287, 339
Dawson, C. A., 103
Dayton City Plan Board, 424
de Aberle, S. B., 104
DeBoer, S. R., 287
de la Blache, P. V., 71, 87, 157–58, 194
Devereaux, E. C., 419
Dewey, R., 395, 424, 427
Dickes, E. W., 370
Dickinson, R. E., 390, 391, 397
Dodge, S. D., 71, 248
Dublin, L. I., 127, 145
Dunham, W., 90
Durkheim, E. I., 196, 208, 209

433

SUBJECT INDEX

Abyssinia,
  colonization of Italians in, 170
  correlation of natural and culture
    areas, 86
Accessibility,
  effect of change in, 244
  highways, 417
  in cities, 387
  interdependence, 163, 236
  measured by time-cost distance, 238,
    288
  need for, 245
  residence location, 280–81
  route intersections, 242–45, 387
  secondary business districts, 394
  specialization, 277
Adaptation; *see also* Maladaptation
  a continuous process, 17
  and capacity for change, 324
  communal, 18, 29–31, 66, 178
  defined, 16, 18, 29
  genetic, 19–21
    compared to somatic, 21
    of man, 20–21, 24, 55, 177
    overspecialization of, 21
  individual, 18–29
    as related to communal adaptation,
      30
  necessity of, 18, 21
  of rhythms, 290–91, 295
  somatic, 19, 21–29
    behavior as, 22–29
    compared to genetic, 21
    imperfections of, 26–29
    of man, 22–29
    specialization of, 25–26
  to habitat, 194
  to time, 288
  types, 18–30
Adoption,
  as kinship equivalent, 213
  as a population control, 159
Africa,
  census in, 92
  colonization of Germans in, 169–70
  culture areas in, 83
  density of population, 96
  early migrations into, 158
  estimated population (1650–1935), 106
  growth of population, 105
  lag of organization in, 201
  race division of labor in, 189–90
  subsidies to immigrants by, 170
Age,
  as basis of functional differentiation,
    183–84

  compared to influence of sex, 186
  physiological cause of, 186
  composition patterns, 131–40
  ecological significance of, 143–48
  effect of war on, 140–42
  effect on service structure, 380
  flexibility of behavior by, 25, 147
  grading of, 186–87
  in cities, 142–43
  in stationary population, 129–30
  labor force, 145–48
  migration, 340, 341, 343
  mortality, 112–113
Agriculture,
  acceleration of tempo in, 308
  as type of economy, 56
  changes in proportions employed in,
    375–76
  competition with urban land uses, 414
  decline of, about cities, 358
  density of population in, 151
  displacement from, 359
  effect of business cycles on, 313
  effect of technological change on, 308
  migration, 330–31, 359
  timing in, 300–301
Airplane, comparative efficiency of, 352
Albania,
  population growth, 134
  surplus population in agriculture, 166
America,
  density of population, 96, 97, 100
  dumping ground for surplus popula-
    tion, 118
  growth of population, 105
  settlement pattern, 268
Andaman Islands,
  age grading among natives, 187
  economy of, 58
  extent of adoption in, 213
  nomadic pattern in, 239
  population decline, 106, 160
  size of groups in, 197
  time reckoning in, 295
Animal,
  community, 41
  ecology, 6, 8
Annexation, decline of, 426
Anthropogeography, 70, 84-86
Anthropomorphism, 59
Arapesh, 184
Arctic circle,
  agriculture in, 62
  Eskimos in, 56
Area,
  administrative, 258–59

439

number of, 255–57
of political areas, 259
overlapping of, 249
Brazil,
decline of native population in, 160, 188
race-caste structure in, 189
Buffalo, population increase by distance from center, 398
Bulgaria,
birth rate, 108
death rate, 108
immigrants from, 342
net reproduction rate, 108
population,
growth, 108
surplus in agriculture, 166
Bushmen, time reckoning by, 295
Business cycle,
correlations with, 311, 313–14
effect on agriculture, 313
effect on dependent community, 312
loss of efficiency, 313

Cairo, rise of, 244
Canada,
birth rate, 108
census in, 92
death rate, 108
famine among Indians, 155–56
infanticide, 157
land available in, 162, 336
net reproduction rate, 108
population,
distribution, 95, 100
growth, 108
subsidies to immigrants, 170
Canals,
effects of, 357
freight rates on, 357
Capital cities, location of, 245
Carthage, size of, 371
Caste,
as categoric unit, 217
Hindu, 189
in Brazil, 189
in preliterate society, 197
Catastrophic theory of change, 320
Categoric unit; *see also* Caste; Class
as a system of relationships, 219–20
based on commensalism, 210
competition, 211, 218
defined, 210
distinguished from statistical category, 210
dominance of, 222
effect of motor vehicle on, 419
extension of principle of, 218
function of, 211
in dependent community, 228–29
in independent community, 223, 224
membership characteristics, 217
number of, 217, 229

relations to other units, 220–22
segregation of, 274–75
symbiosis in, 219
temporal relations in, 299
Celibacy, 15, 159
Census,
beginning of, 92
conditions favorable to, 92
defined, 92
enlargement of, 93
international comparisons, 94
origin and diffusion of, 92
reorganization of, in United States, 207
resistances to, 93
Centers,
dominance of, 418
juxtaposition of, 429
nucleation in, 273
number in independent community, 268–75
persistence of, 244
rise and fall of, 244–45, 416–17
specialization of, 273
Central America, estimated population (1650–1935), 106
Central and axial growth, 382–84
Central business district,
change in composition of, 390
Chicago, 394
growth of, 387–93, 400
movement of, 394, 417
Philadelphia, 278–79
rebuilding of, 390–91
segregation of units in, 273, 278–80
specialization in, 277
succession, 400
withdrawal of manufacturing from, 391, 392
Centralization,
development of, 241
differentiation and, 221
requisite conditions for, 242
route intersections, 242–43
Centrifugal movement,
effect on service costs, 426–27
expansion, 348, 359, 360, 405
families, 397
intracommunity, 421–25
manufacturing, 410–13
recreation services, 419
relation to rental values, 424
transportation costs, 427
urban population, 395–97
Centripetal movement,
expansion, 348, 359
factors in, 424–25
growth of cities, 373, 376
relation to rental values, 424
Change; *see also* Community; Expansion; Migration; Population; Transportation
catastrophic theory of, 320